Art Explorations: Pigments of my imagination

Shirley Mc Daniel

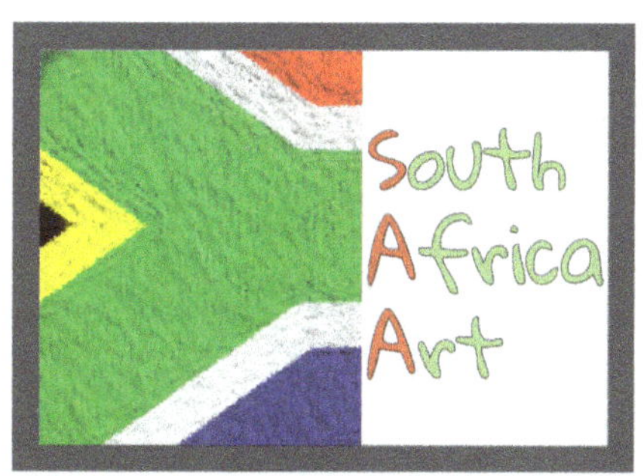

Published by South Africa Art

a division of South Africa Writing

Cape Town - London - Los Angeles

www.southafricawriting.com/art.html

ISBN-13: 979-8-9902721-2-5

For my Beloved Barry.

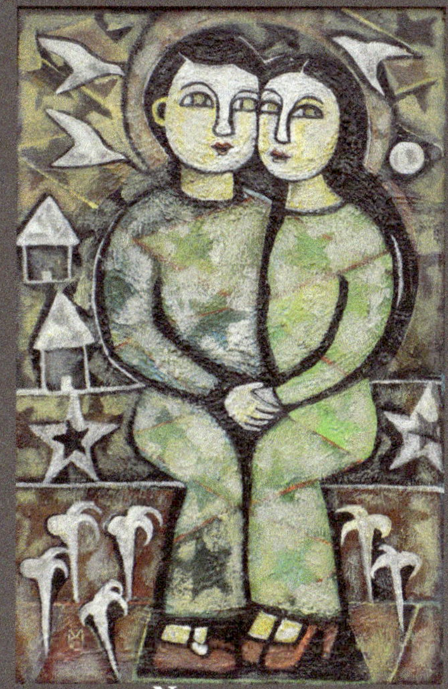

Nearness
(55cm x 36cm)

Boundless bonds connect us forever . . .

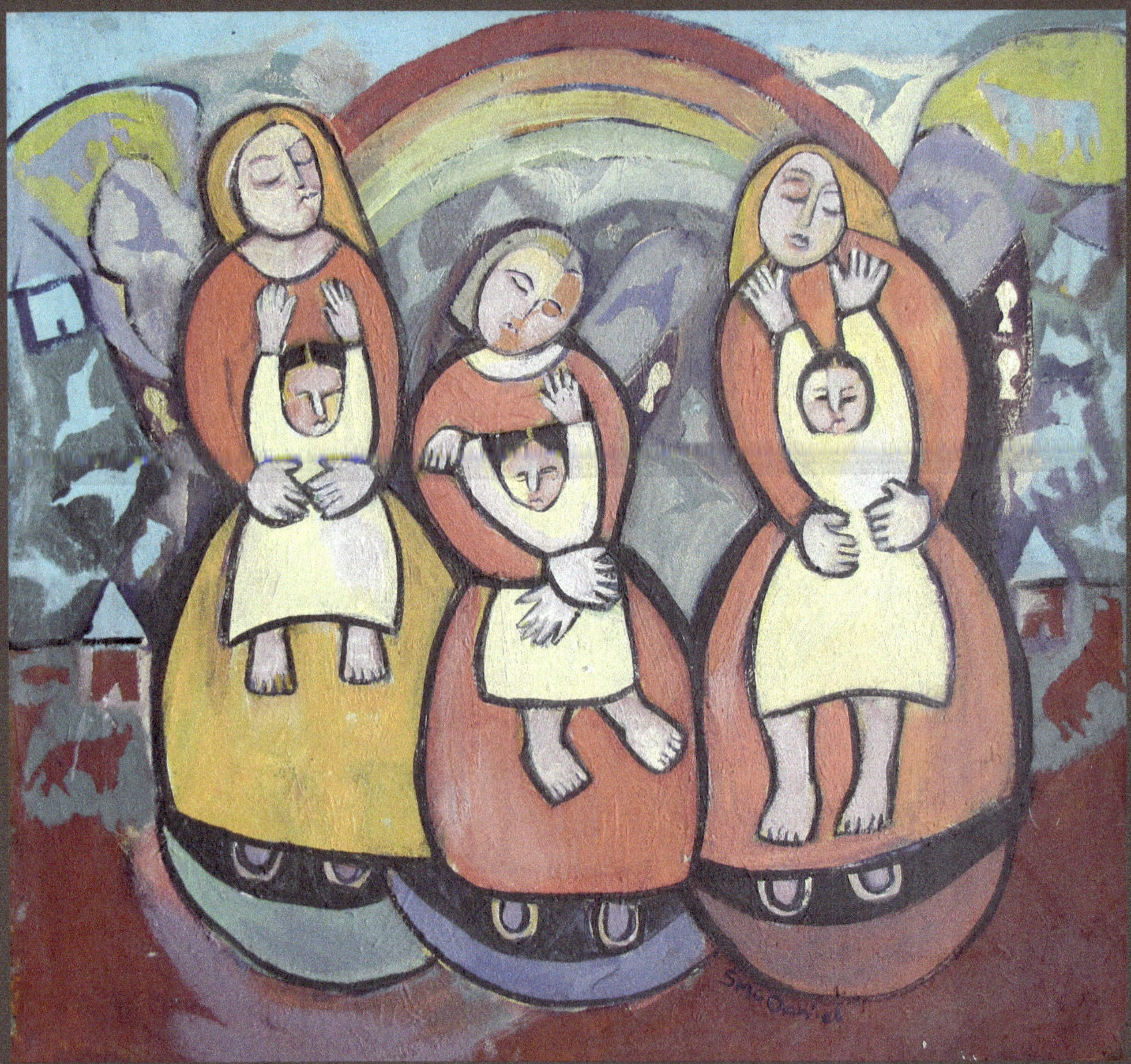

Maternal Allegory
(70cm x 80cm)

Table of Contents

Introduction by Jayne Galassi -
Artist and Author of Ezulwini: Place of Heaven

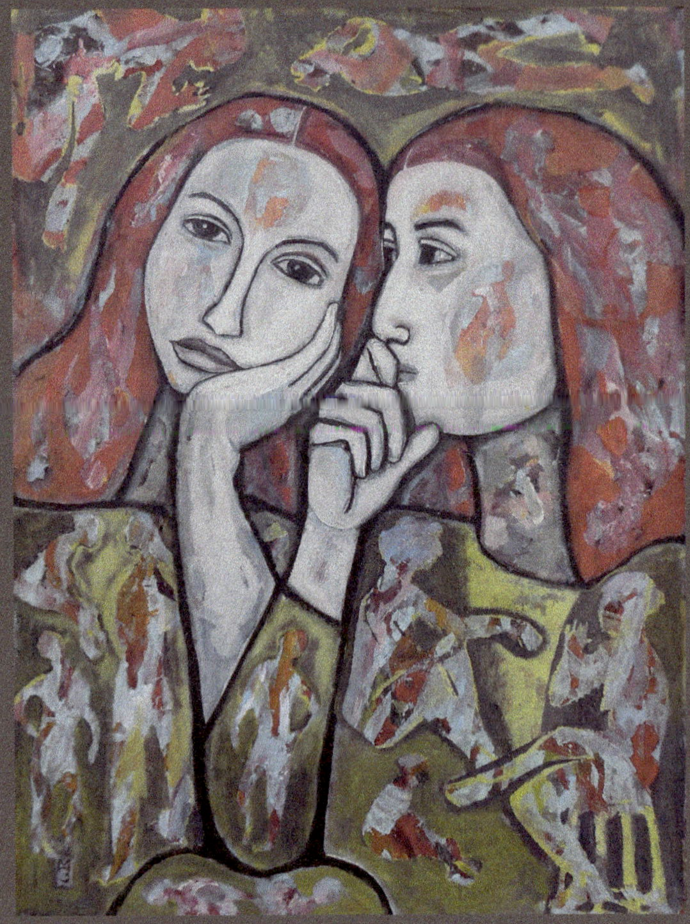

Activists
(101cm x 76cm)

The Artist Shirley McDaniel

To come upon a singular friendship that lasts a lifetime is rare, but to find an enduring love that is born of a connection that belies everything and everyone that came before and after the tender age of thirteen is and was, for me, a remarkable synchronicity.

Here, on our first year of high school, Shirley walked in, seemingly shy and self-conscious, her large eyes averted, her long dark hair that framed an unusual face. She reached over to my desk and clasped my hand in hers.

'Hello *Scrim*...' Her eyes smiled warmly. It was a small class and mine was the only new face.

I had been at the school as a border for a couple of years as a junior, so my old nick name had followed me.

'I'm Shirl.'

It was the small gesture of taking my hand in hers, and I warmed to her immediately.

To begin with, Shirley was a day scholar, so that her day at school ended while the borders gathered into clubs and groups, study and meals. We had few opportunities to get to know each other. But later, Shirley persuaded her parents to allow her to board and that meant late afternoons and late-night chatting. We both loved French and English classes, but Art was by far our favourite – the studio was open all day and Shirl and I spent many an afternoon finishing off projects.

Shirley, the artist. She was also eccentric, witty and immeasurably wise. We slipped so comfortably into an enduring friendship that has lasted almost a lifetime, sharing a love of art, literature, and philosophy. Even as a young girl Shirley had a maturity and a sense of self far beyond her years. We both loved Shakespeare, poetry and writing. We poured over Kahlil Gibran's lyrical verse and we talked of the philosophers of the day.

I was introduced to her family and often spent evenings sprawled on comfy couches or cross-legged on the carpet surrounded by her warm and accepting family. She was the youngest of five children and the only girl. Music was central to the Newmans. Peppered with laughter and banter they all sang along to old melodies, with Shirley playing the guitar and the piano (self-taught and using mainly the black keys!) My own childhood home was somewhat formal and restrained, so I was mesmerized by the warmth and humour of my best friend's family.

Double Art Classes were a taste of freedom from academics, with instruction in every medium, from sculpture to lino cut, plaster cut reliefs to drawing and painting. I settled into a more traditional style as realism came quite naturally to me. But Shirl was spontaneous, fearlessly experimenting with colour and bold composition. Her figures were abstracted and her style seemed effortless as if she held a hundred delightful sketches in her head, expressive but harmonious figures that danced along the page in a sort of musical rhythm.

Shirl had an innate sense of style. And even today is instantly recognised as her unique style that has changed little over the years, if not more mature in subject matter, colour harmony and figure composition so often infused with compassion for maternal subjects, integrating birds and animals with a rendering that reflects a natural sympathetic compassion for all of nature.

As schoolgirls on the brink of adulthood we gave little thought to the conventions of girls pursuing smart careers or early marriages to suitable partners. We were much more inclined to travelling, exploring the arts, and having clandestine love affairs. We had no doubts about enrolling in Art College after school.

But life intervened as so often happens when you try and chase goals that you have simply dreamed up. Shirley fell in love before we finished our last year at school.

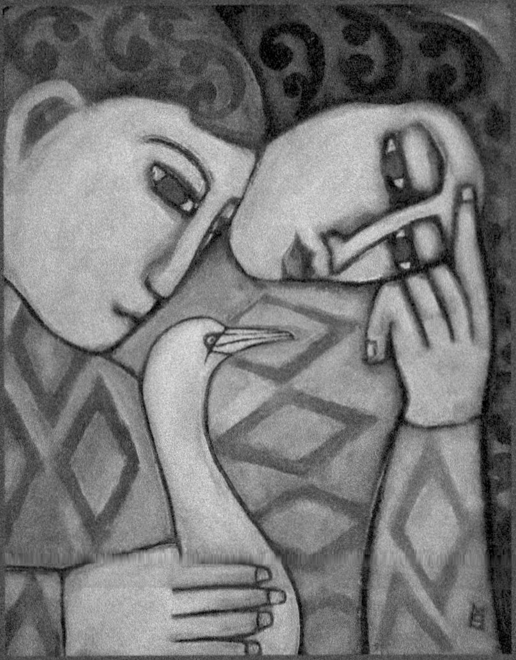

Gannet Gaze
(61cm x 48cm)

Barry

Barry Mc Daniel was not only calm and self-assured, but he also easily matched Shirl's sense of humour and her love of music. He was gentle and self- effacing but with a determined sense of wisdom and practicality, clearly delighted with Shirley's eccentricities and compassionate nature. Everyone loved Barry. They were a hand to glove match, and he clearly adored her.

Years later when I met them both on the South Coast that relationship had sustained in all the years in between, the laughter, the gentle compassion between them had lasted as if they were sewn into each other's hearts.

The house that the Mc Daniels built was nestled in the heart of Trafalgar, surrounded by the lush subtropical vegetation so common to the South Coast of Kwazulu Natal, with a view of the sea and the rolling hills in various shades of greens, and a wild menagerie of wildlife and birds. Vervet monkeys were prolific and frequented the surrounding gardens with abandon, as did a variety of snakes.

The land of the Zulu was bountiful and colourful, most of the ethnic inhabitants had few modern conveniences. Mothers walked miles to and from their villages, carrying their large bags of provisions on their heads, their young children tied to their backs or traipsing behind holding hands. Shirley's many depictions of the rural women, their persistent strength in hardship, the acceptance of a simple life, and yet, their warm laughter and their song. Many of her paintings paid tribute to endurance of women, the age-old stories of motherhood. I love the way she names her subjects, bringing into recognition their own independent lives.

Shirley peppered the backgrounds with naïve depictions of cows and sheep and traditional thatched houses and birds that wove their wings through the landscapes and across the skies.

The three of us sat in their lounge drinking copious cups of tea, immersed in conversation, years of shared stories of our lives of friendship, of love and loss and laughter. Bound by an enduring love and familiarity matured by age and hopefully wisdom.

There were so many memories, stories of loved ones lost and children beloved and philosophy to share. There was laughter. There were tears. Time was precious and we spoke avidly for three days. I knew that this may be our last time together as I was leaving the country to join my family in Australia. Every conversation felt like an embrace.

The house was a treasure trove of their history with an orchestra of art works on every wall and door. From mirrors made of knickknacks and objet-trouve to delightful abstract sculptures made of metal and wooden tools and findings, and paintings painted on cotton fabric, paper and whatever available surface. The house was a gallery, and they just happened to be there, bringing that sense of warmth and humanity to a world of sheer imaginings. The walls and even doors were simply structures, like mirrors that reflected imagined worlds born in the mind of the artist.

In nature circles and spirals occur mathematically. In the ancient worlds, from the early Greeks to historical lands of the Middle East, Asia and India, the symmetries of universal rhythms of circles and spirals became fundamental to art down the centuries. In drawing and sculptures of every medium it is the discovery of that underlying motion that imbues an artwork with an underlying comprehension of this phenomena – the harmony that delights the eye as the composition is integrated in the flow of line.

Shirley has that natural flare for composition, that balance of form, the linear rhythms, the use of colour. All the elements come together in a symmetry that is natural to the artist's eye. I am certain that this is not a studied integration, but a natural progression of her art, characterized by her awareness of her generous compassion and synchronicity.

Shirley's art has a natural spontaneity, capturing her figures in simplified forms with understated expressions, often captured in a moment of reflection. Even in her complex collage images, that seem impulsive and busy, her seemingly fragile women move through a background world of spontaneous turmoil. Even her flat digital backgrounds accentuate the contrasting and delicately painted figures.

It was about a year after my final visit to their home in Trafalgar that I heard the devastating news of Barry's passing. I can barely imagine the wrench it must have been to our dearest Shirl. Barry was her constant, her rock, her beloved. It was a deep reminder of all who knew him of the fragility of life and the certainty of loss.

Bravely, and perhaps compulsively she still paints, ever driven by the need for the real artist to explore her talent, creating and rediscovering the life and love that is Shirley Mc Daniel.

The Inspiration for the Art -
an explanation by Shirley Mc Daniel

My works involve scrutinising and digging through surfaces, delving through my thoughts and their roots and thus stirring up images. What I depict is highly personal and my imagery is accessed from many sources, both from within and around me. I work towards creating an overall harmony within my paintings, collages and mixed media and do not have any entirely preconceived ideas for my pieces, but allow them to evolve. An example of this evolution is illustrated in a series of found object (objet trouvé) face and figure assemblages I created. I have also created mirror frames, using recycled materials.

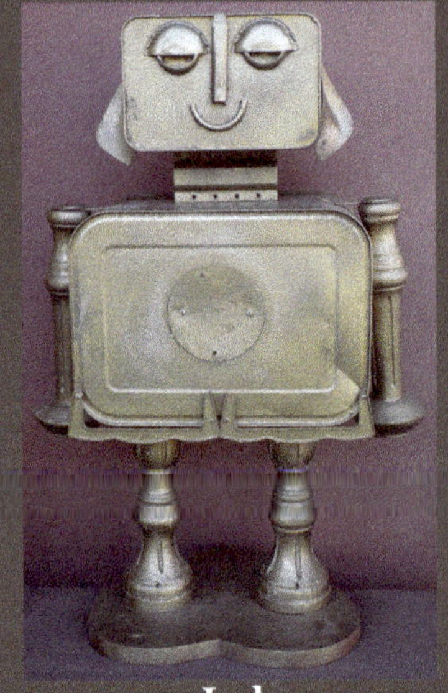

Jude
(73cm x 60cm)

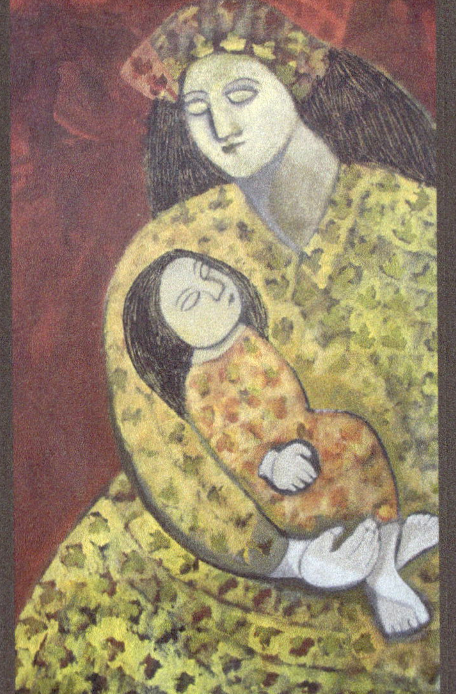

Dreamers
(130cm x 75cm)

Much of my work is representative of human communication and my depictions largely incorporate the female form. My stimulus mostly comprises various aspects of womanhood, represented singly and interacting with others. I portray maternity and motherhood in terms of universal nurturing. My work frequently depicts bounteously pregnant women, as an expression of life energy. My images of women symbolise a connectedness, incorporating inclusiveness and tenderness. The subject of womankind flows from me and has become a recurring theme for my work.

I am inspired by generous womanly contours and tend to simplify the curved female shape into softly-rounded forms, seeking rhythmic lines within these female figure-scapes. My imagery frequently includes angels and various animals, reptiles and birds, as symbols of nature and freedom. I instinctively work towards connecting and linking elements of colour and line into an overall unity, the varied and distinct parts comprising a whole.

Incorporating and embracing elements that evolve, yields spontaneity. I might salvage an entirely unplanned area, or fragments of colour which emerge whilst over-painting. Embracing these unexpected elements may heighten an image, adding subtlety, or depth. Certain limitations may aid and sharpen my creativity in seeking alternatives, experimenting with limited palettes and searching out alternate routes. I might alter an image in order to "tighten" it up, perhaps rendering it bolder, shaping a piece into a more concentrated form, conjuring up chance-elements within the changing picture surface e.g. an area of paint left glimmering through, or an interesting texture which may then consciously become incorporated into a work in progress. Utilising these unexpected gifts and collaborating with chance, is stimulating . . . weaving the planned together with the unplanned.

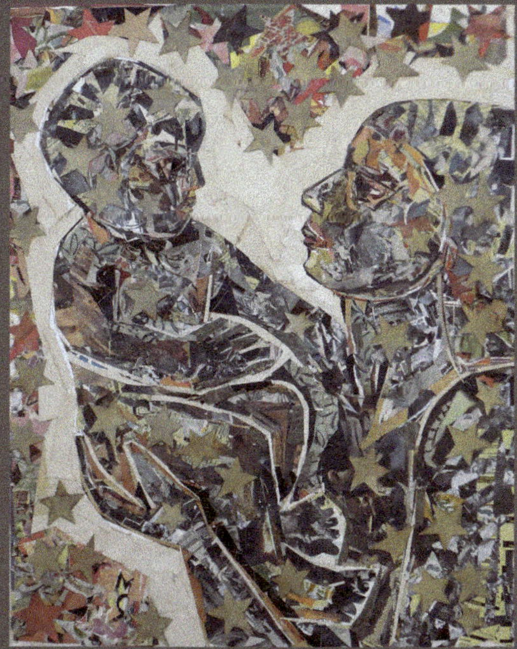

So Soft
(63cm x 51cm)

I am inspired by collage, combining a myriad of juxtaposed facets, building up the imagery, areas of darks, lights, textures, colour and/or patterned surfaces. I overlap elements, creating a cohesive whole from many-layered, or superimposed fragments. My work is largely a blending of various distinct parts, combining and arranging elements into an integrated whole. There are instances where the painting is re-created in a different art-form as is seen on pp.43-44, where the painting on the left called *Tri* is created in a collage form called *Or So I Imagined* on the right. This creation in multiple art styles became the base for digital art which is covered in its own section from pg. 167.

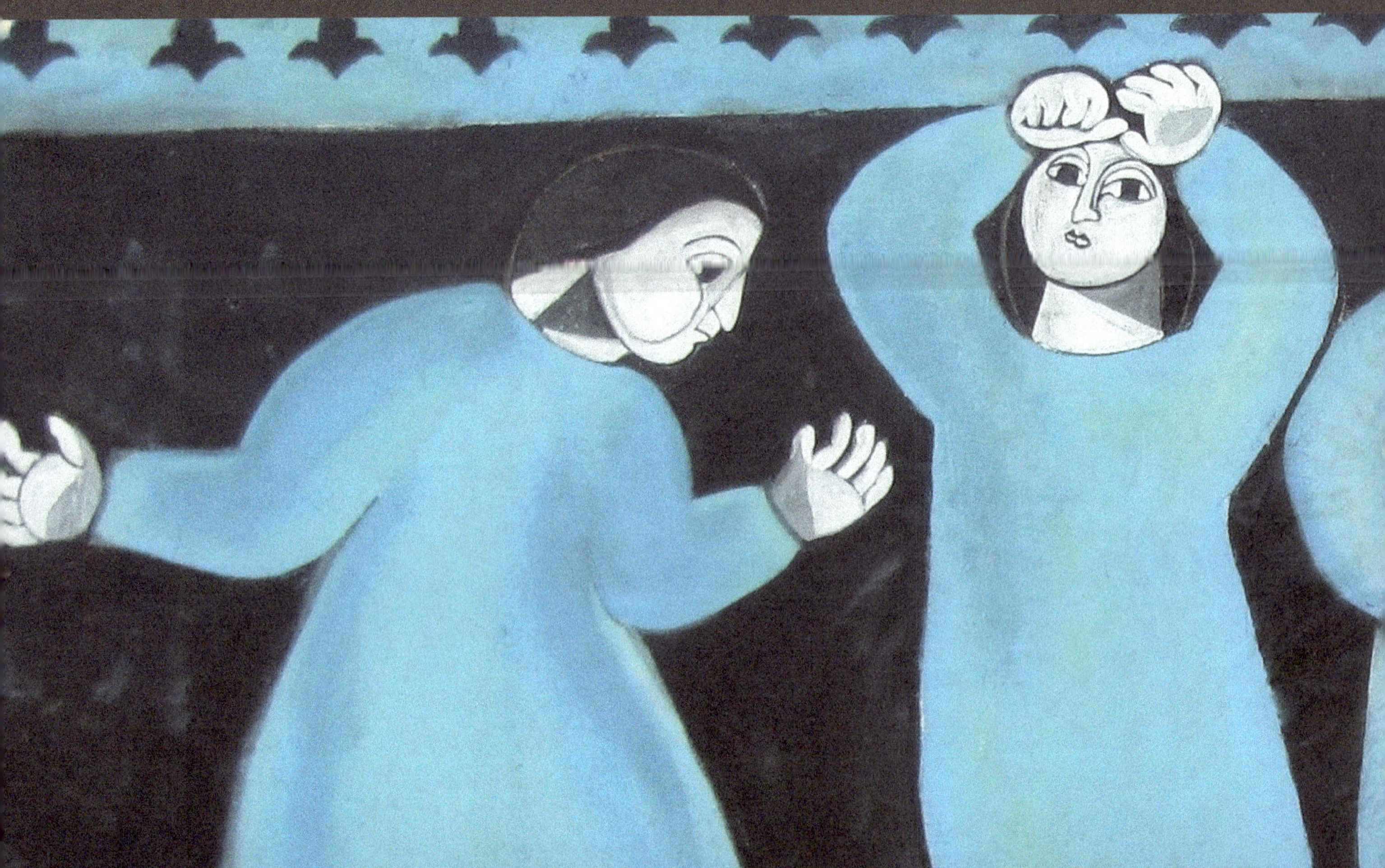

Turquoise Tunics
(130cm x 325cm)
Part digital images on pp.181-182.

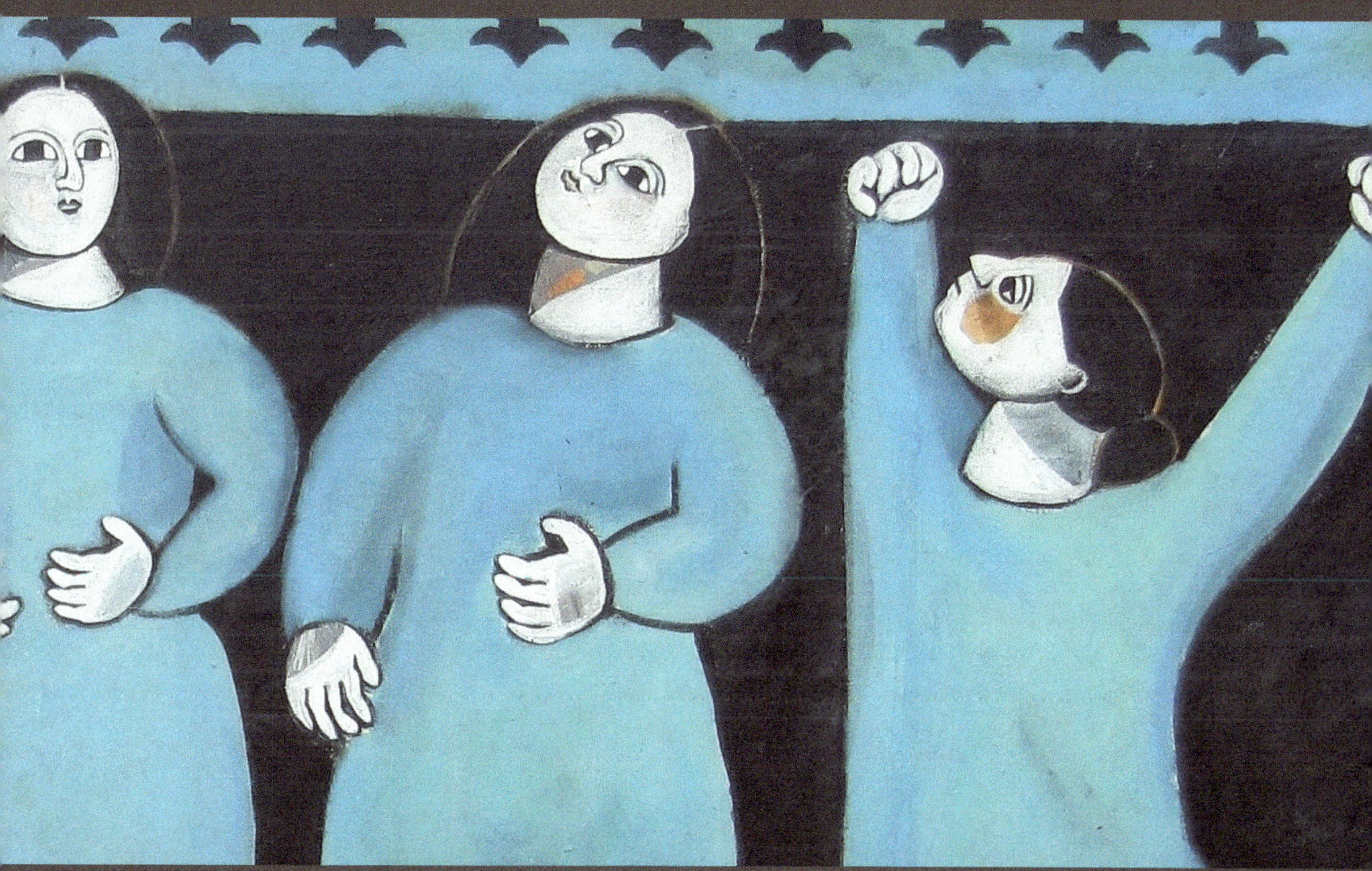

Paintings

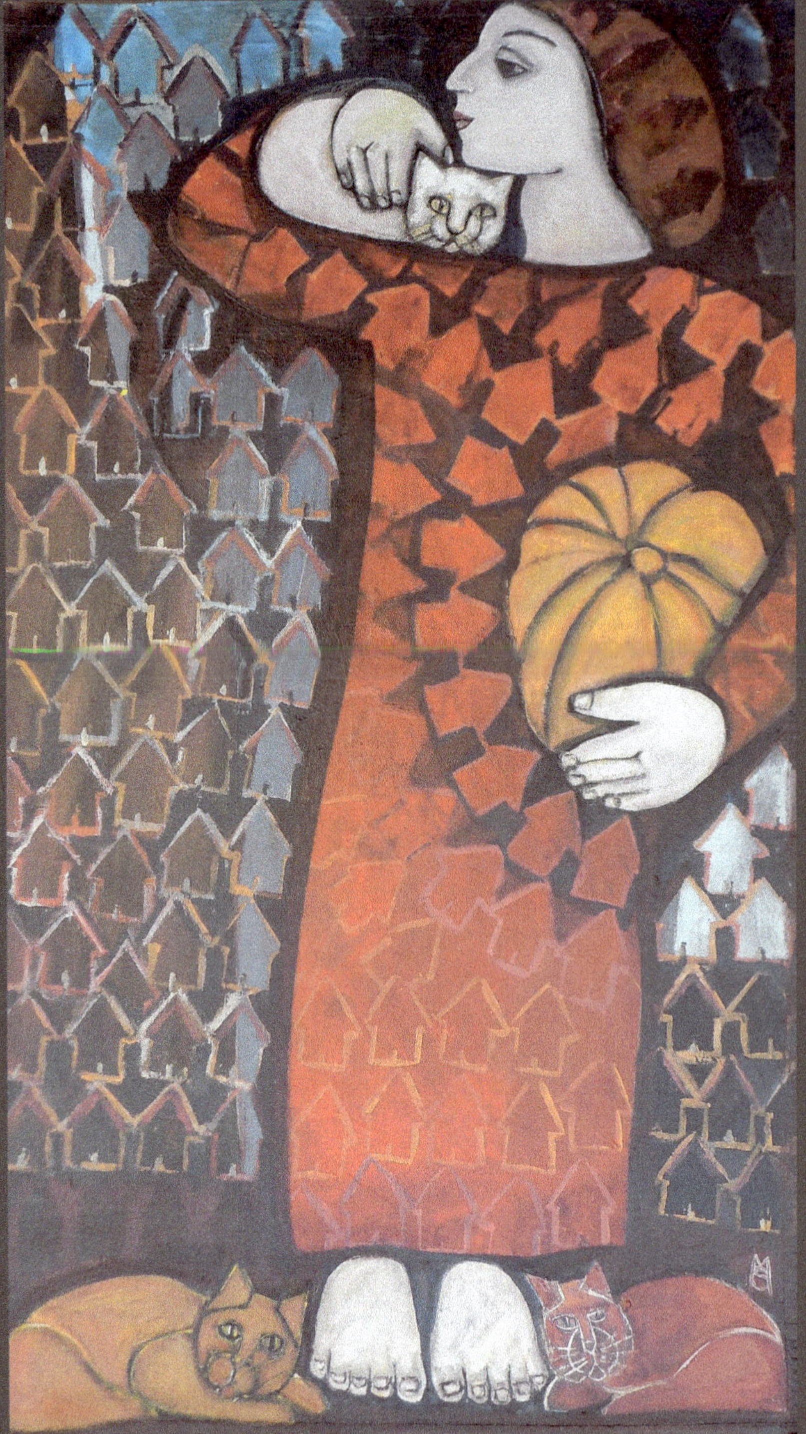

Pumpkin Purrs
(130cm x 75cm)

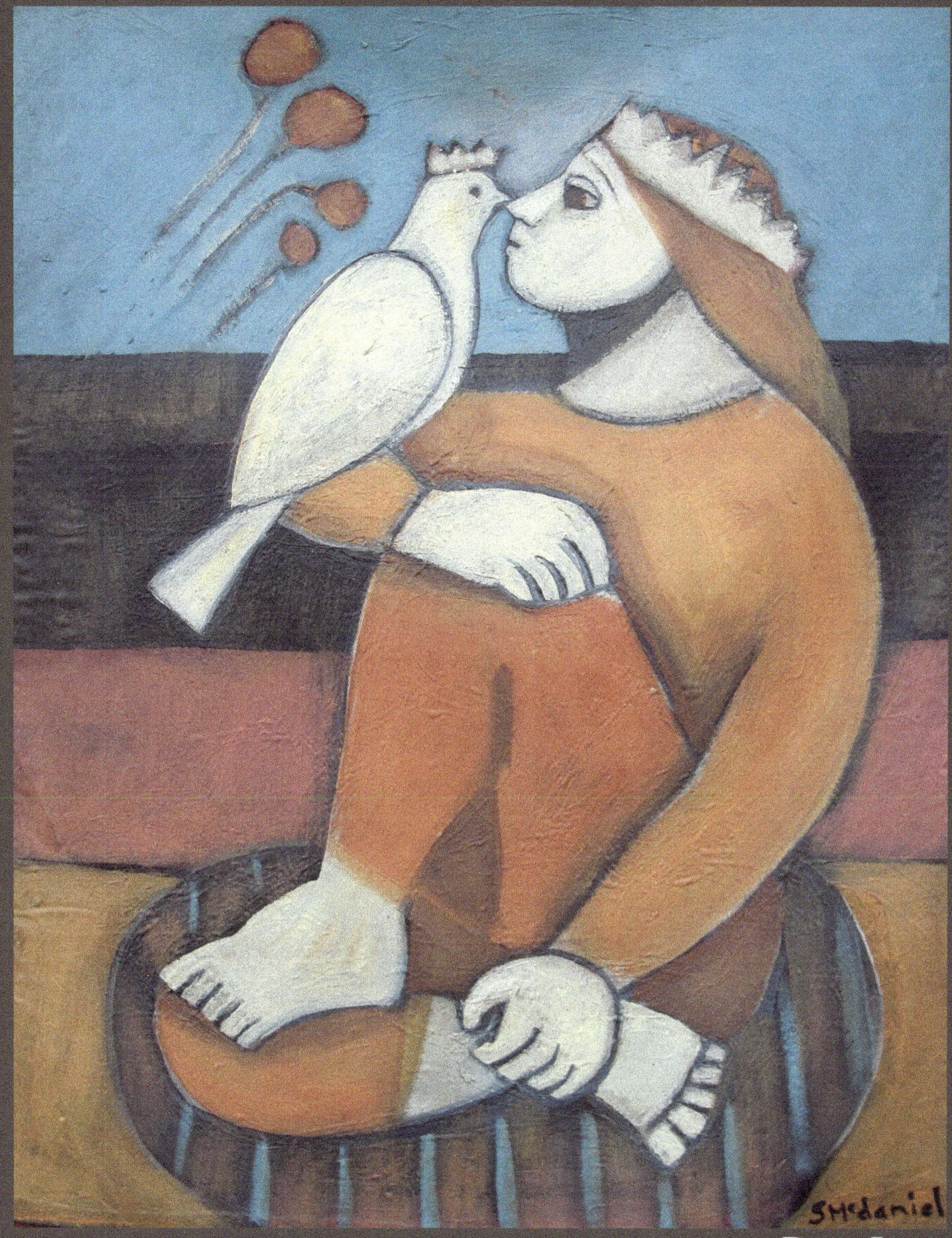

Dove Love
(75cm x 60cm)

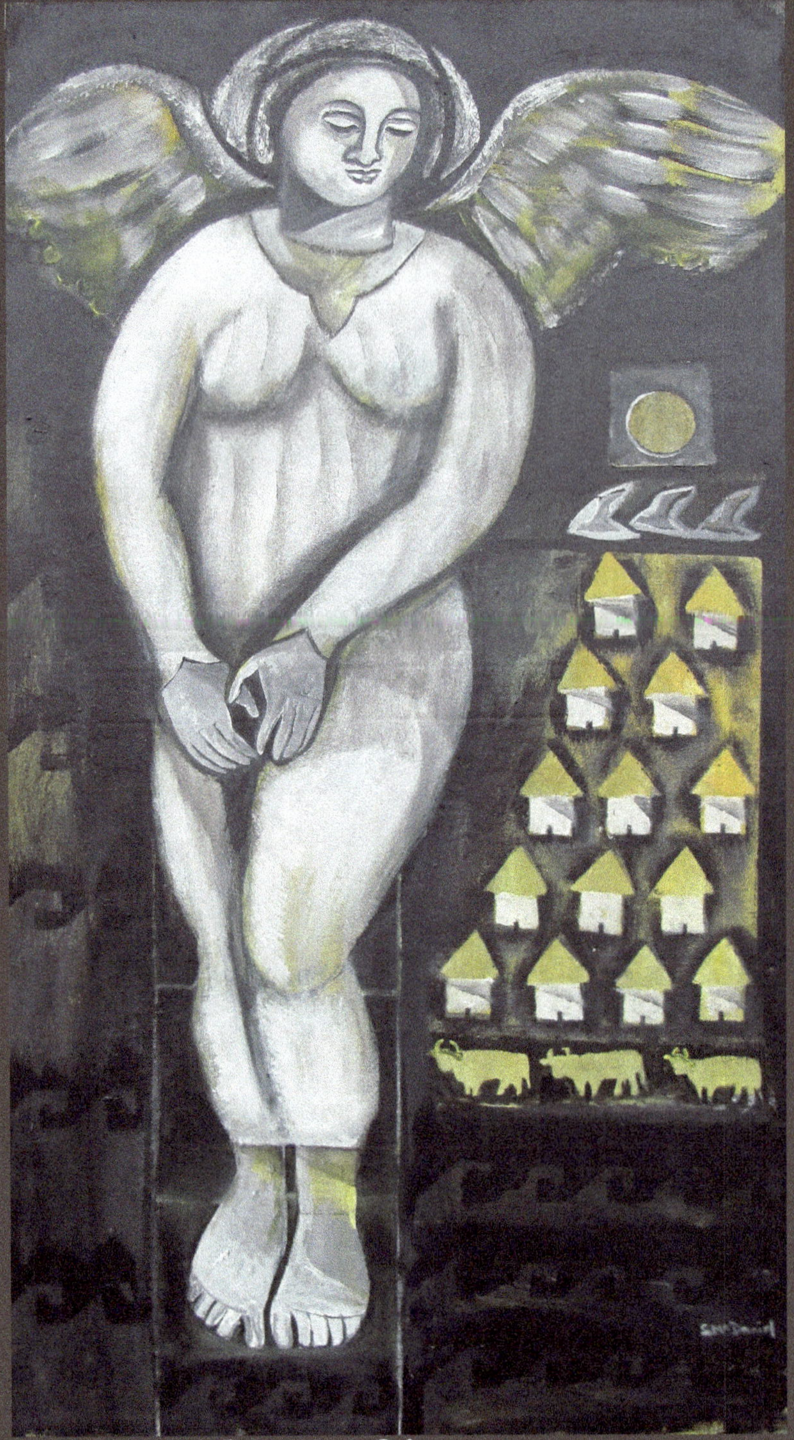

Lool's Angel Over Africa
(135cm x 75cm)

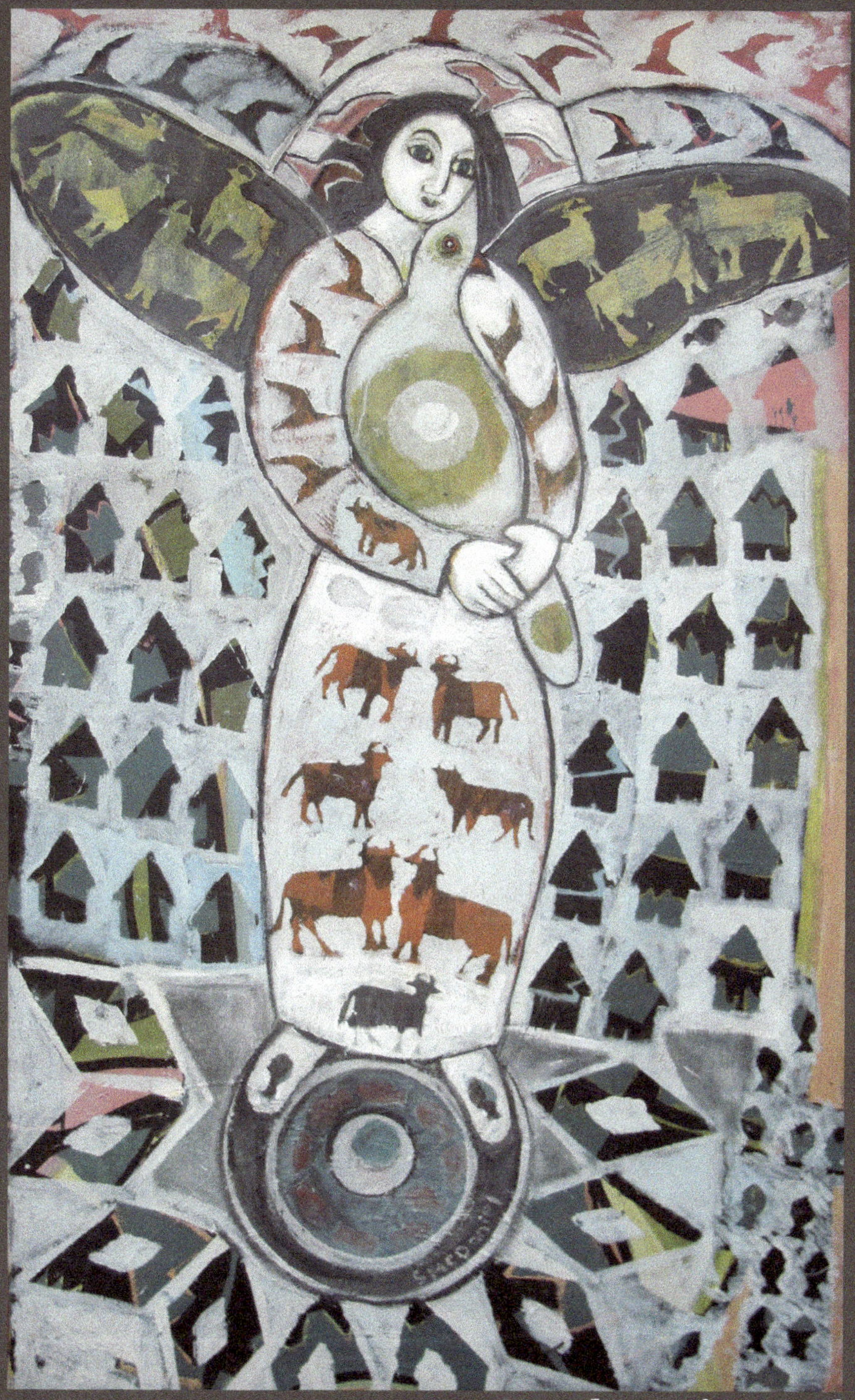

Rural Lourie Angel
(115cm x 70cm)

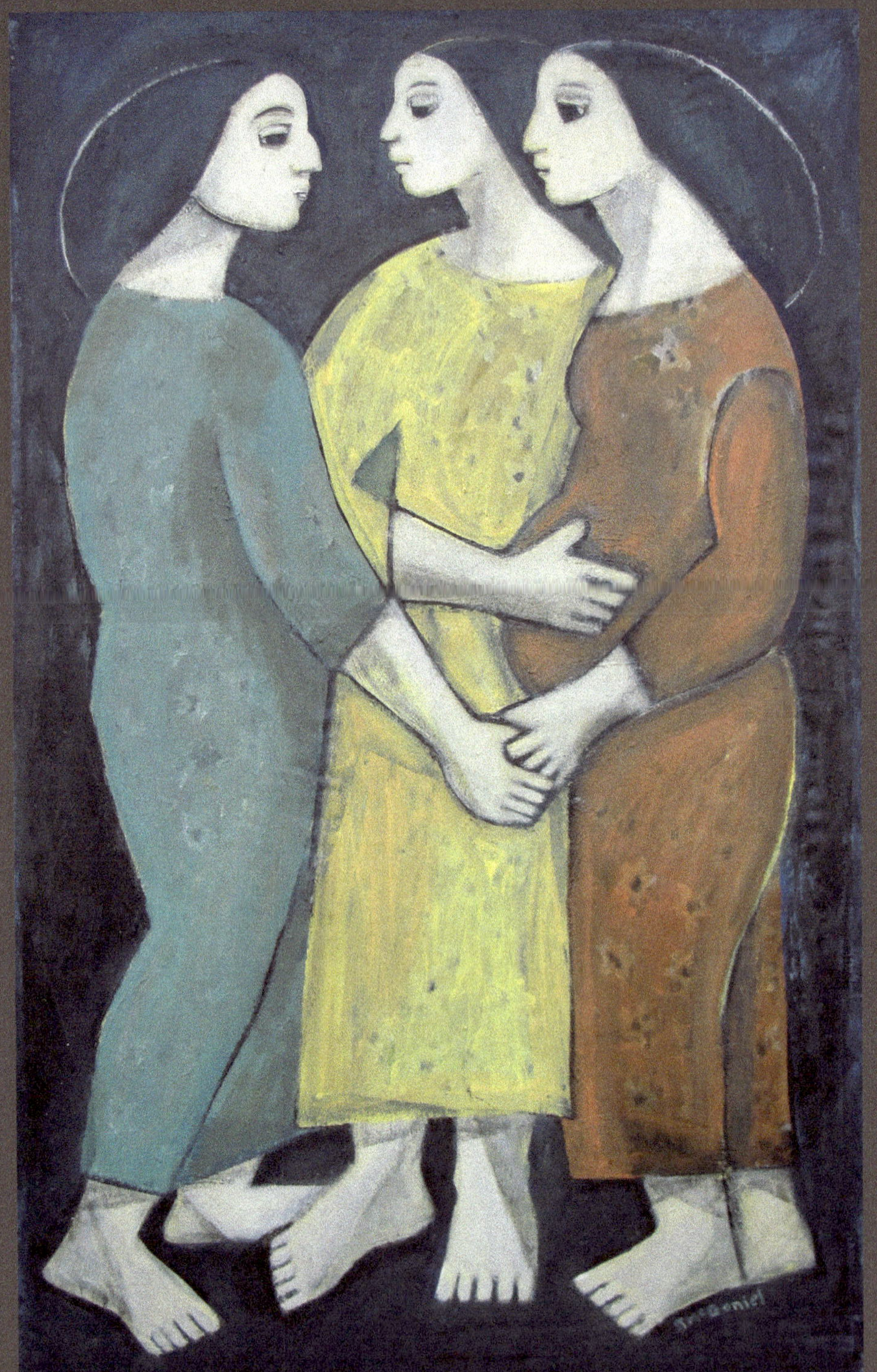

Girl Gathering
(110cm x 70cm)

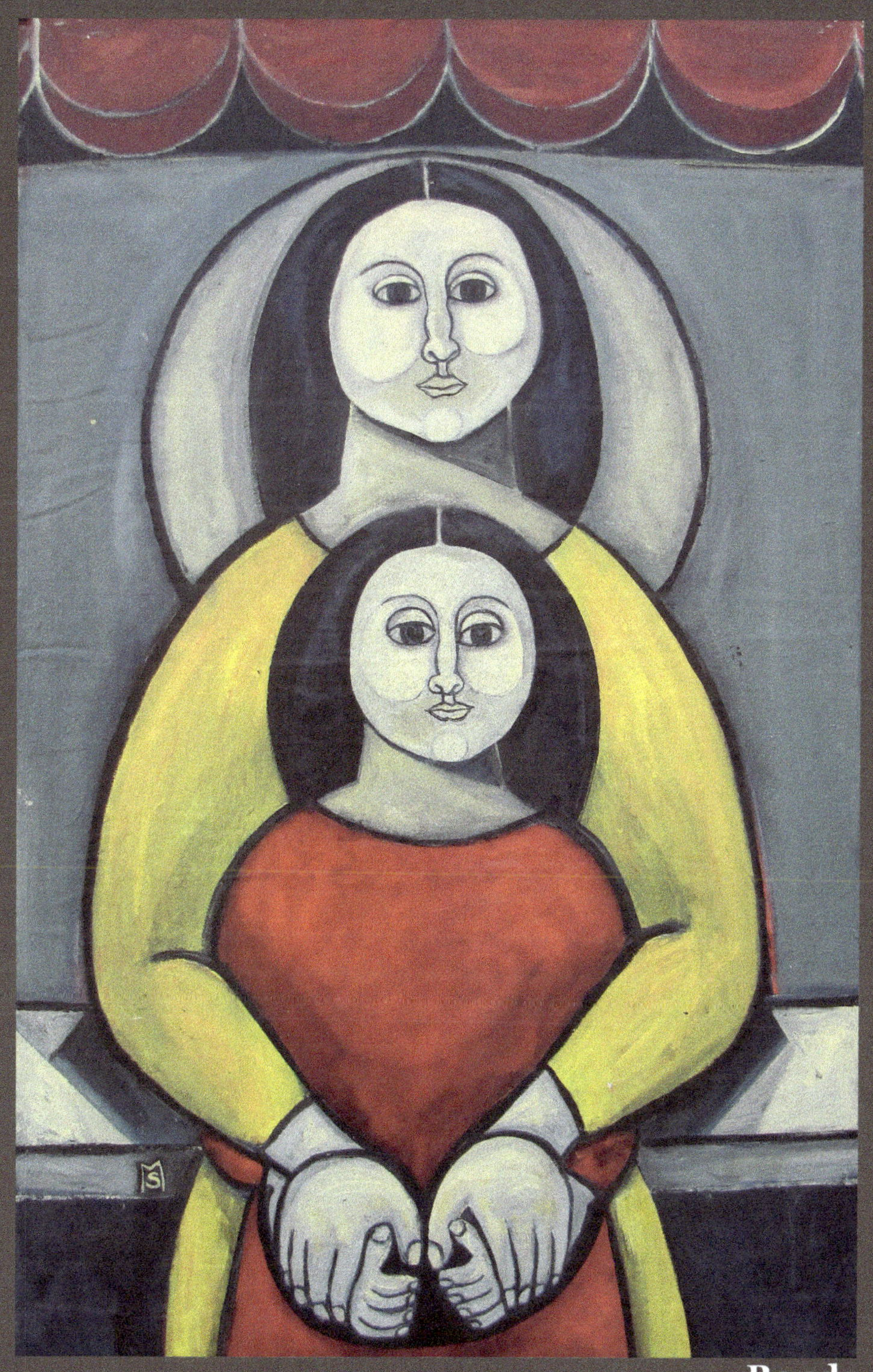

Bonds
(110cm x 70cm)

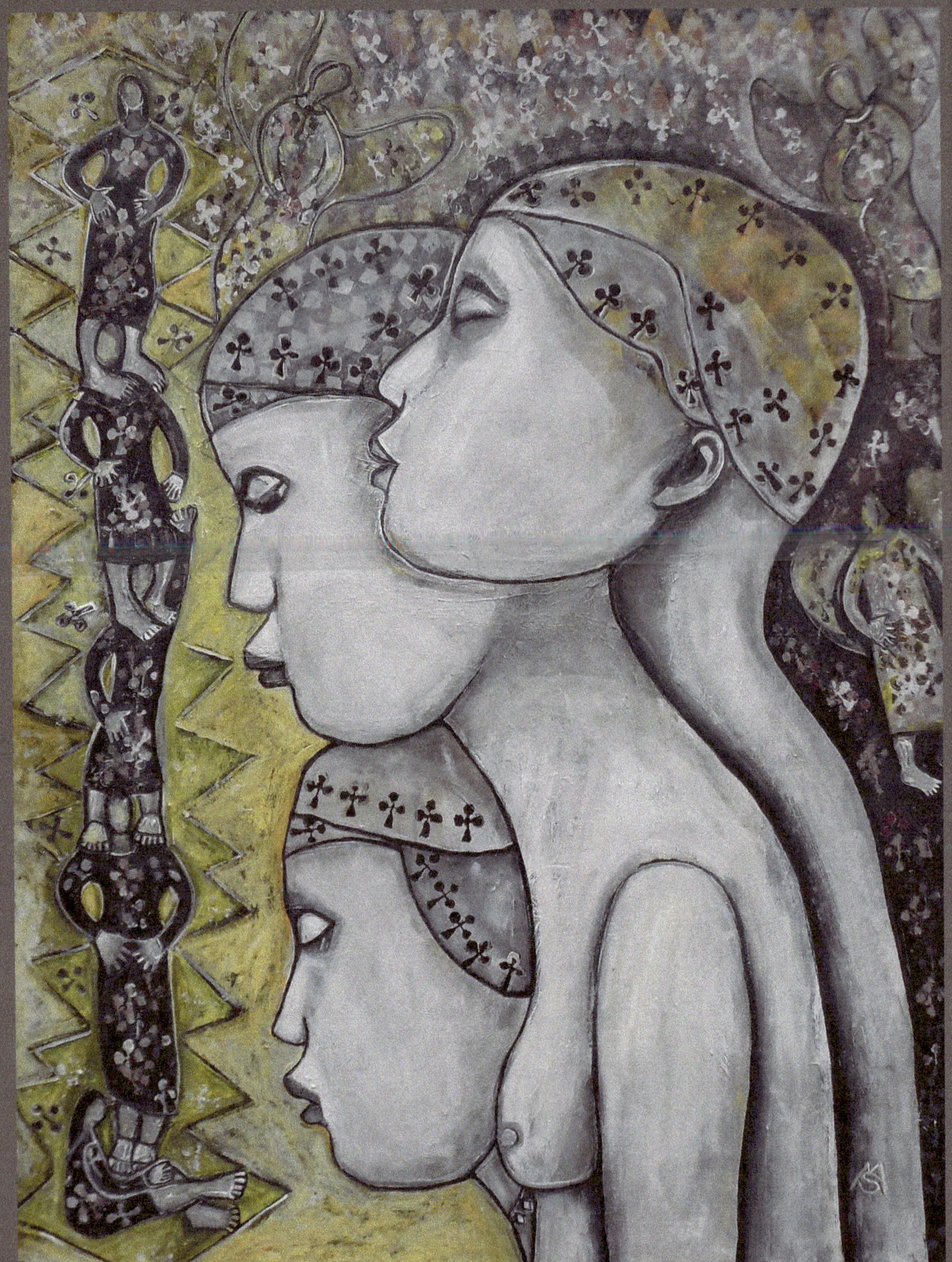

Seeds
(101cm x 76cm)

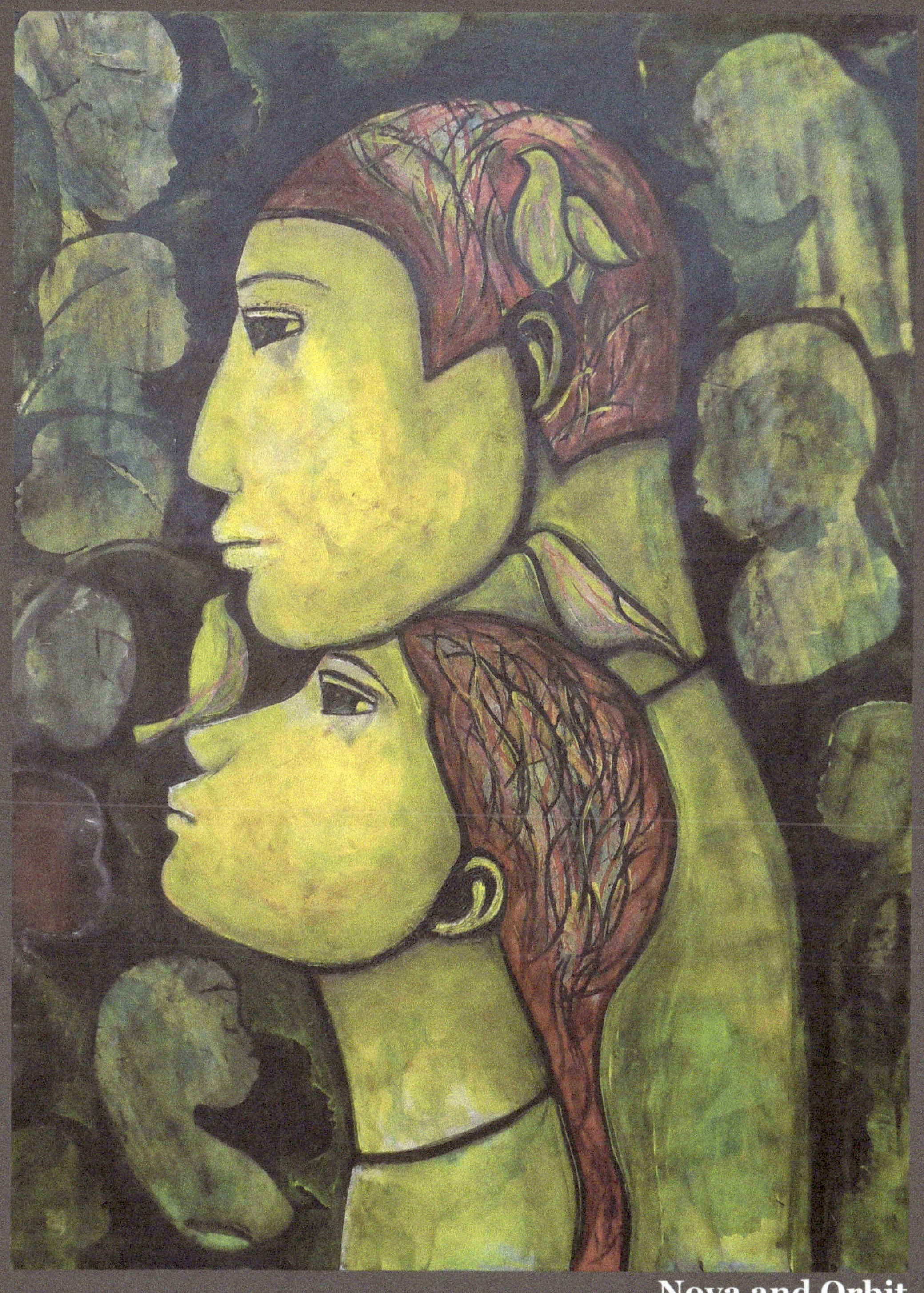

Nova and Orbit
(10cm x 76cm)

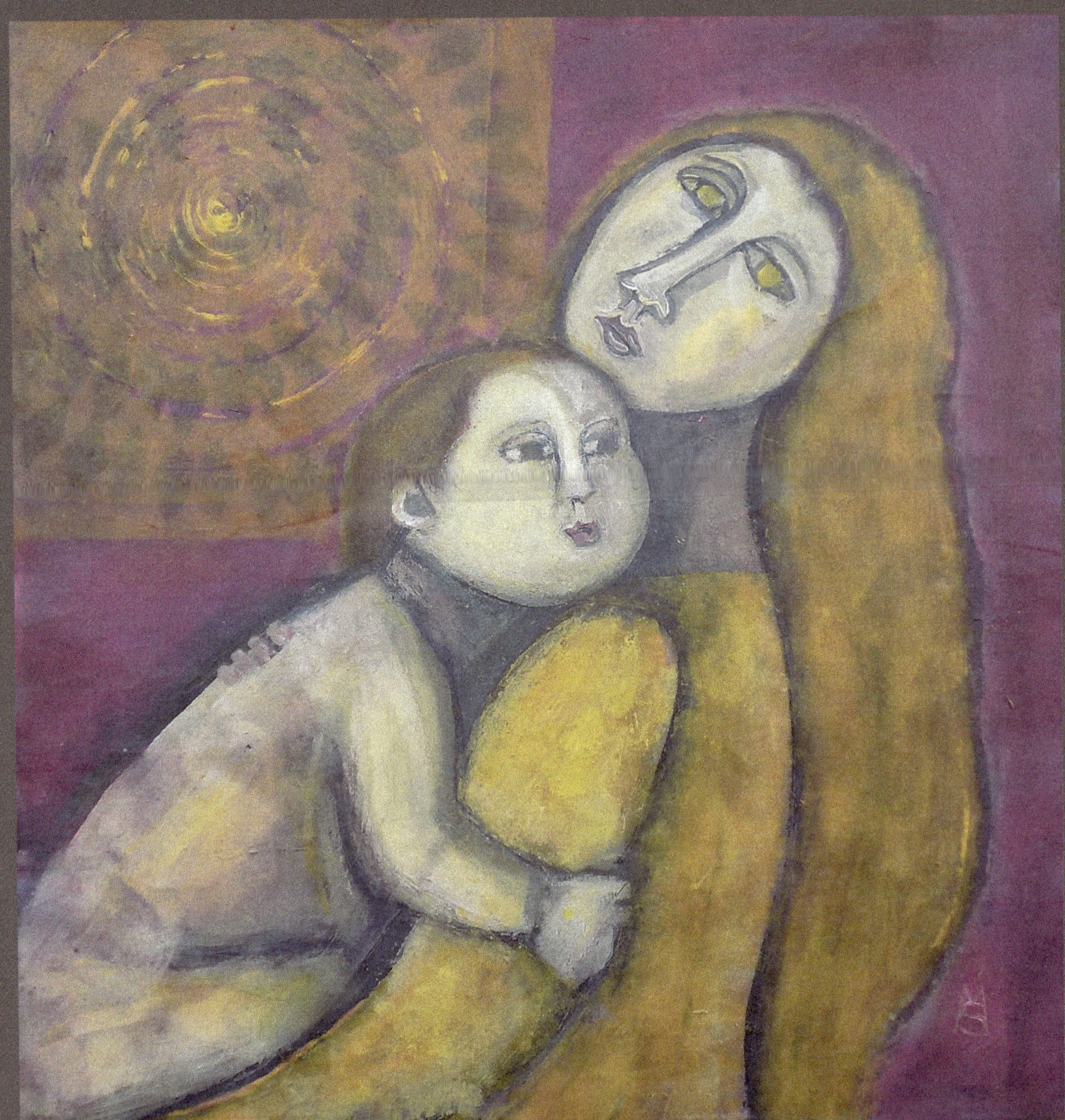

Cadmium and Magenta
(78cm x 76cm)

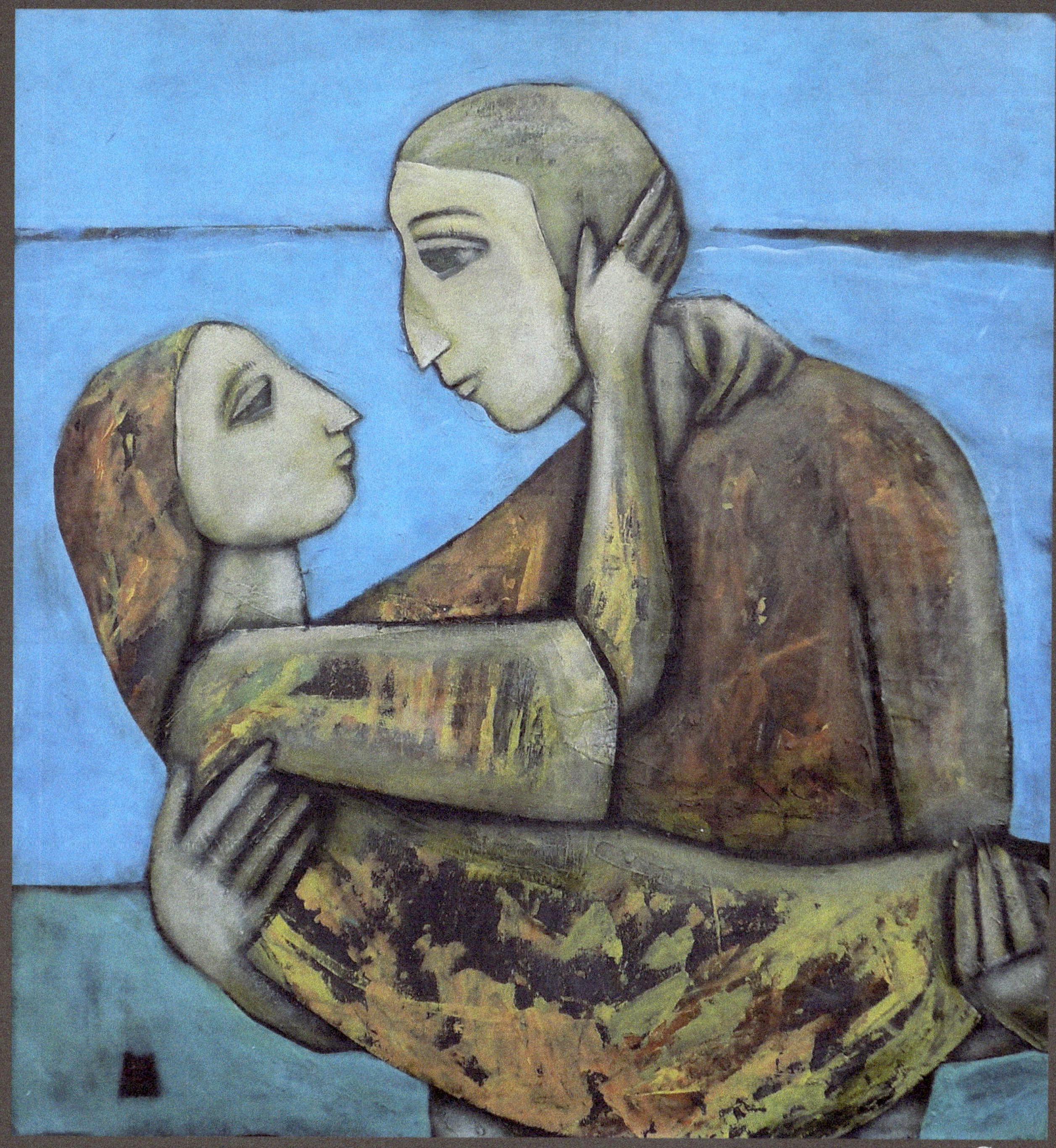

Gaze
(79cm x 76cm)

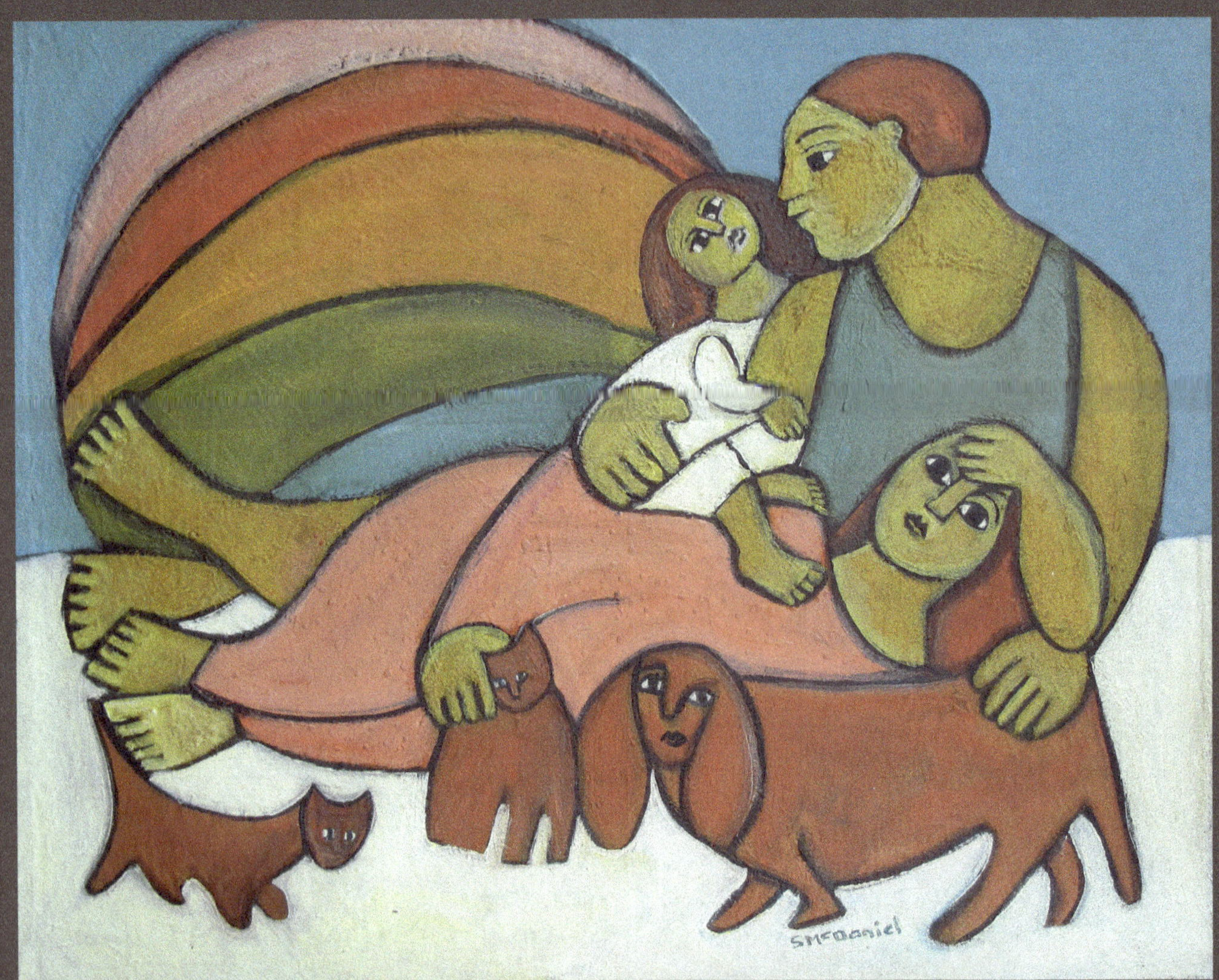

Jani's Rainbow Family
(60cm x 80cm)

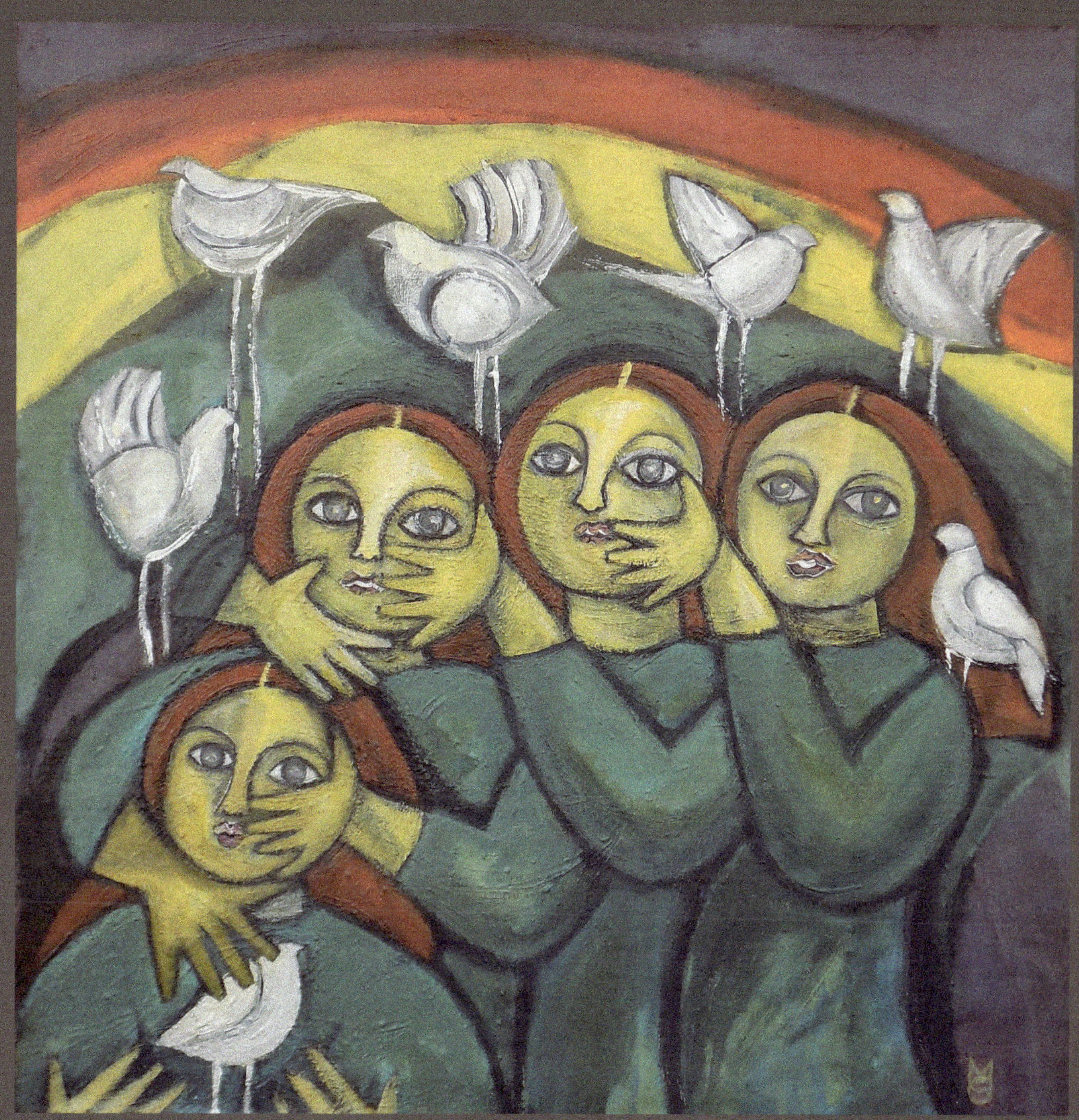

Quatre
(70cm x 70cm)

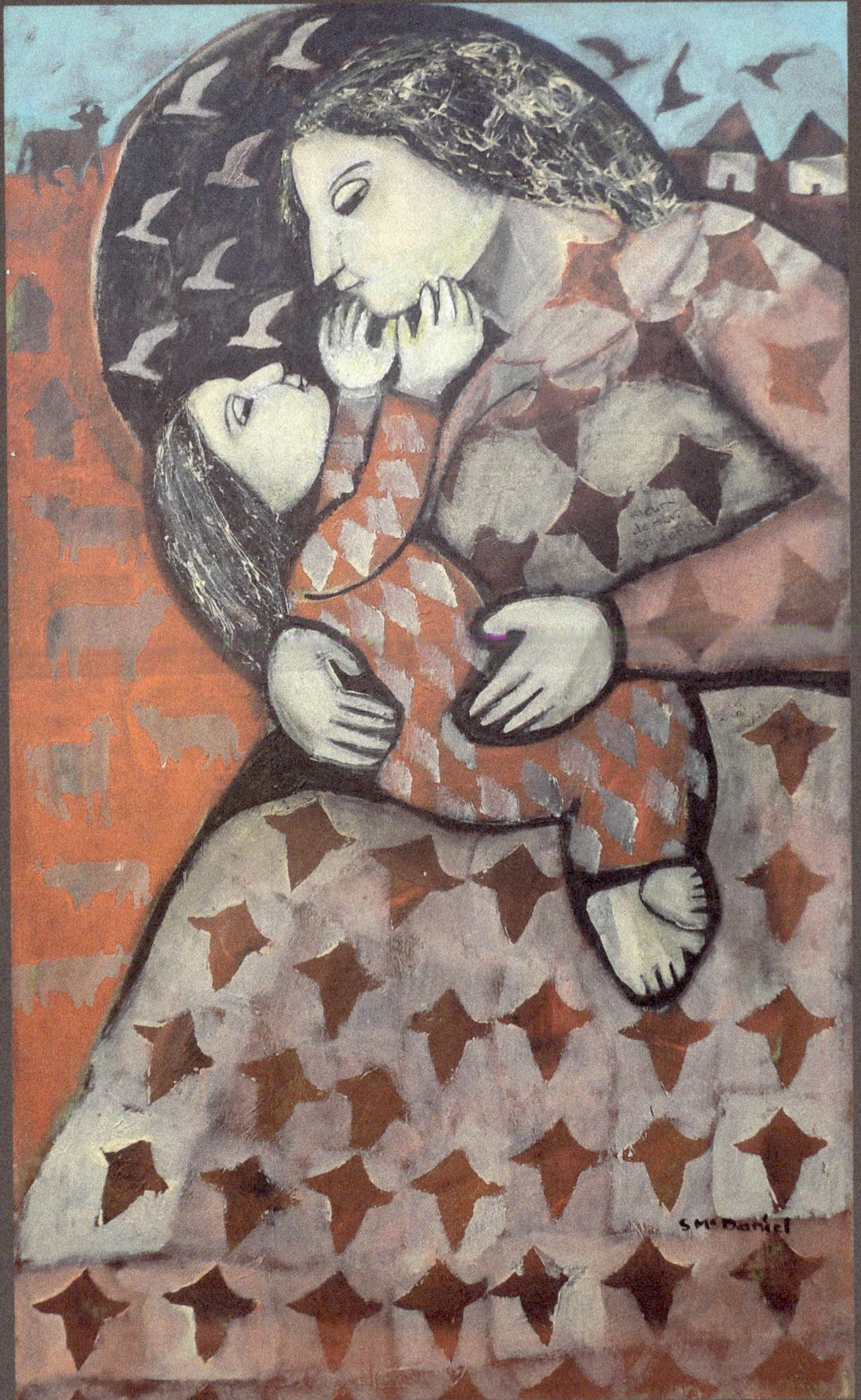

Fleur-de-Lis Madonna
(110cm x 70cm)

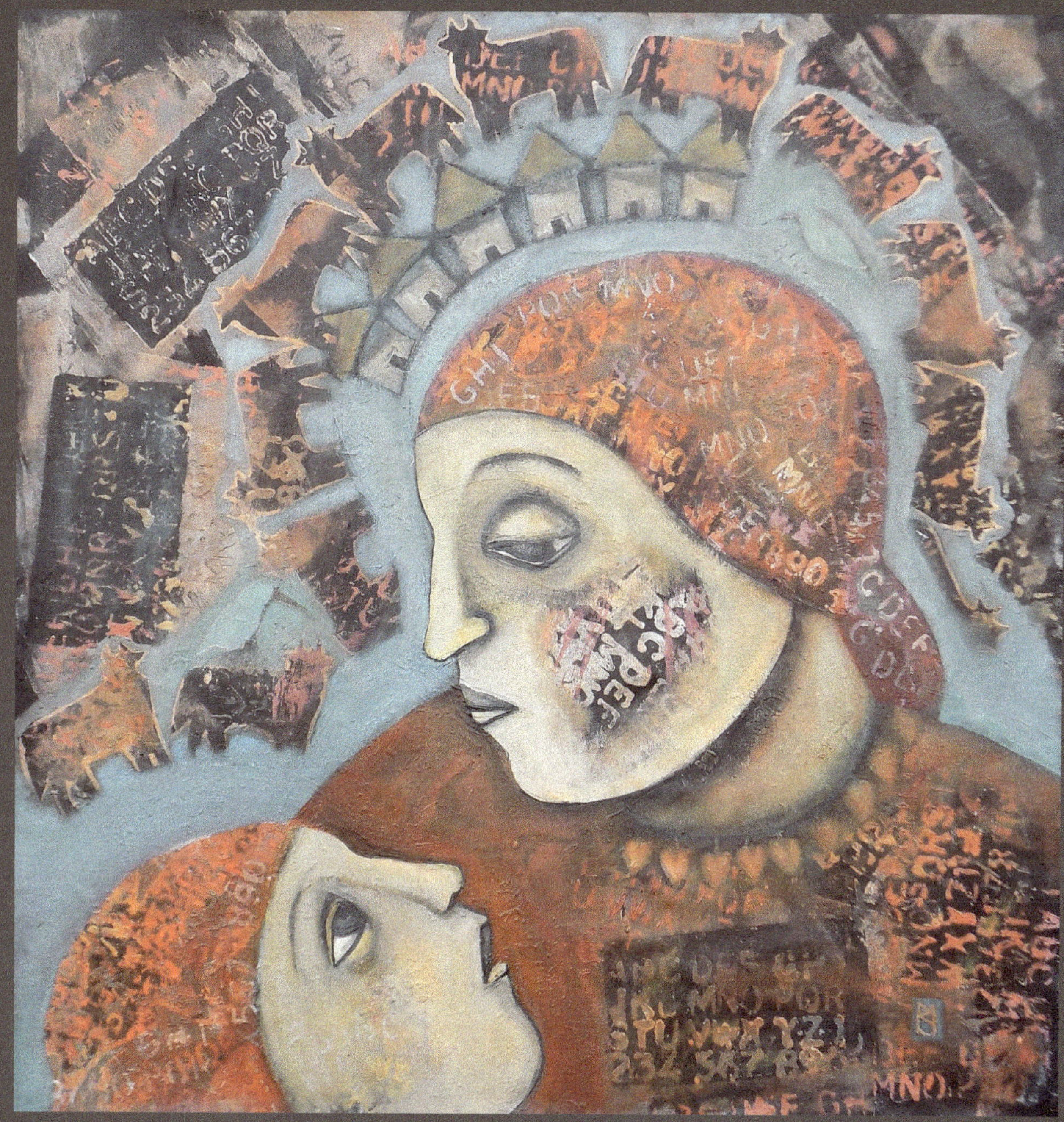

Revelations
(78cm x 76cm)

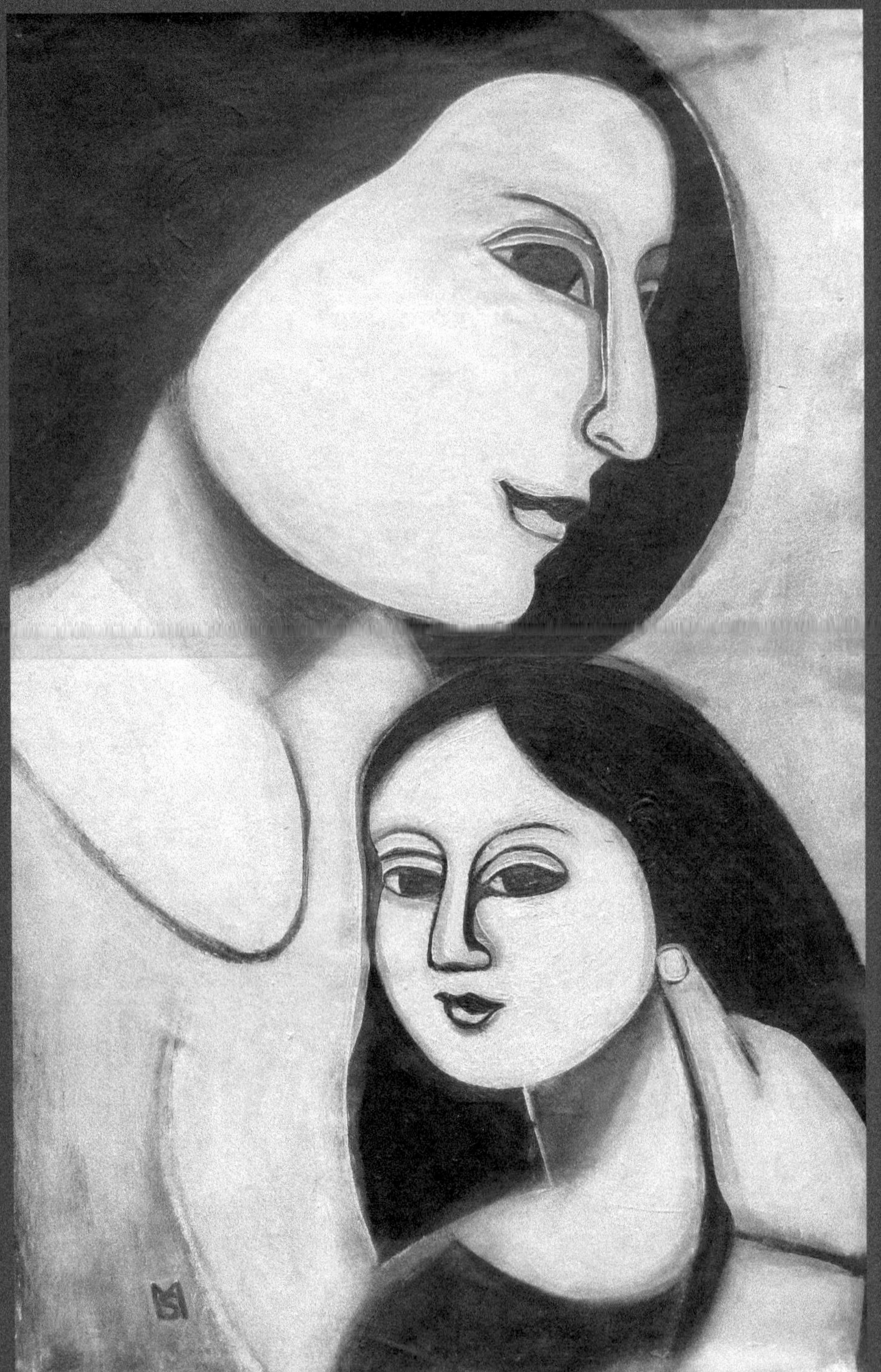

Camilla
(75cm x 50cm)

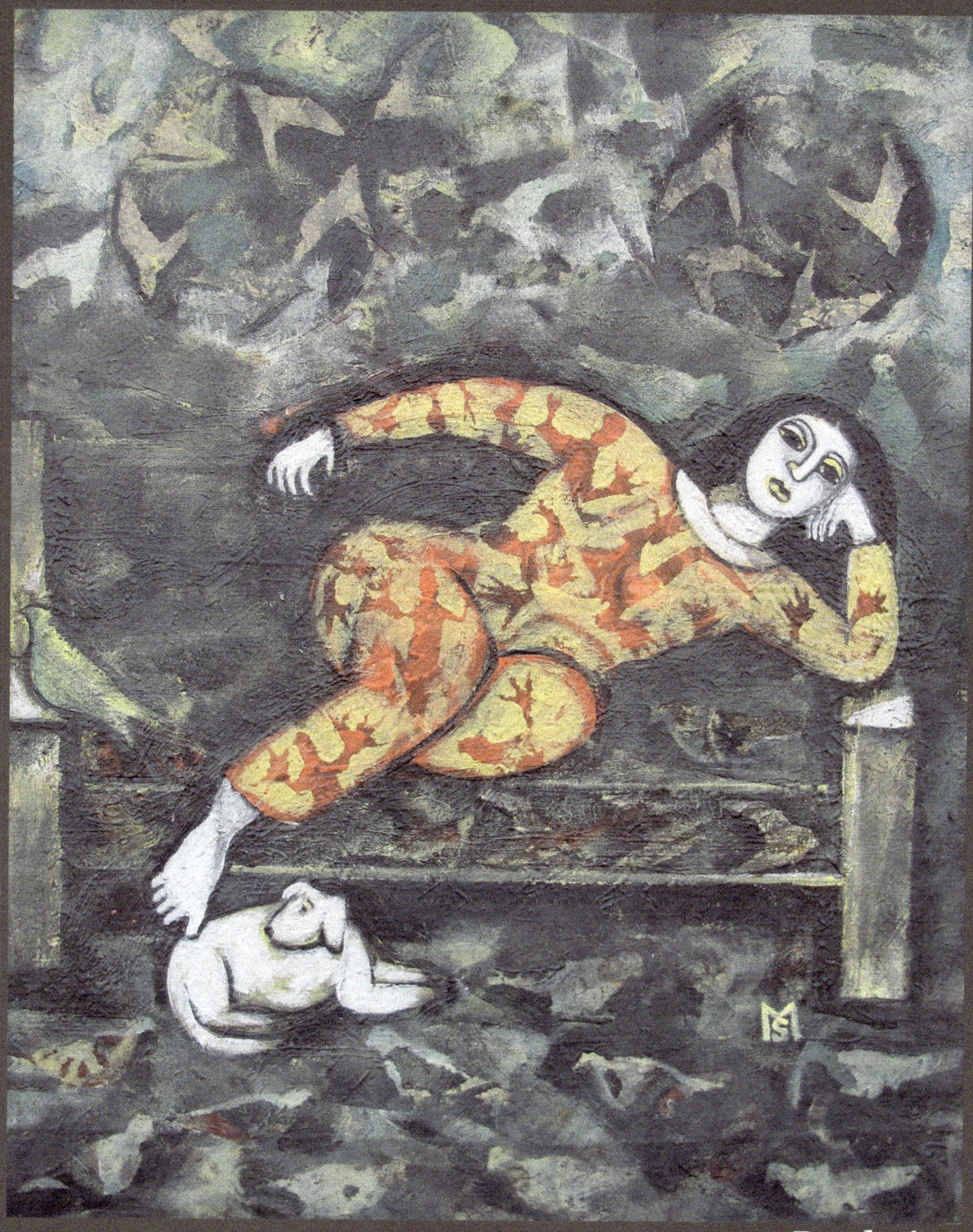

Pondering
(70cm x 55cm)

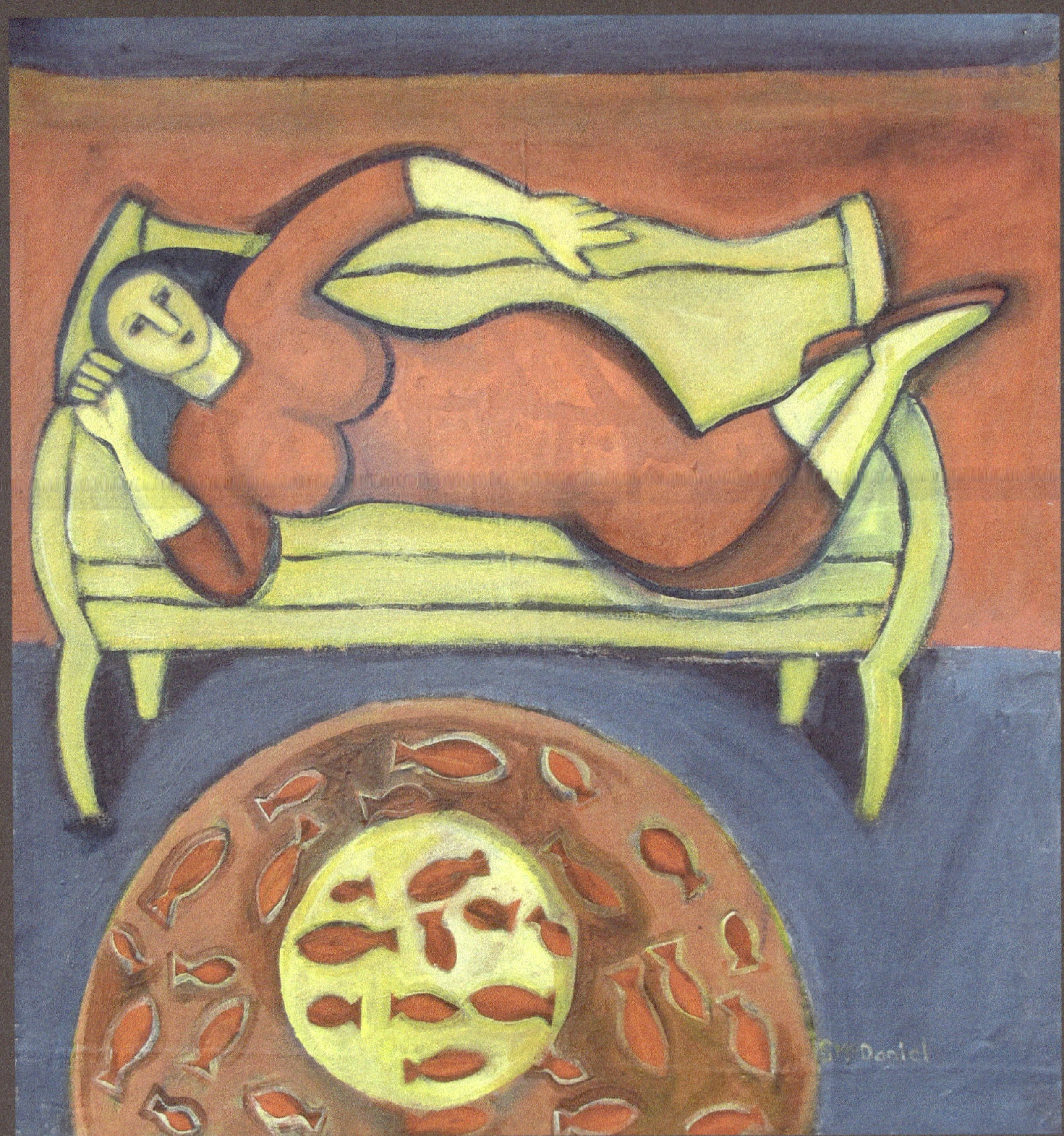

Reclining in Red
(70cm x 65cm)

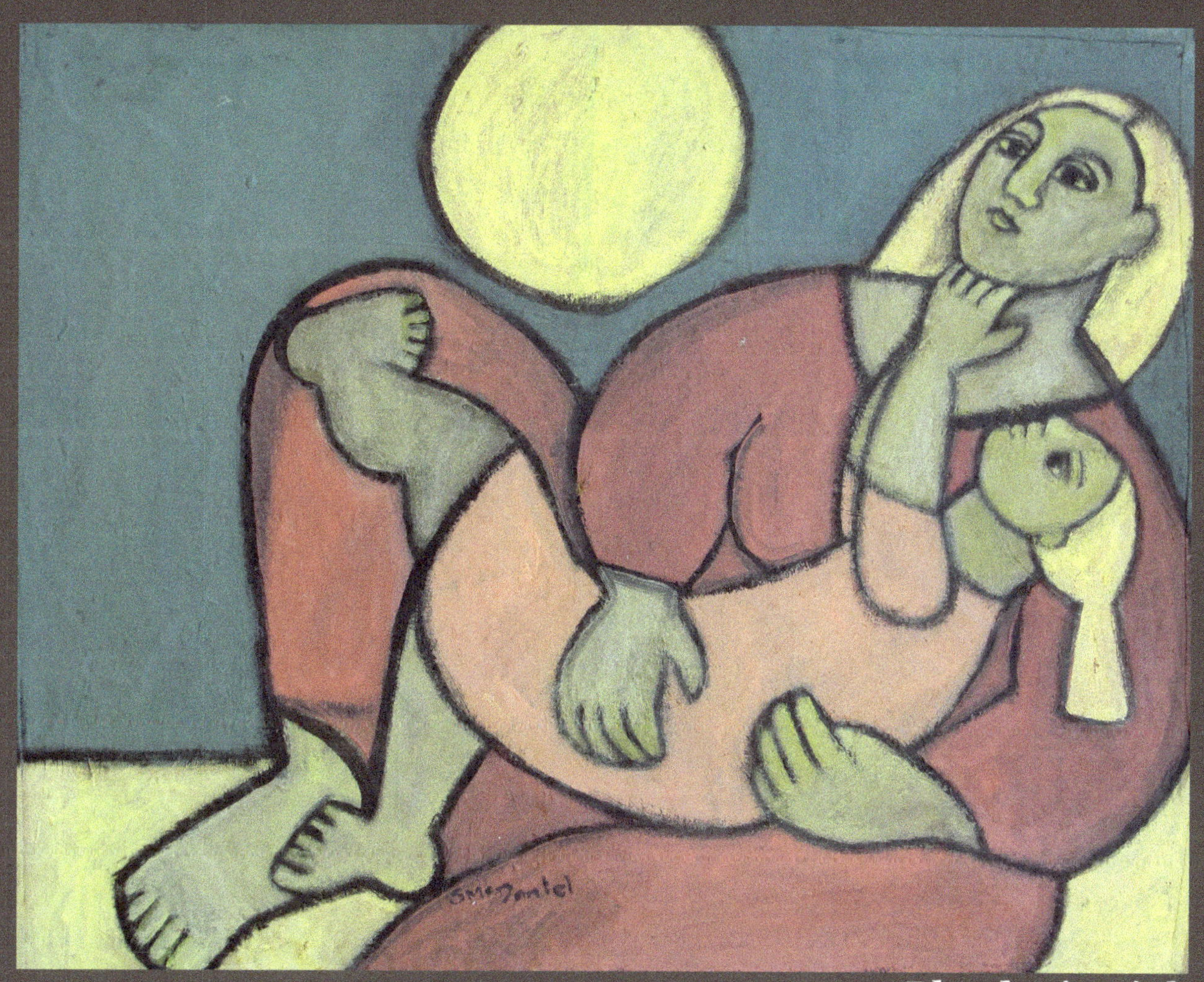

Blondes in Pink
(60cm x 75cm)

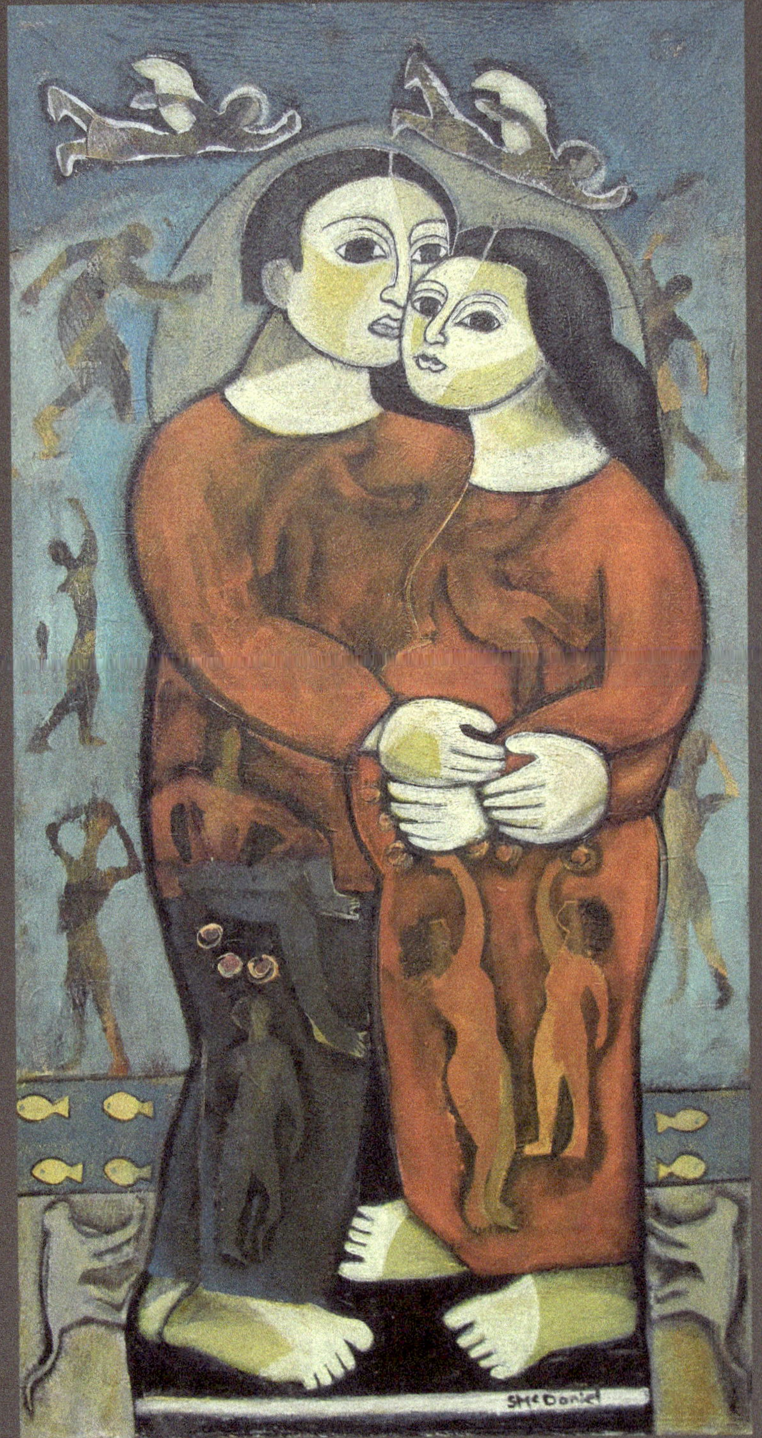

Lingering Love
(130cm x 70cm)

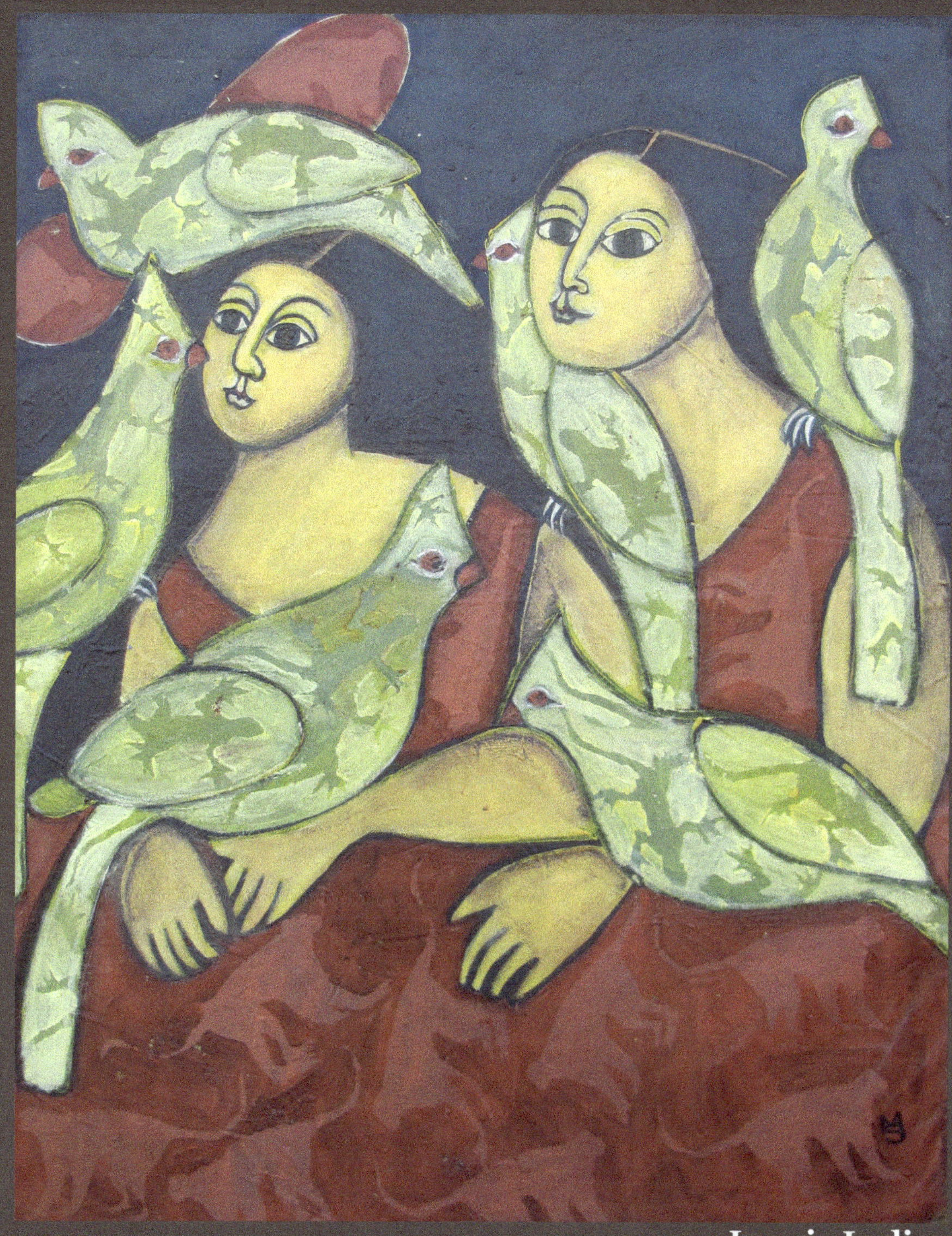

Lourie Ladies
(90cm x 75cm)

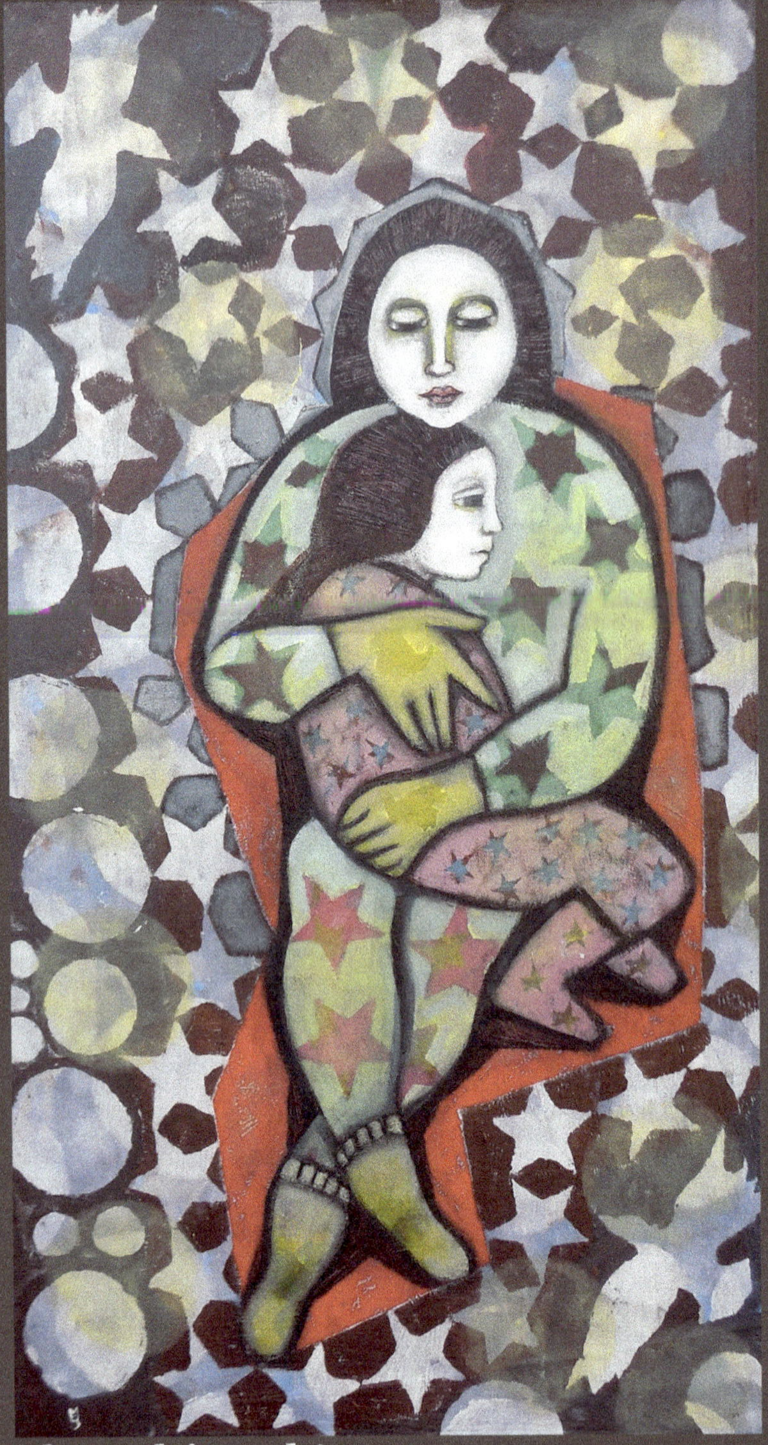

Alexandria and Ayanna
(70cm x 30cm)

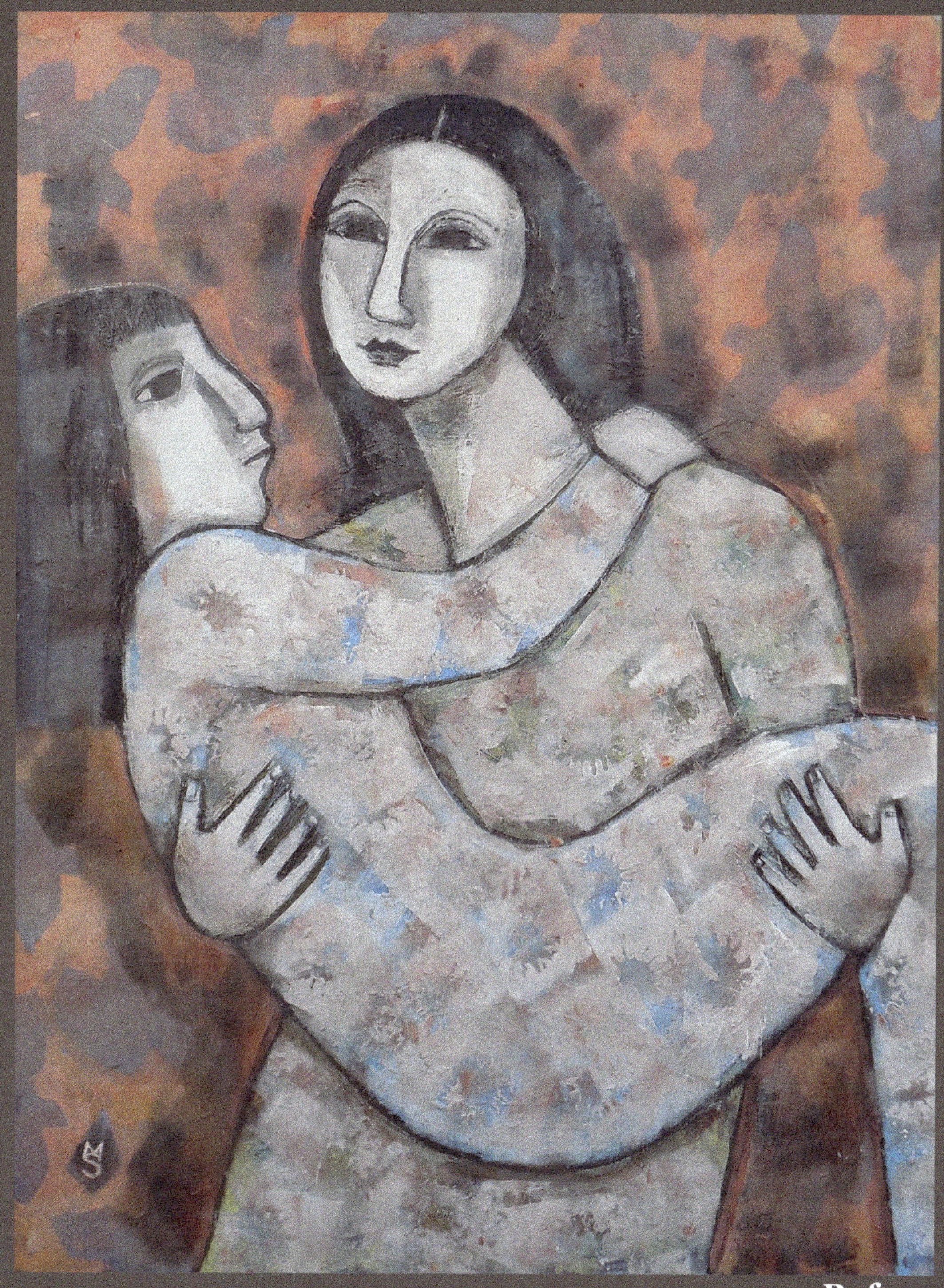

Refuge
(101cm x 76cm)

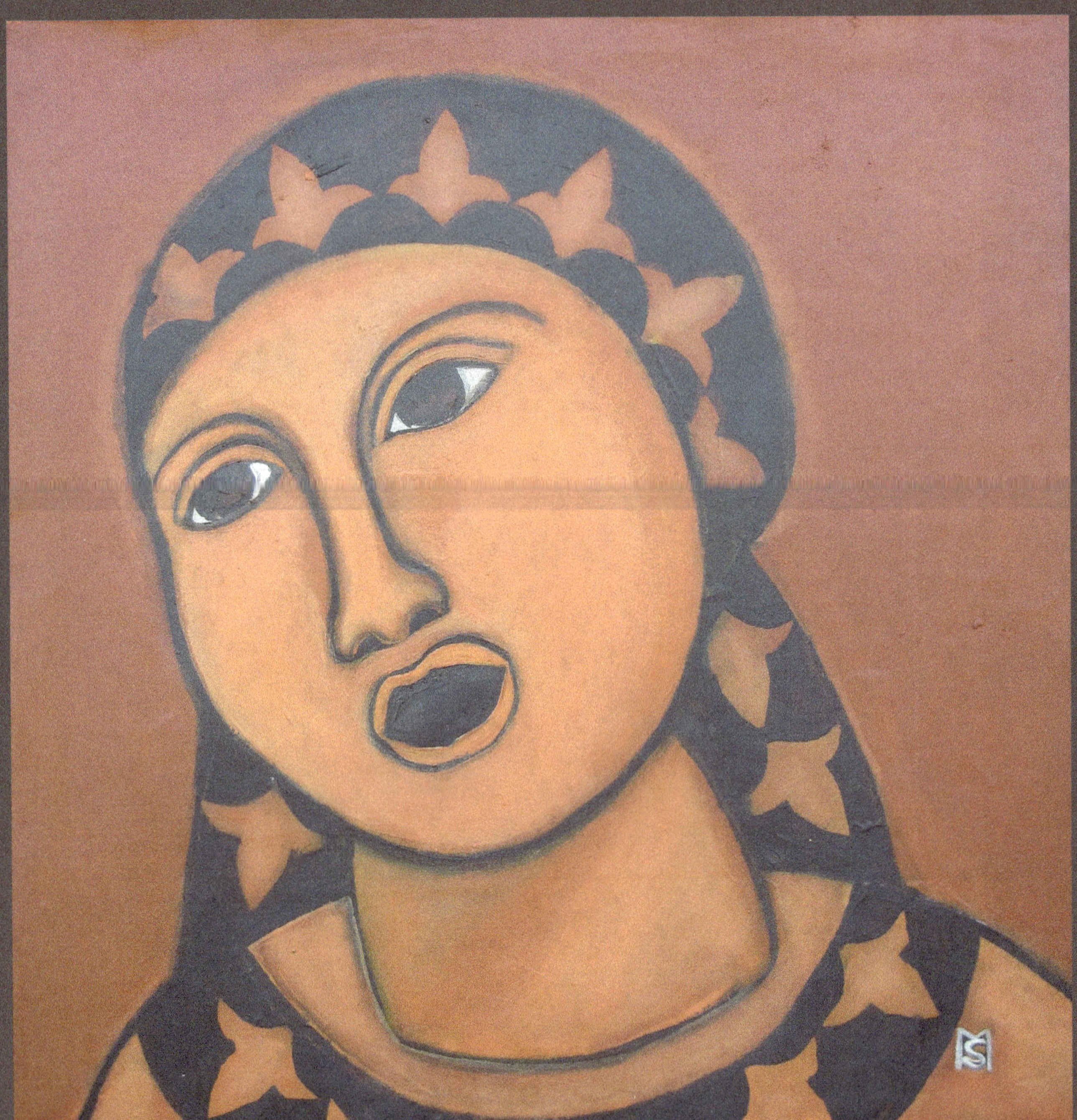

Girl Song
(75cm x 75cm)

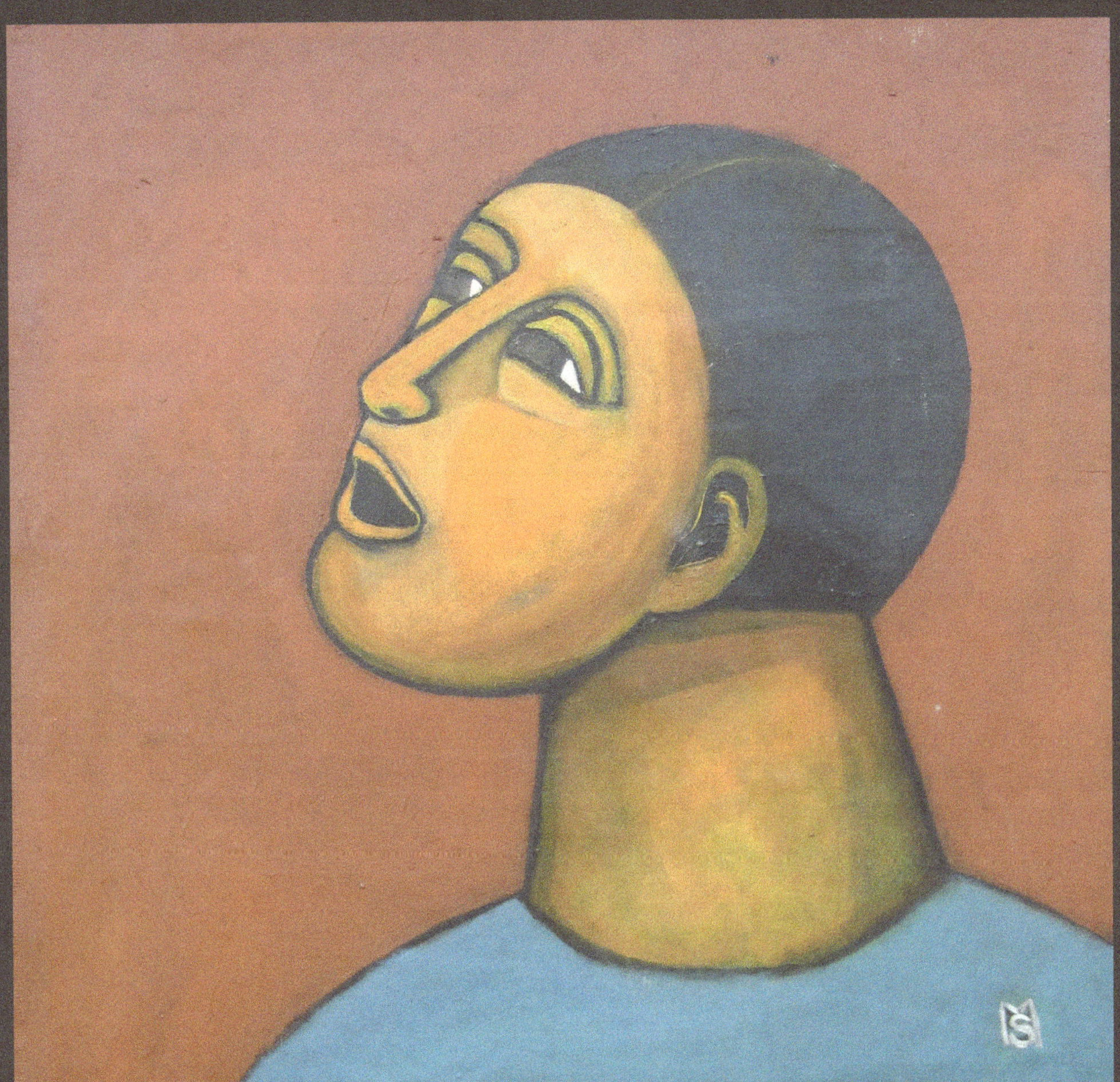

Boy Song
(75cm x 75cm)

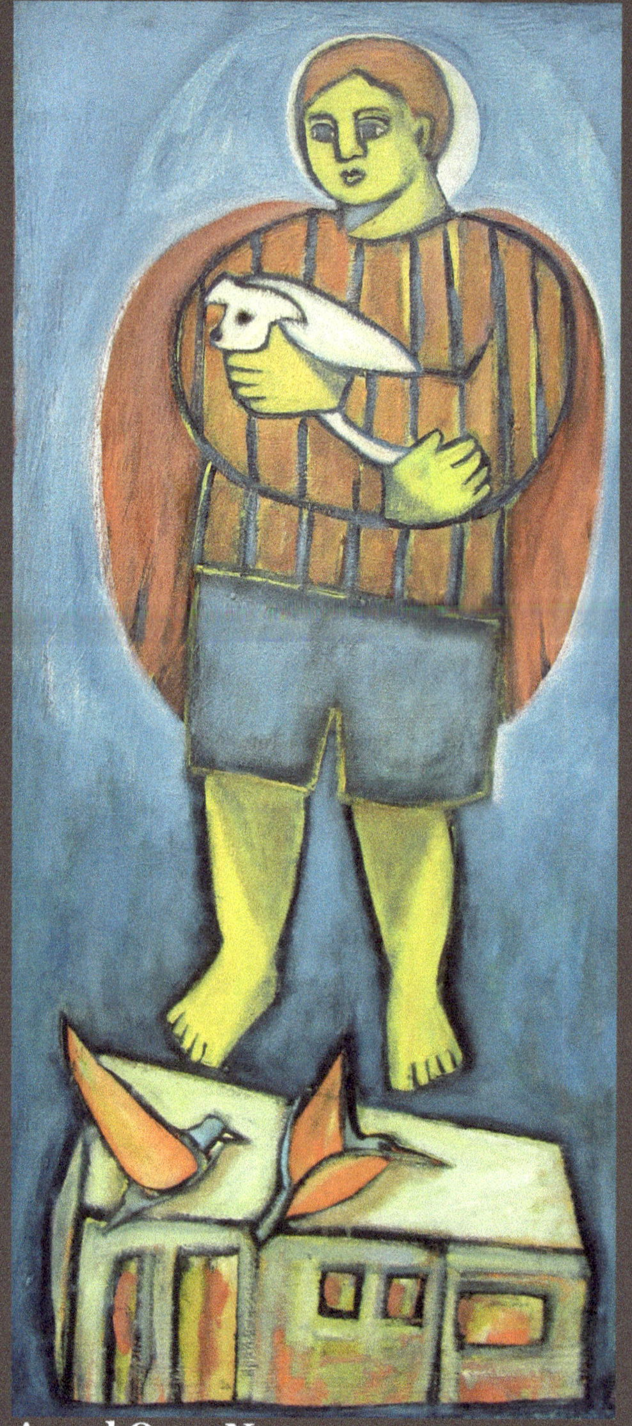

Angel Over Novena
(130cm x 60cm)

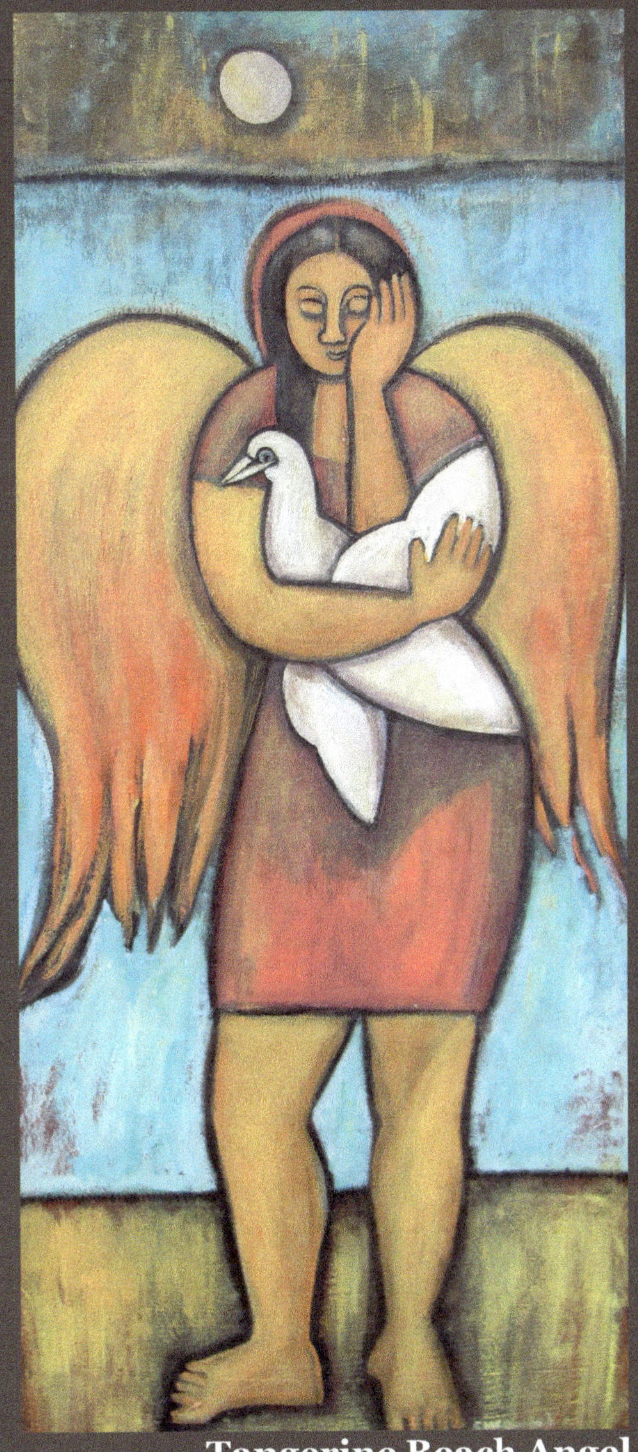

Tangerine Beach Angel
(130cm x 60cm)

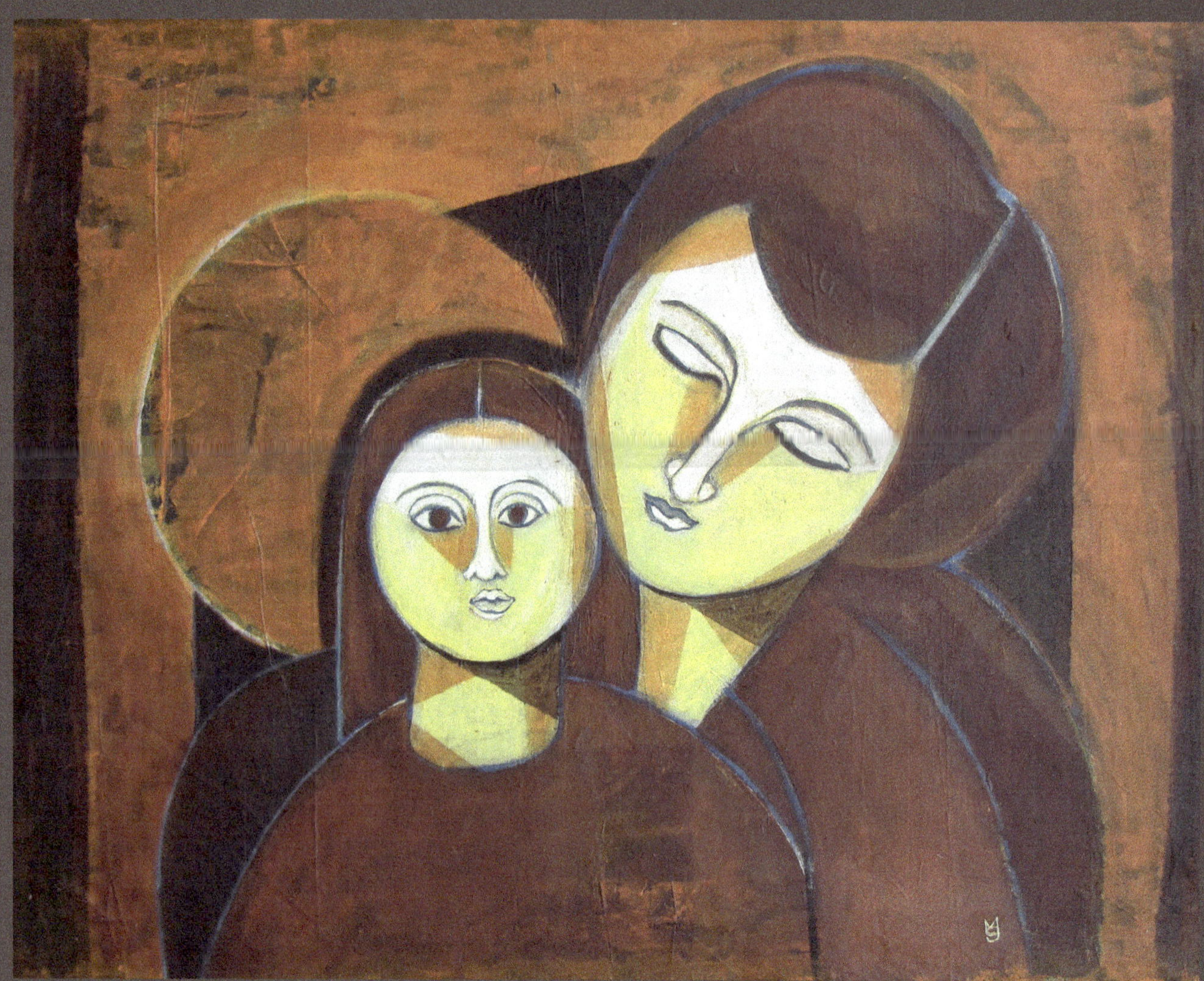

Caramel Motherhood
(95cm x 130cm)

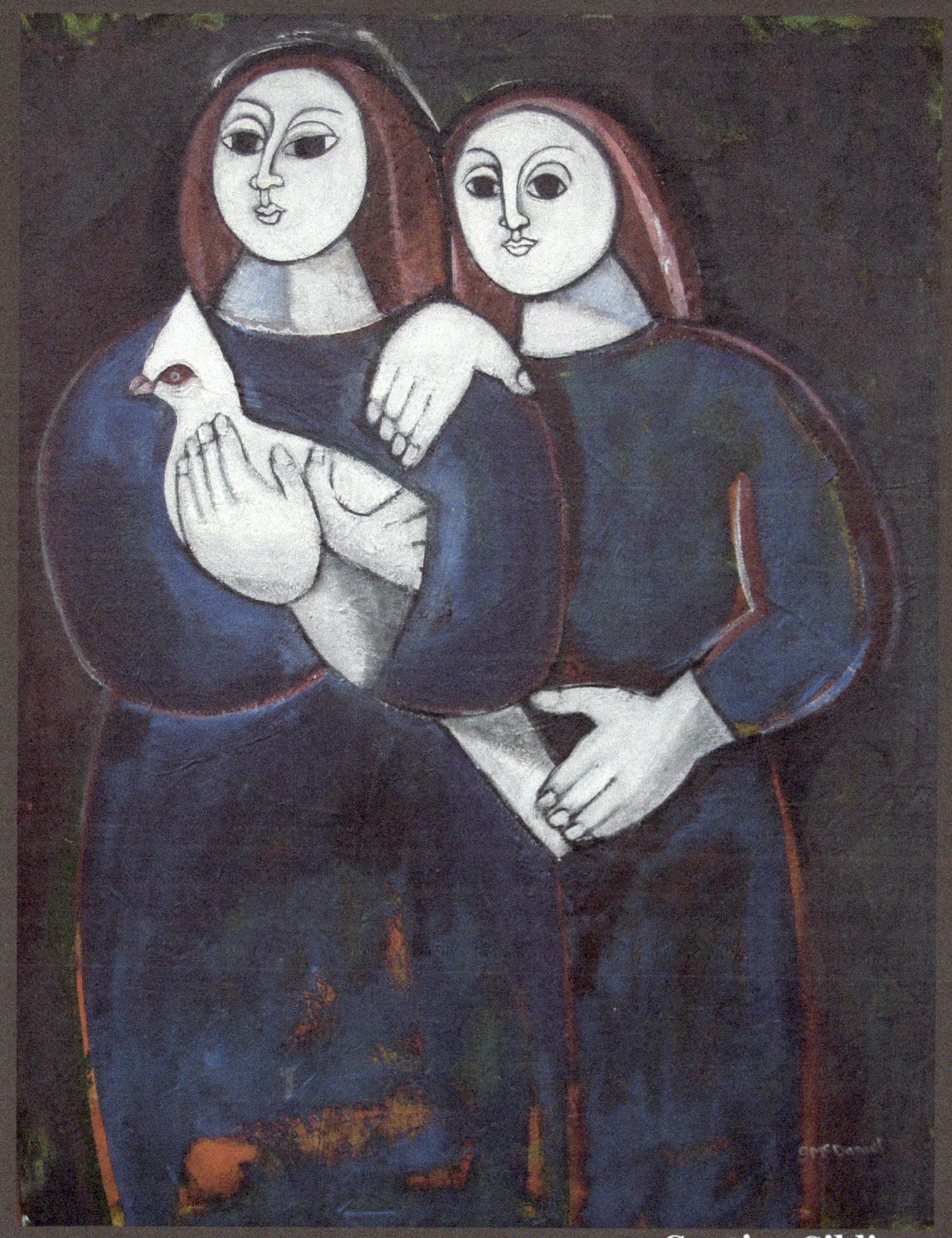

Gentian Siblings
(95cm x 75cm)
Digital version on pg.174.

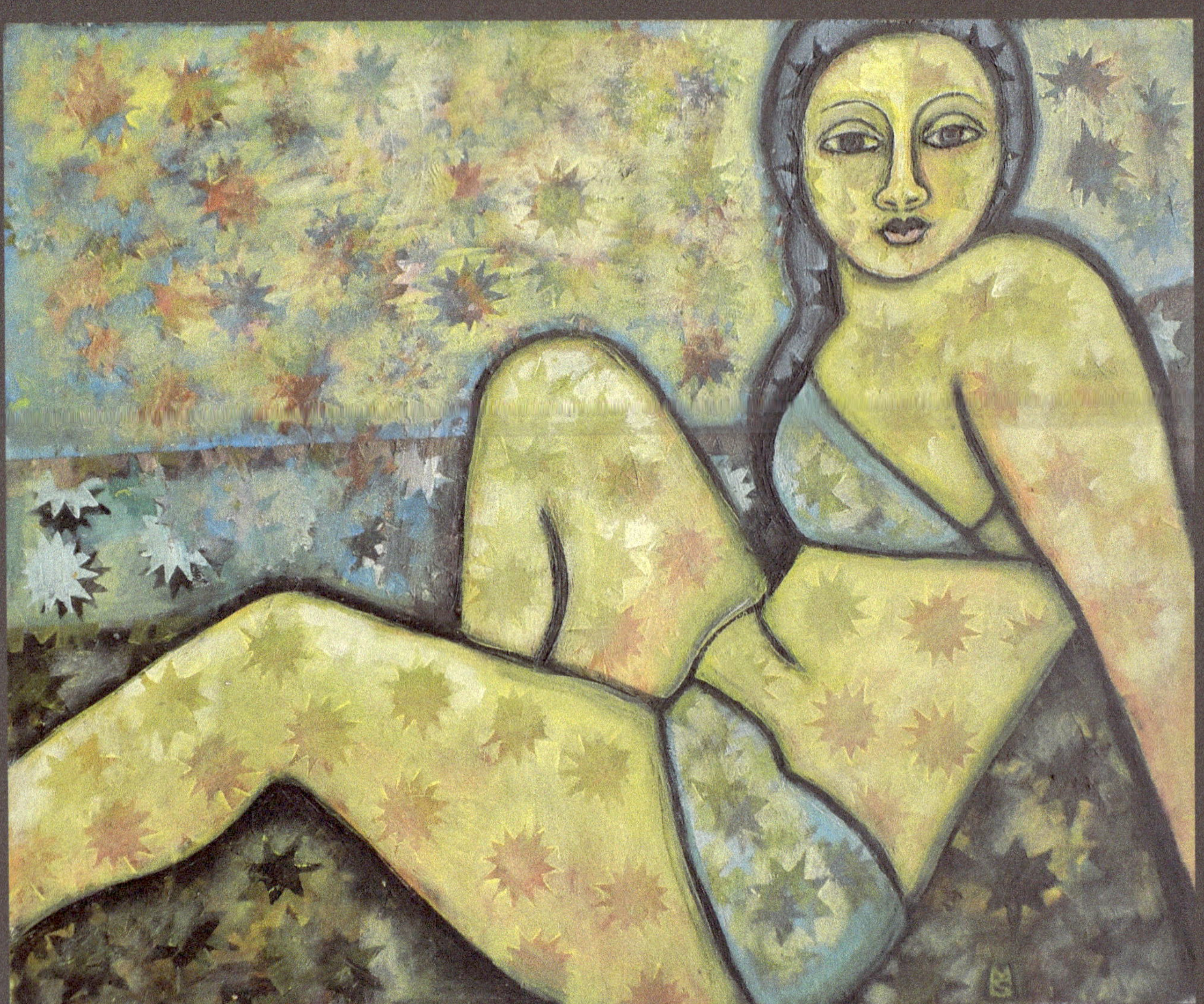

Sunlight
(49cm x 61cm)

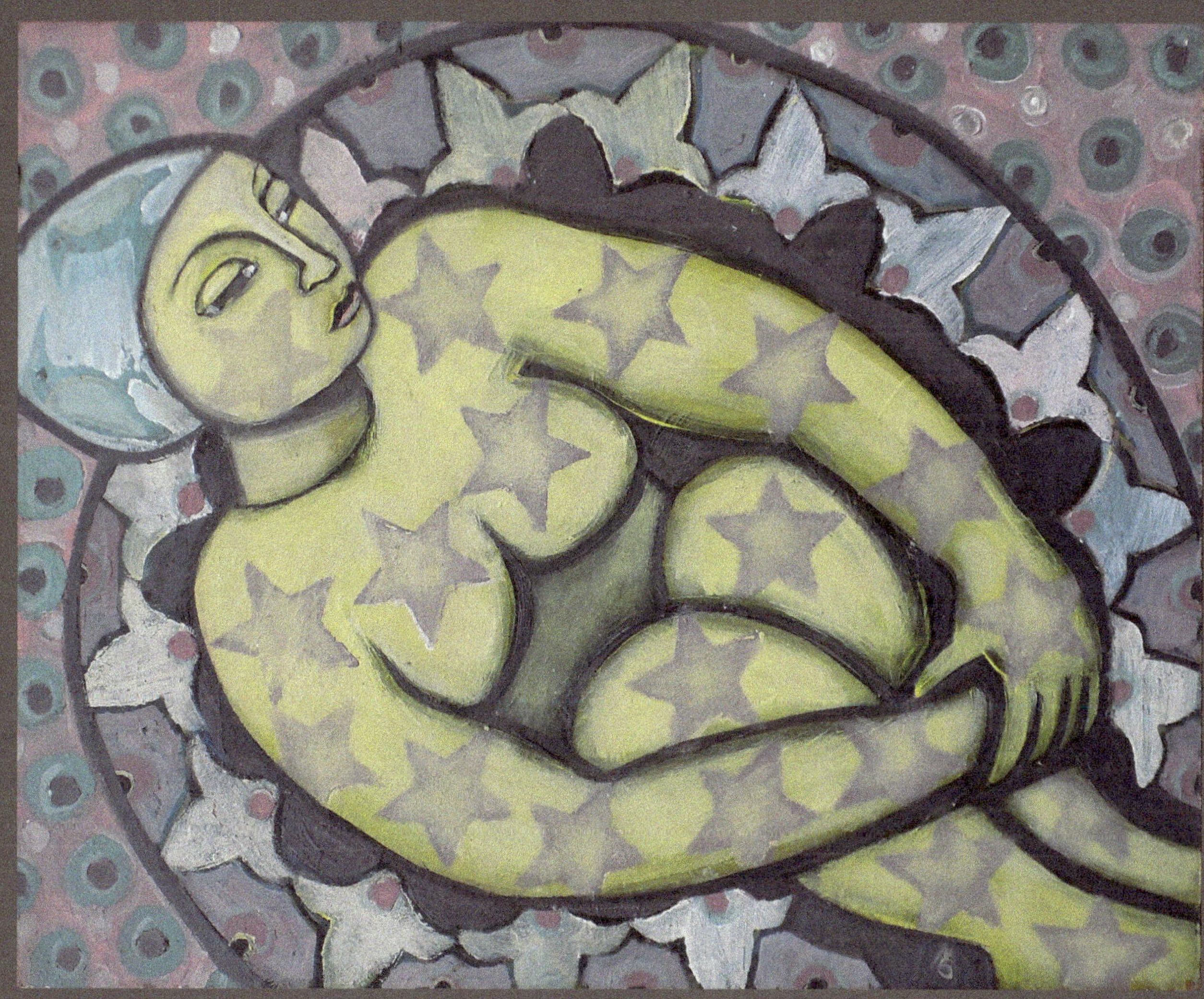

Starlight
(49cm x 61cm)

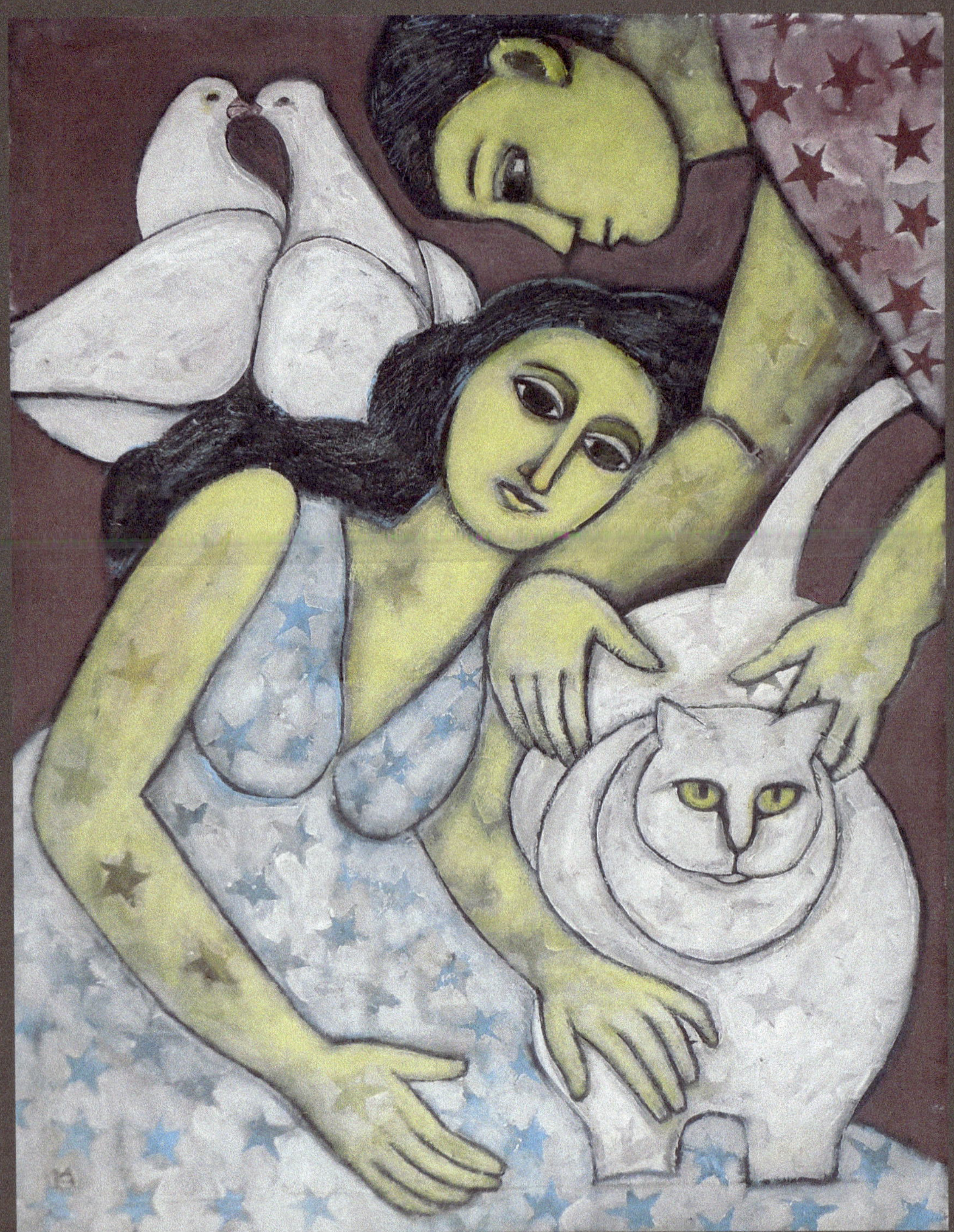

At Peace
(99cm x 78cm)

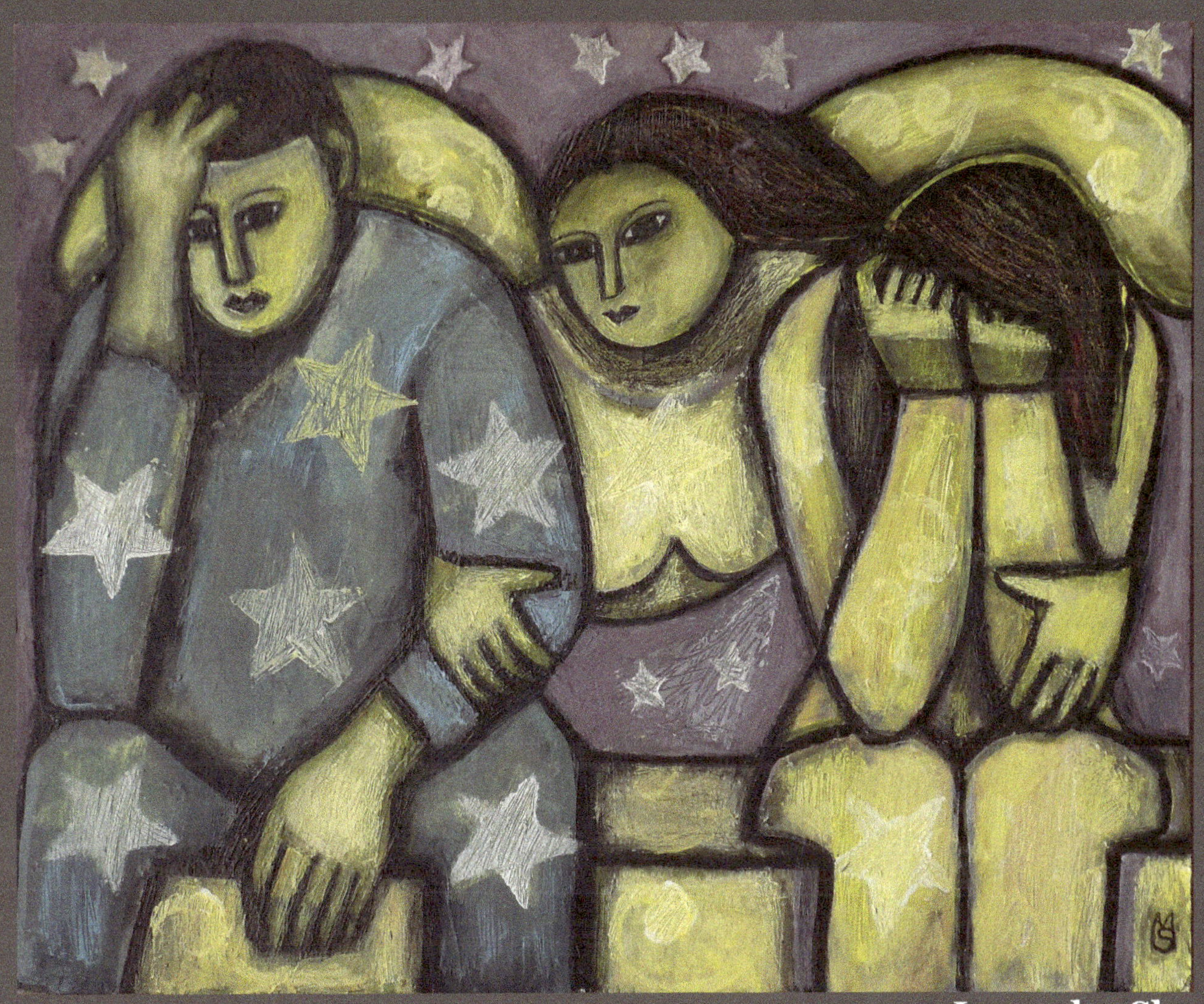

Lavender Sky
(49cm x 61cm)

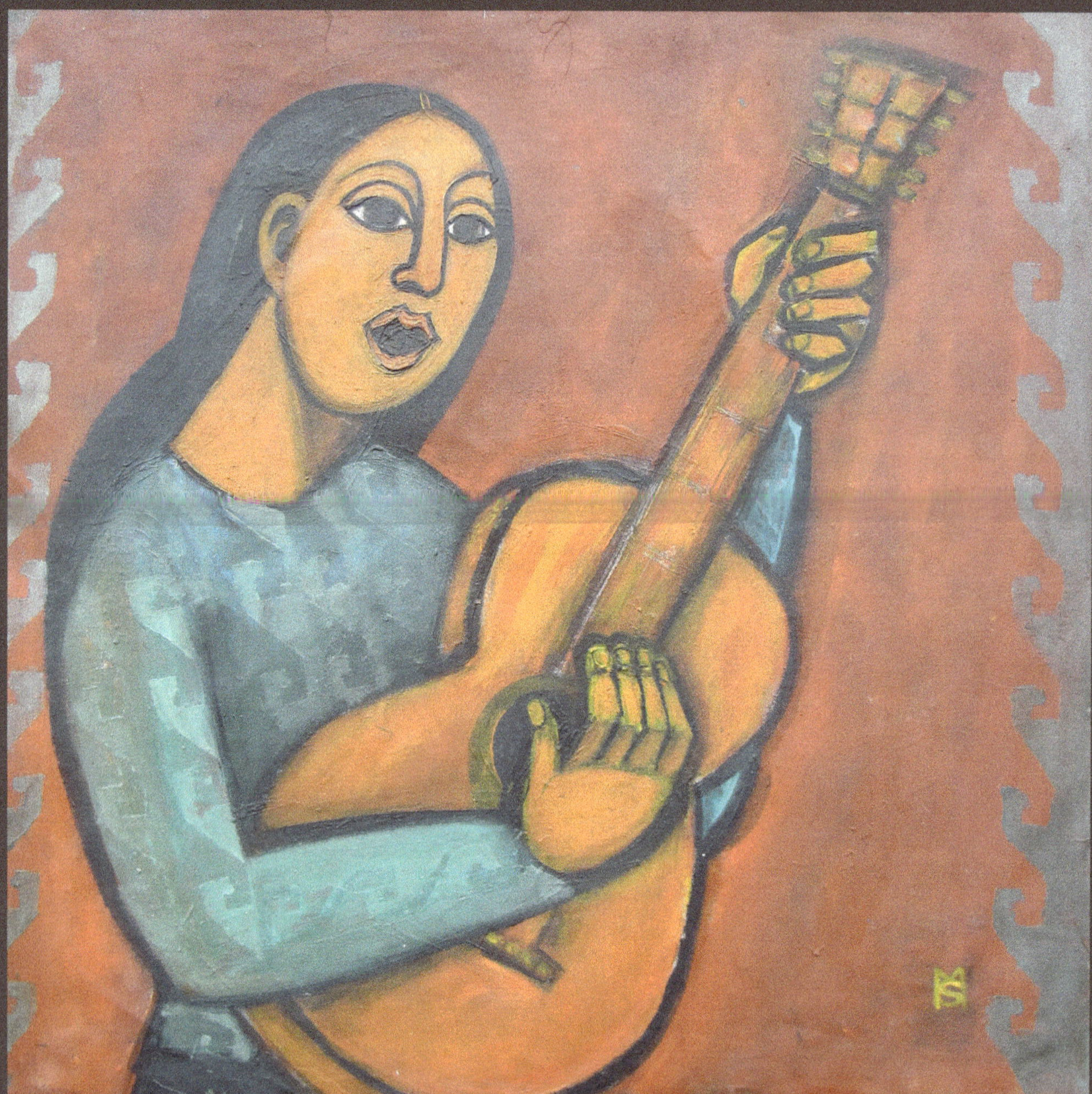

Guitar Girl
(75cm x 75cm)

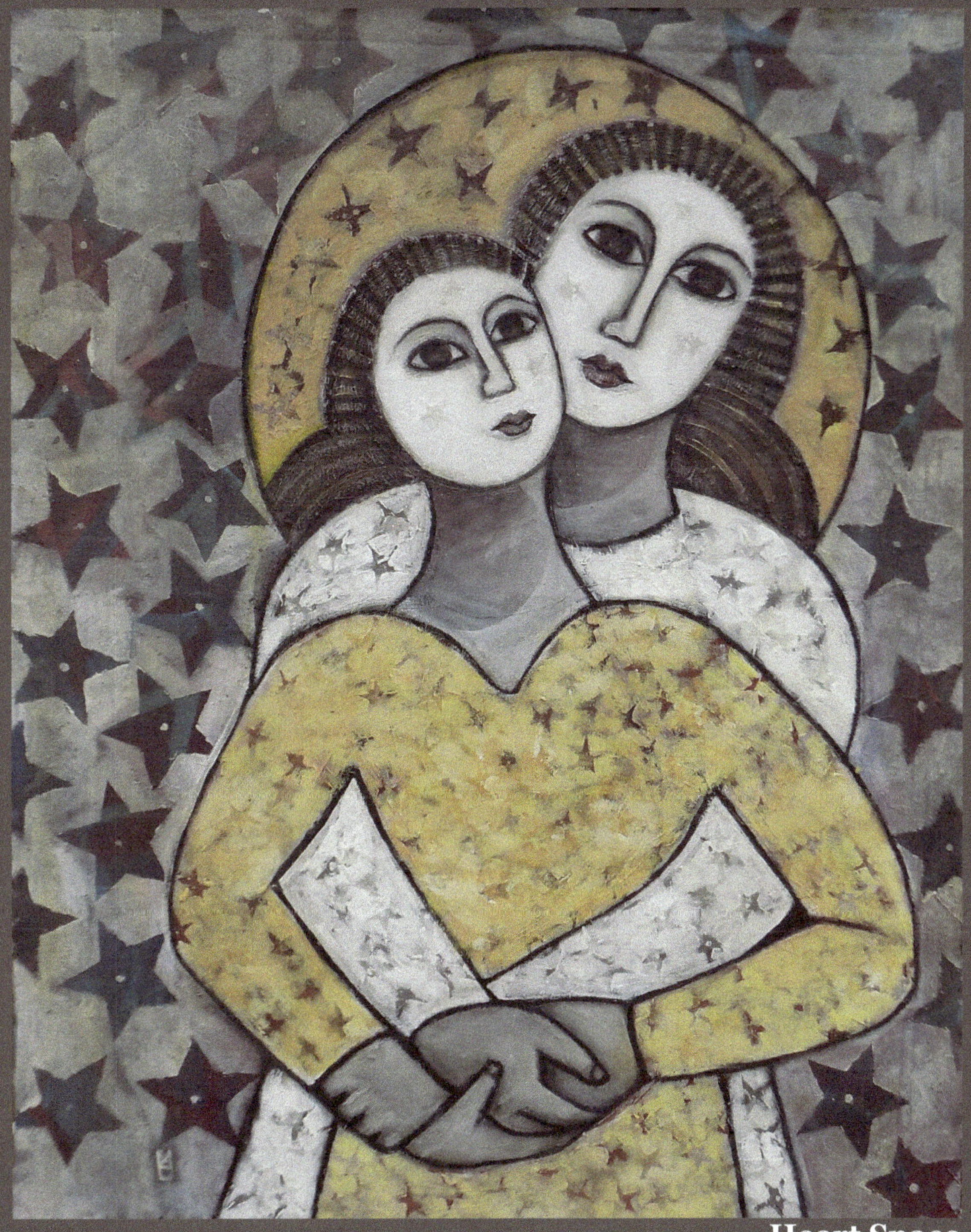

Heart Space
(92cm x 74cm)

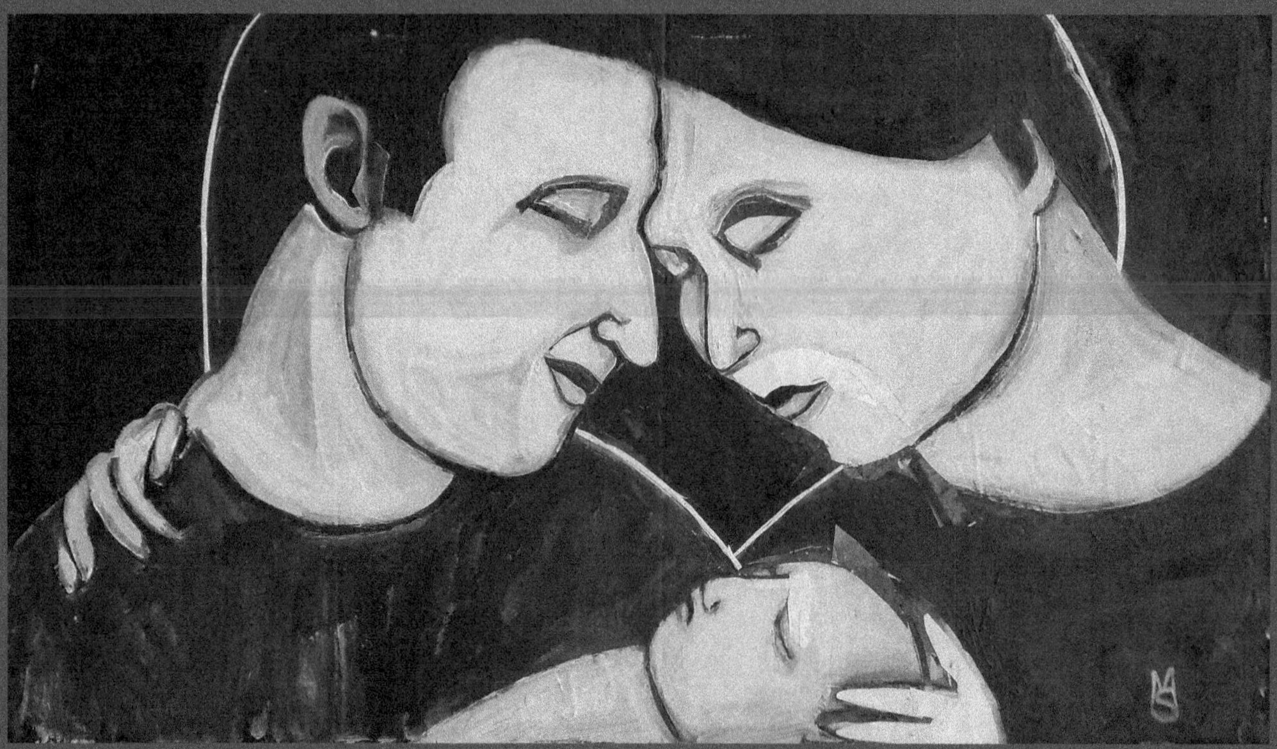

Tri
(46cm x 83cm)
The original painting which is done in a collage form on the next page.

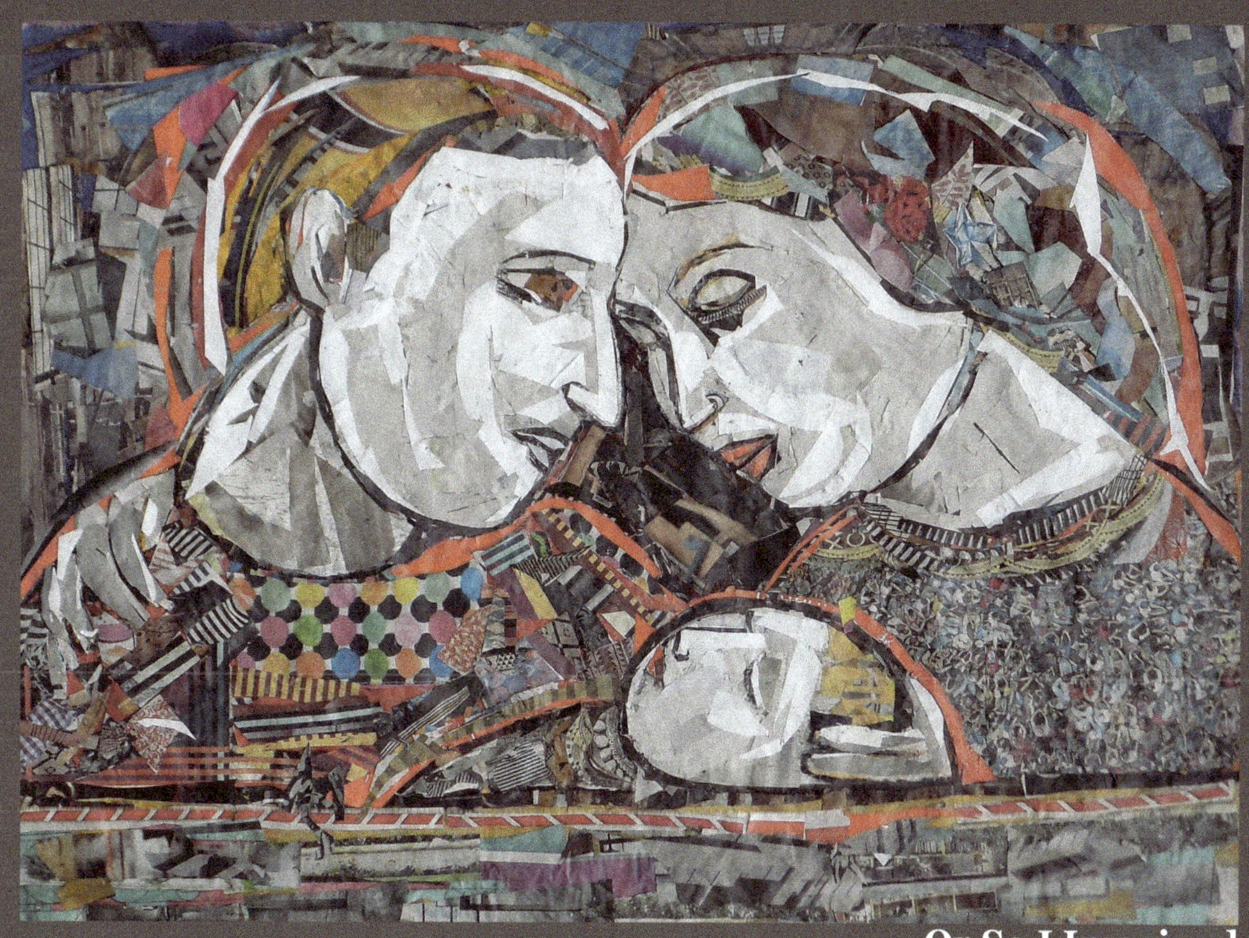

Or So I Imagined
(58cm x 83cm)
A collage form of the painting on the previous page.

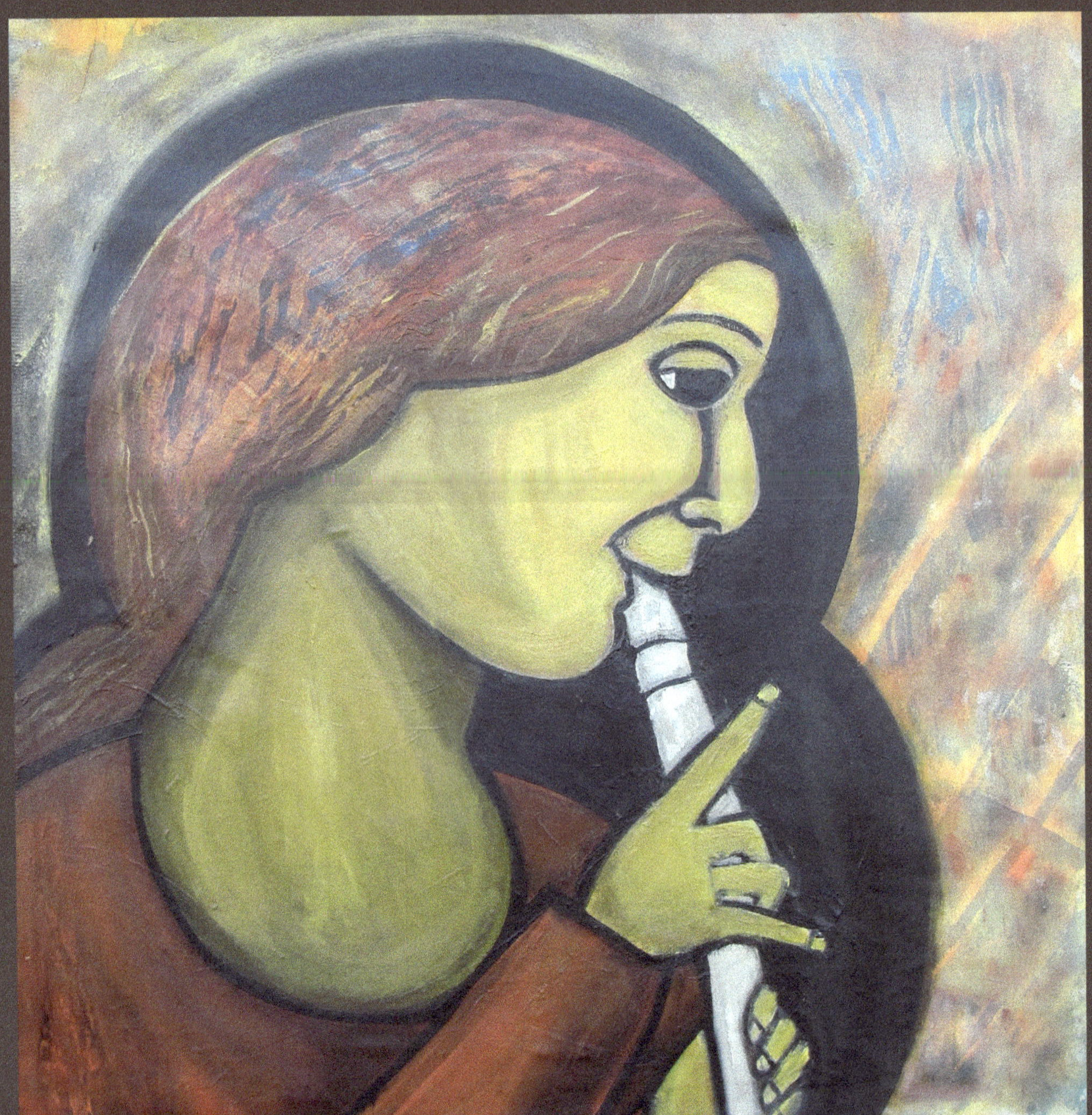

Saffron
(75cm x 75cm)

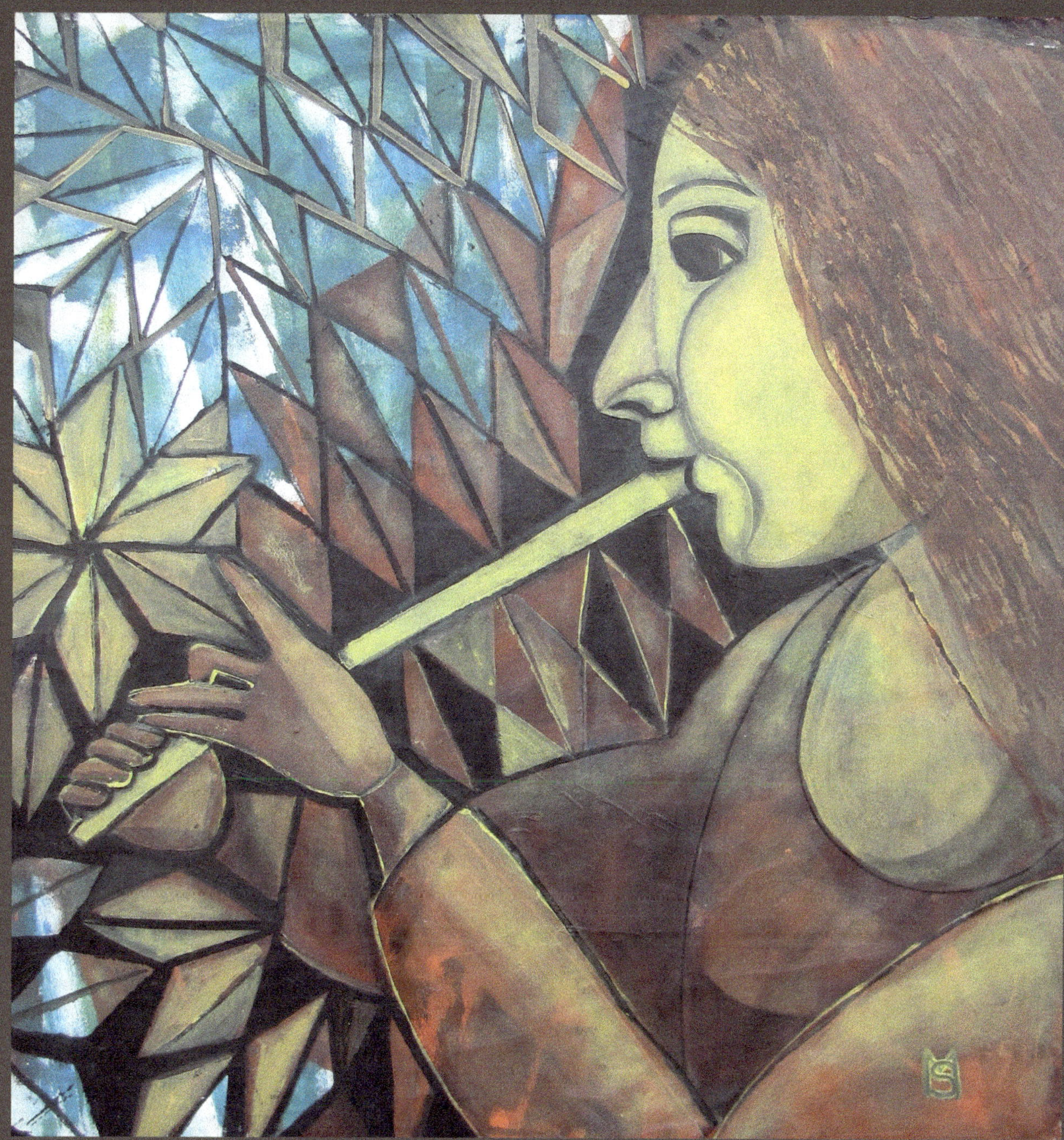

Jezameen
(75cm x 75cm)

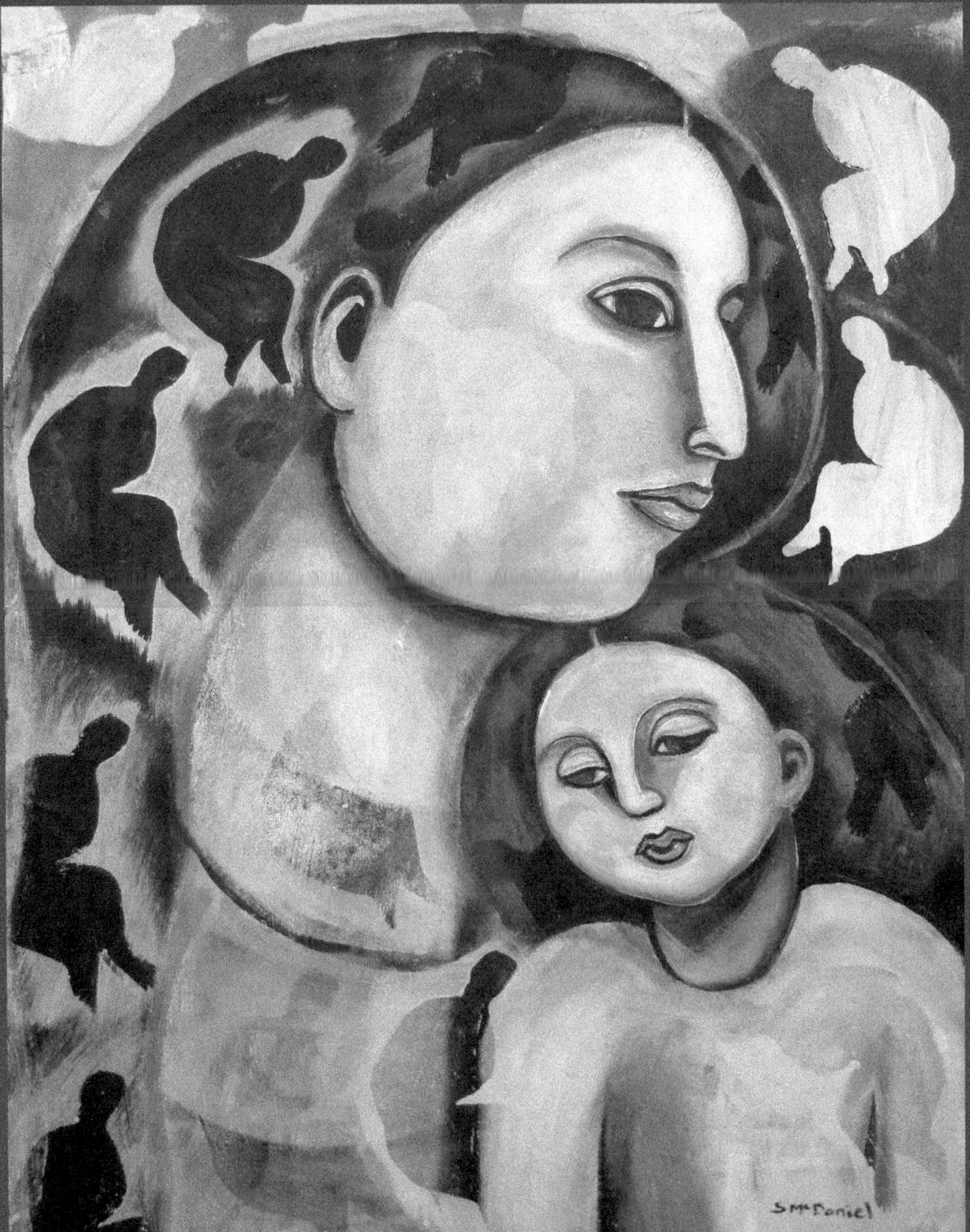

Inherent Harmony

(95cm x 75cm)

Digital version on pg.189.

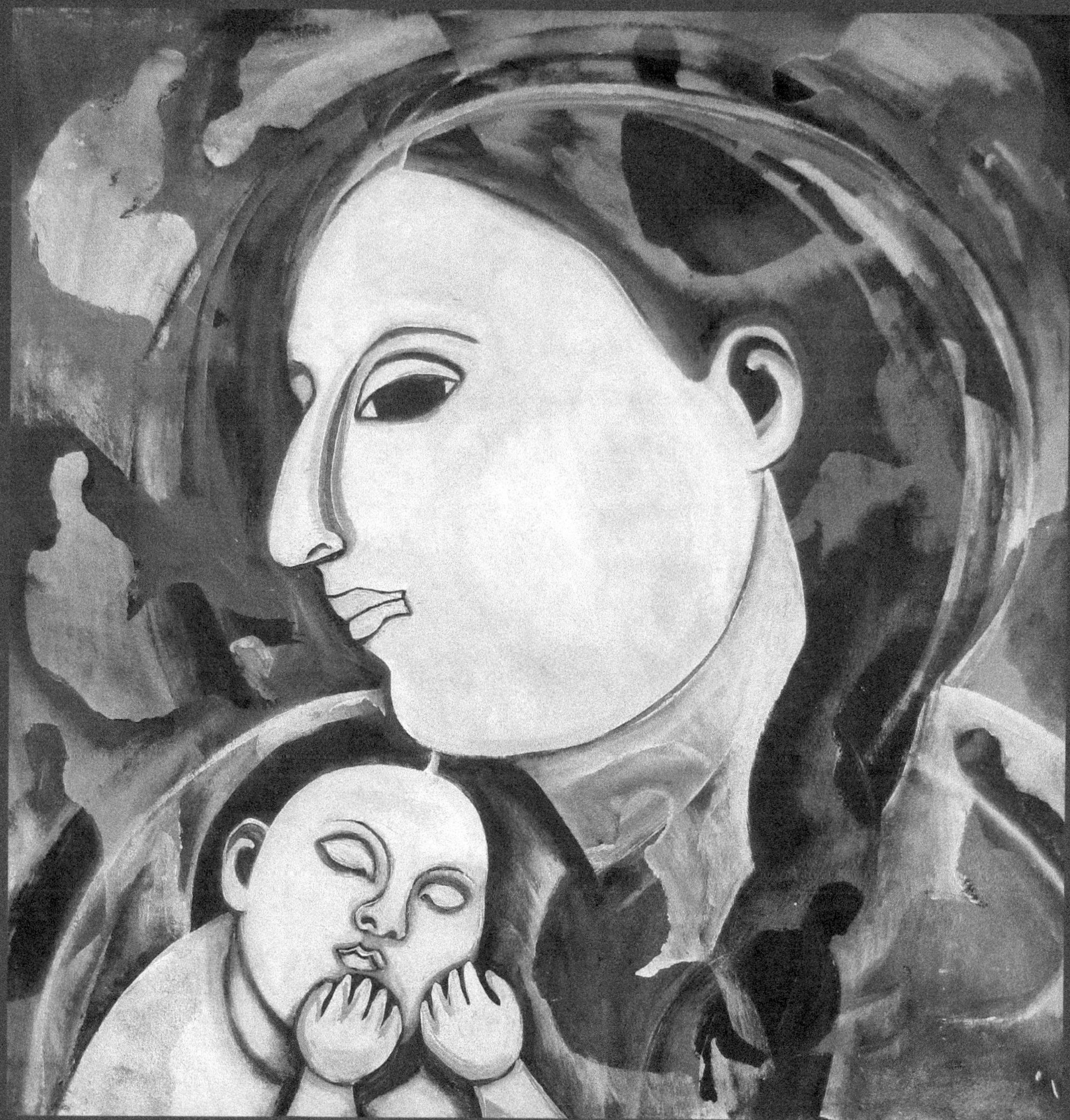

Global Eyes
(75cm x 70cm)
Digital version on pg.190.

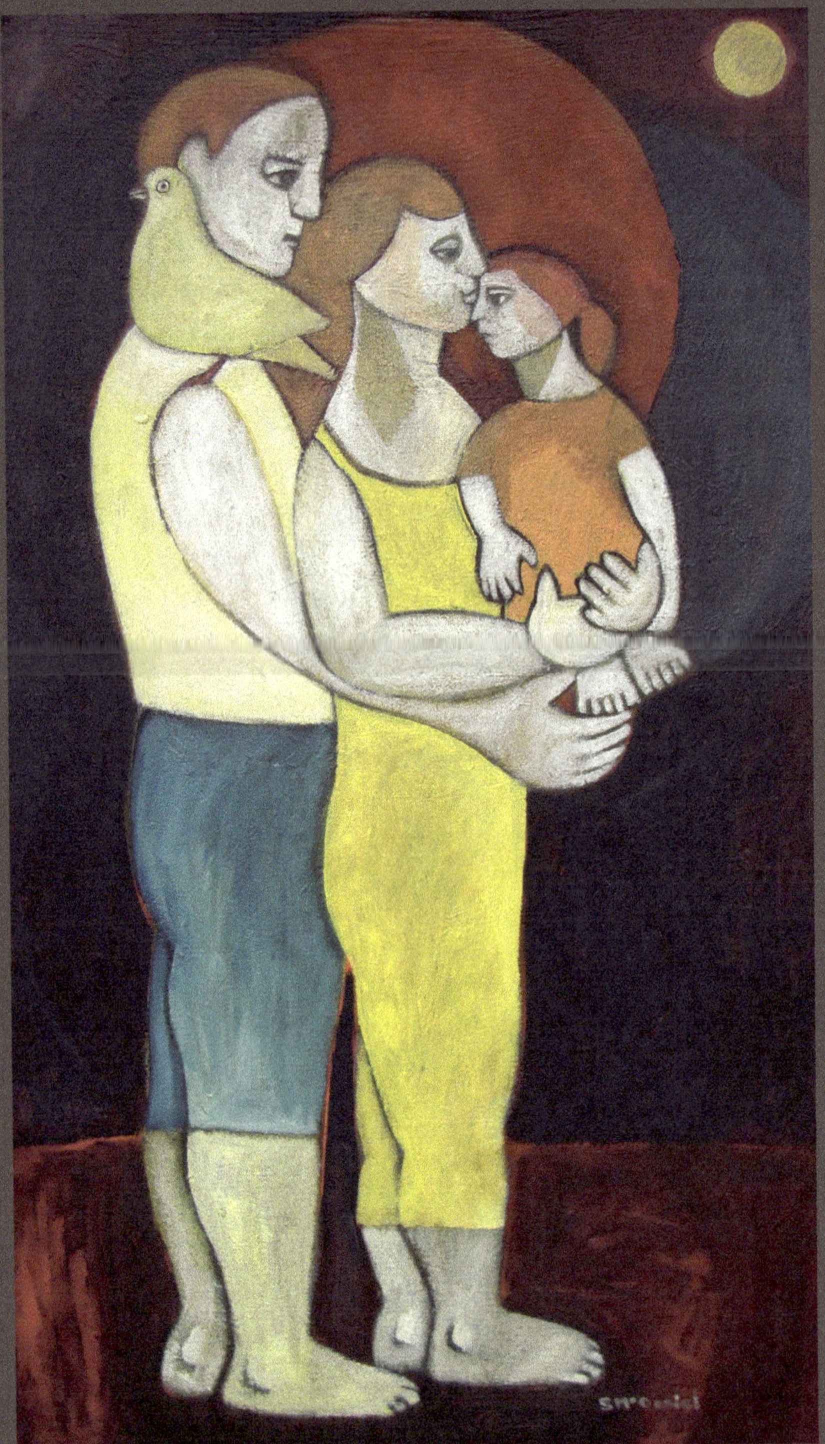

Trinity
(140cm x 85cm)

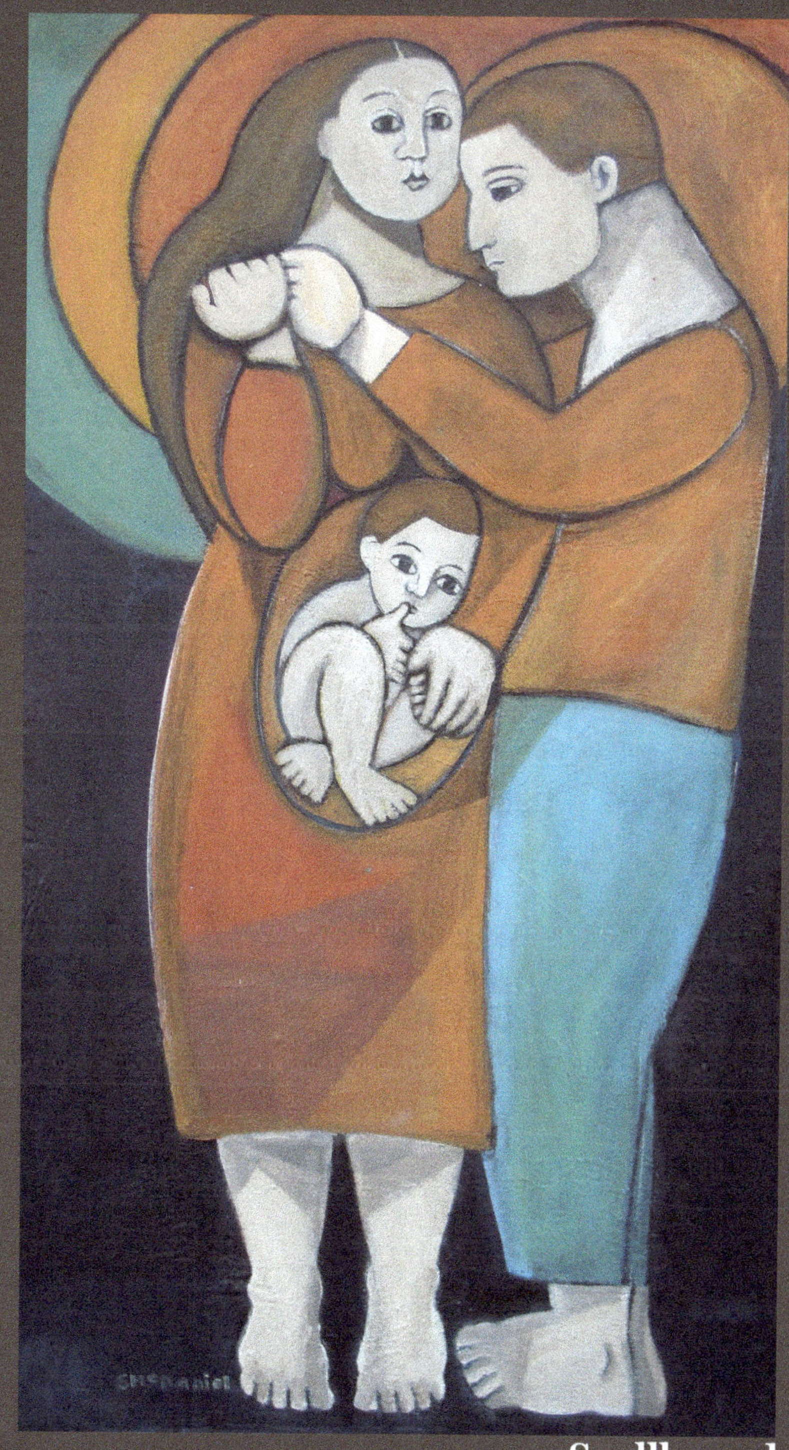

Spellbound
(130cm x 75cm)

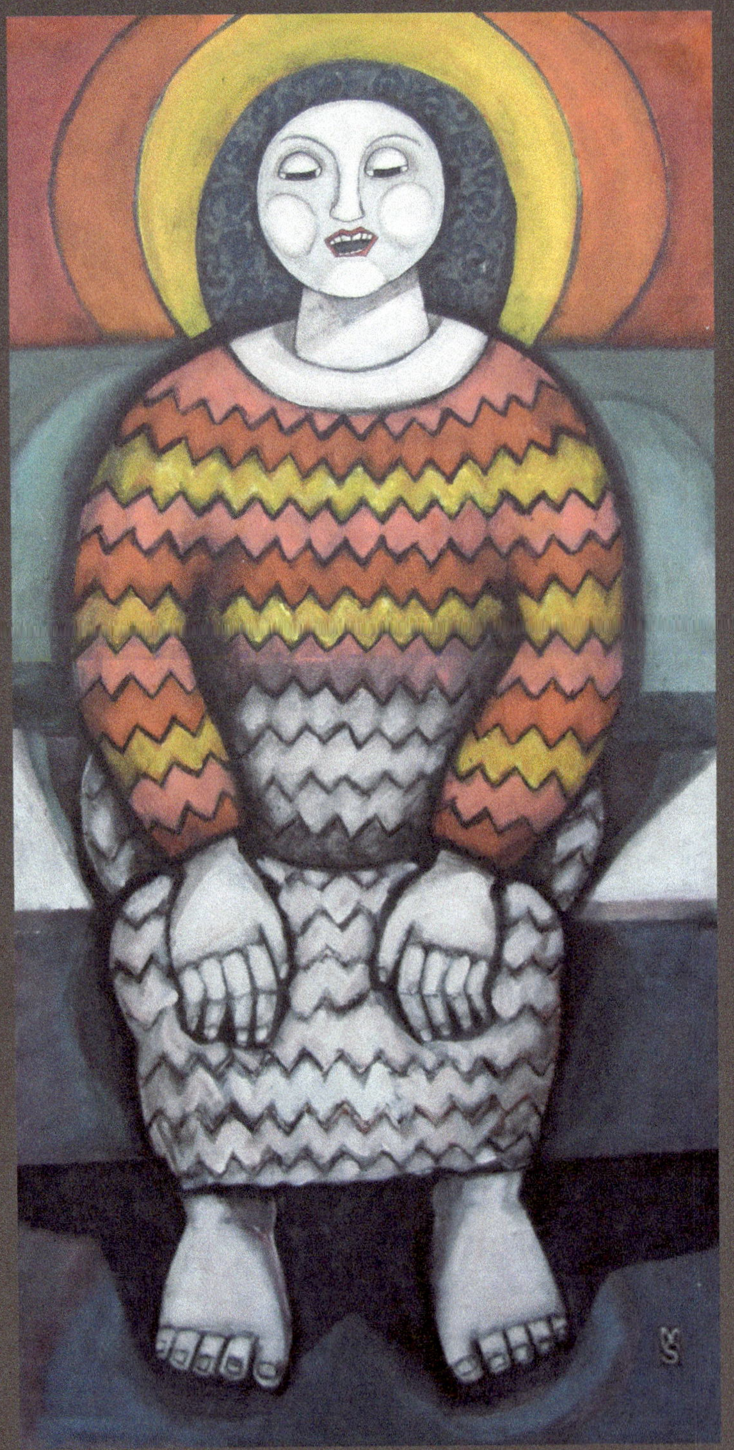

Norneena
(145cm x 75cm)

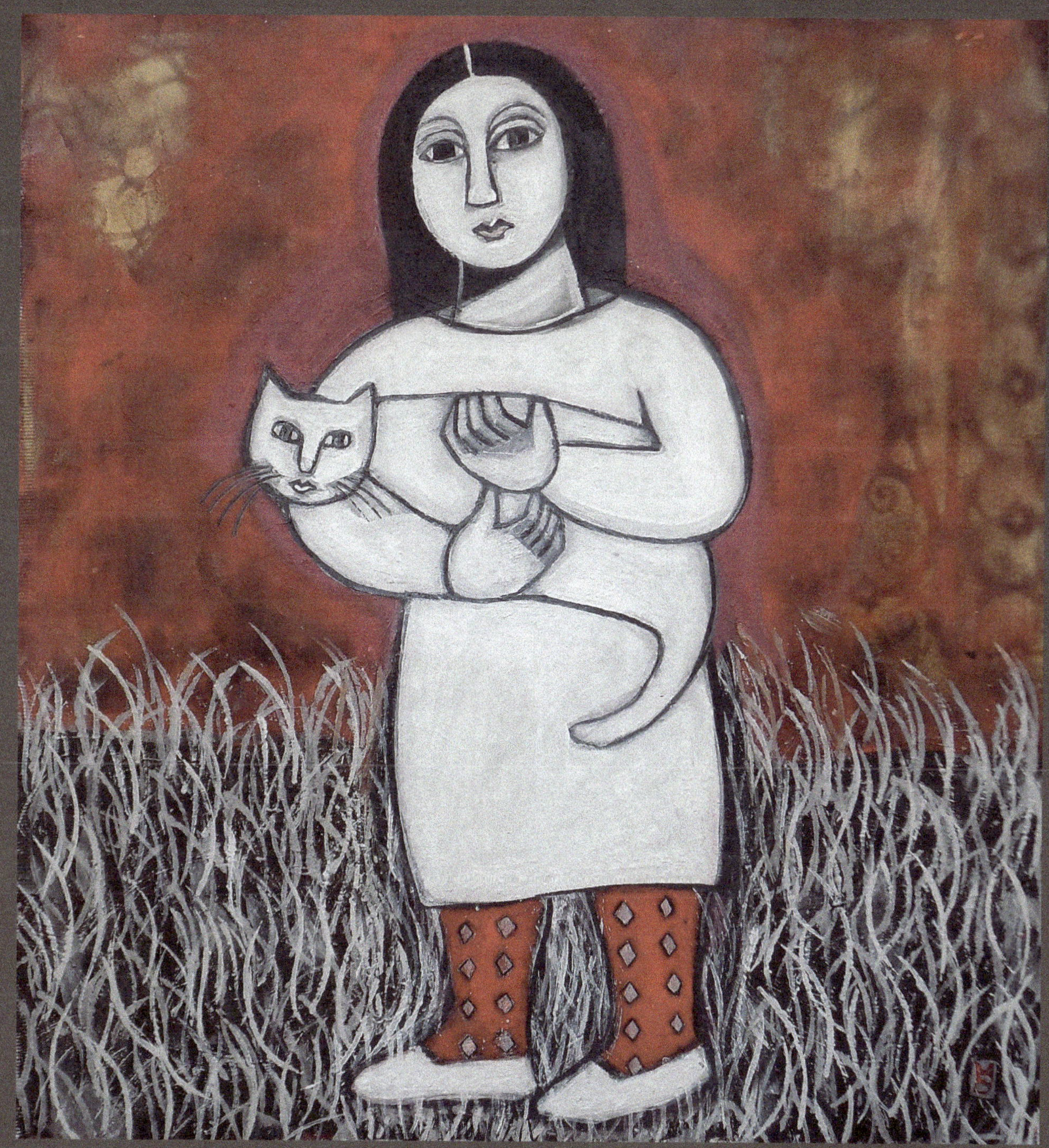

Zoey
(80cm x 75cm)

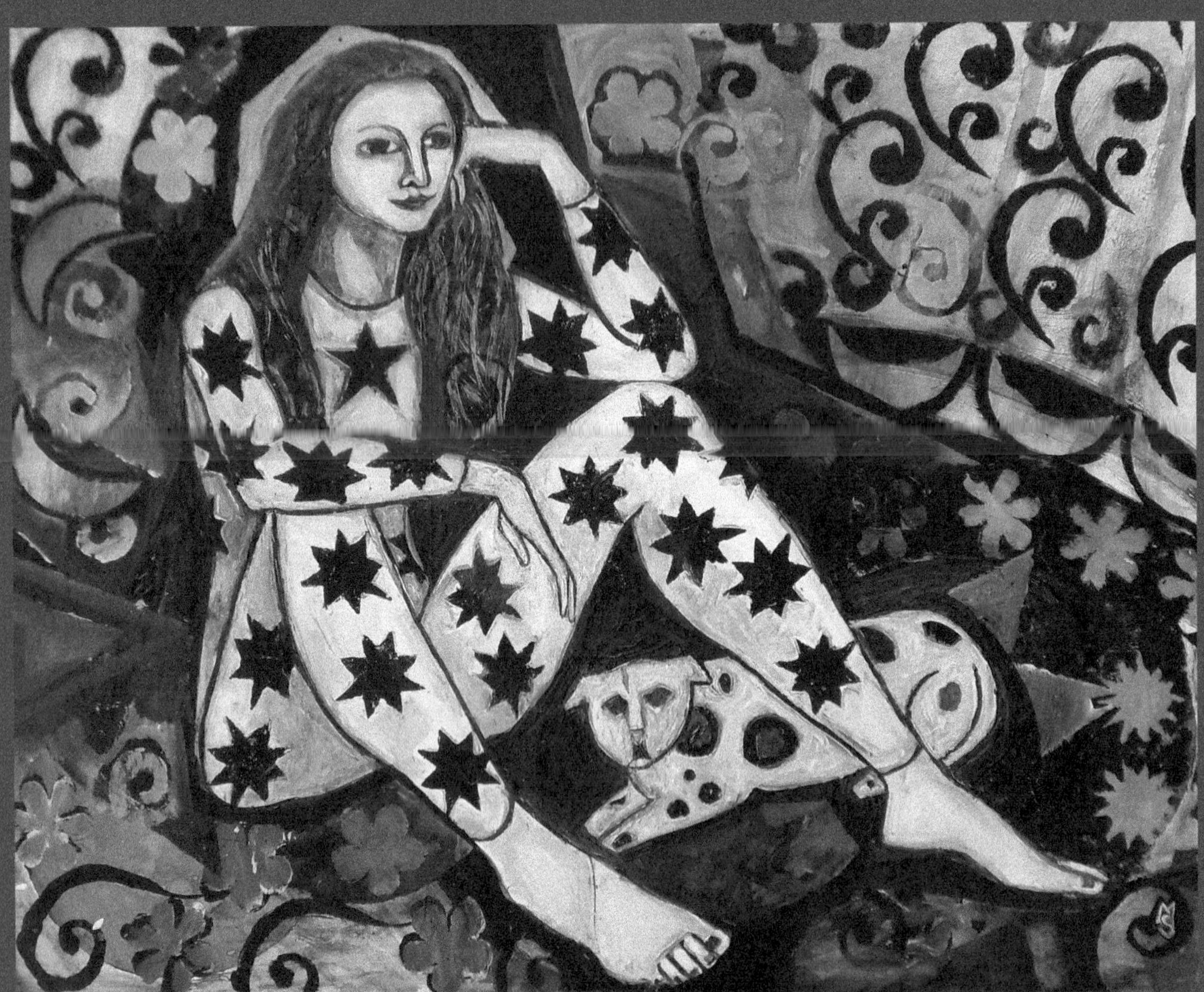

Spot the Dog
(49cm x 61cm)

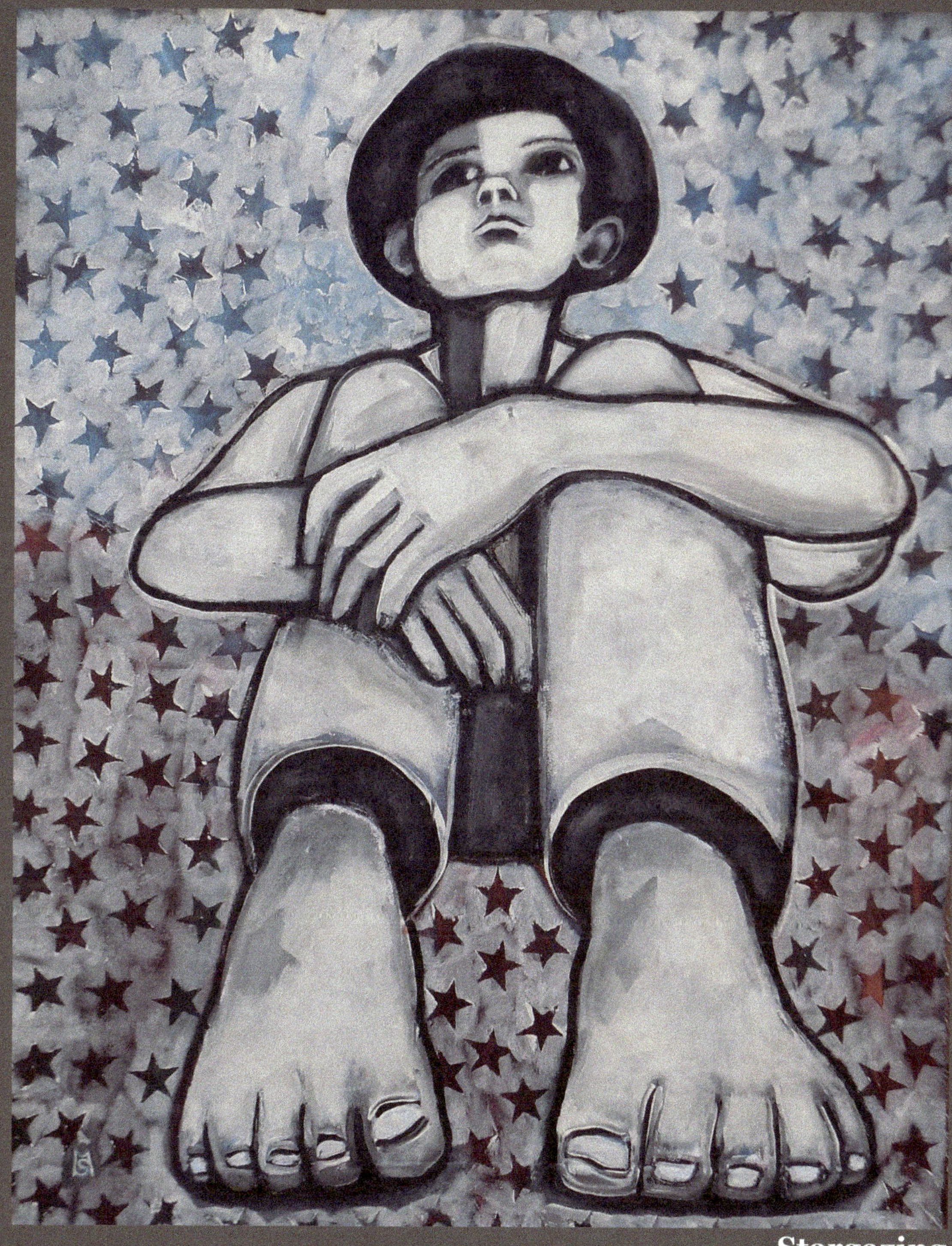

Stargazing
(98cm x 78cm)

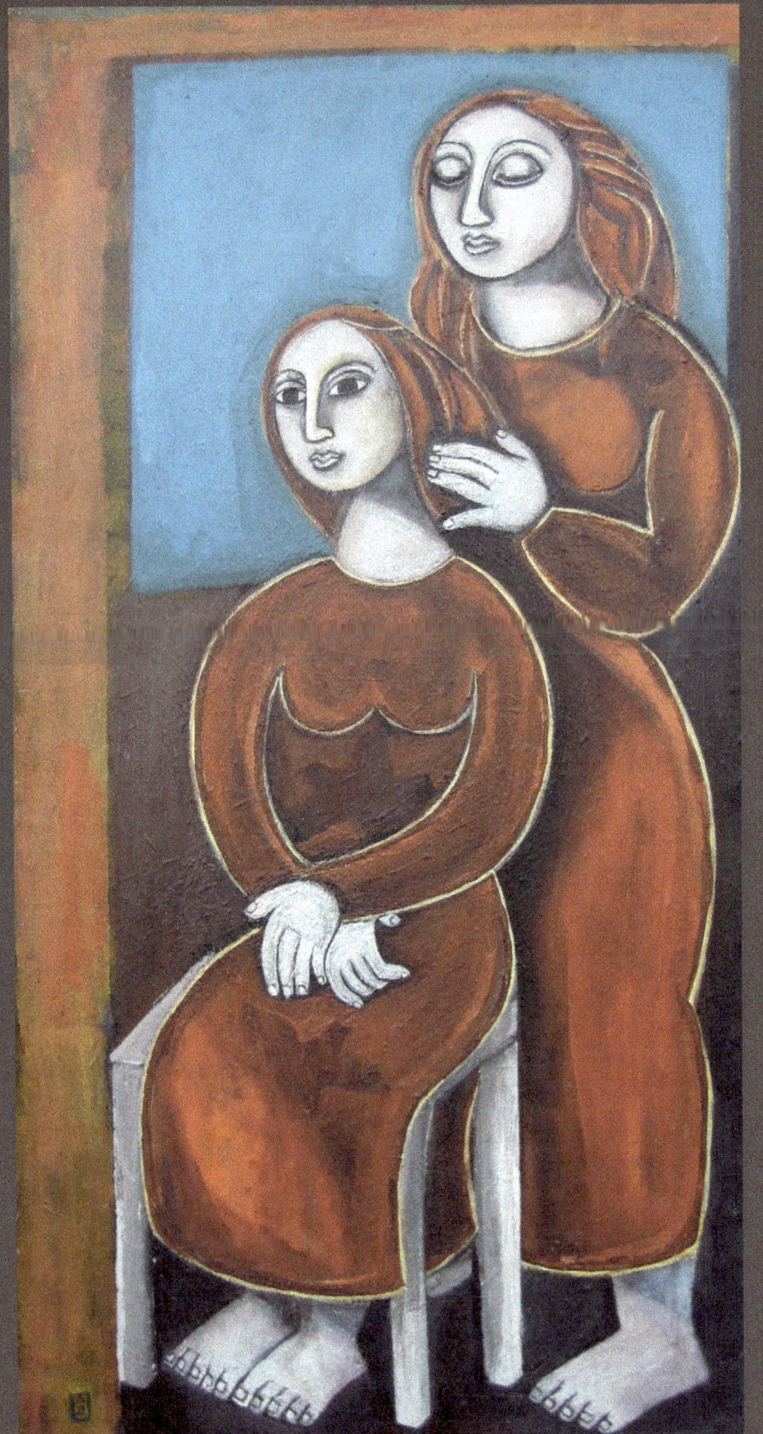

White Chair
(145cm x 75cm)

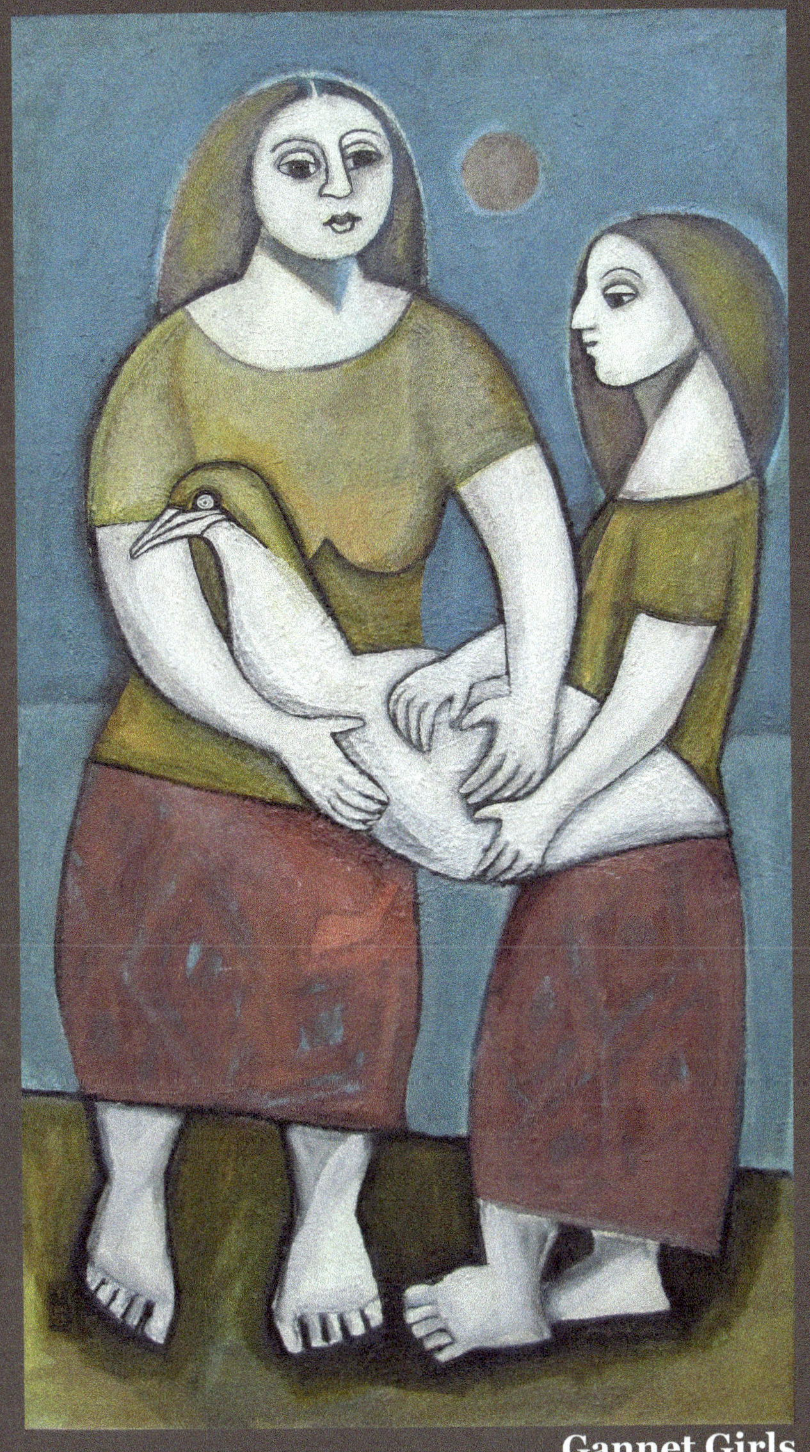

Gannet Girls
(120cm x 70cm)

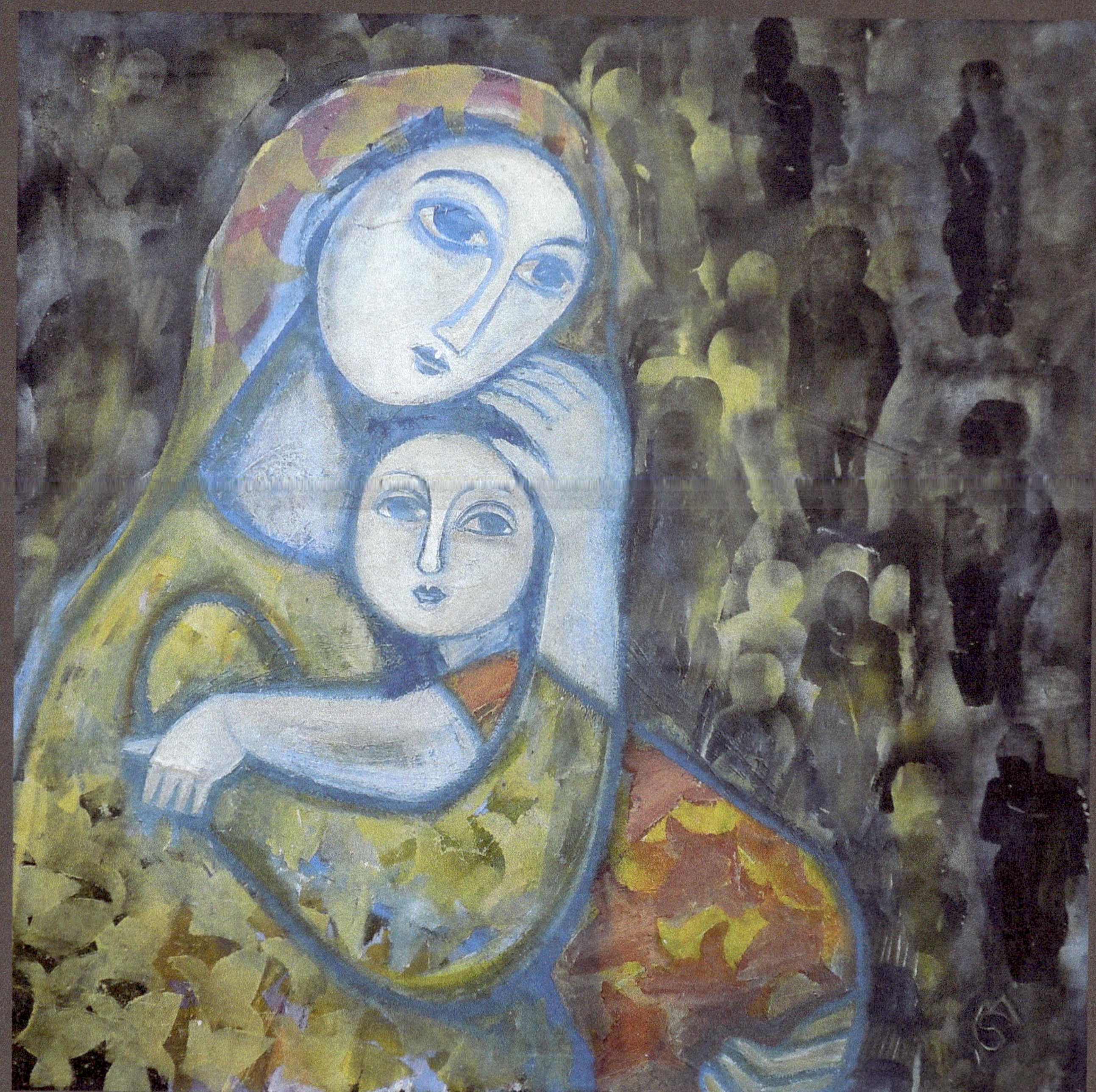

Dwelling Place
(76cm x 78cm)

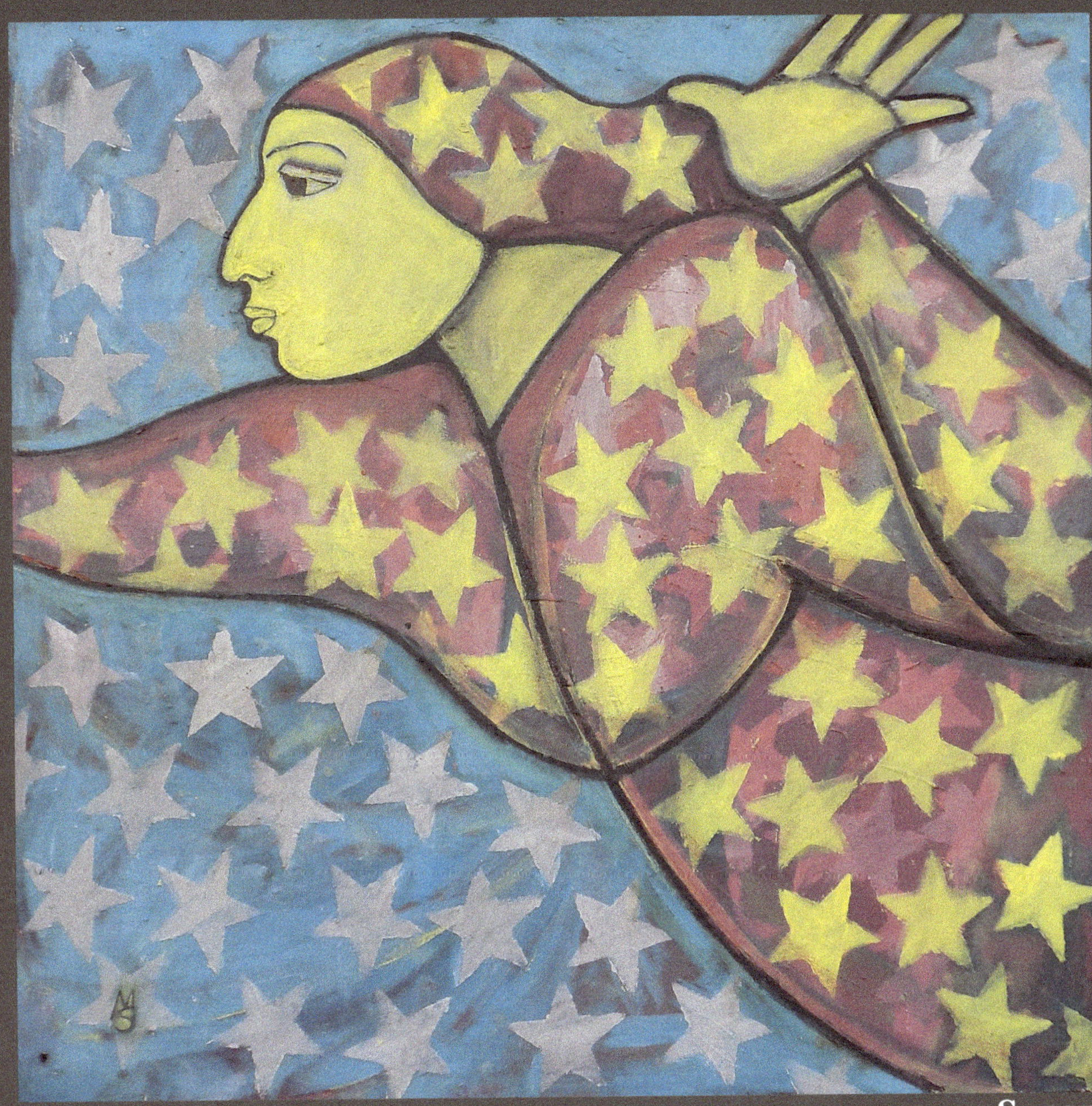

Super
(76cm x 78cm)

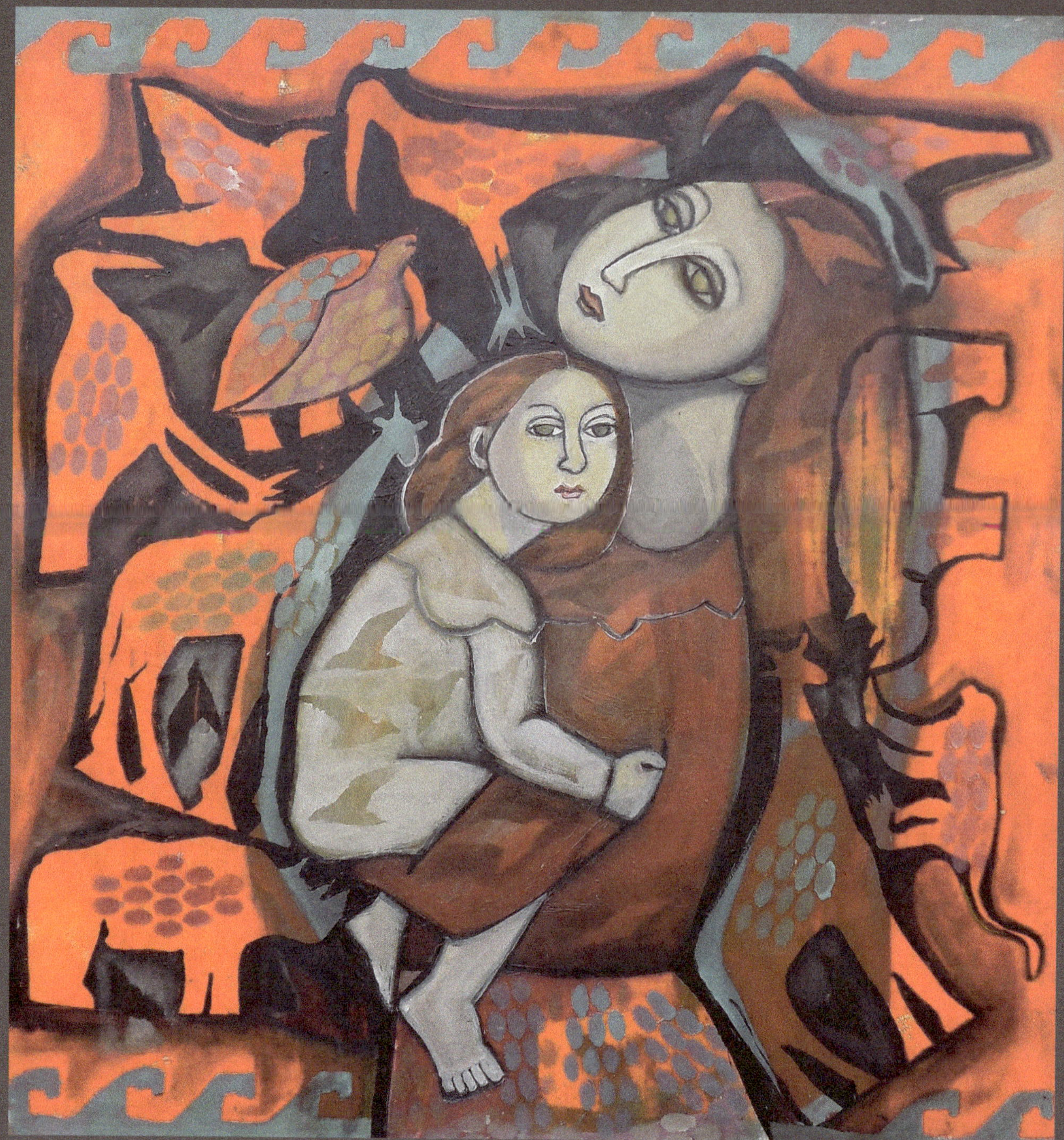

Meanings
(79cm x 76cm)

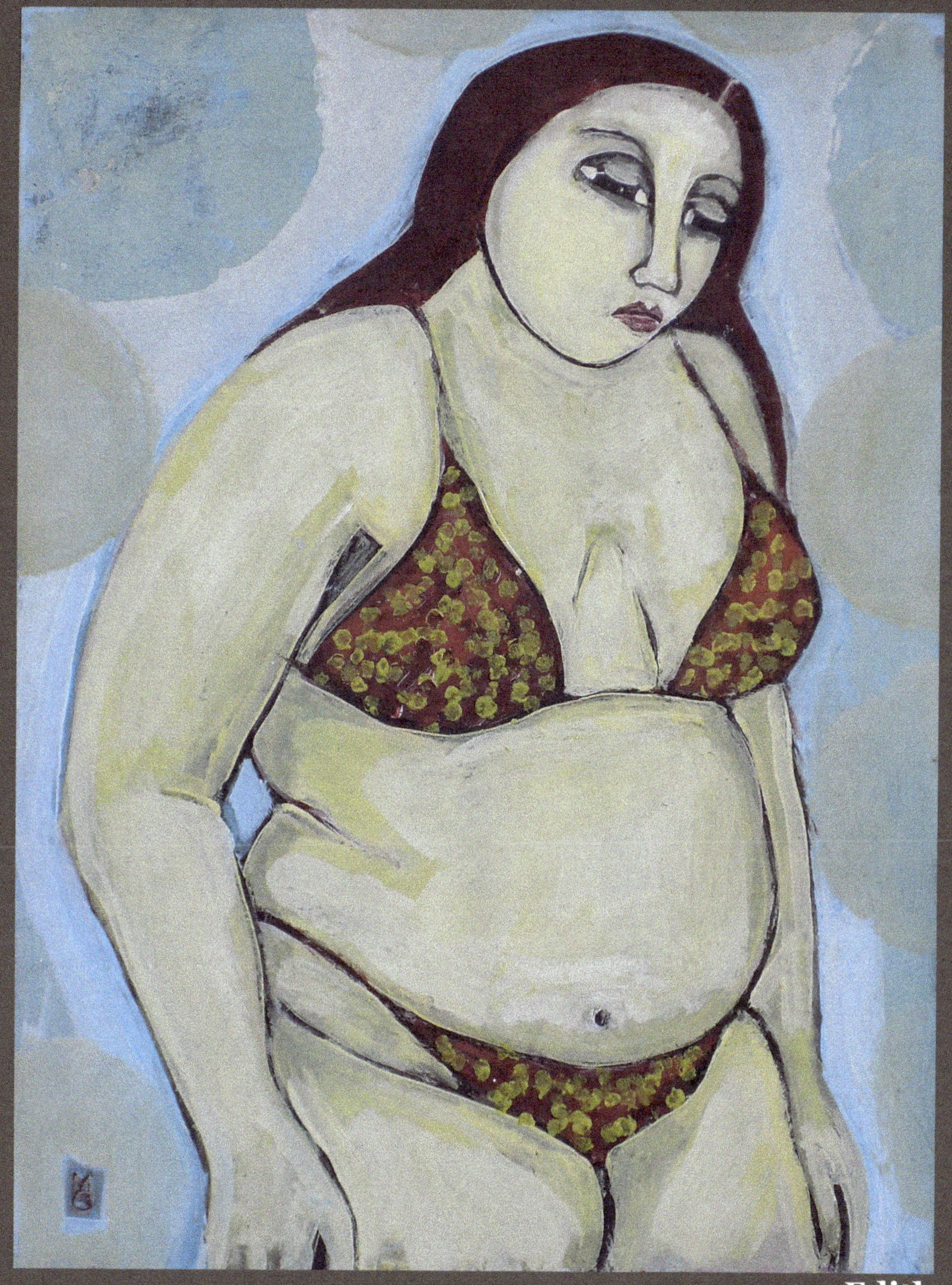

Edith
(51cm x 38cm)

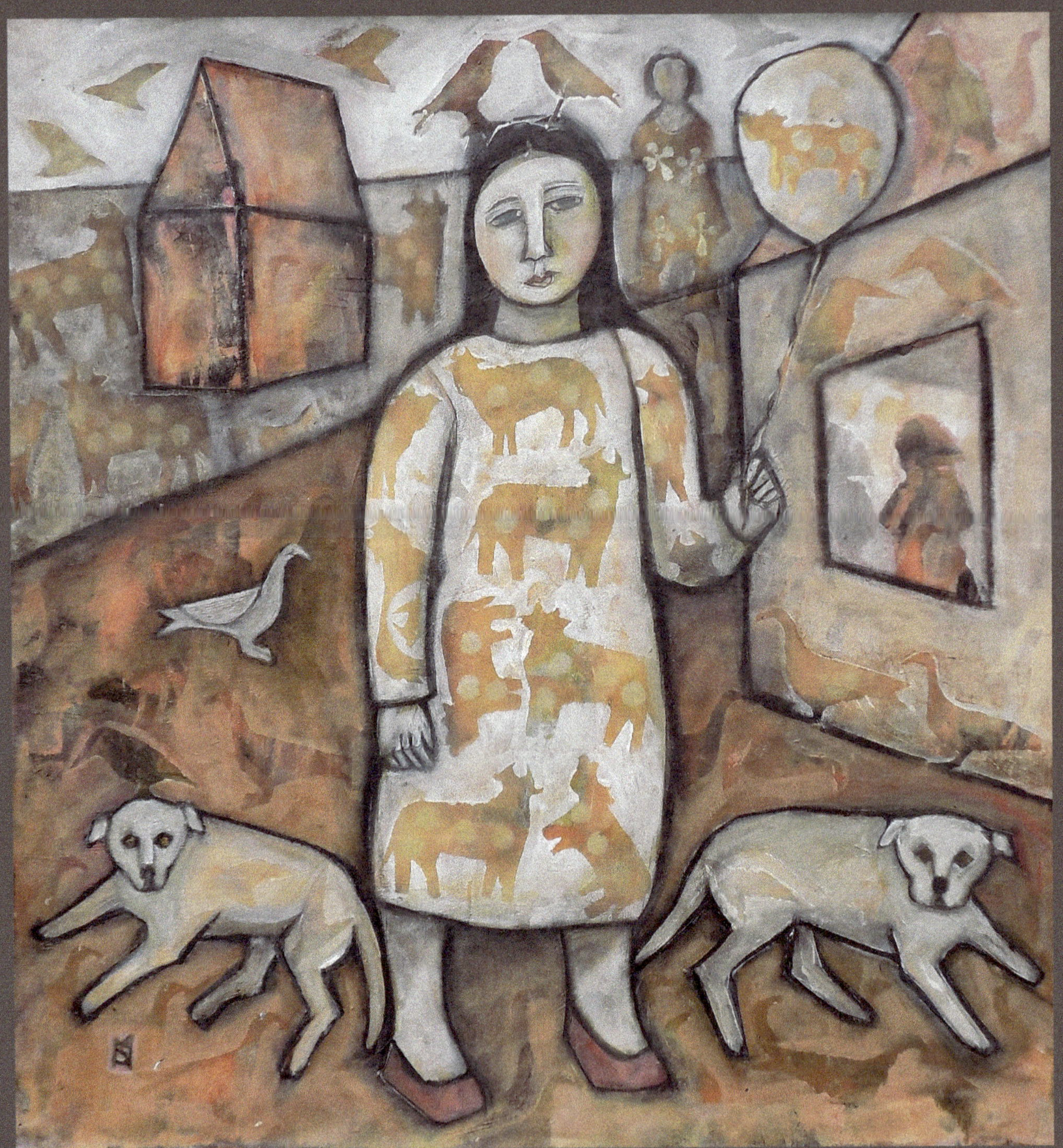

Josette
(79cm x 76cm)

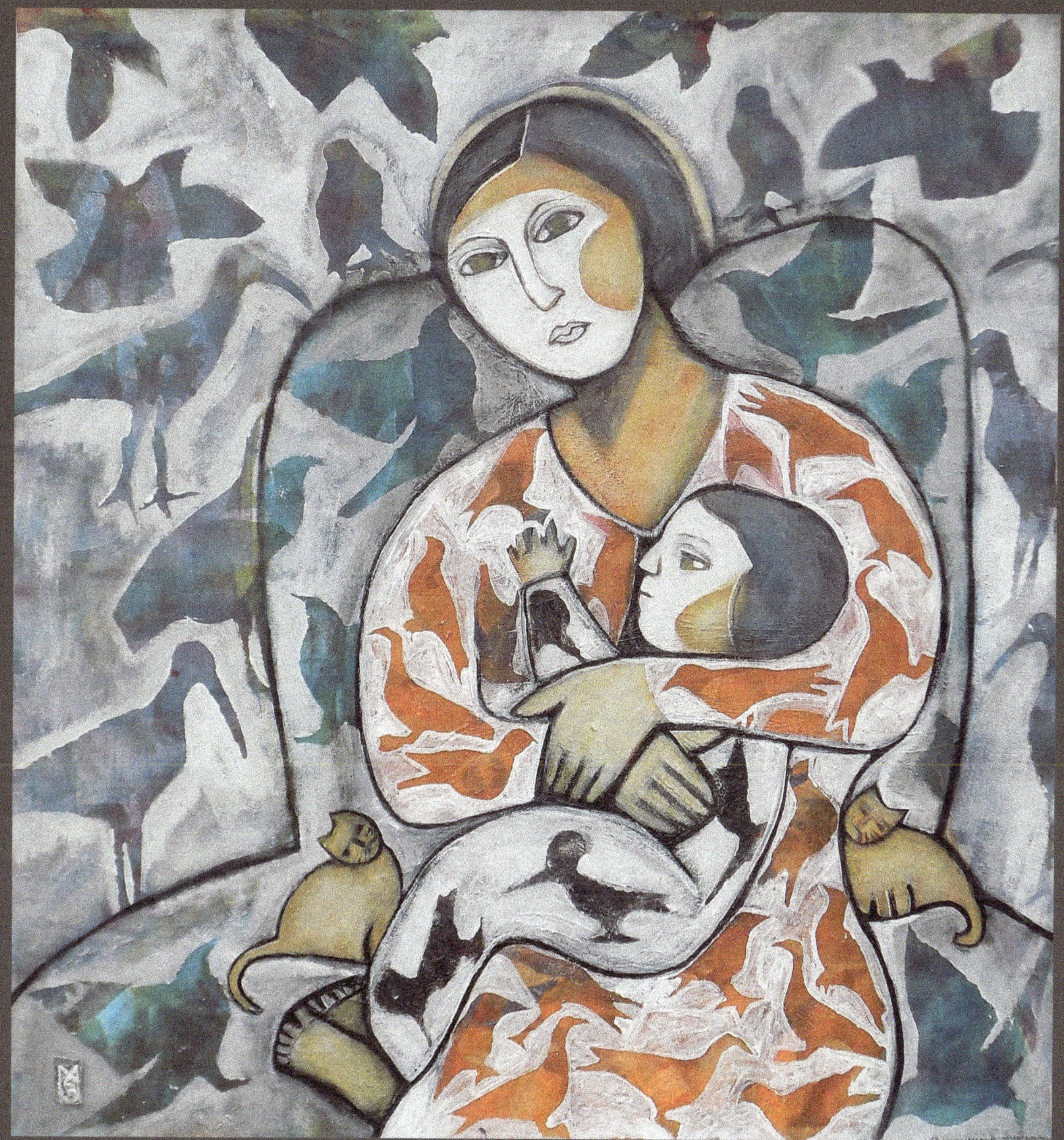

Mila
(78cm x 75Xcm)

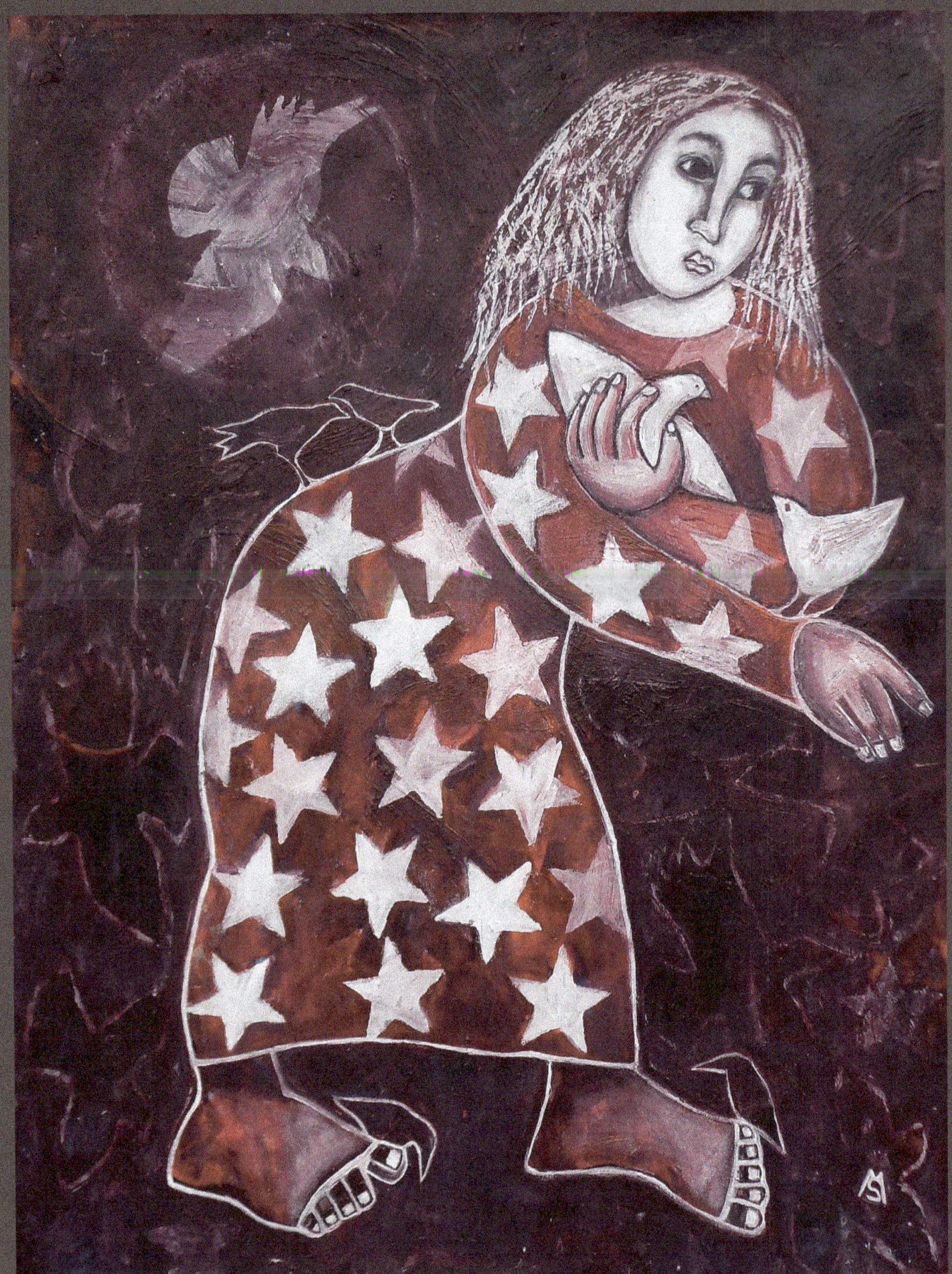

Frankie
(101cm x 76cm)

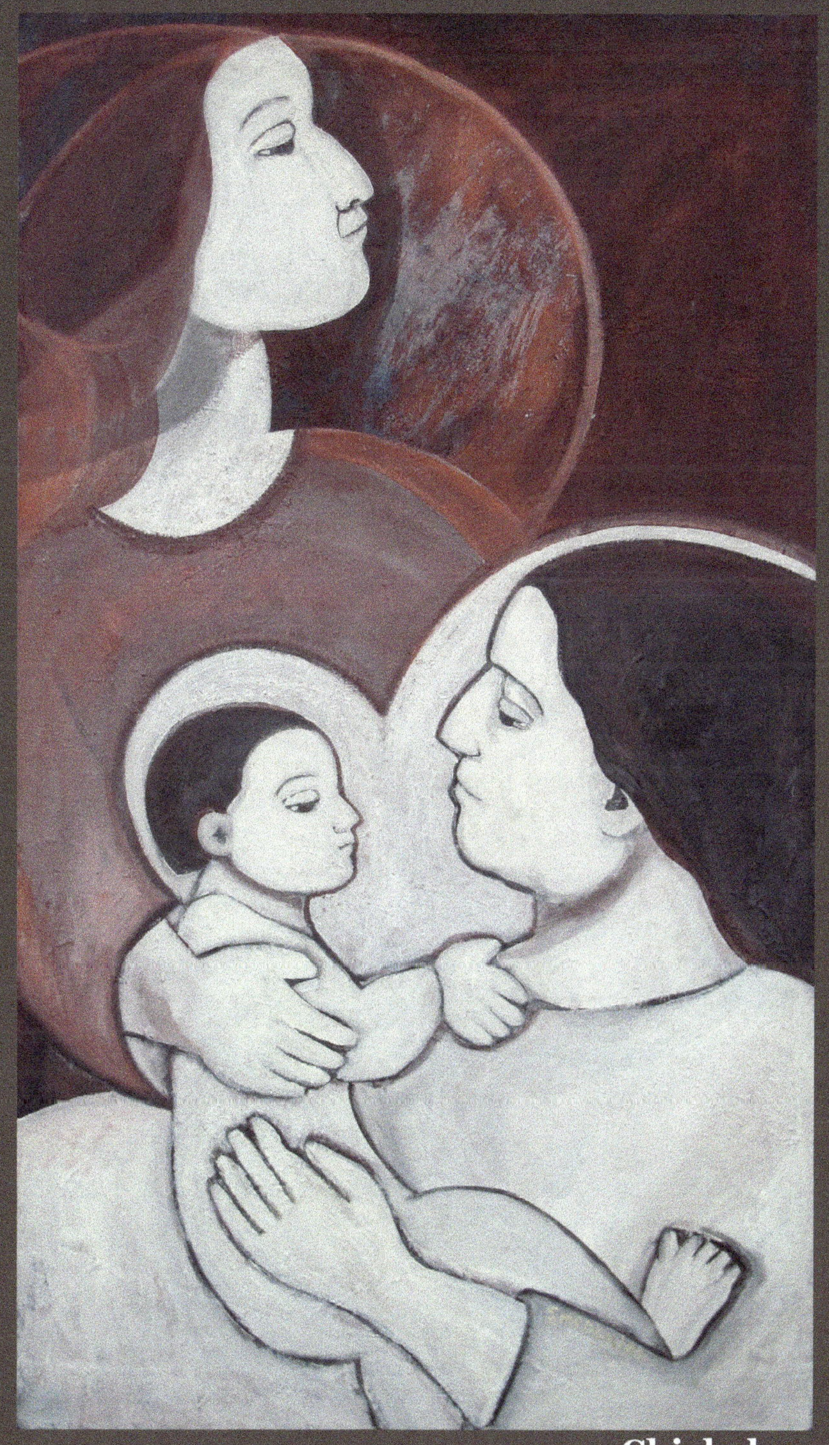

Chickabee
(115cm x 65cm)

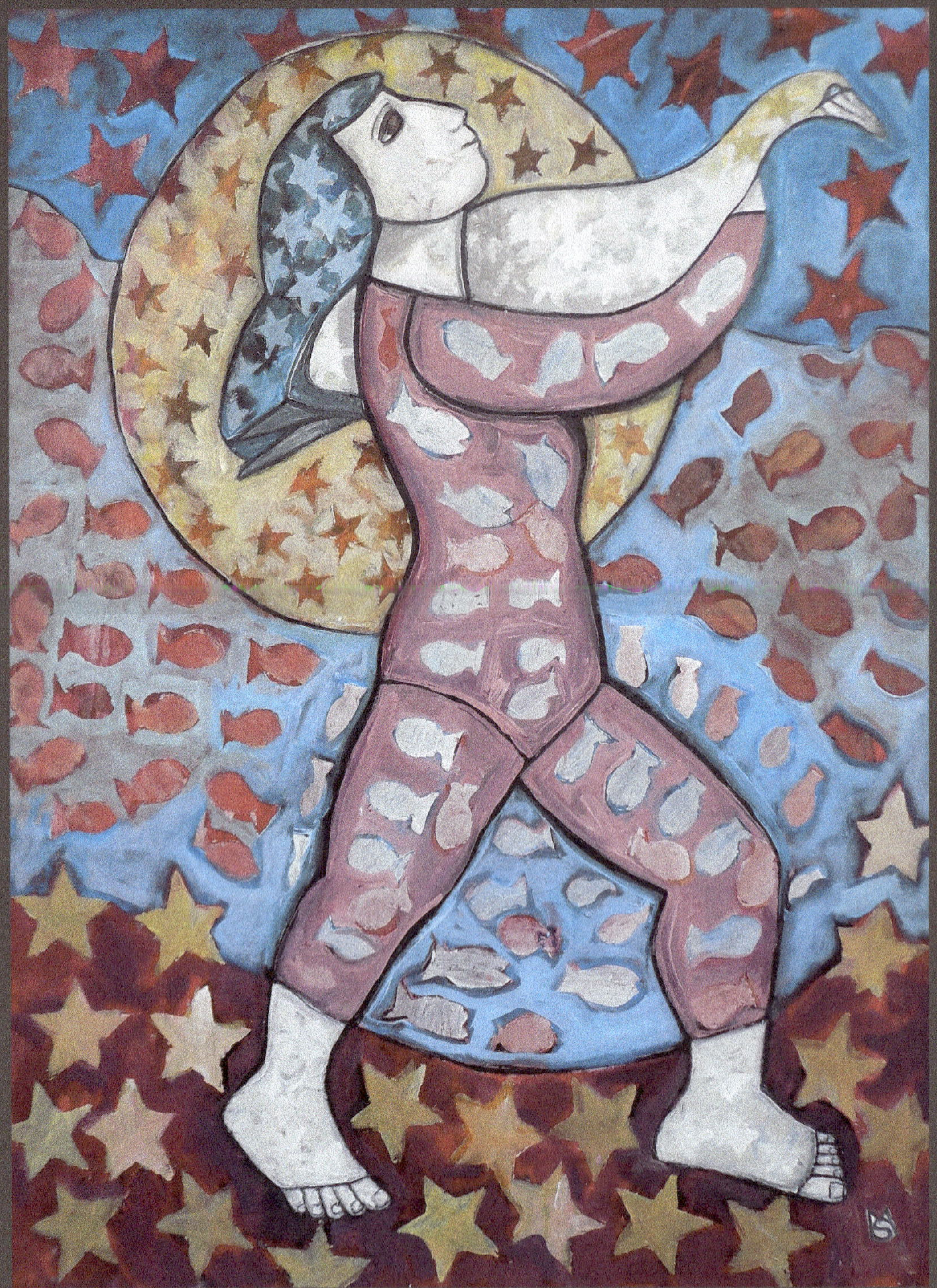

Star Walk
(101cm x 76cm)

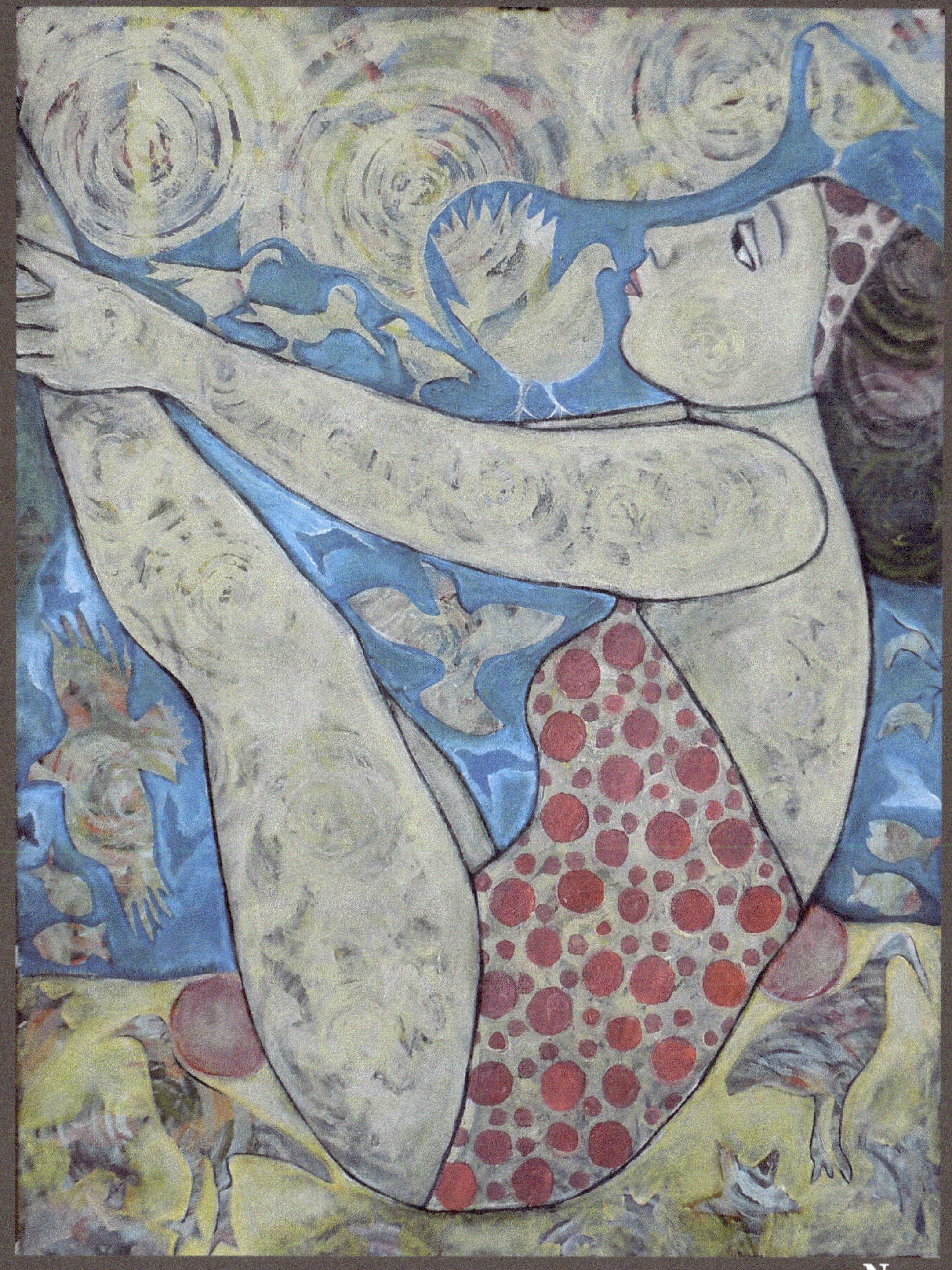

Now
(101cm x 76cm)

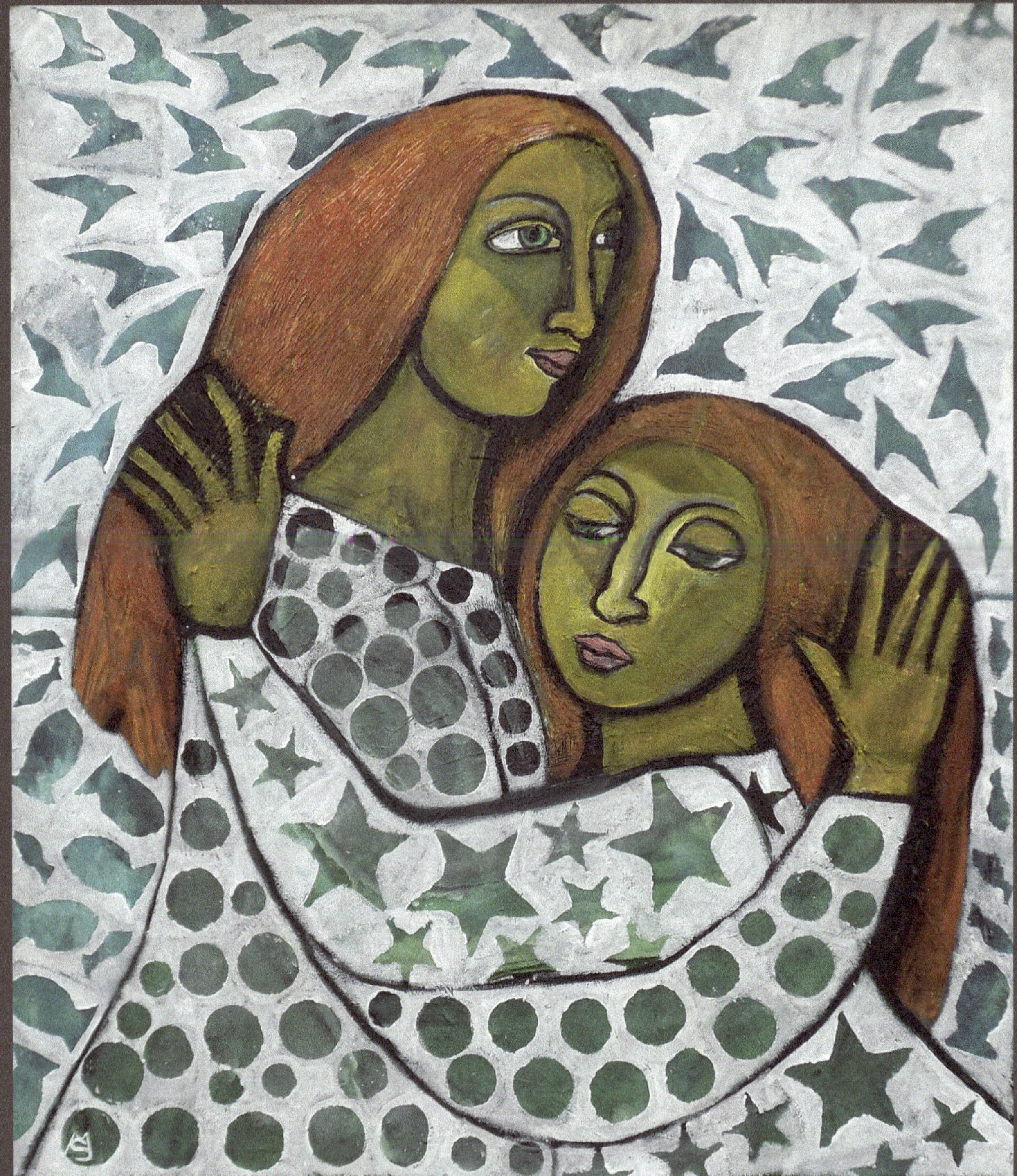

Kamala and Christine
(79cm x 70cm)

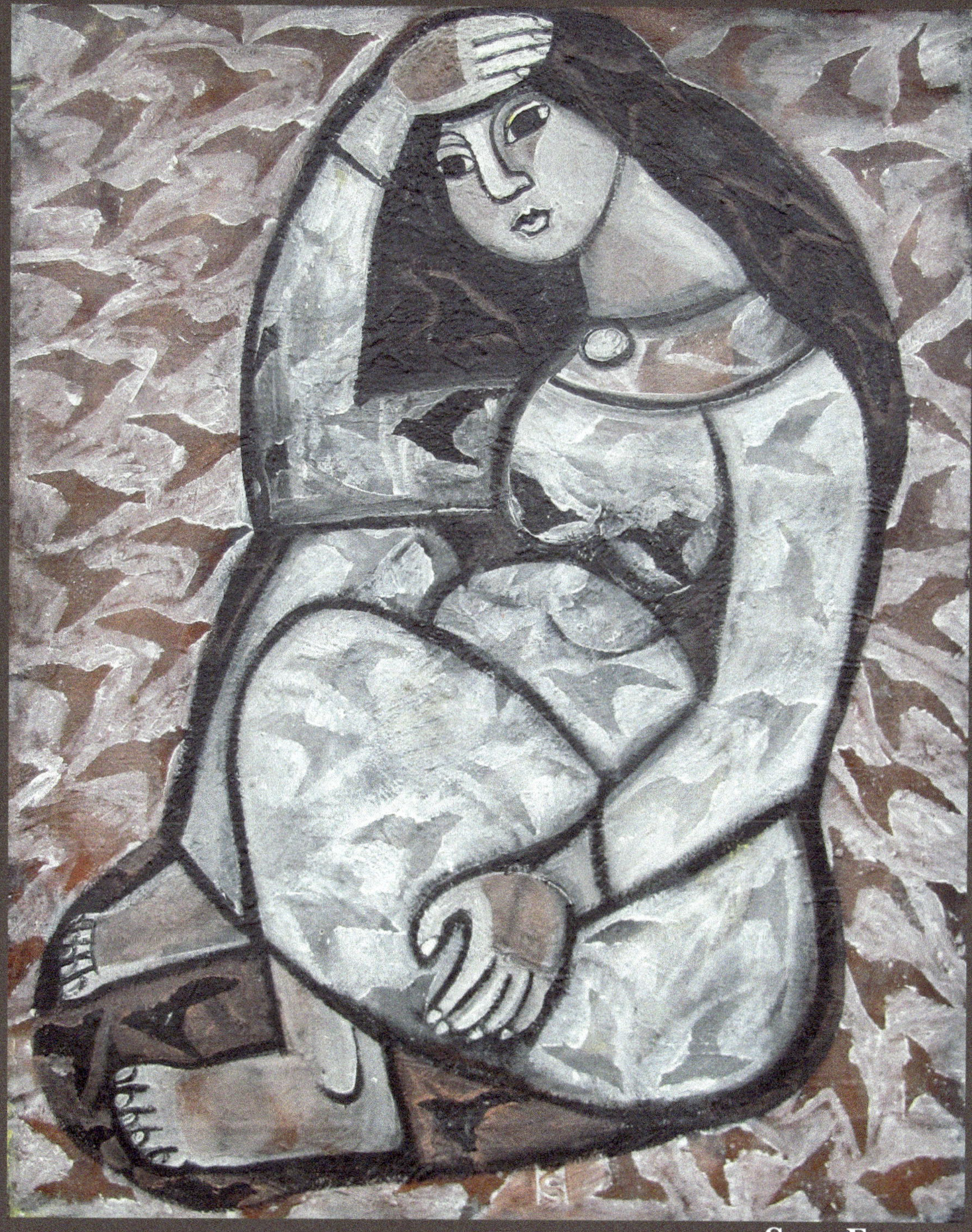

Sage Femme
(70cm x 55cm)

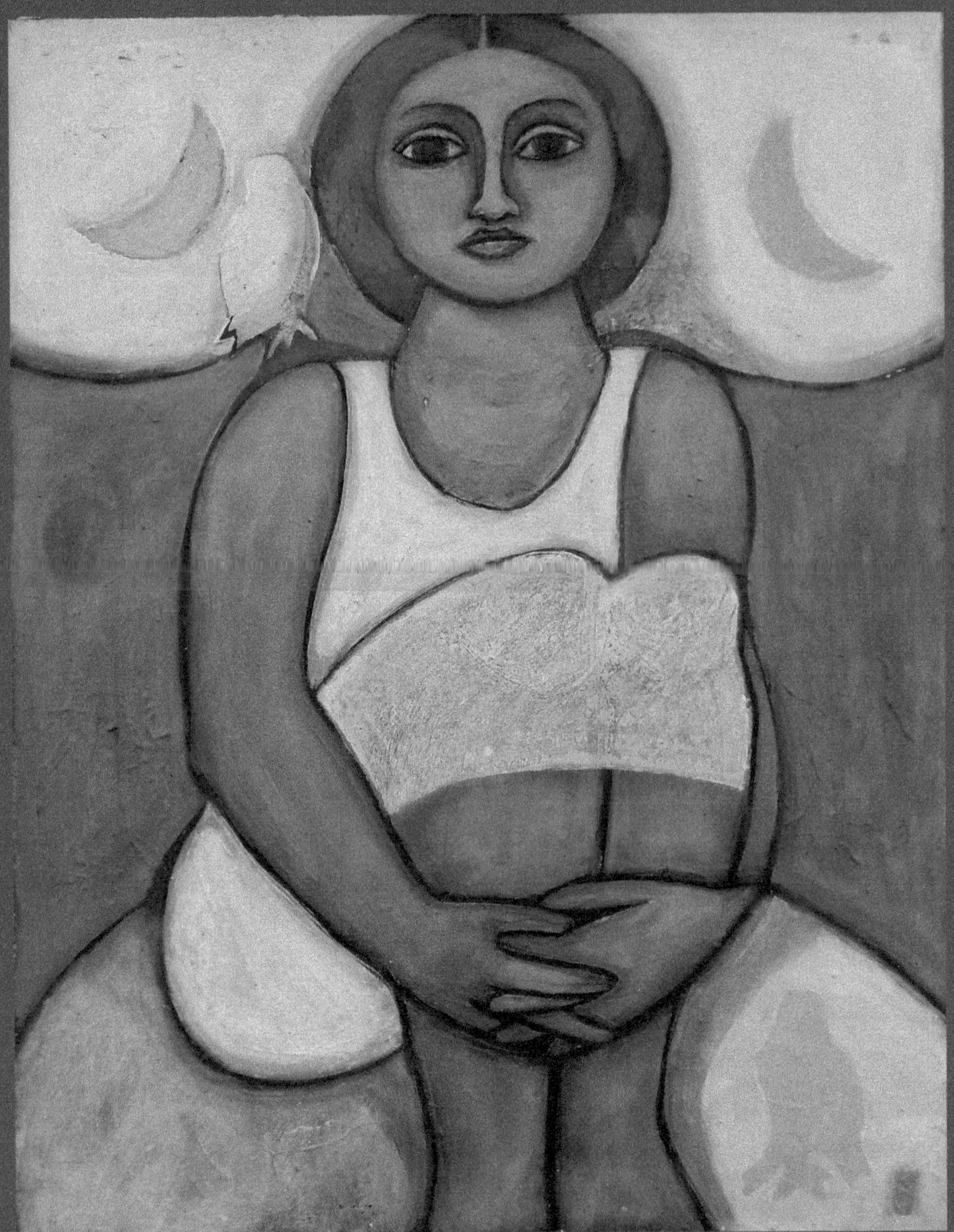

Moonlight
(61cm x 49cm)

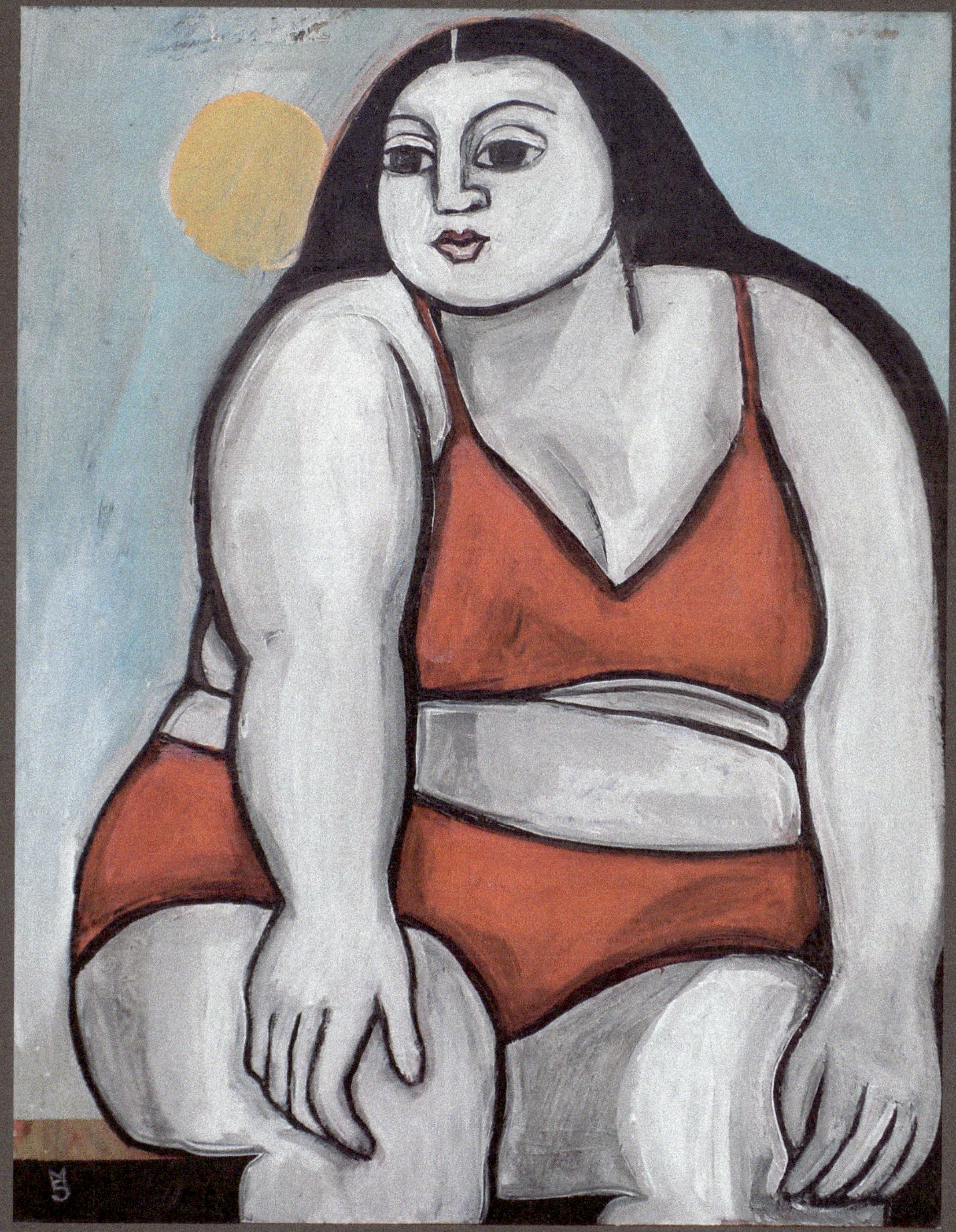

Violet
(61cm x 49cm)
Digital version on pg.230.

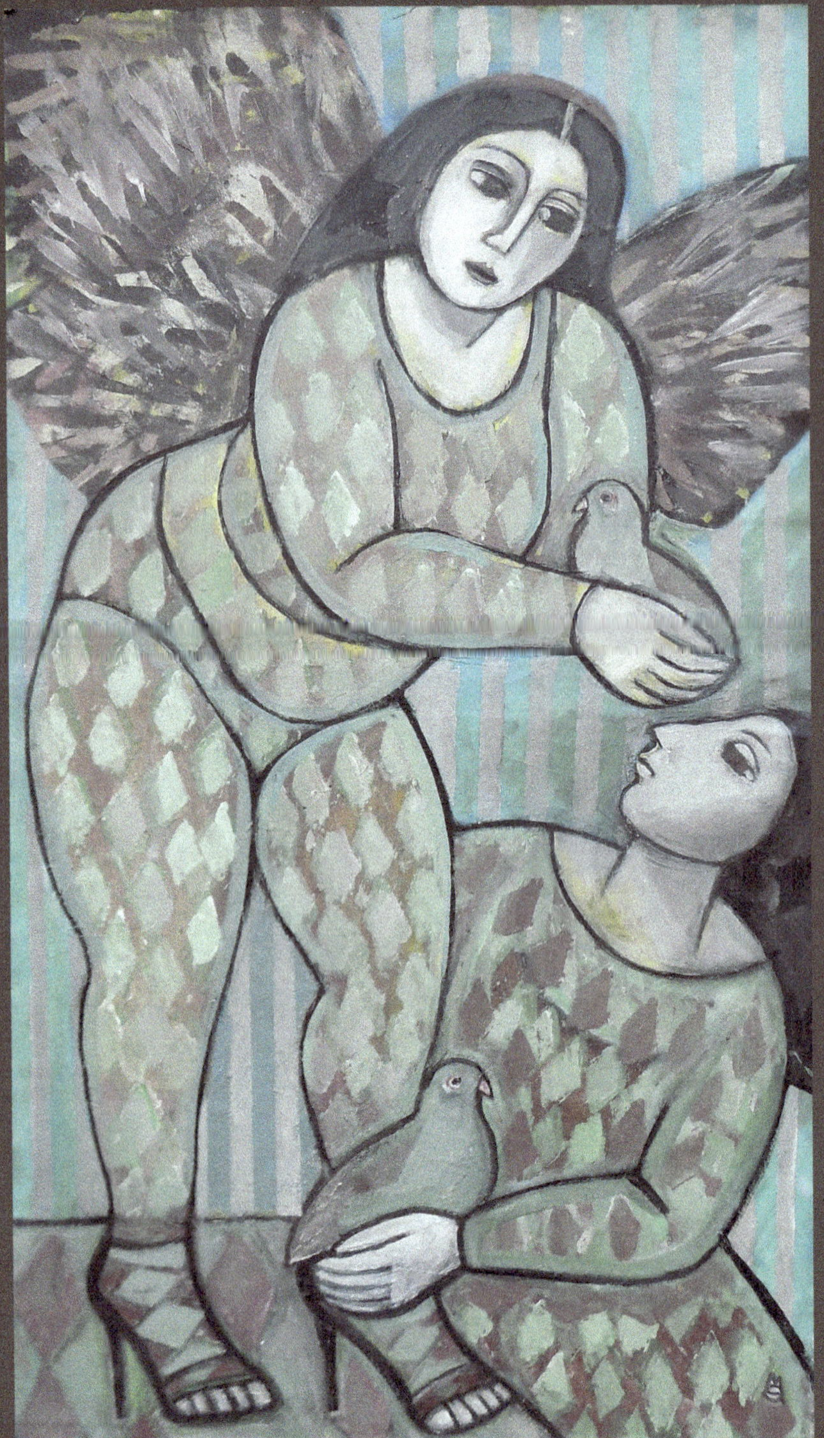

Sage
(114cm x 66cm)

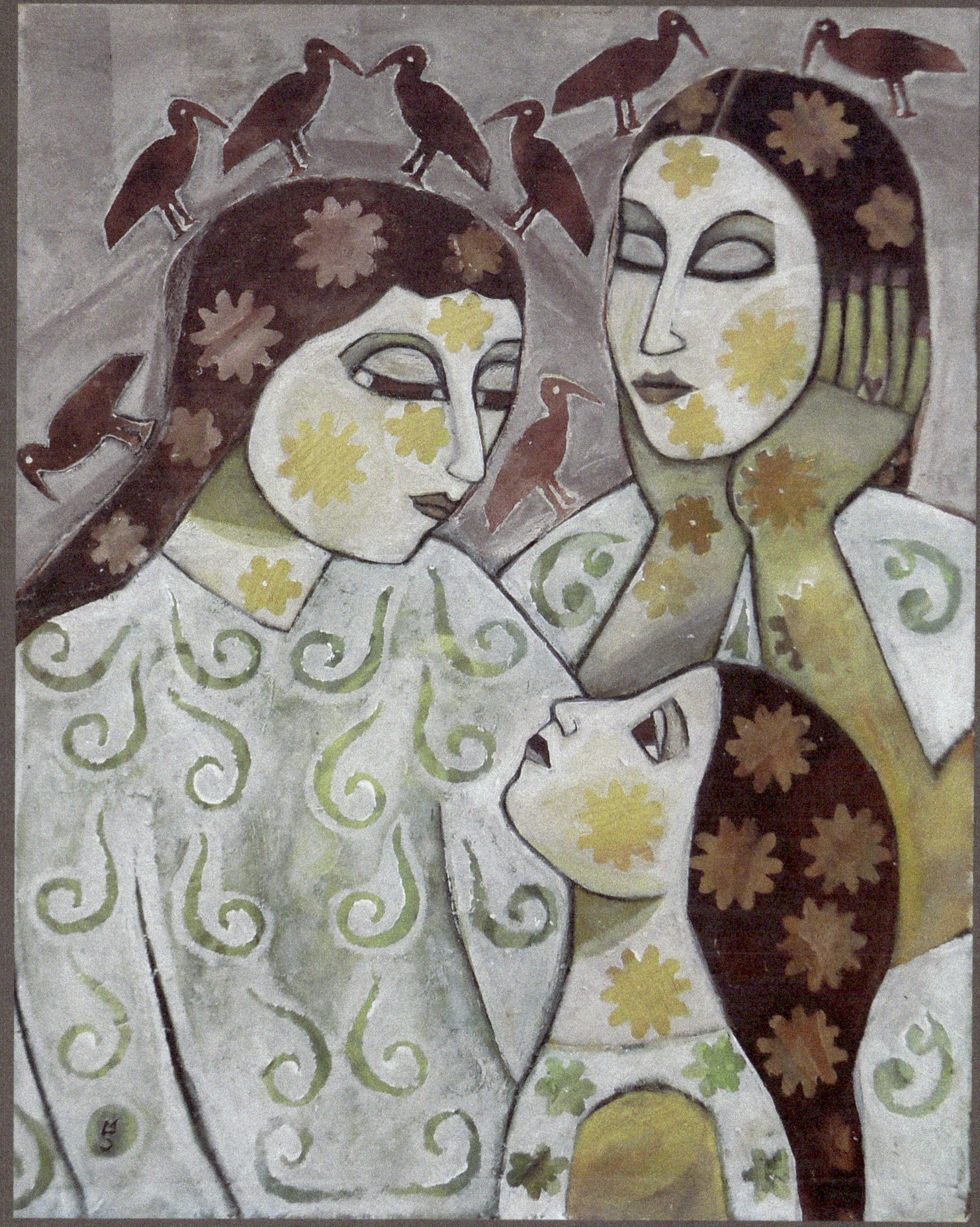

Verde
(90cm x 75cm)

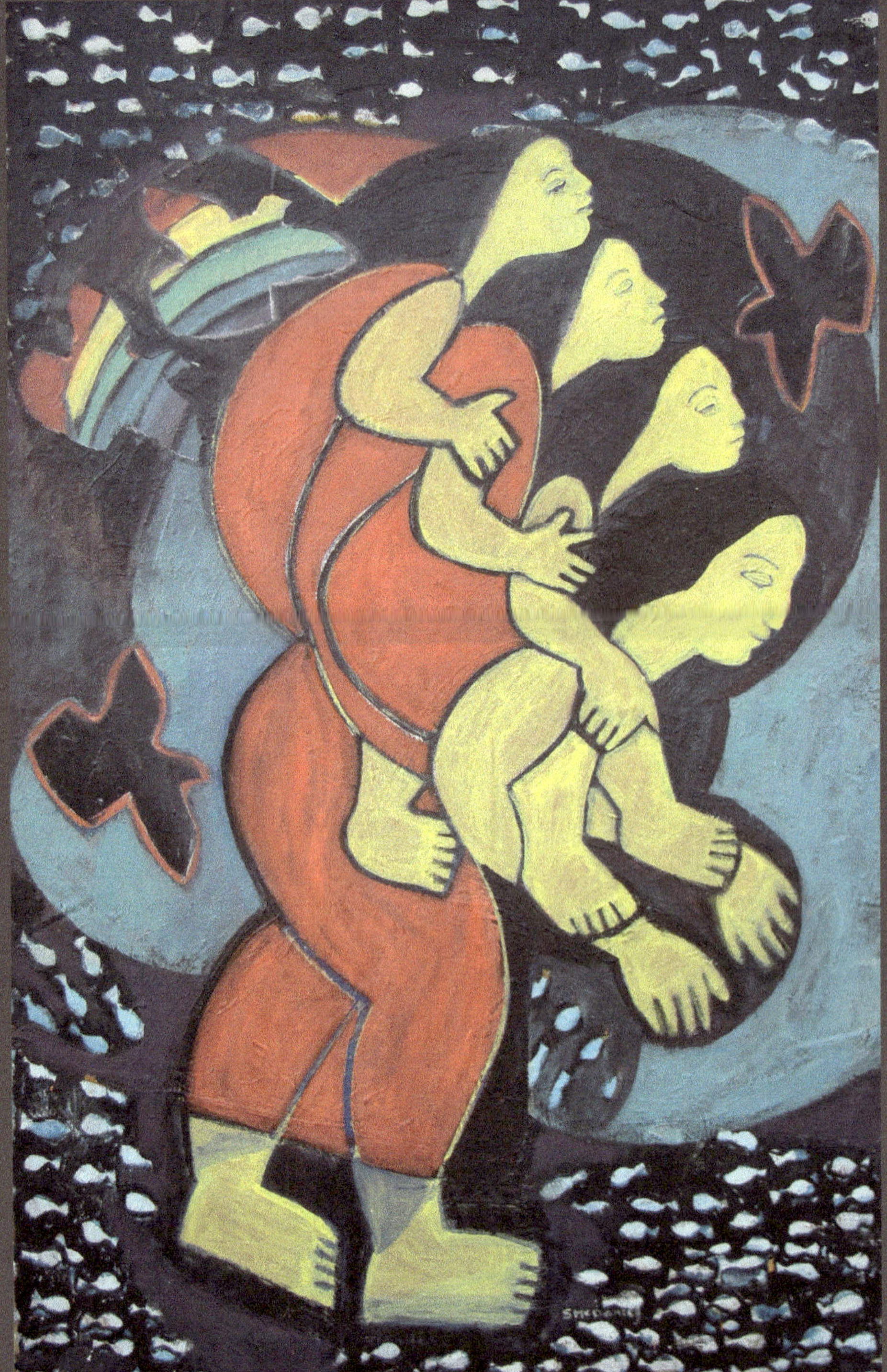

Totem Pole Sisterhood
(115cm x 70cm)

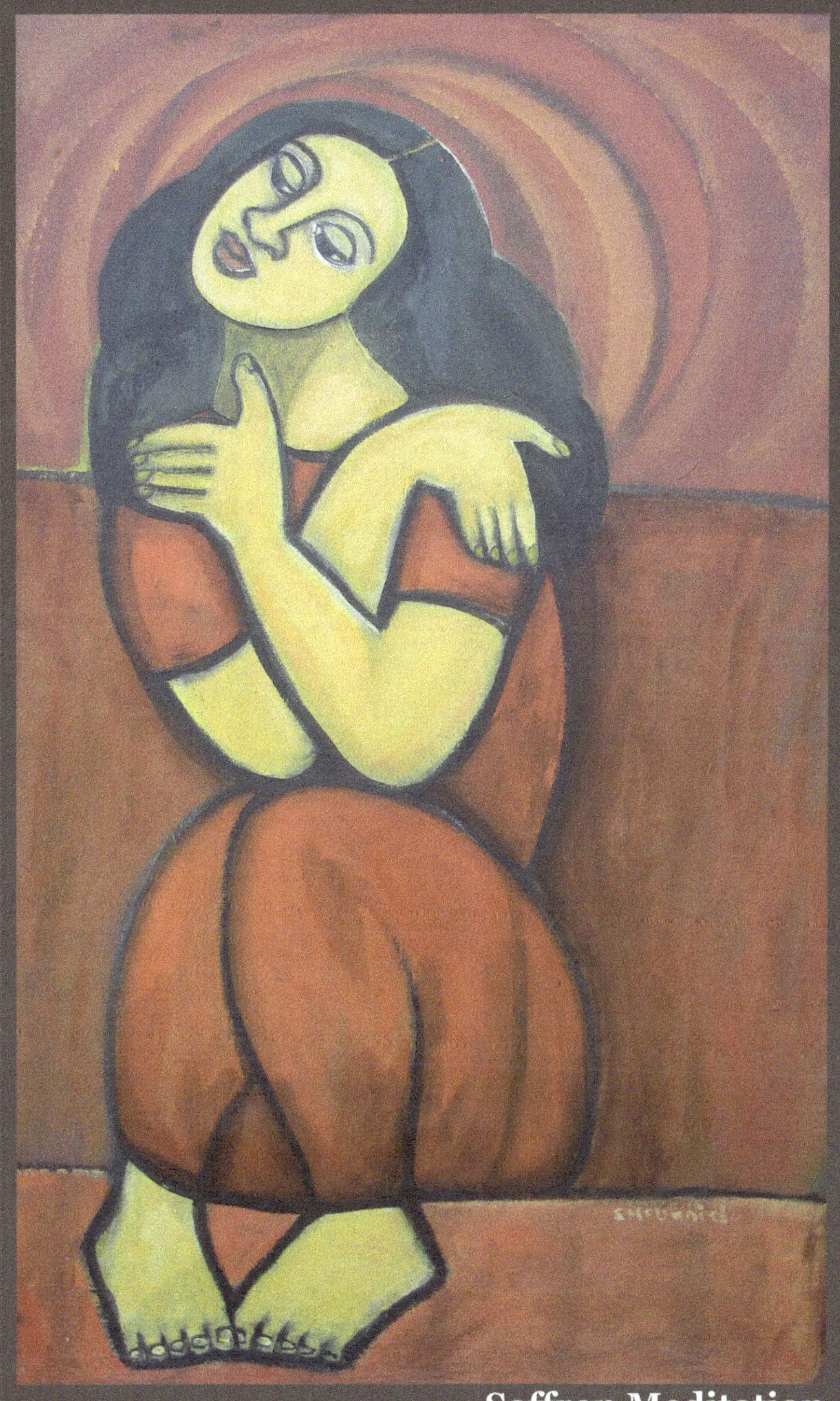

Saffron Meditation
(130cm x 80cm)

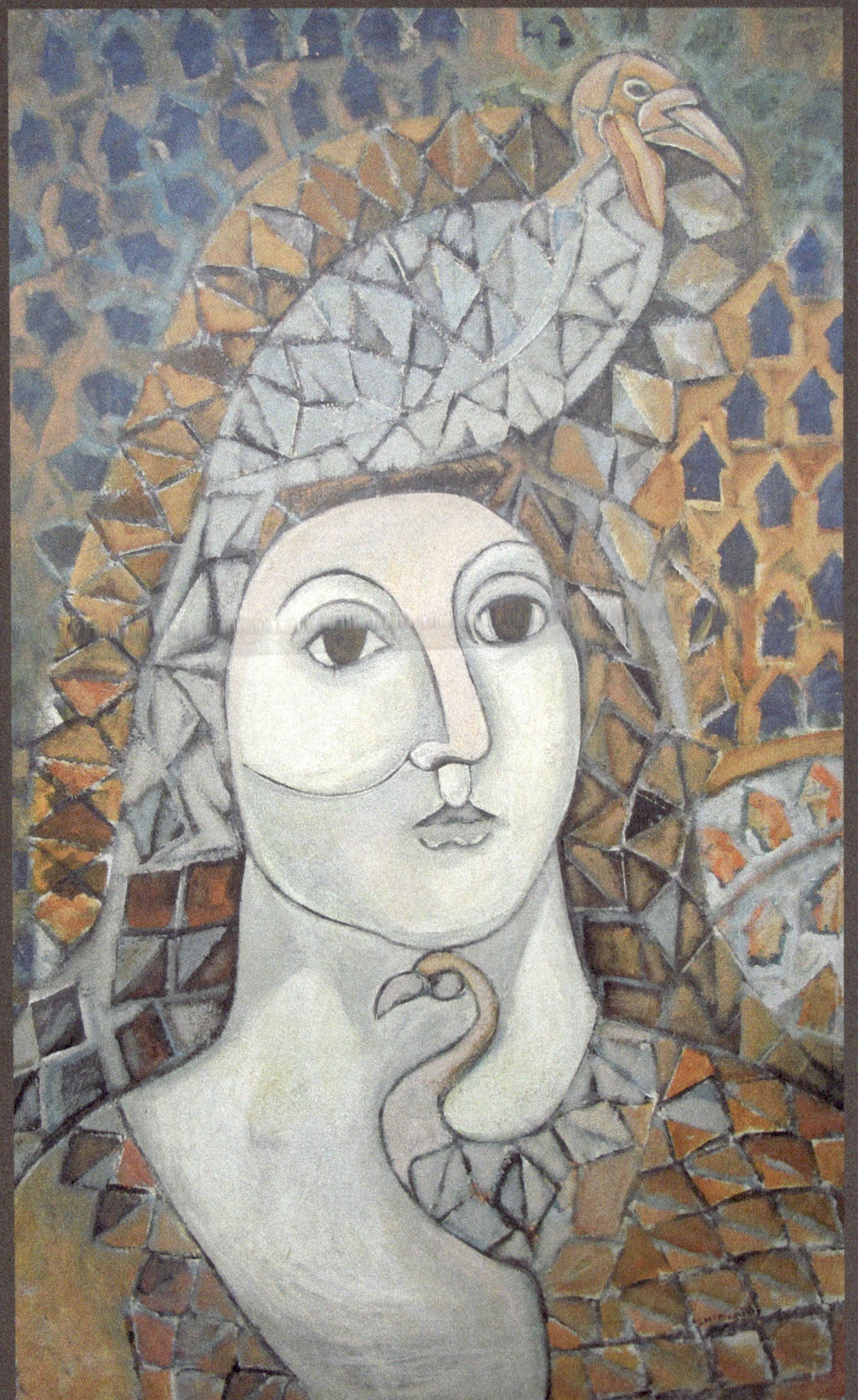

Bird Bedecked
(135cm x 80cm)

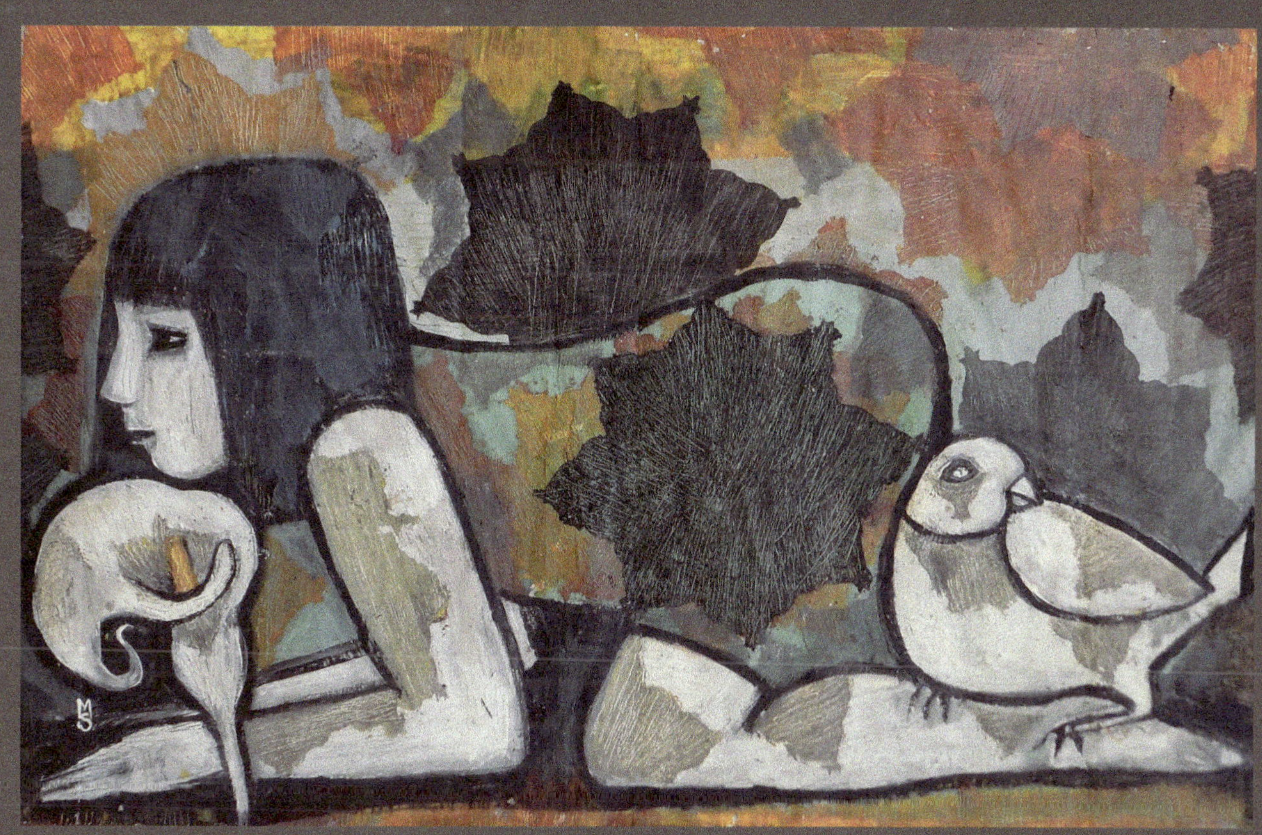

Autumn
(45cm x 72cm)

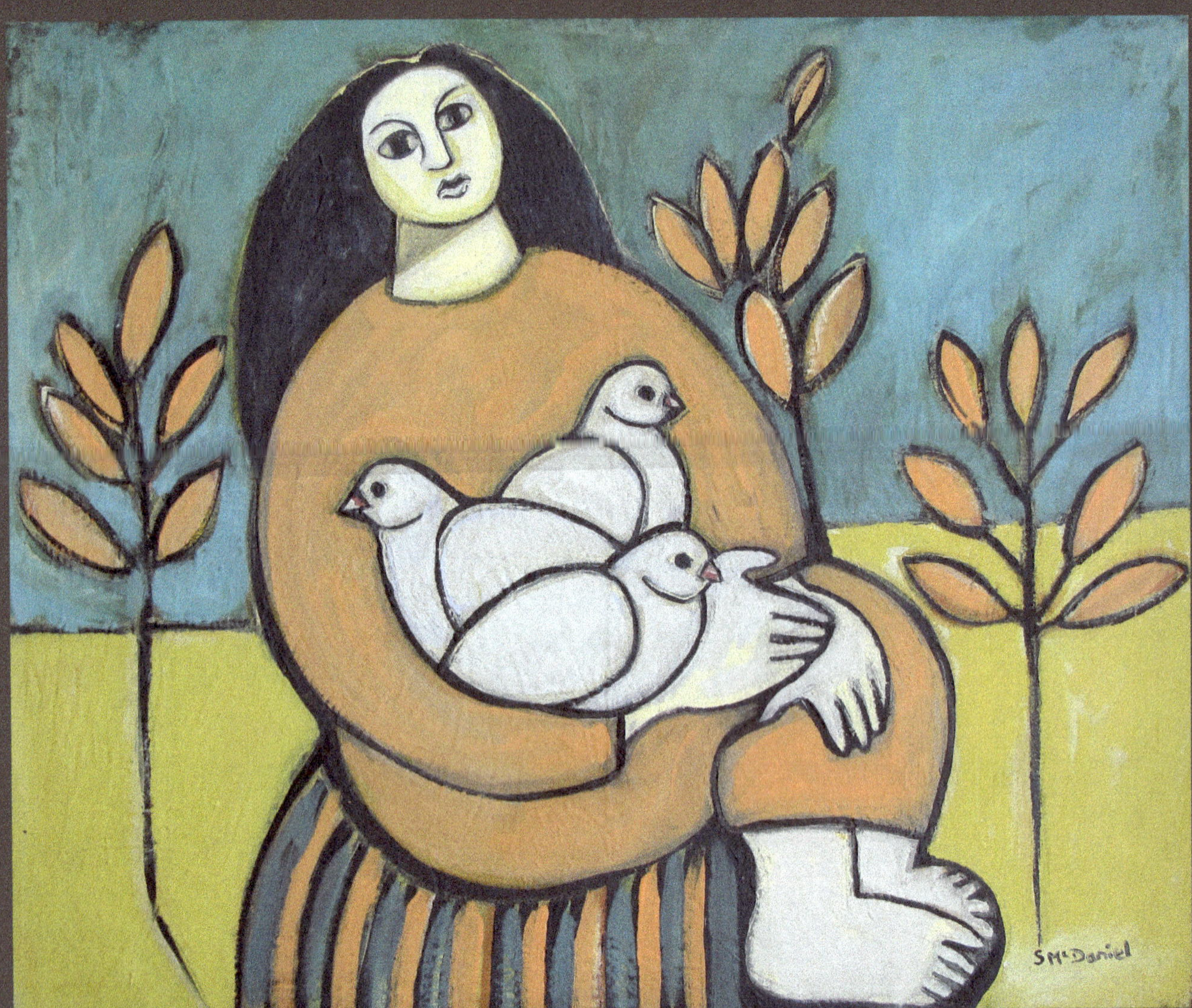

Dove Tale
(75cm x 90cm)

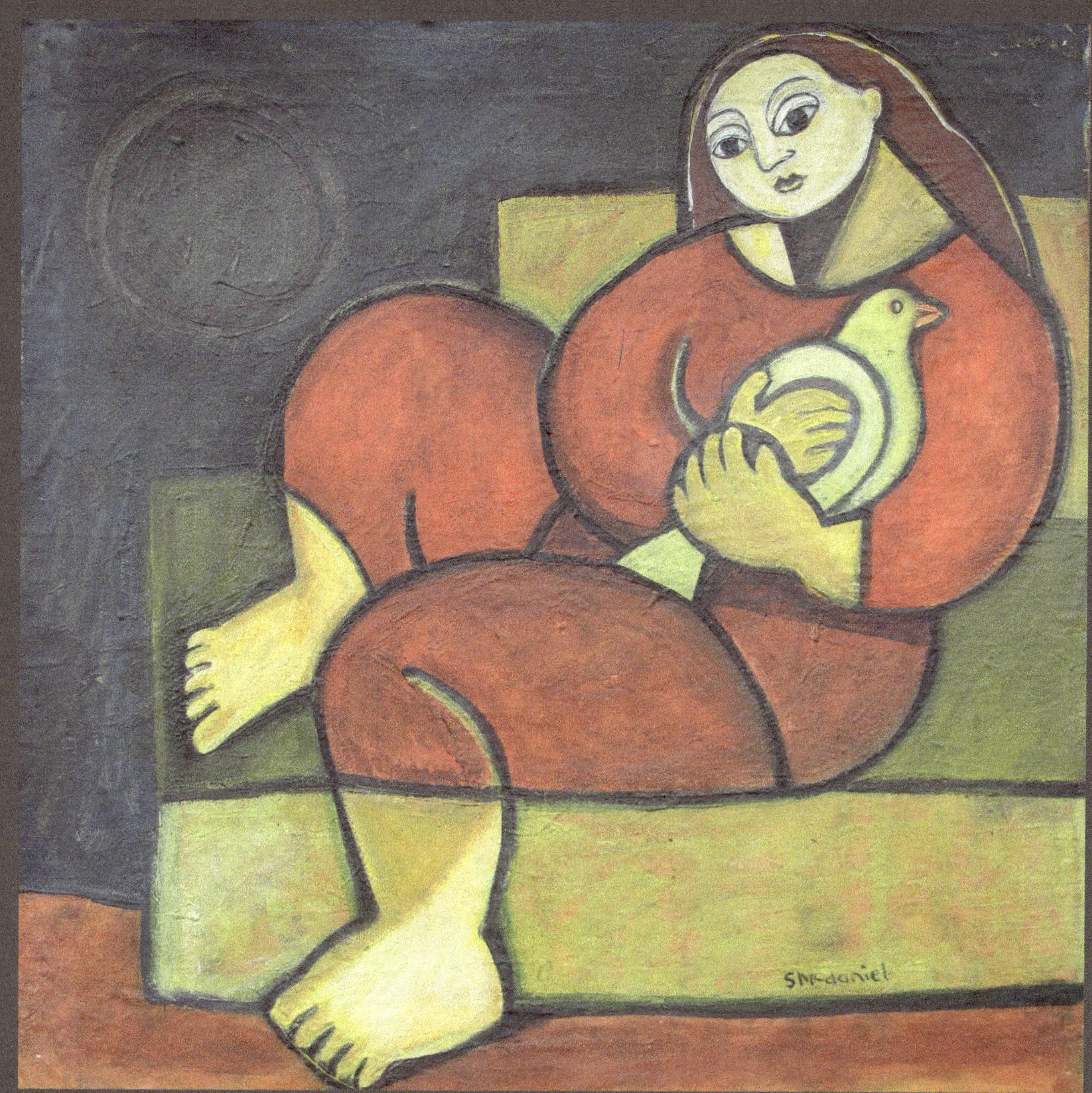

Gentle Genesis
(70cm x 70cm)
Digital version on pg.173.

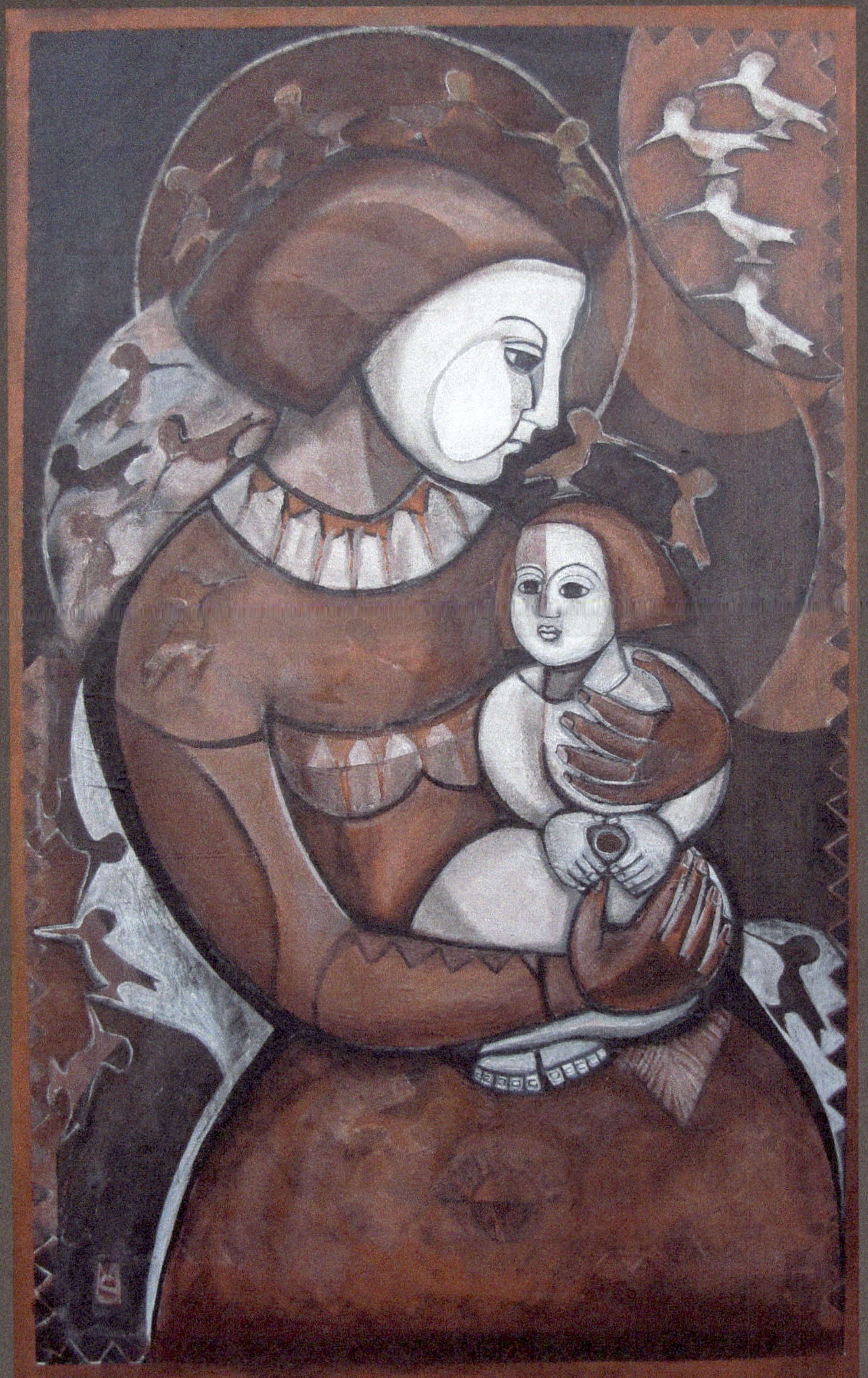

Abiding Love
(130cm x 85cm)

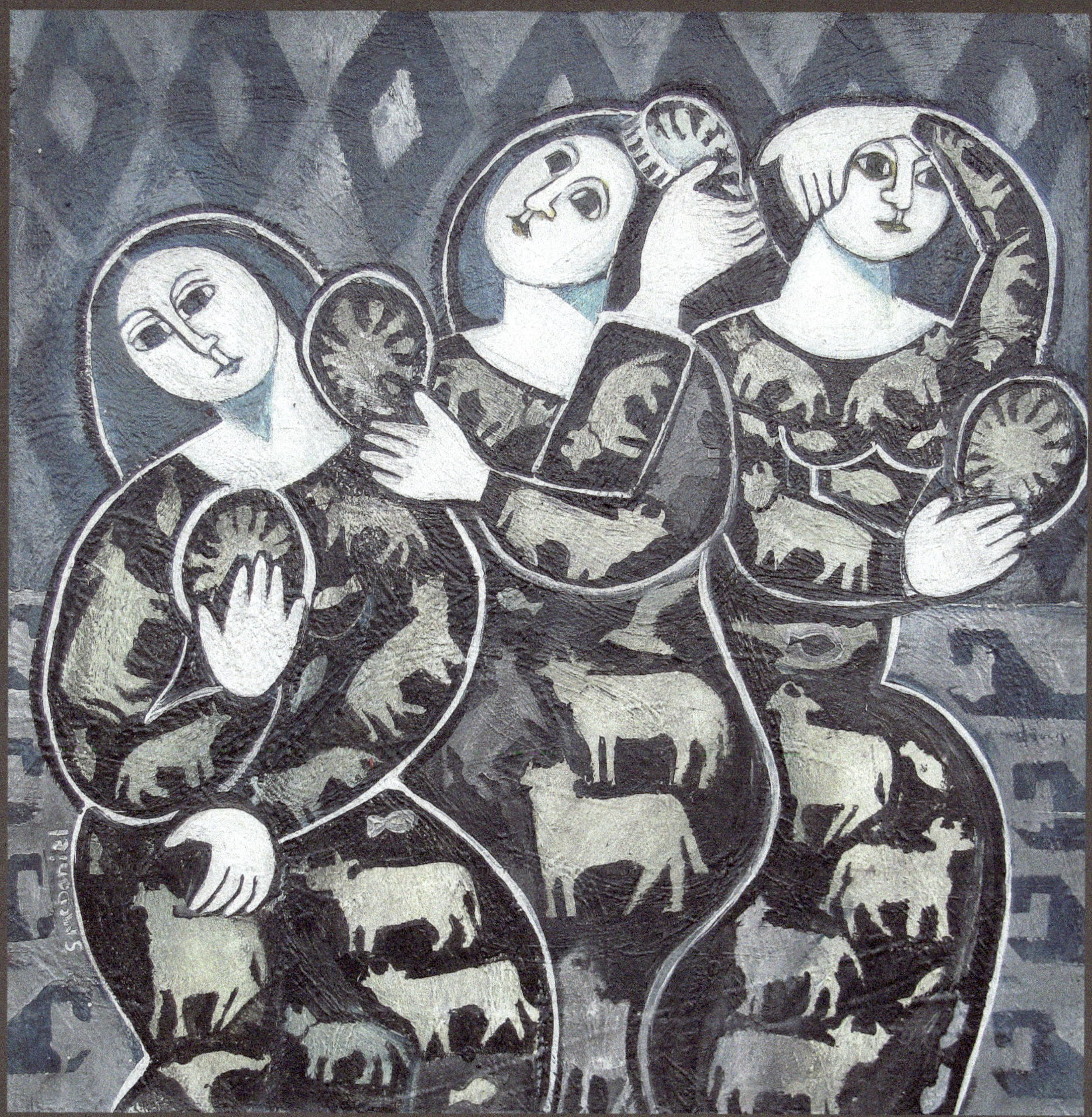

Cow Girls Boudoir
(60cm x 60cm)

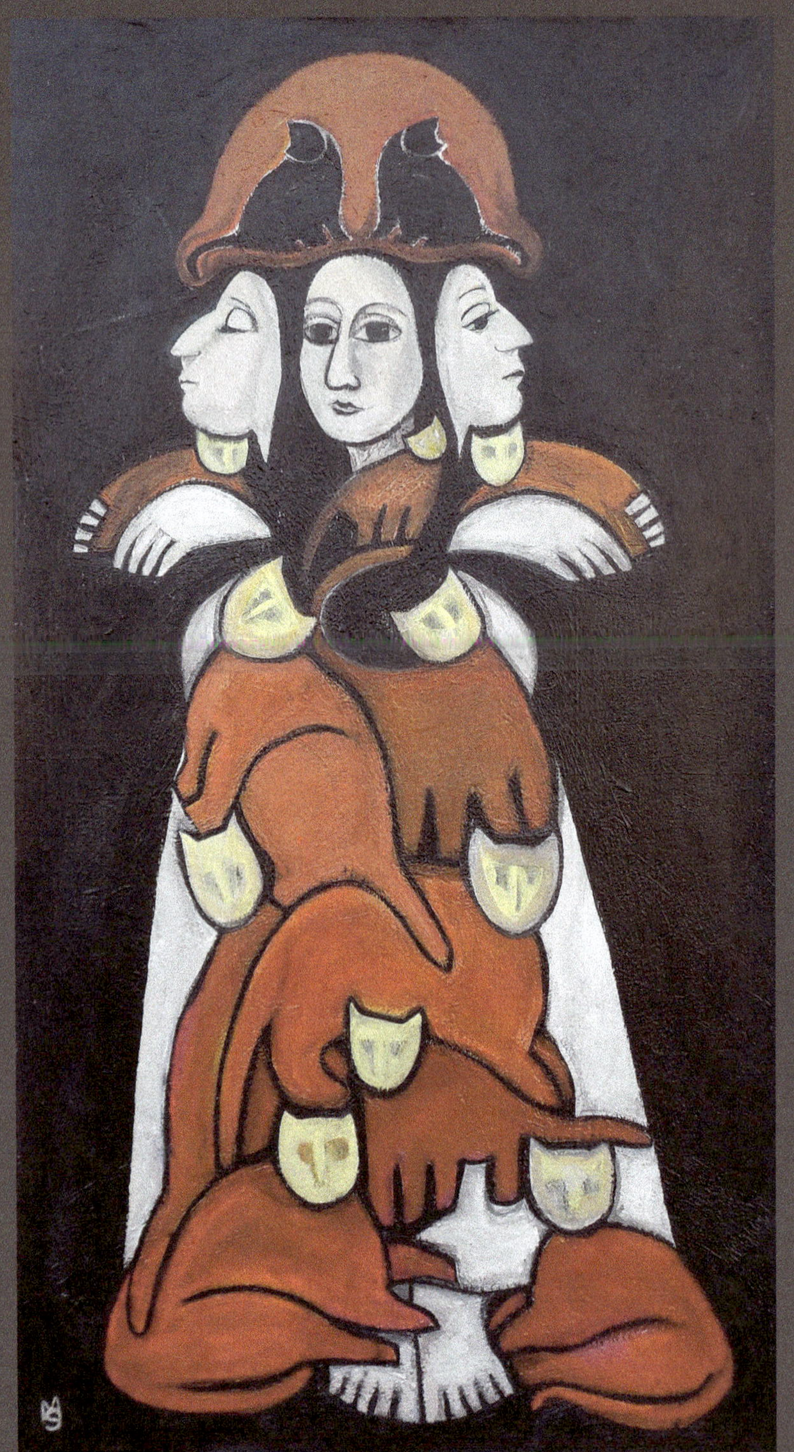

Feline Turban
(110cm x 60cm)

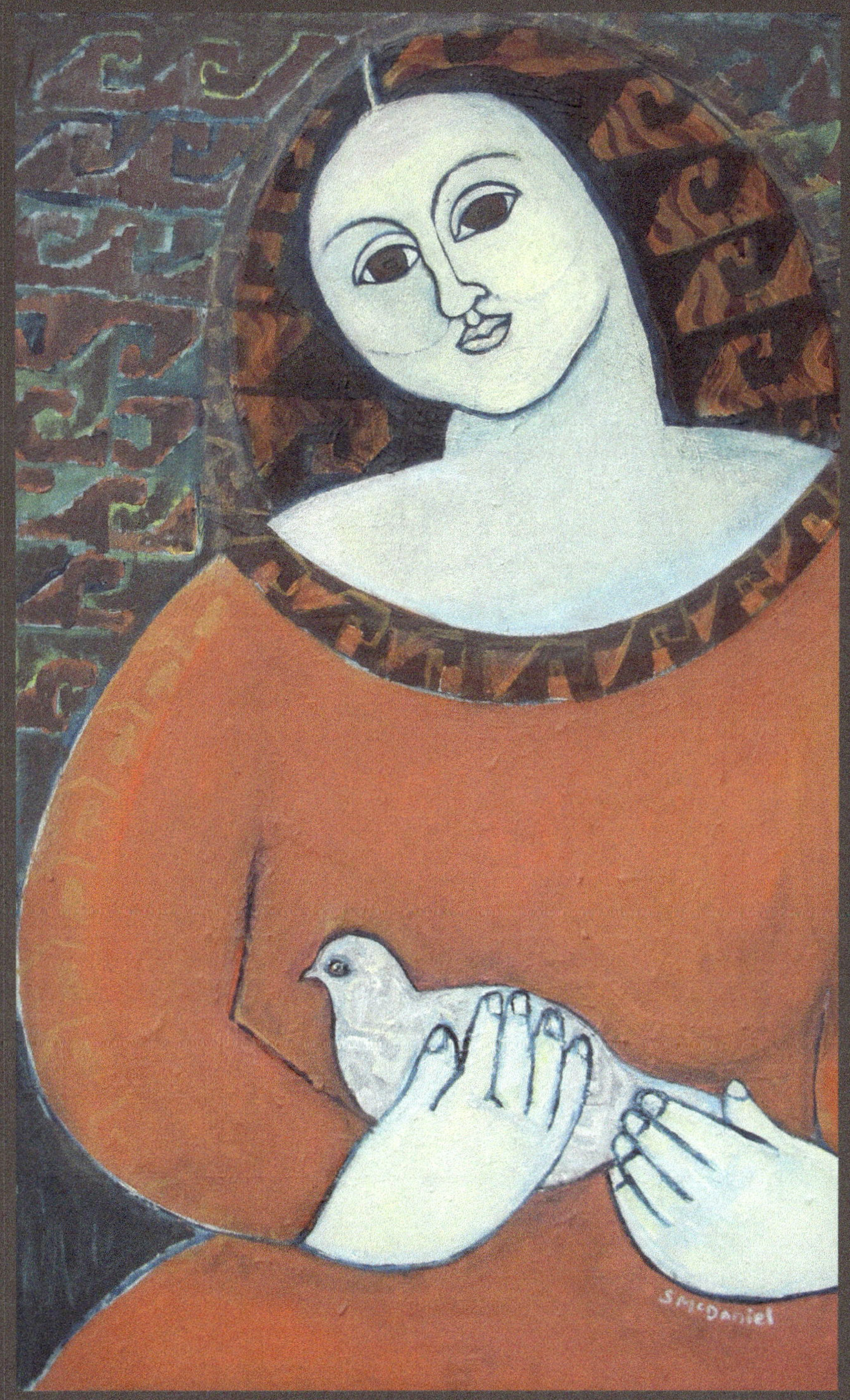

Still Life
(85cm x 55cm)

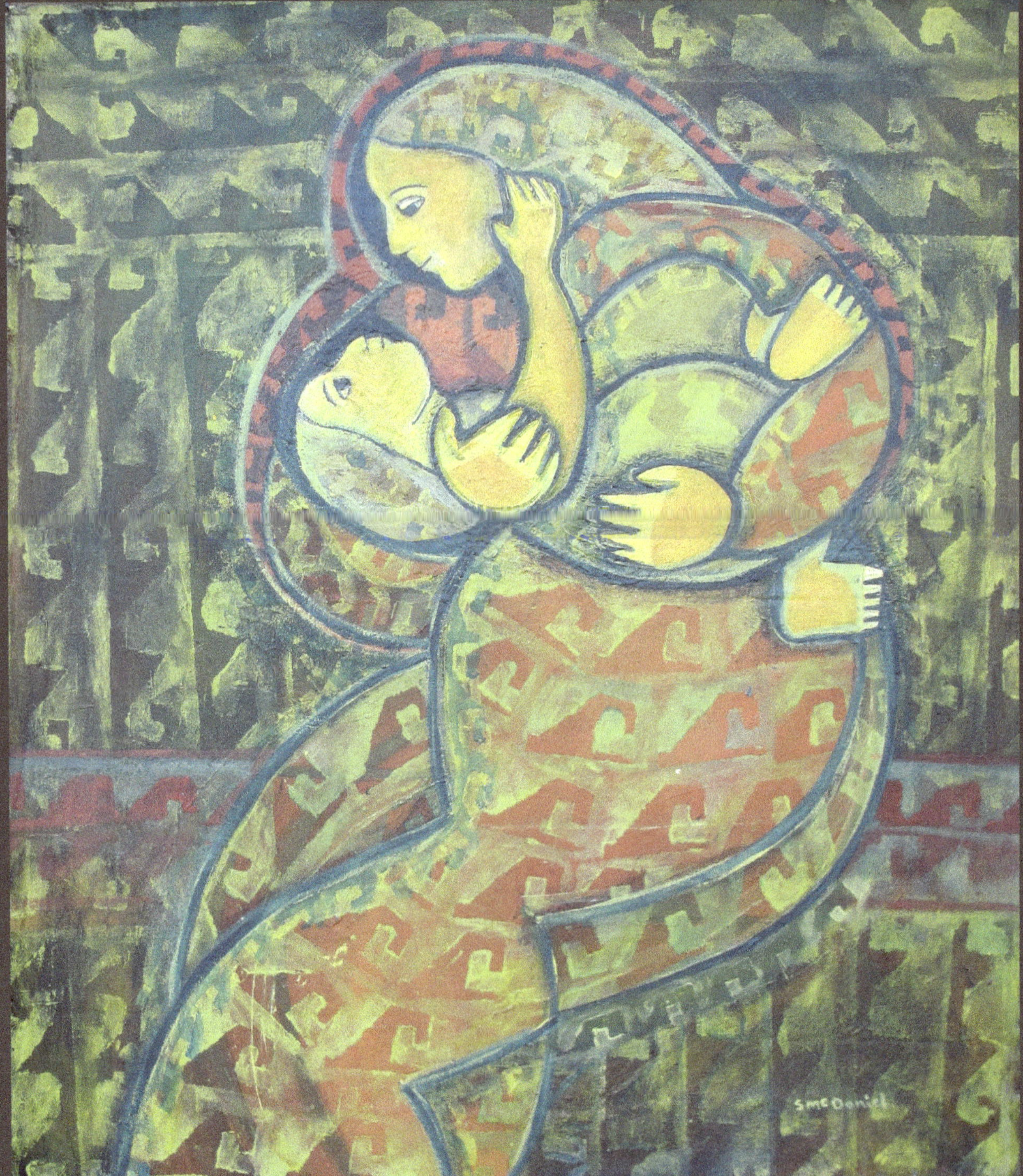

Embracement
(90cm x 80cm)
The image on the cover of this book.

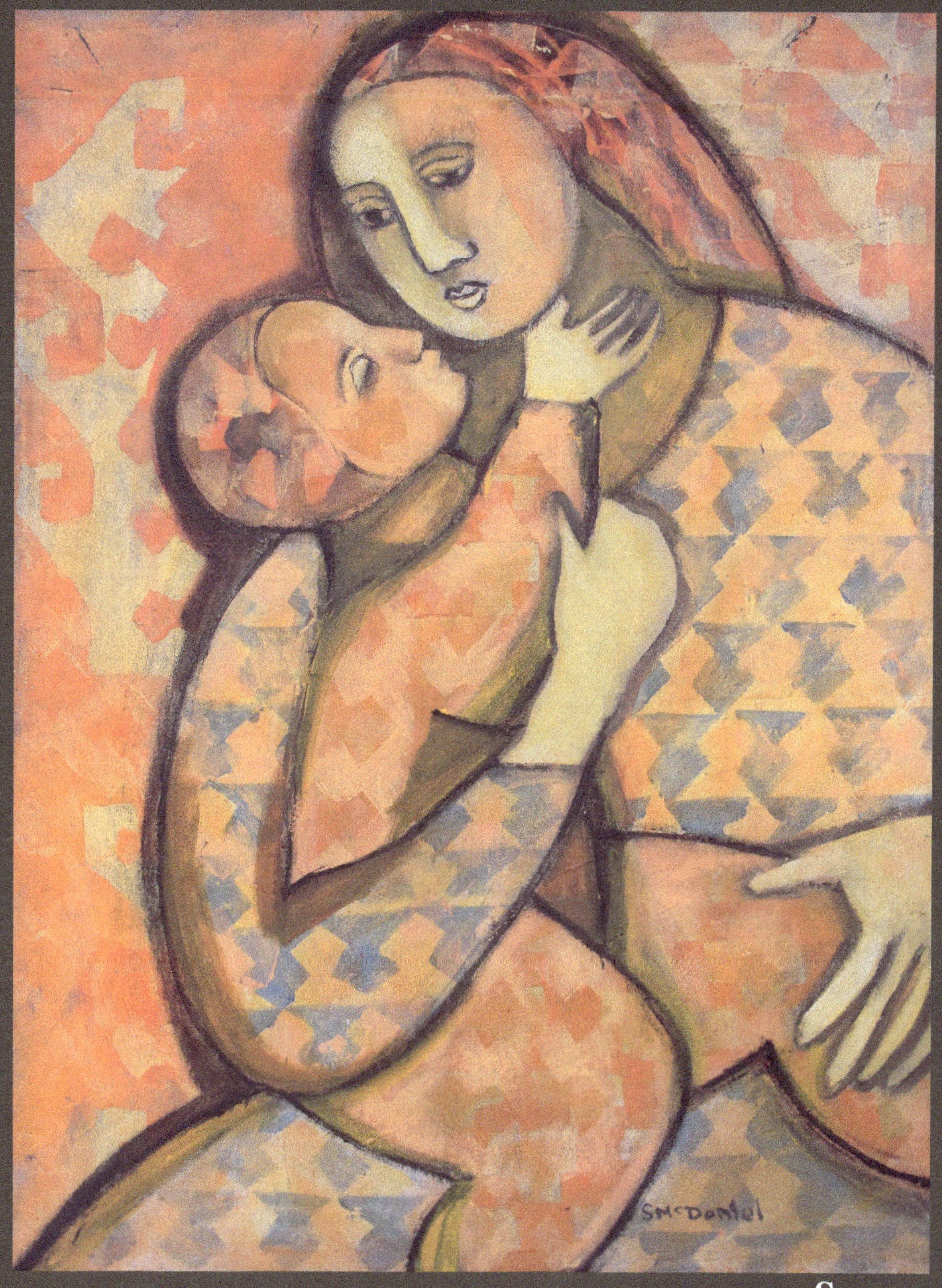

Serena
(75cm x 65cm)

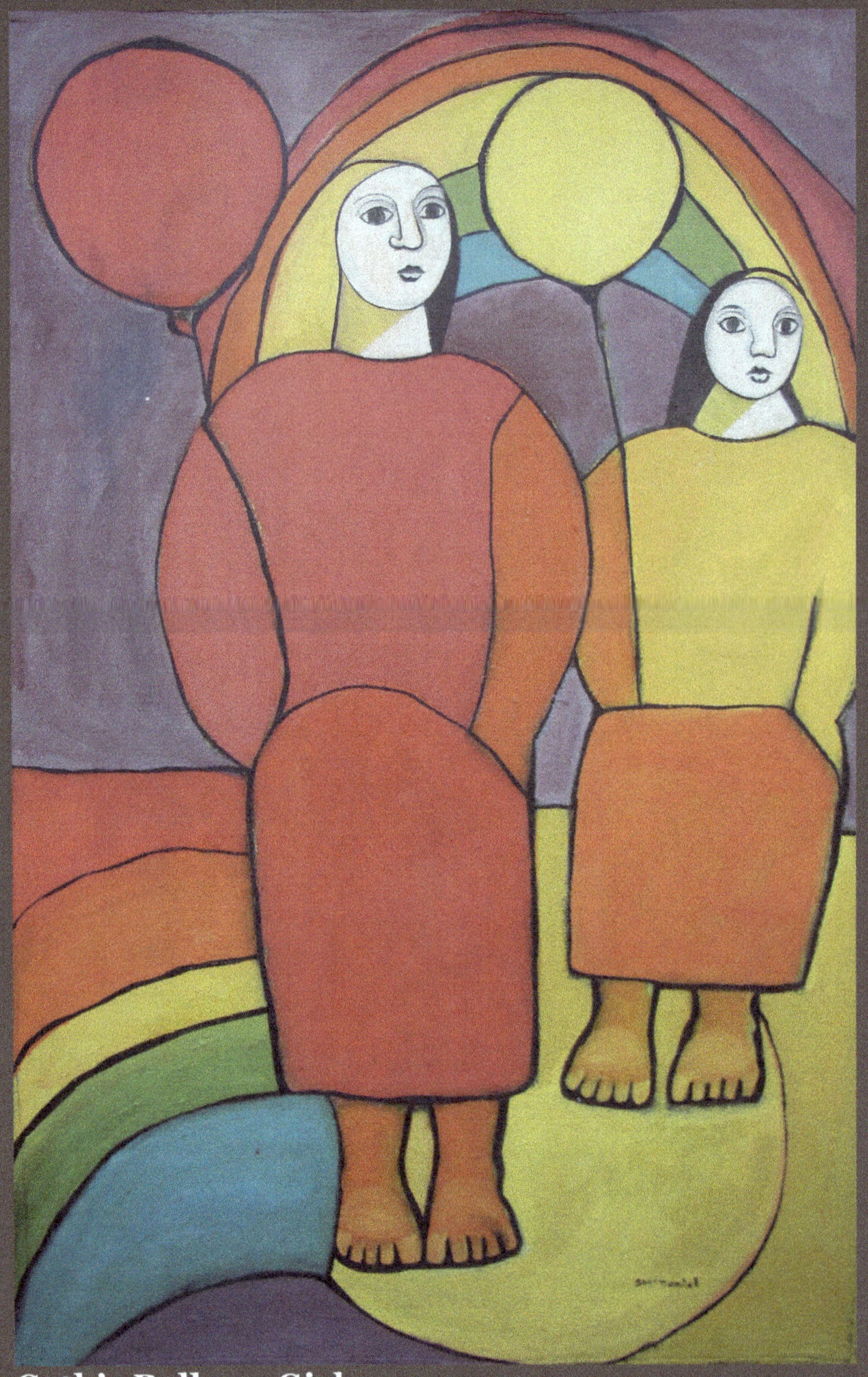

Cath's Balloon Girls
(125cm x 80cm)

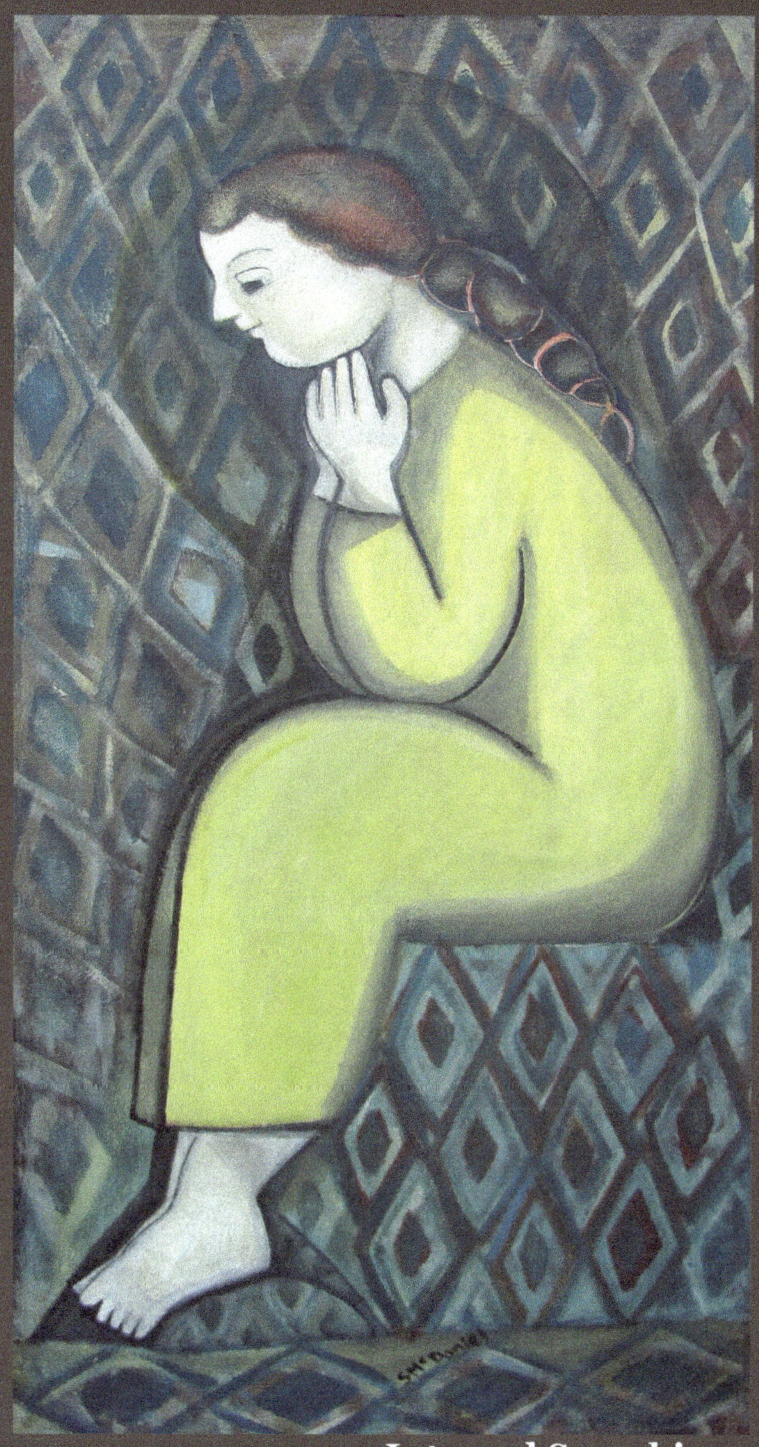

Internal Searchings
(130cm x 70cm)

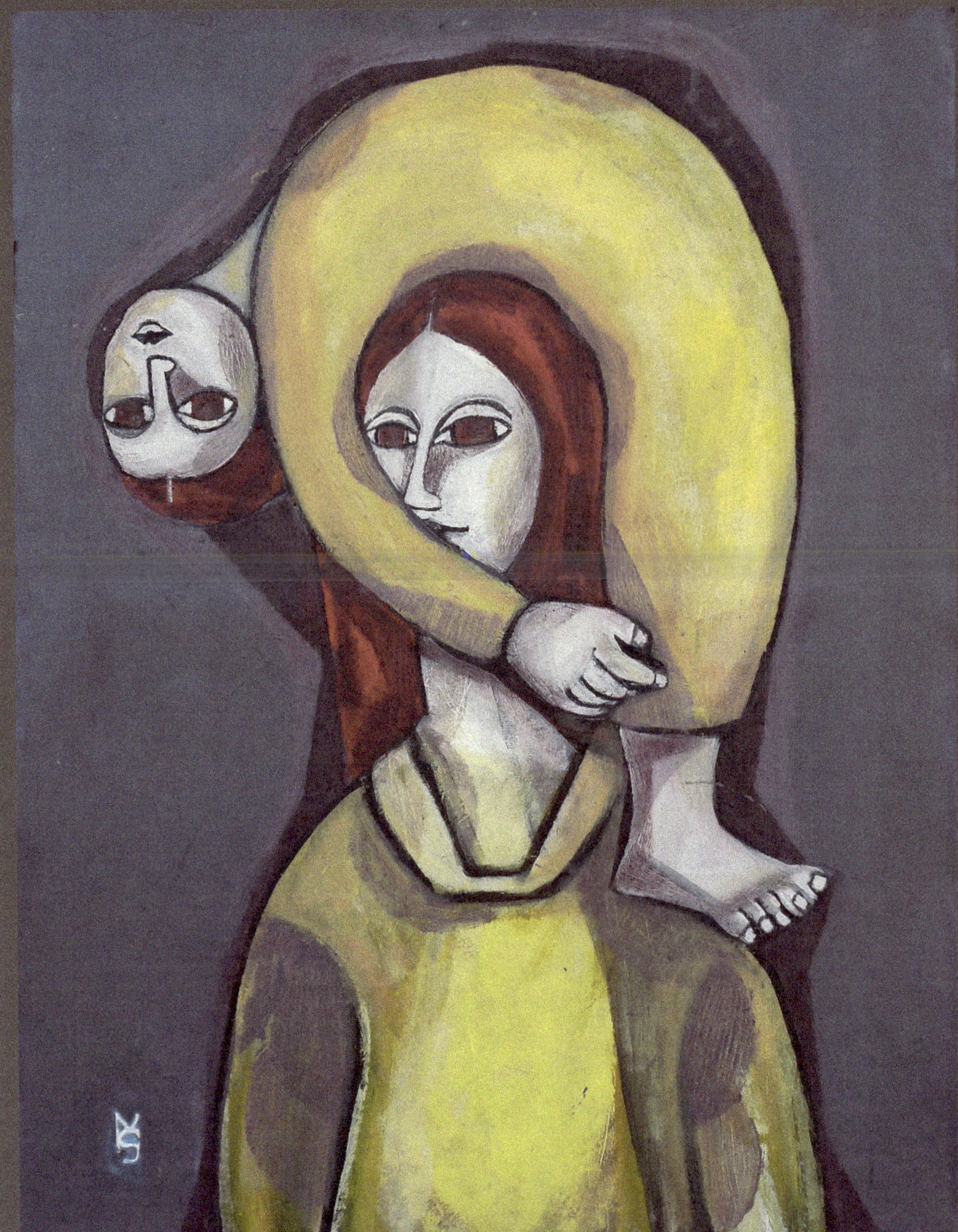

Draped
(95cm x 75m)

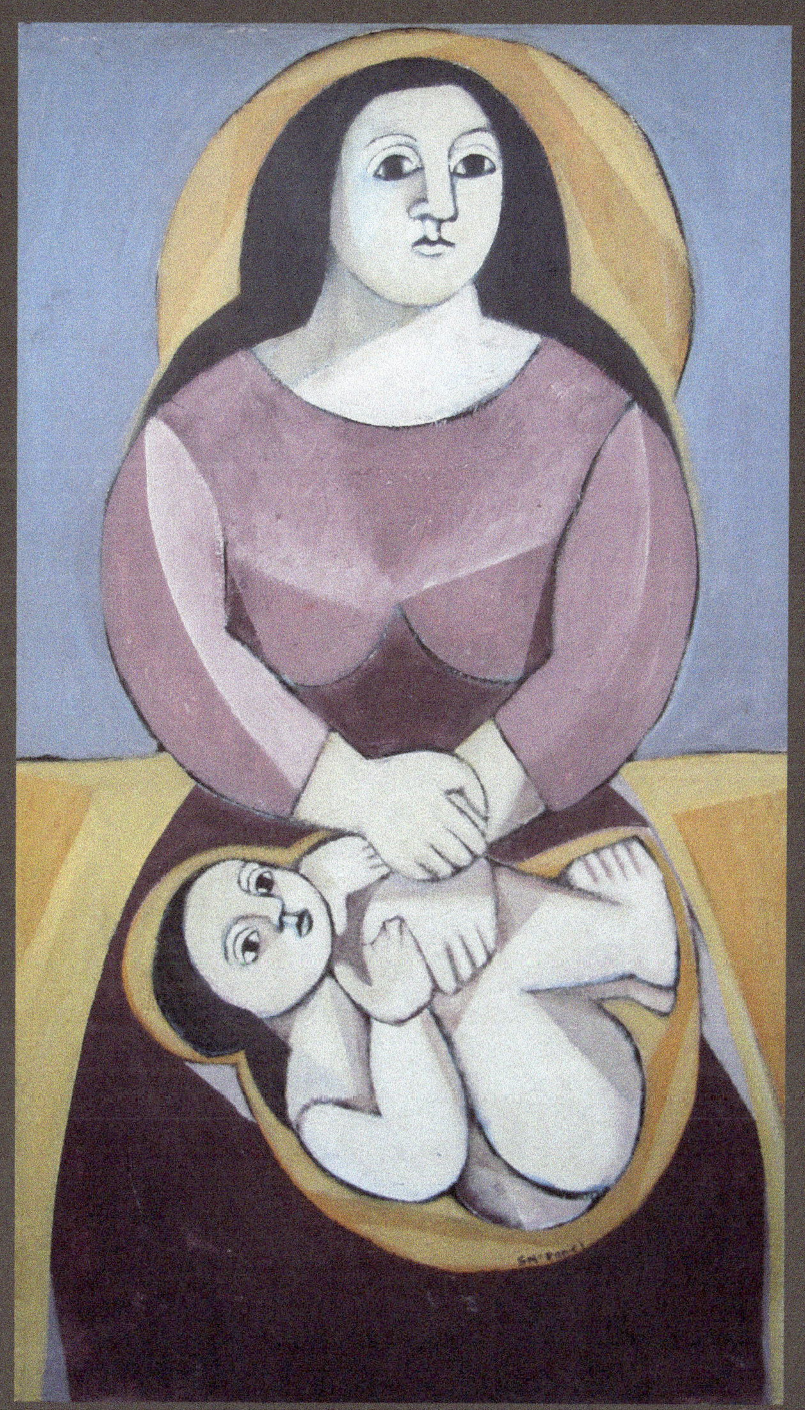

Maternity
(130cm x 75cm)
Digital version on pg.199.

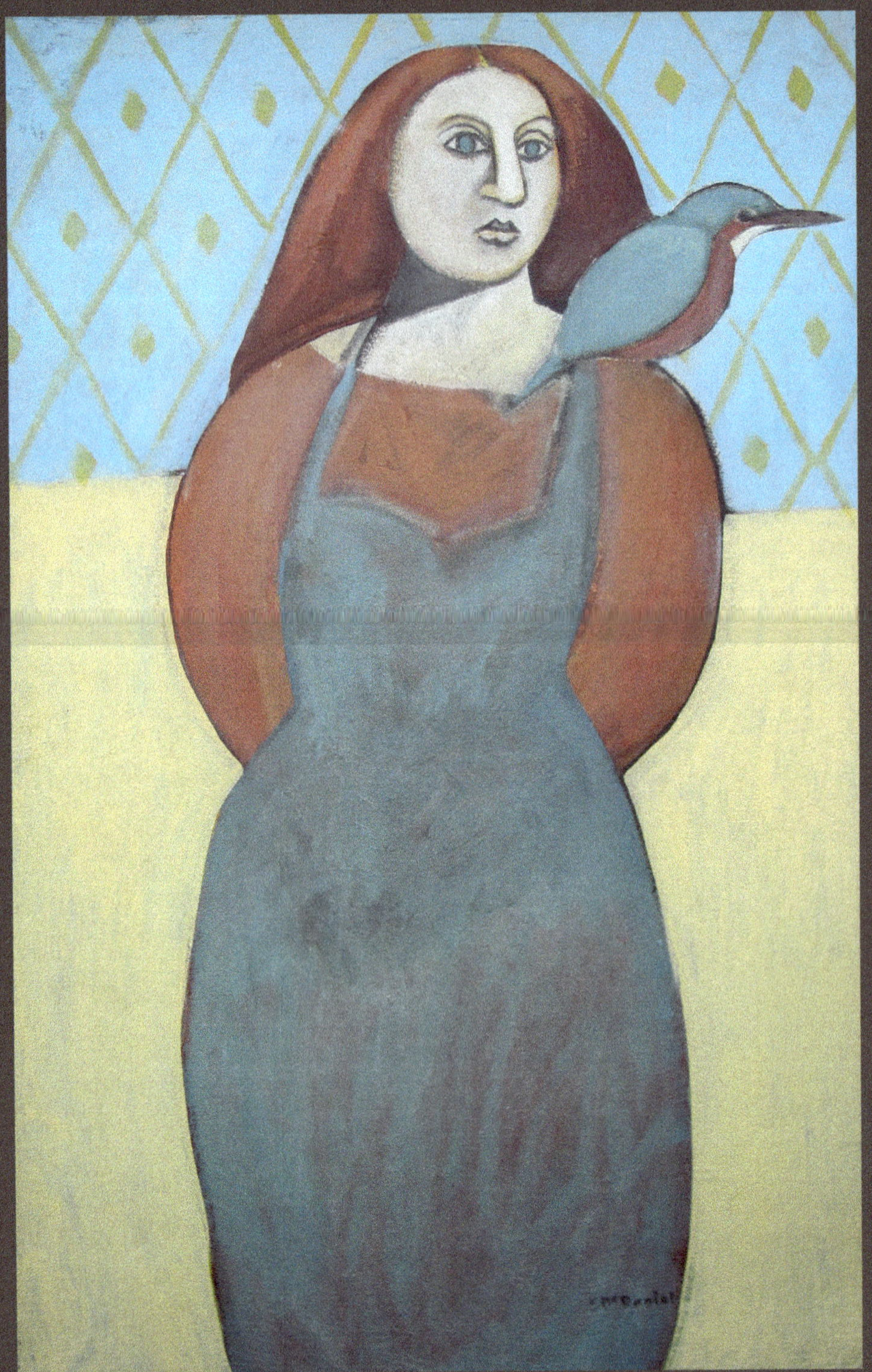

Shoulder Perch
(130cm x 80cm)

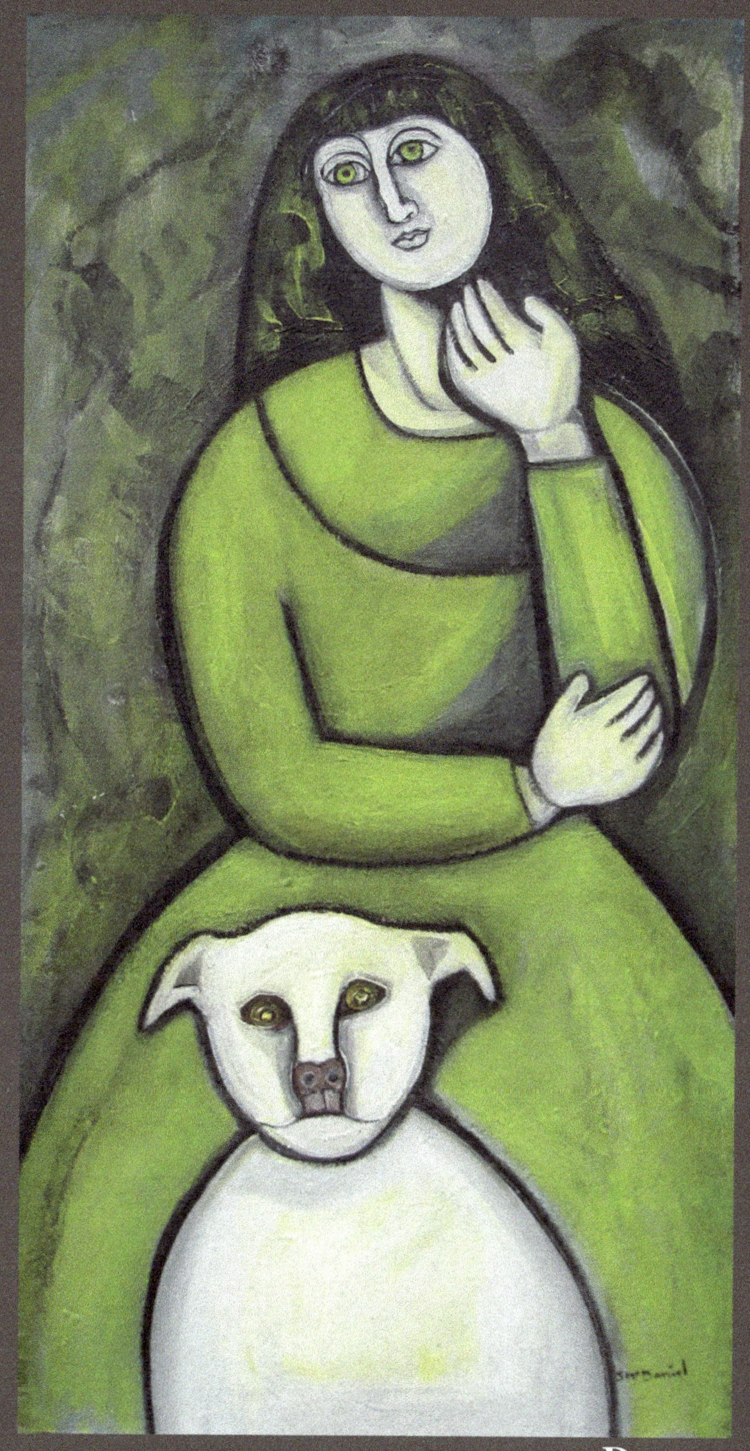

Dogma
(105cm x 55cm)

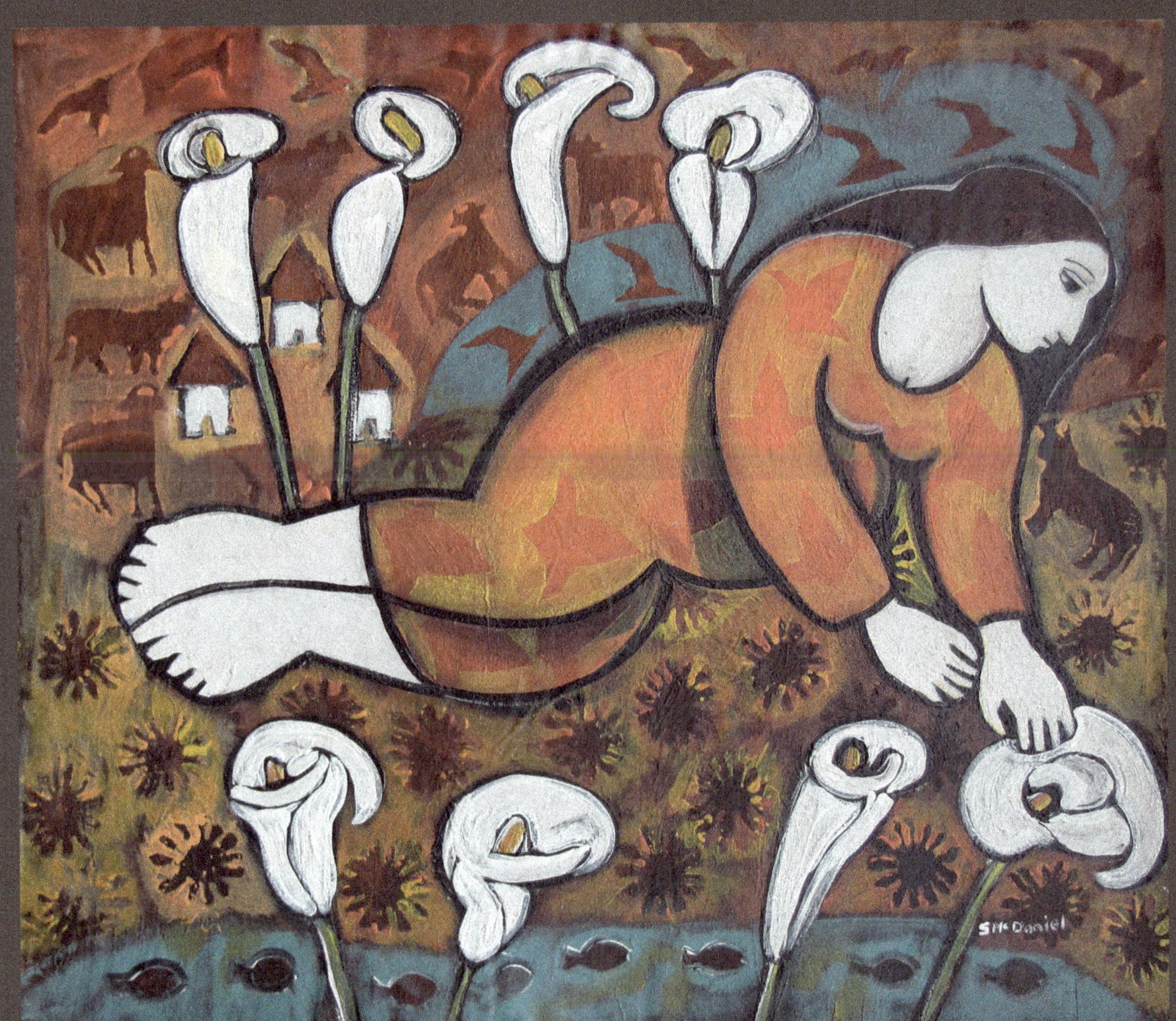

Lily Lady
(70cm x 80cm)

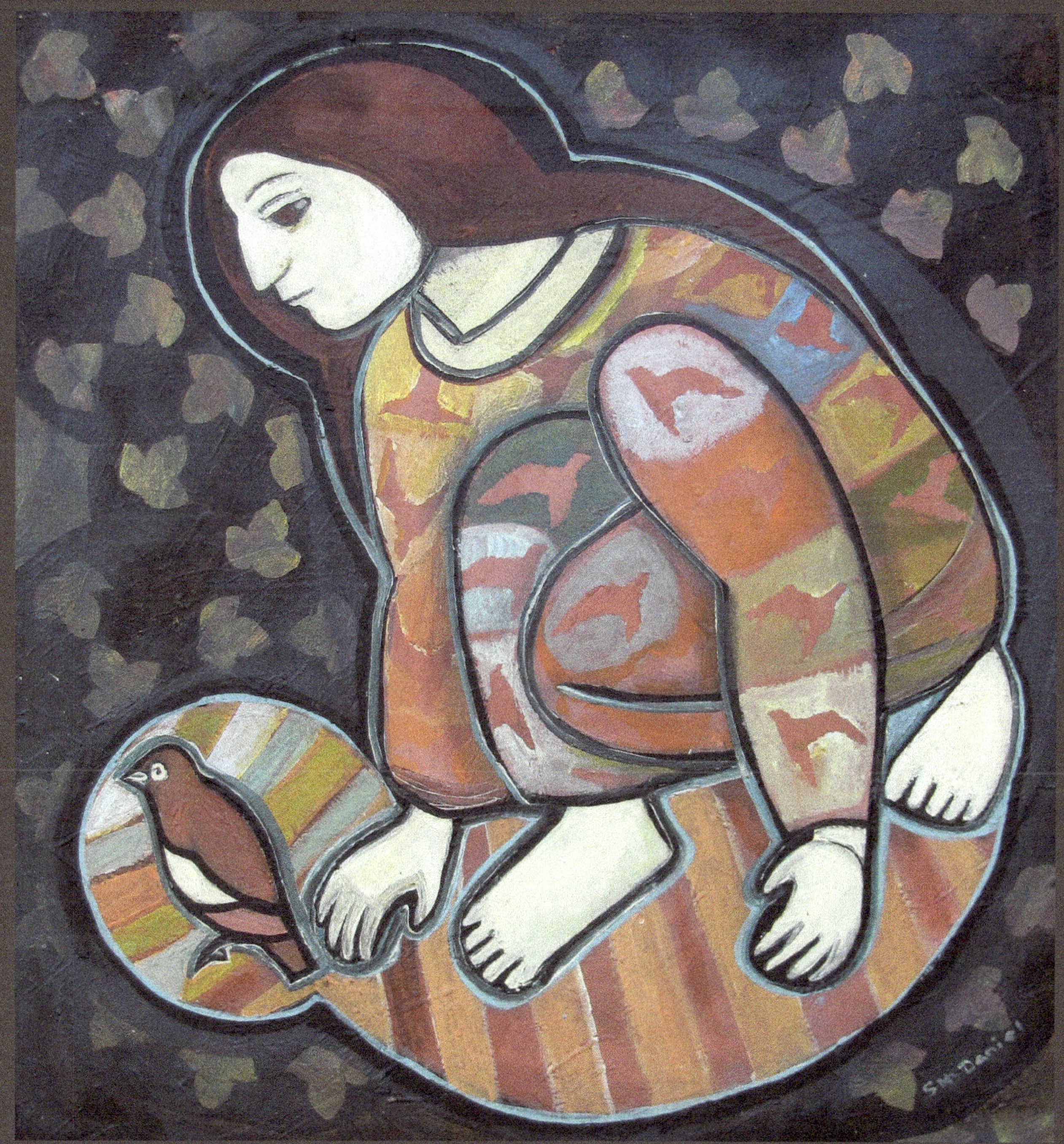

Bird Hush
(60cm x 60cm)

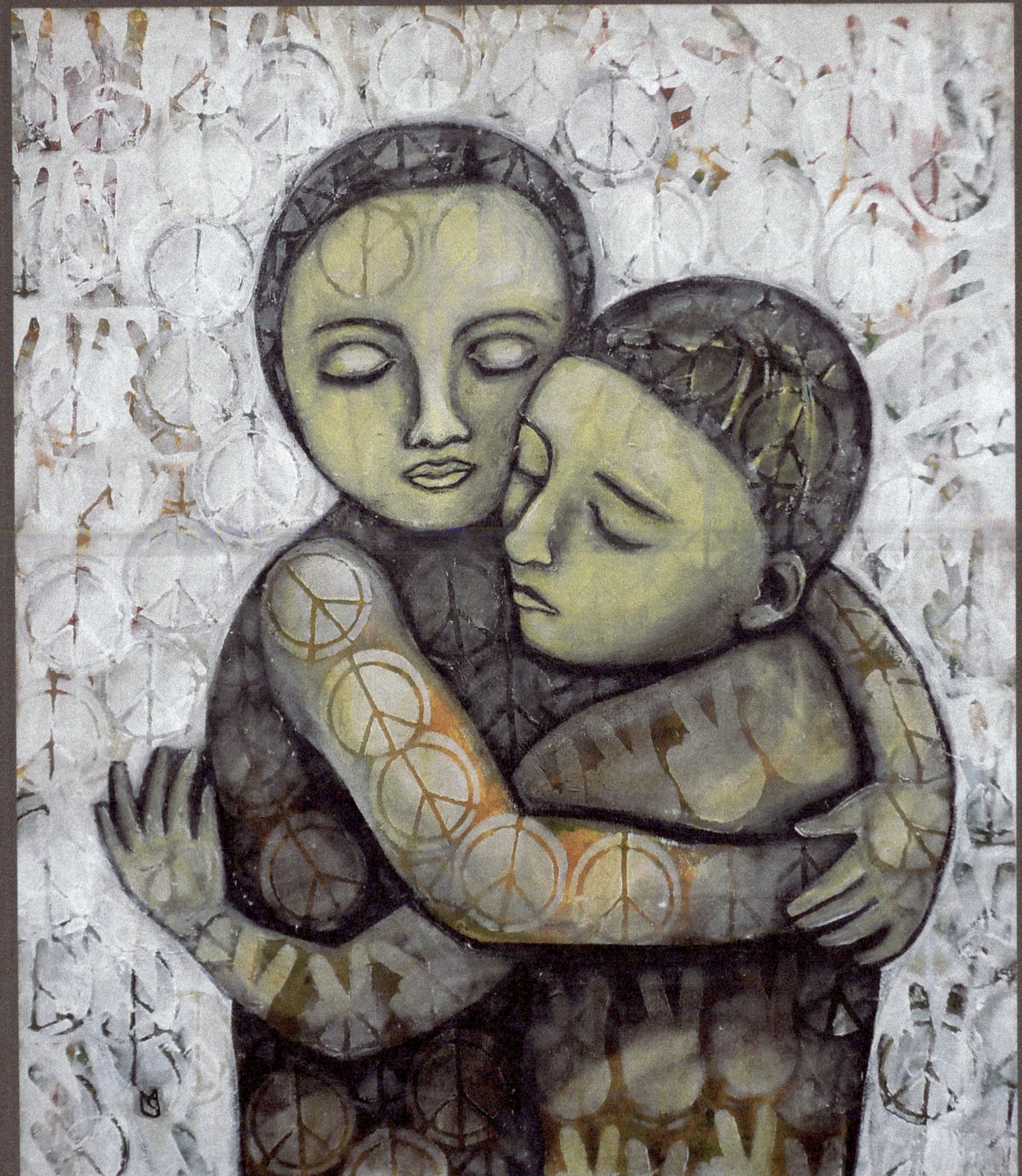

Painting Peace
(79cm x 70cm)

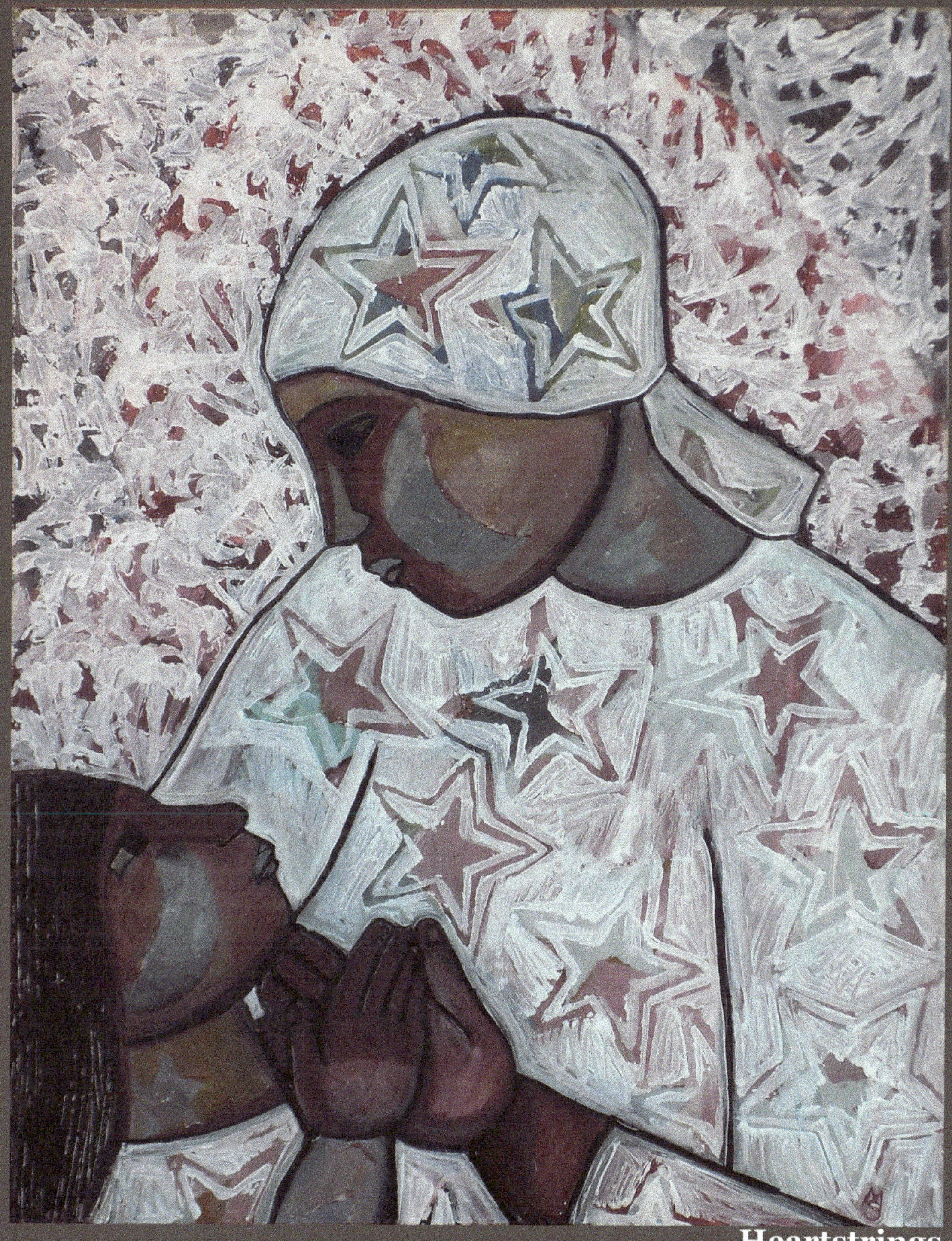

Heartstrings
(61cm x 49cm)

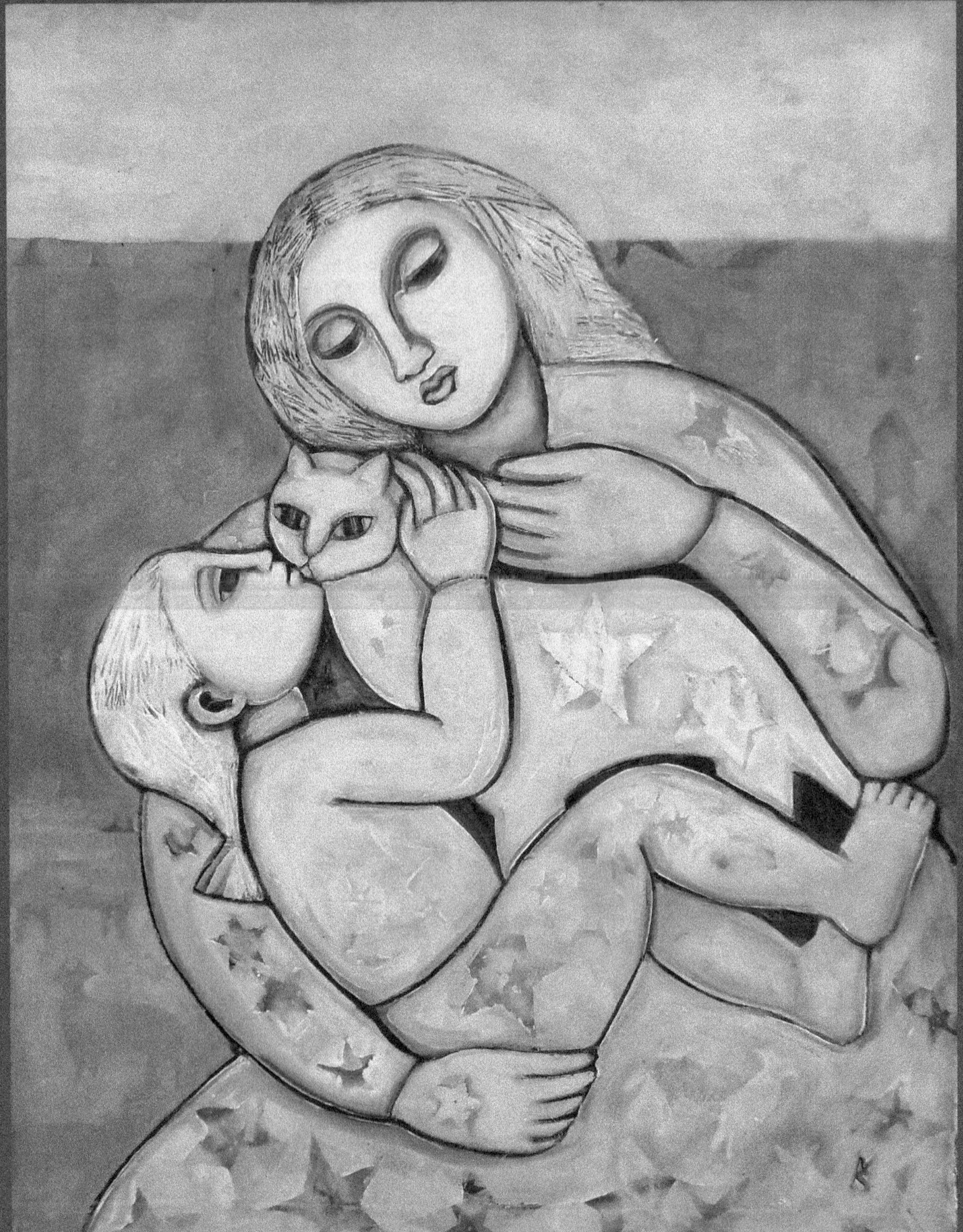

Cat Caress
(92cm x 72cm)
Digital version on pg.211.

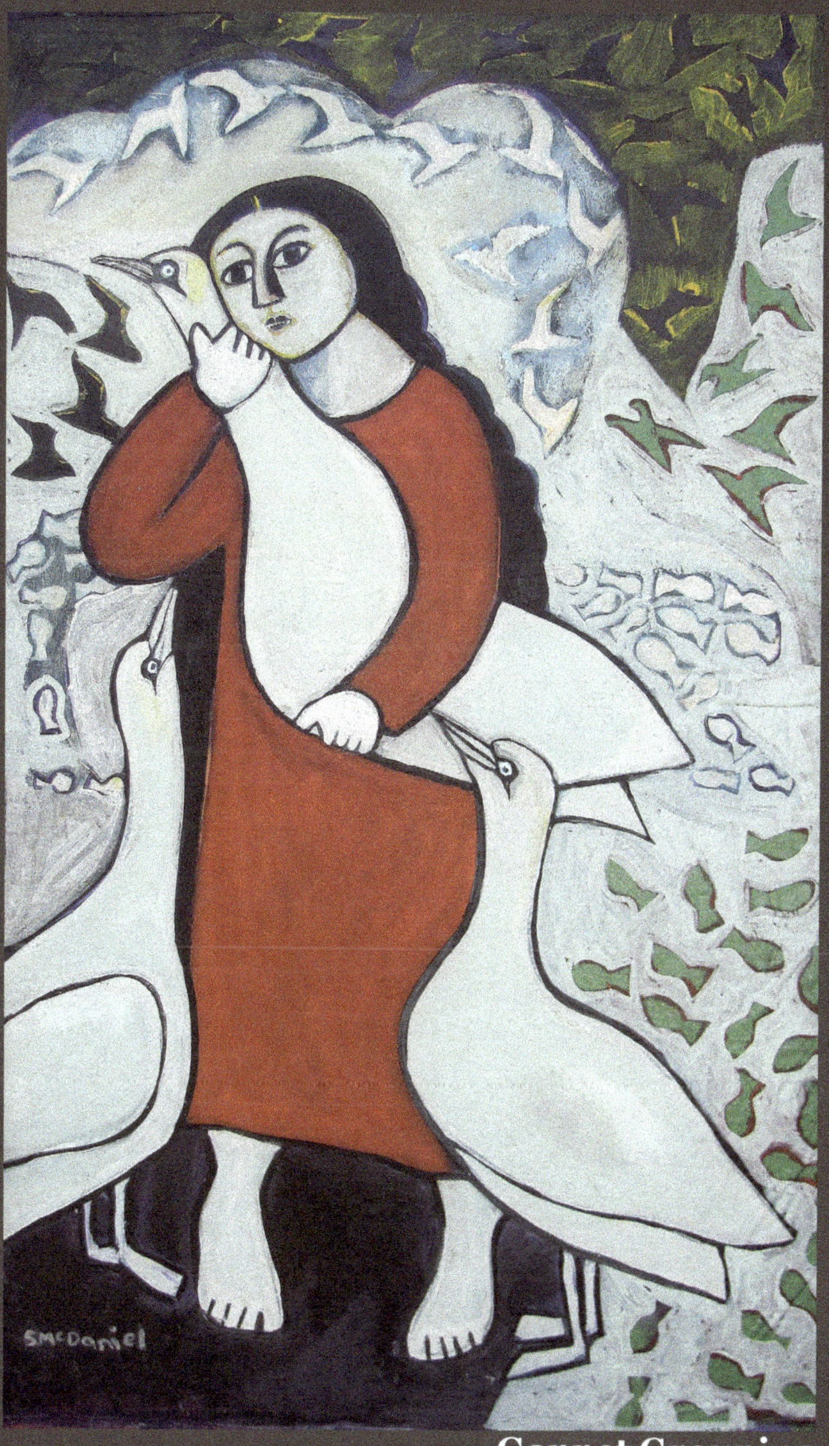

Gannet Grouping
(95cm x 75cm)

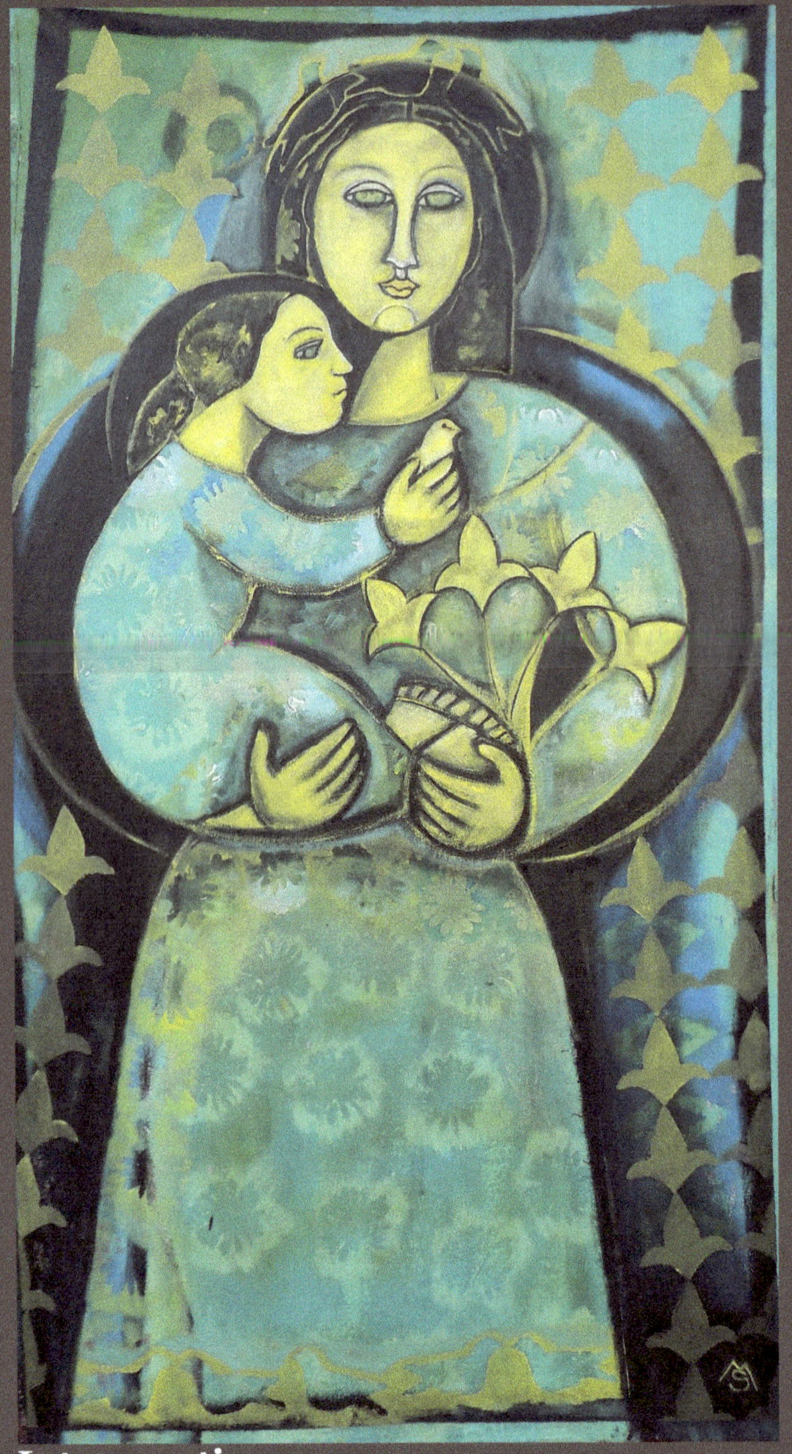

Introspection
(130cm x 75cm)

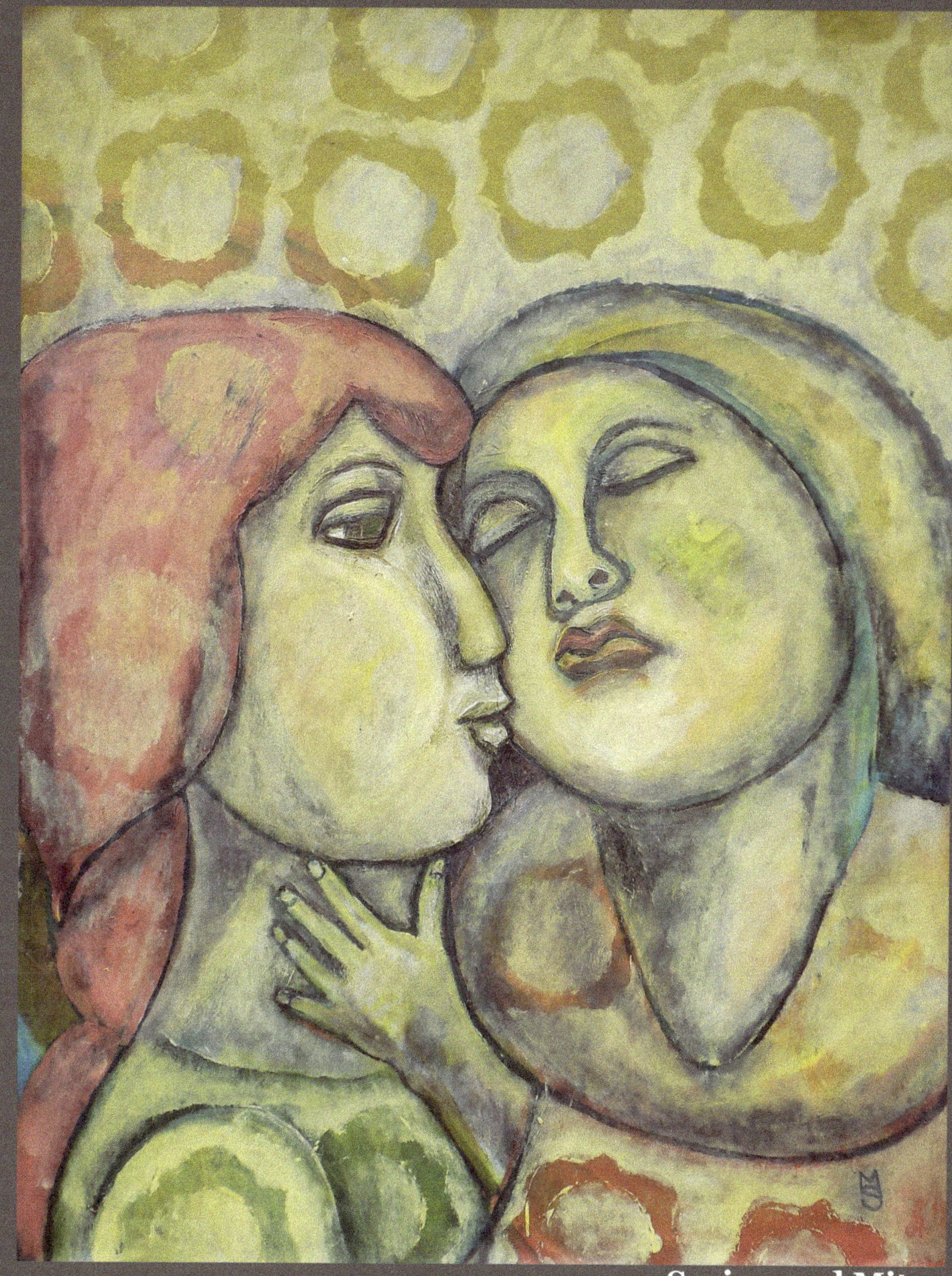

Sarina and Mitra
(104cm x 79cm)

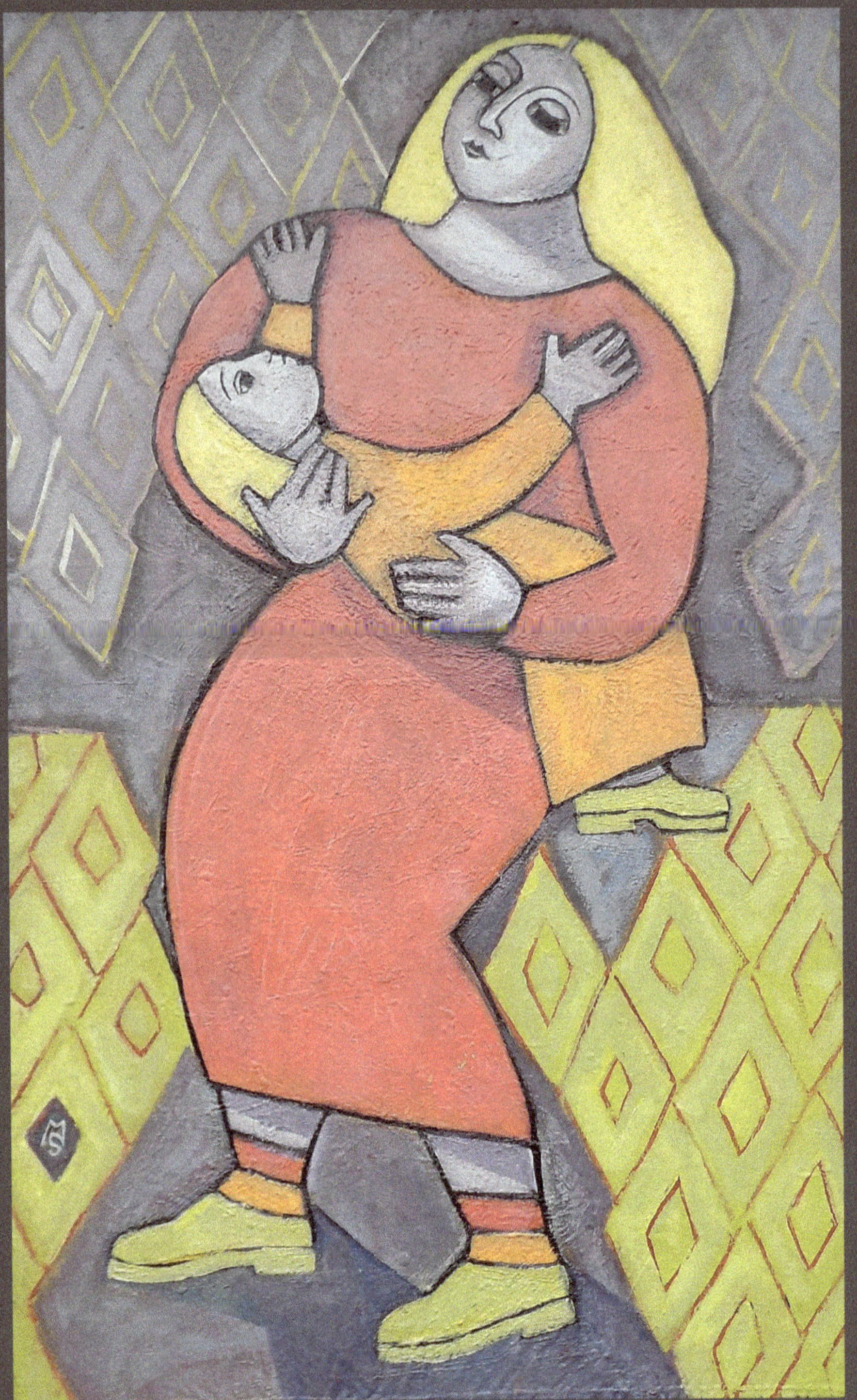

Stripe Socked Madonna
(120cm x 75cm)

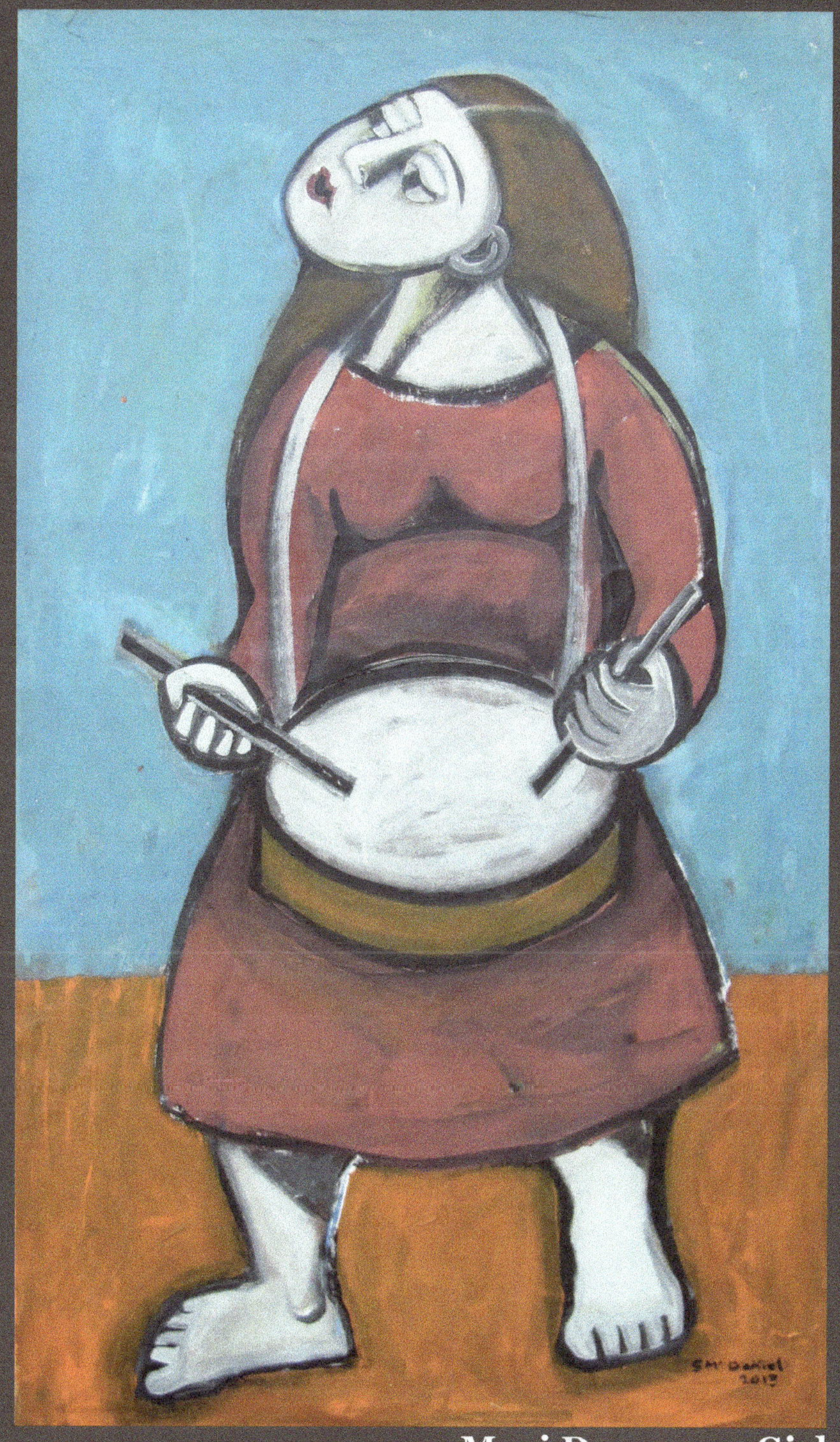

Maxi Drummer Girl
(125cm x 75cm)

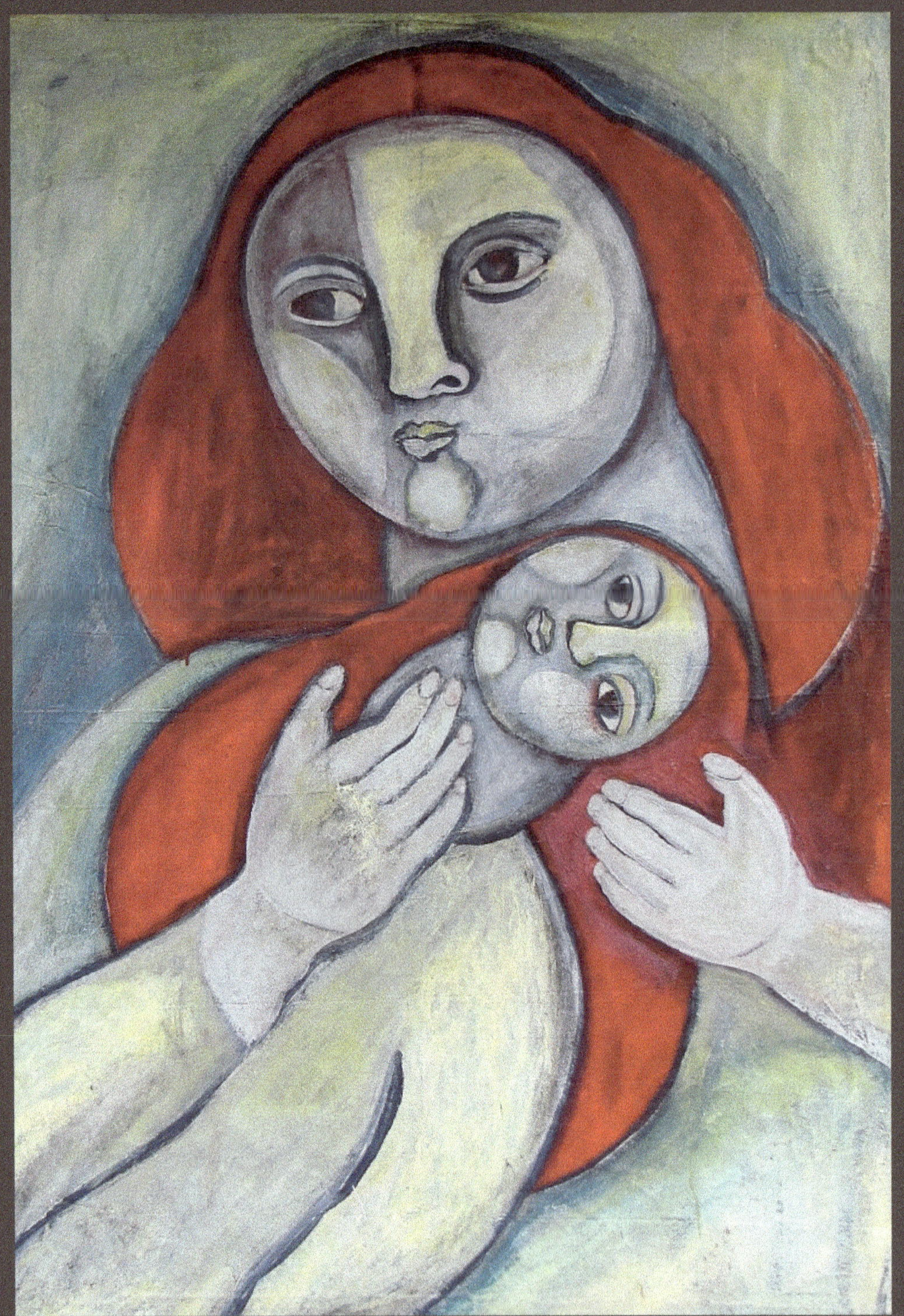

Red Madonna
(130cm x 75cm)

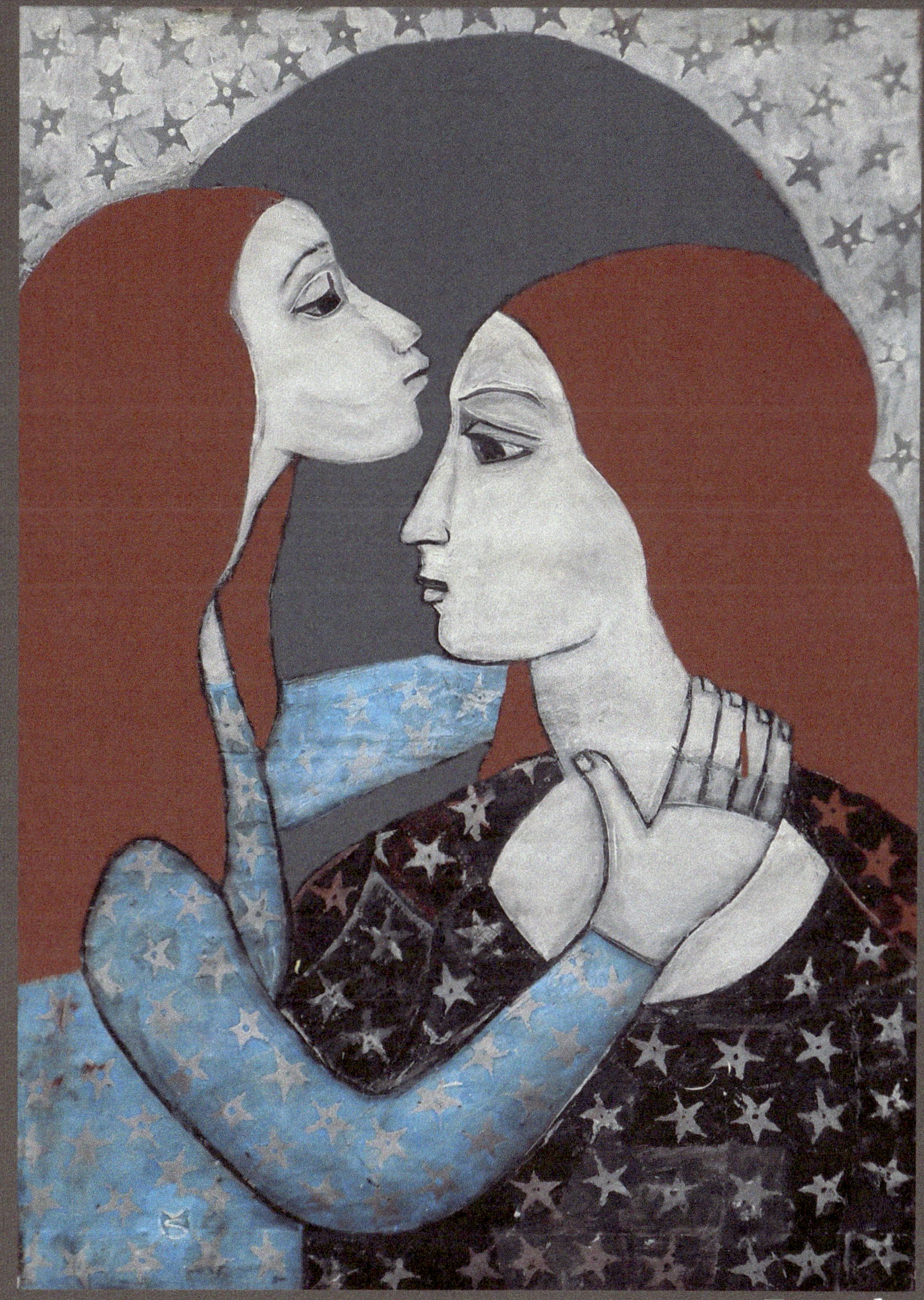

Empathy
(71cm x 51cm)

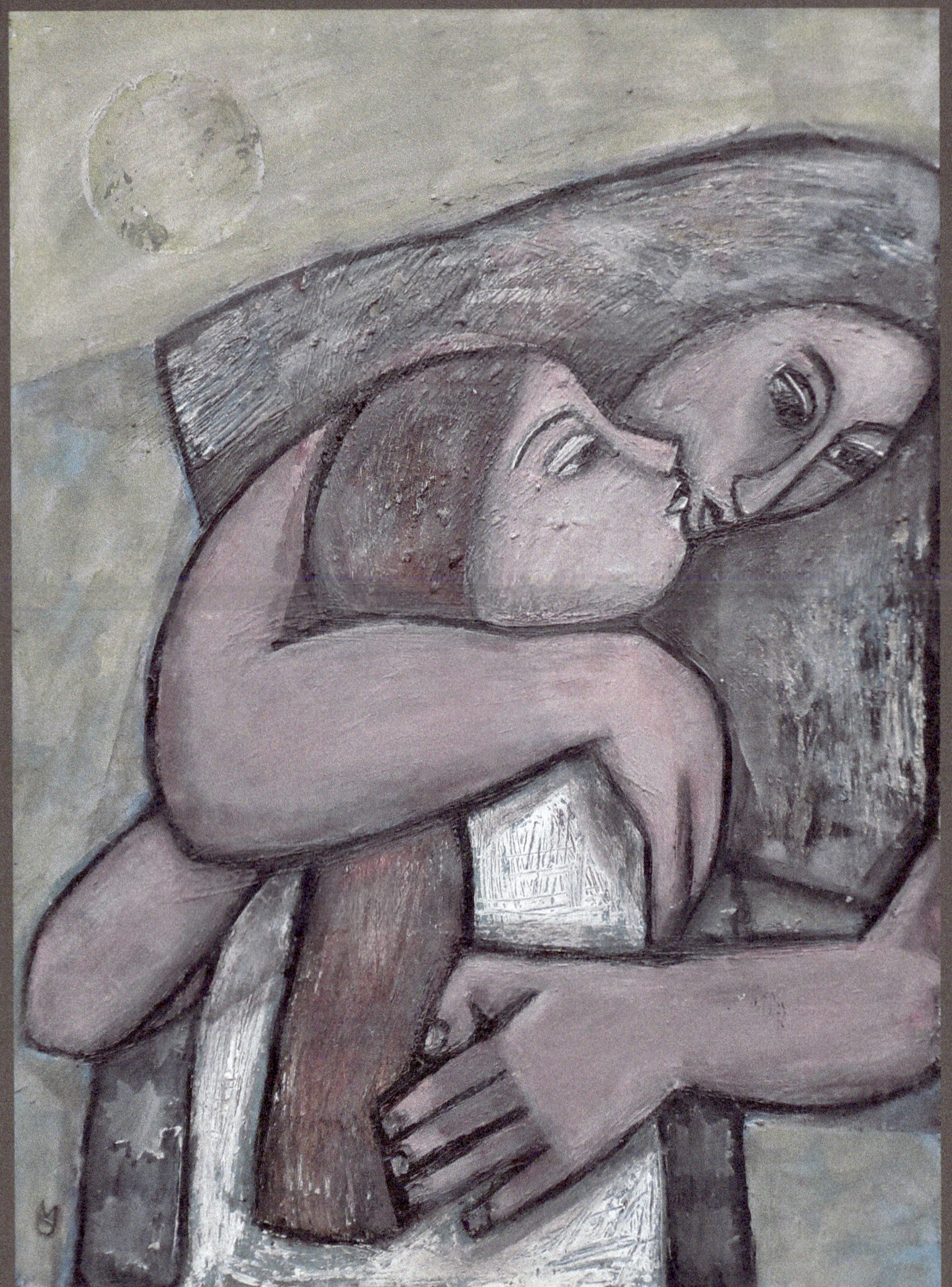

Palabra
(61cm x 46cm)

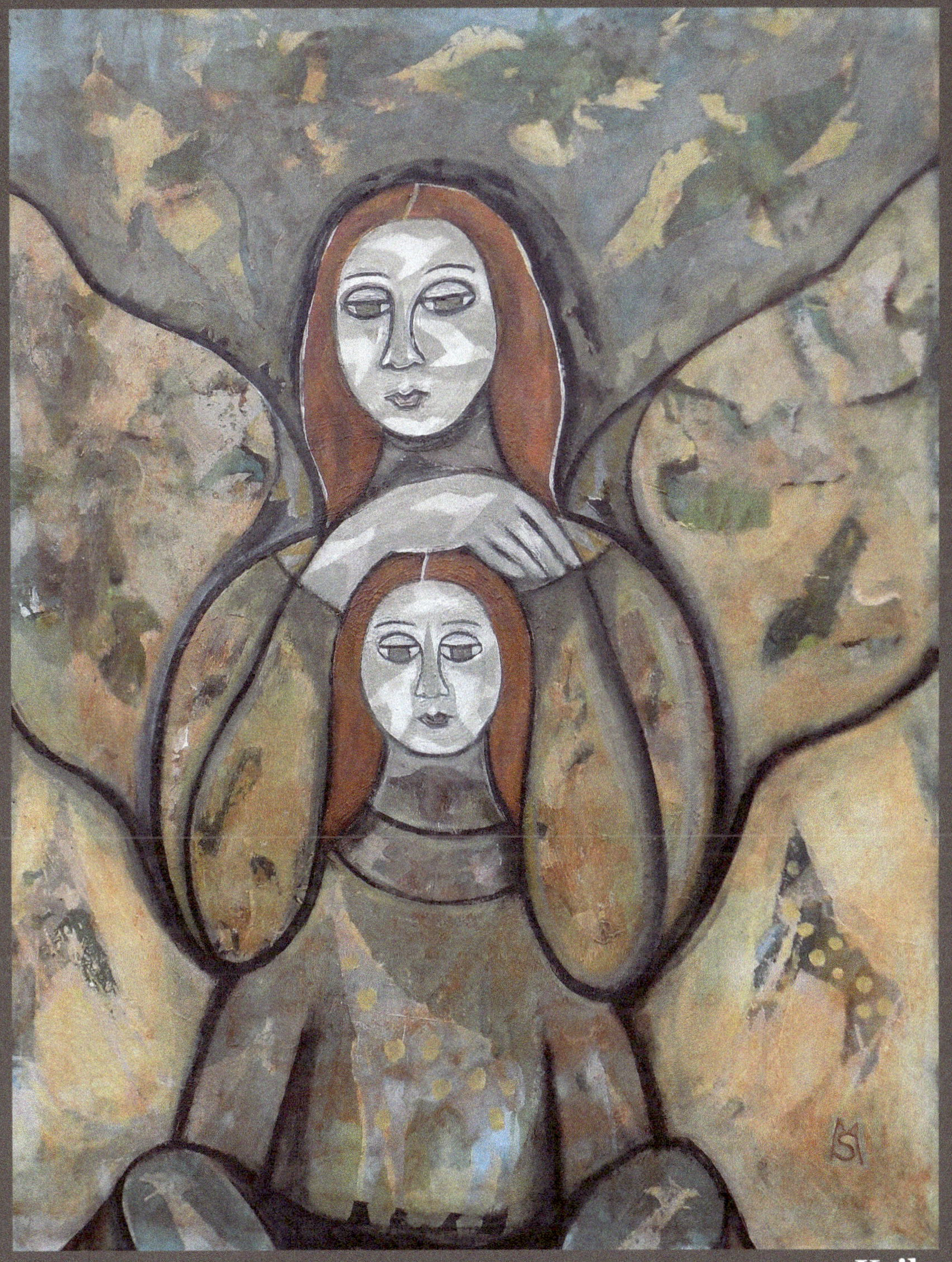

Krilo
(104cm x 79cm)

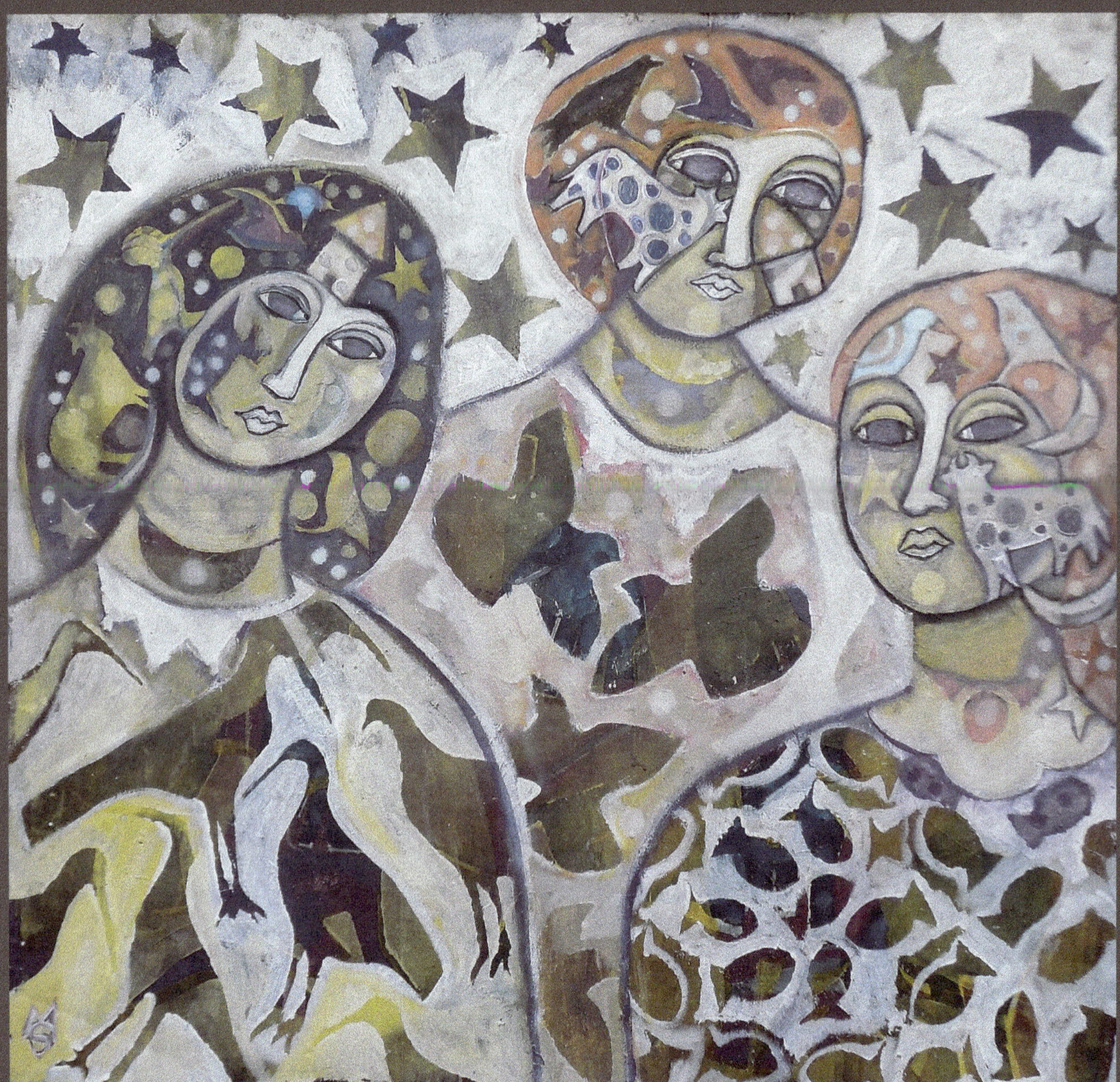

Amethyst Eyes
(75cm x 79cm)

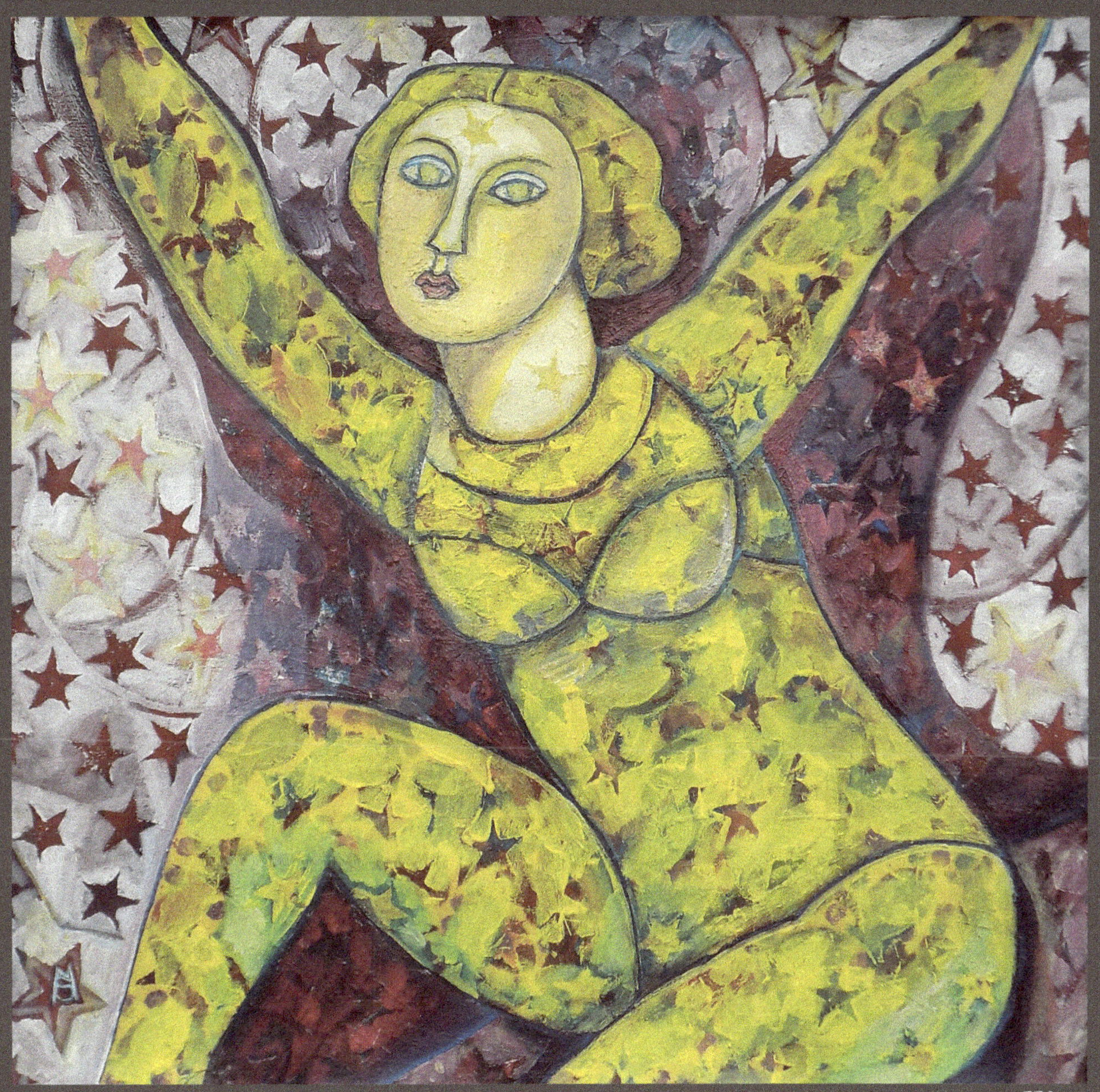

Estrellita
(76cm x 79cm)

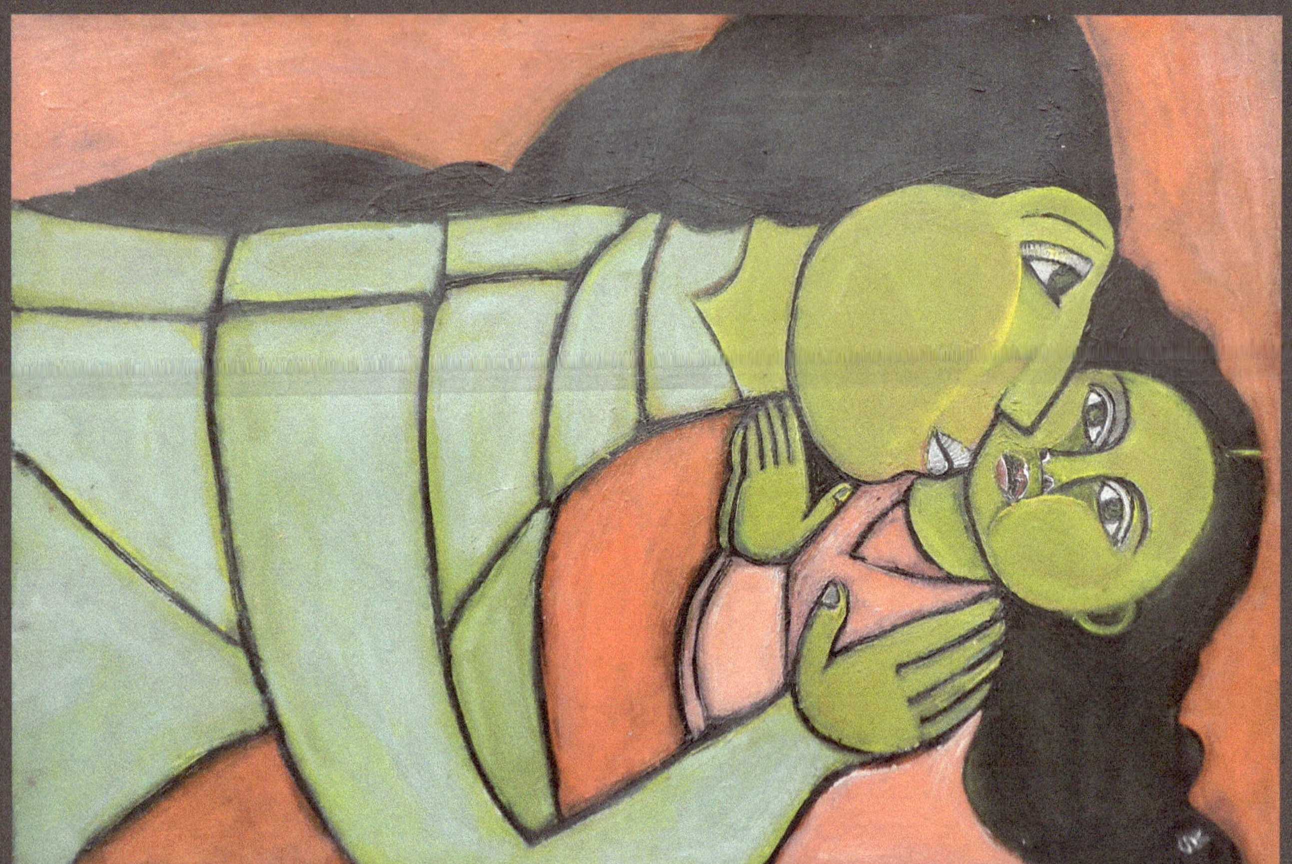

Te Quiero
(50cm x 76cm)

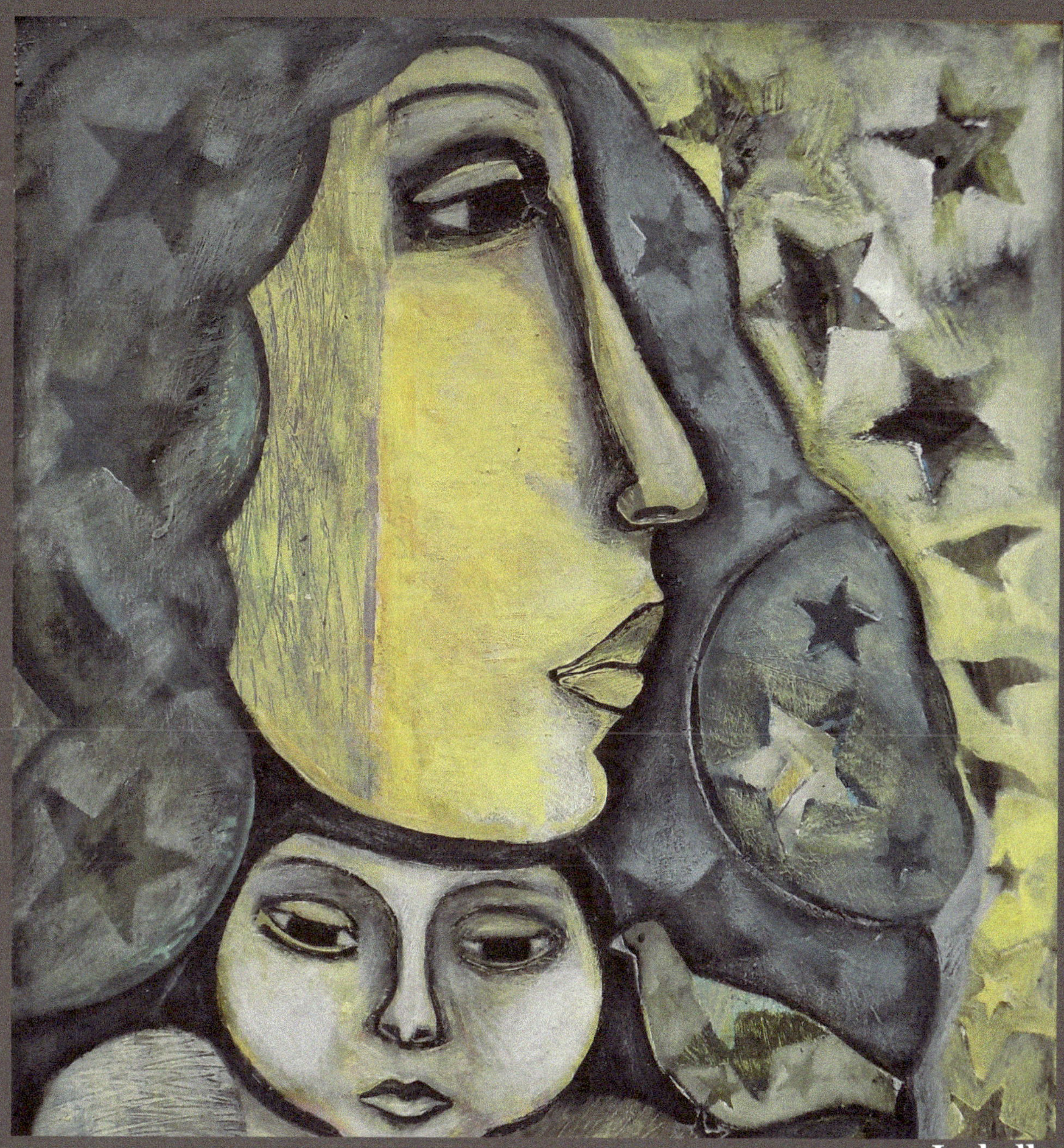

Isabella
(75cm x 51cm)

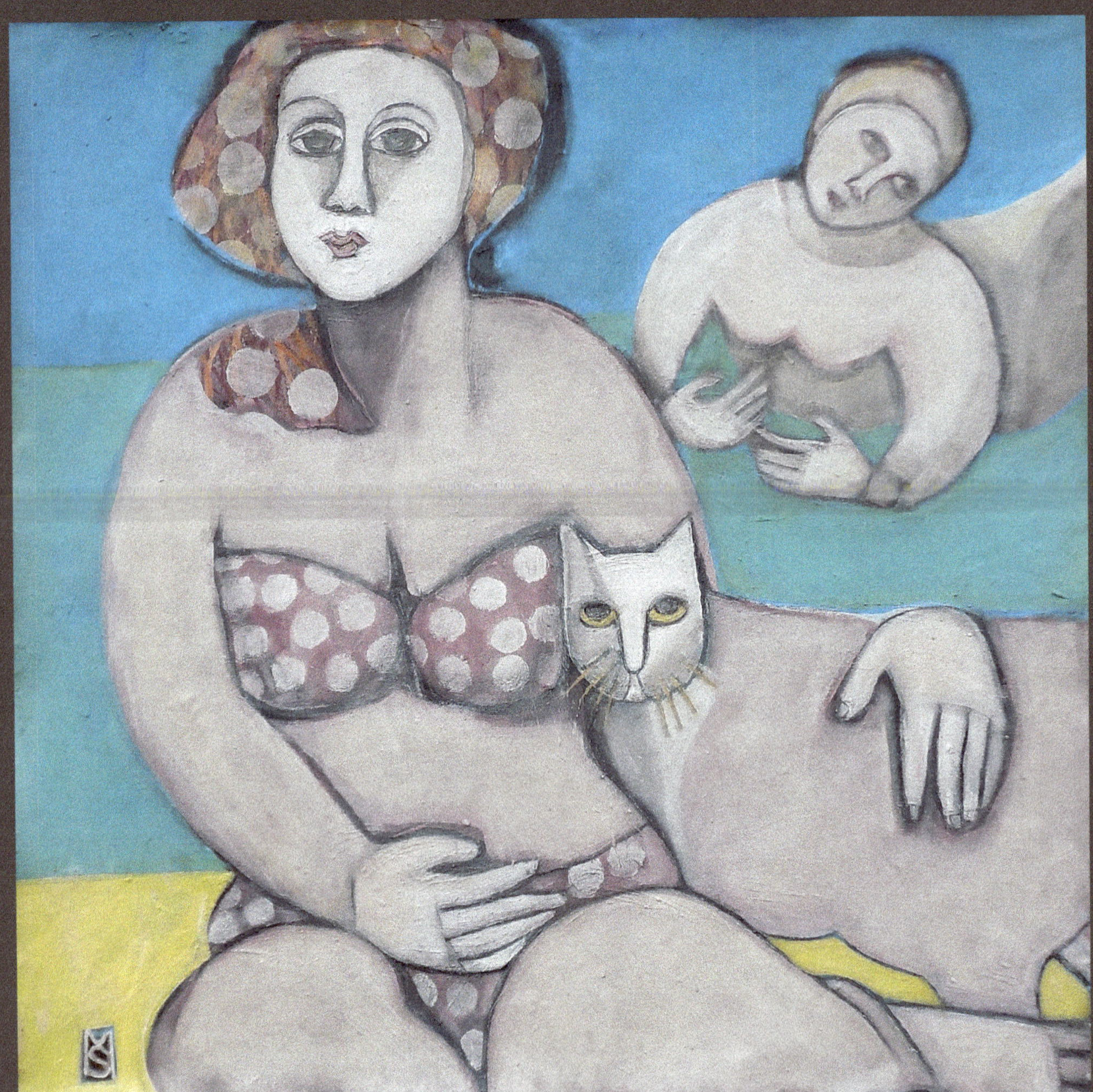

Beach
(77cm x 79cm)

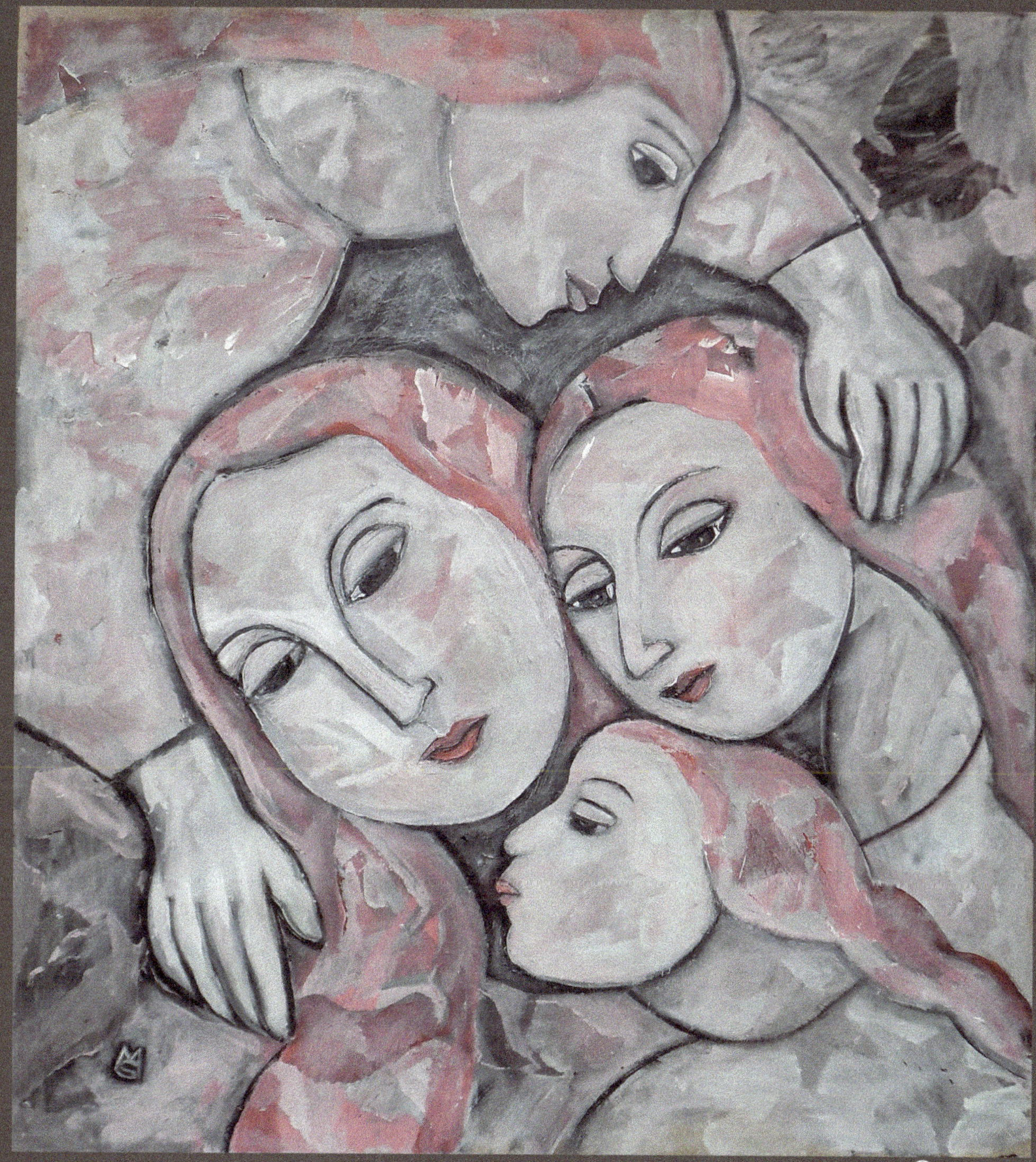

Quattro
(76cm x 70cm)

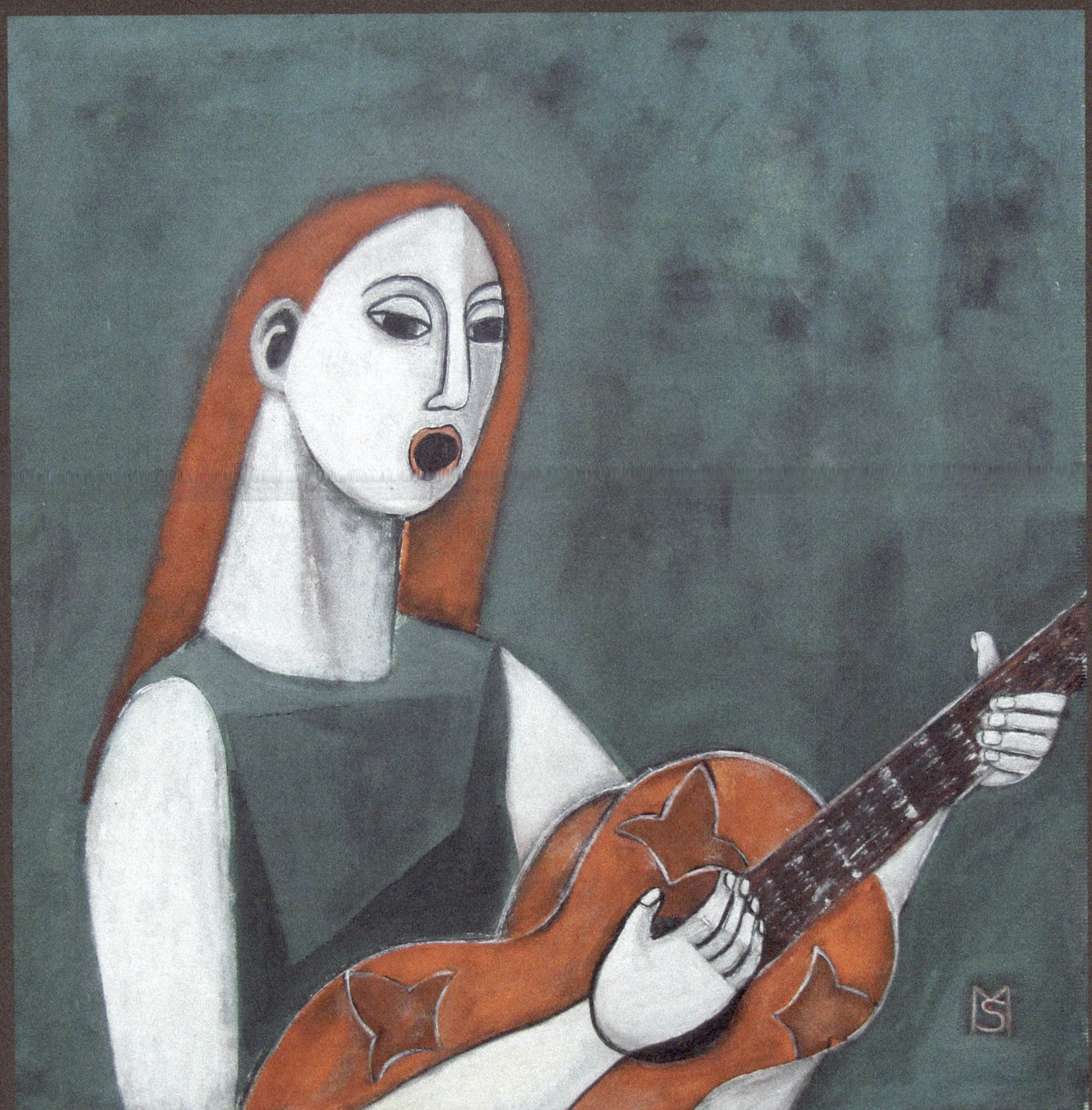

Guitar Girl
(75cm x 75cm)

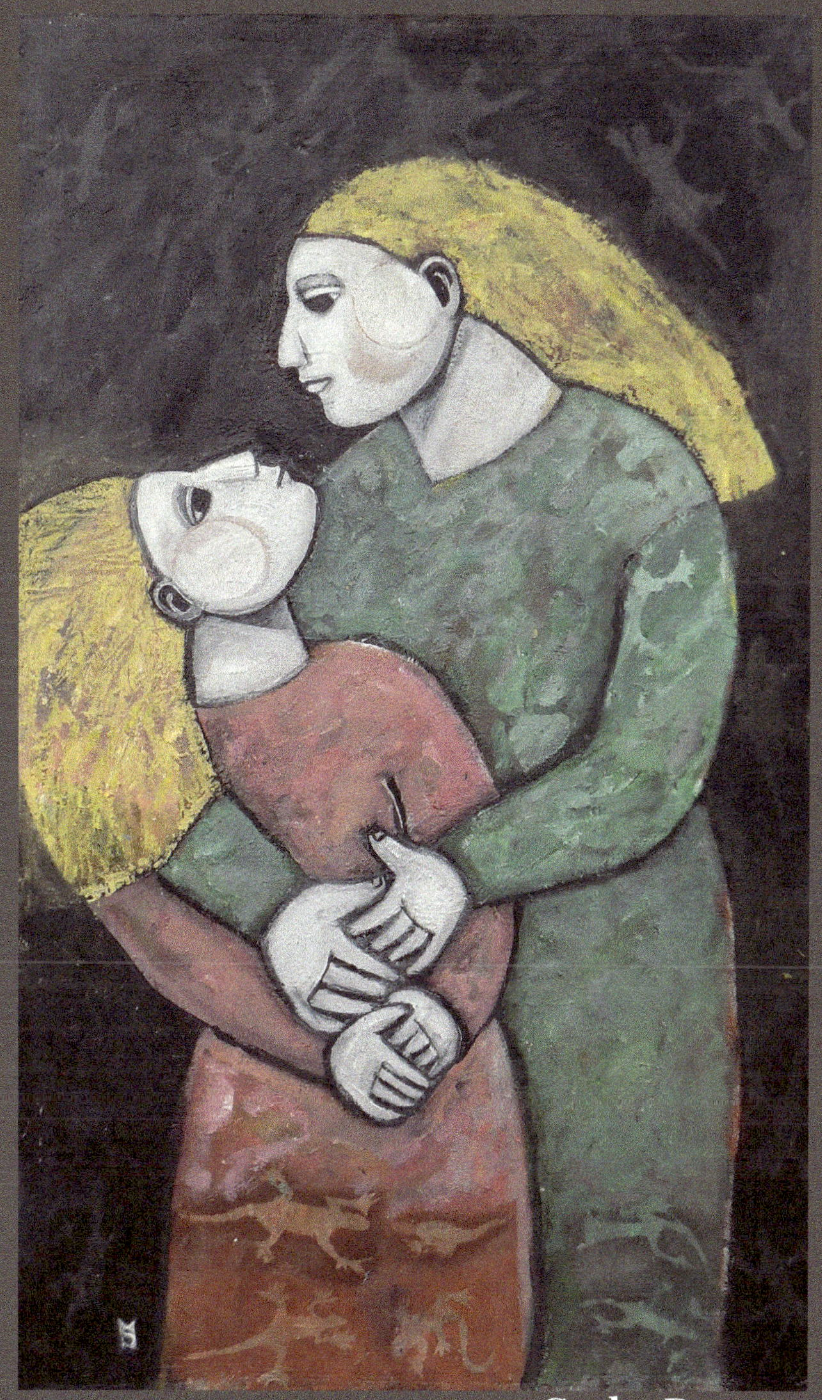

Gecko Dresses
(130cm x 80cm)
Digital version on pg.232.

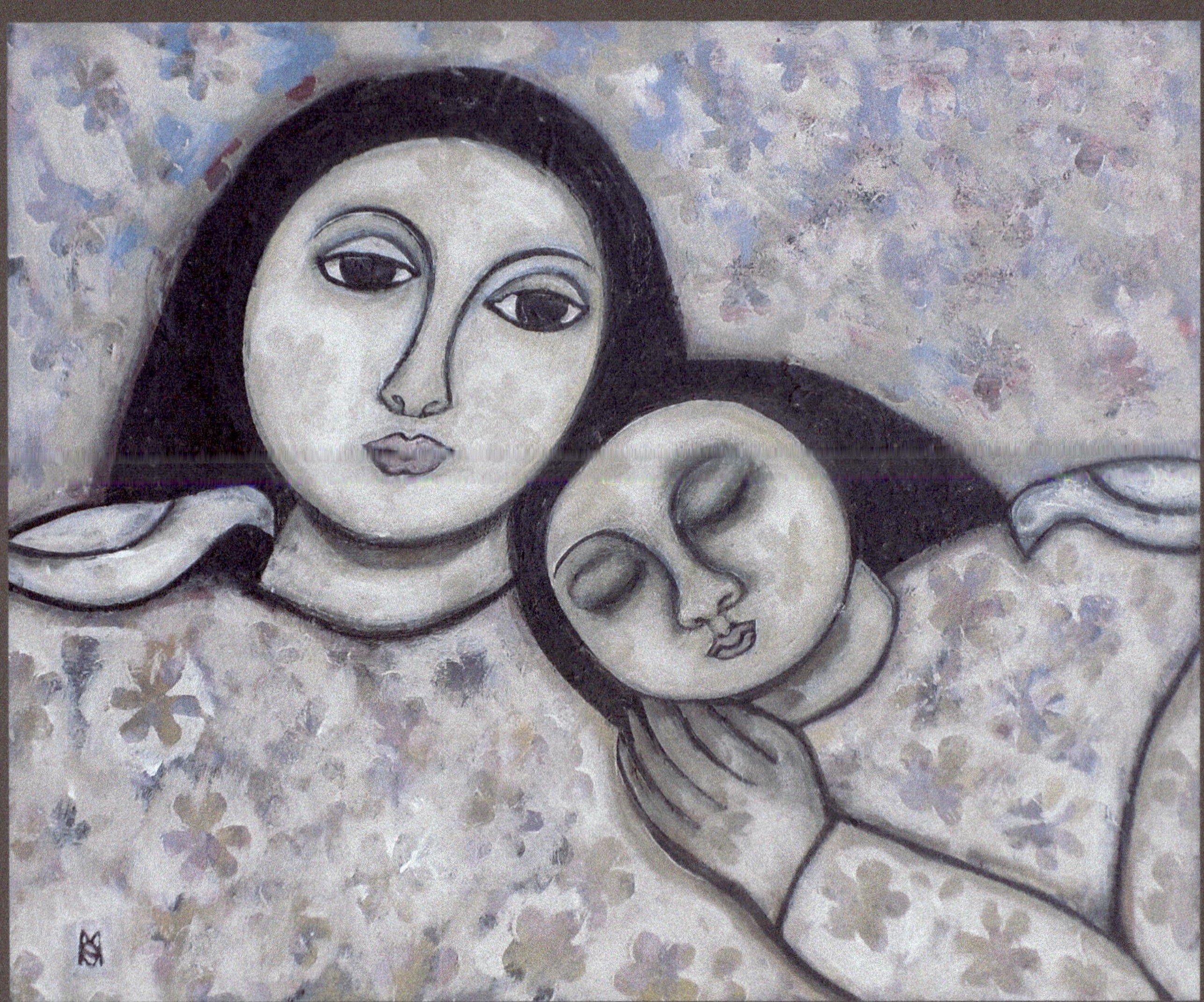

Vigil
(49cm x 61cm)

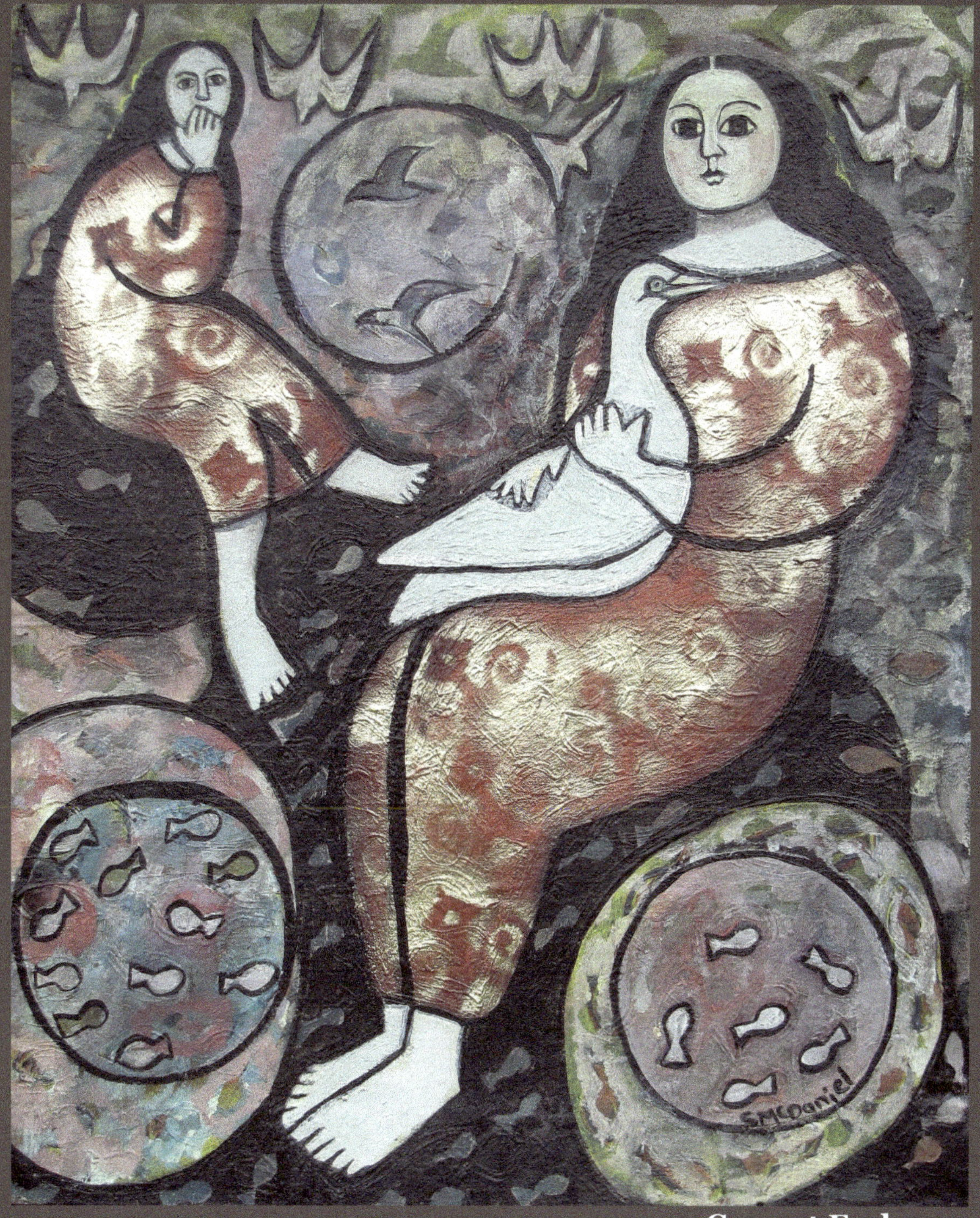

Gannet Embrace
(70cm x 55cm)

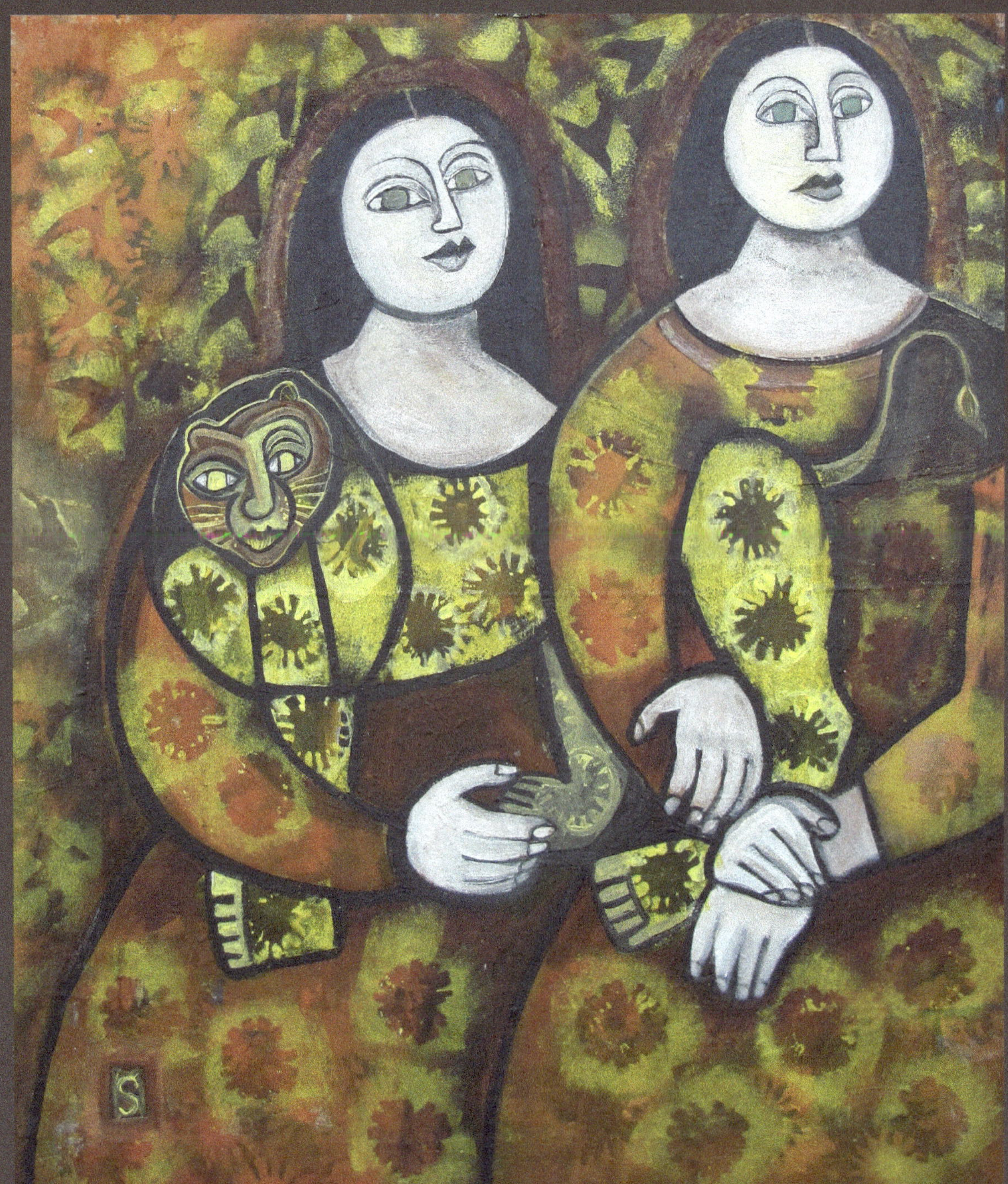

Lionhearted
(80cm x 85cm)

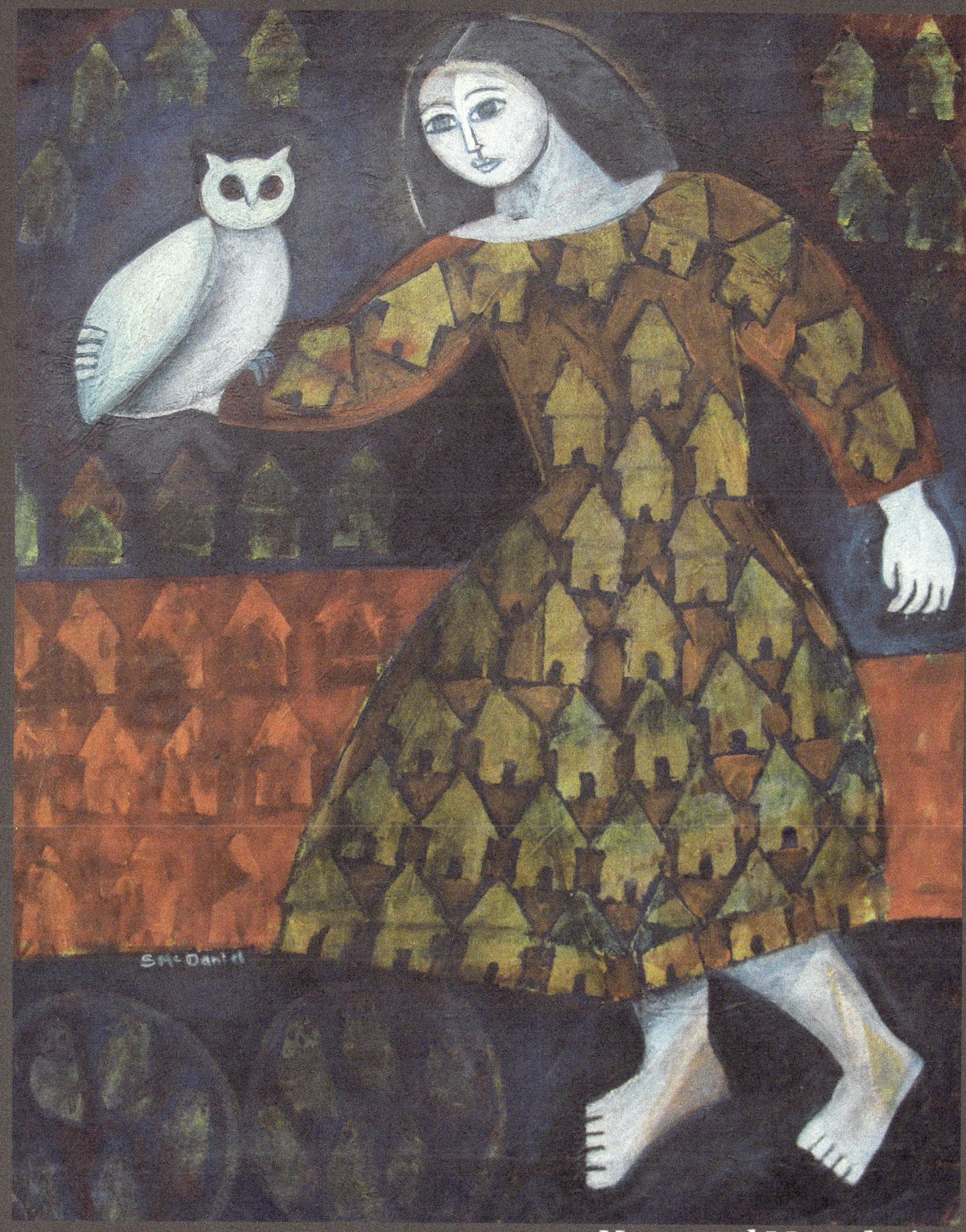

Nocturnal Meandering
(85cm x70cm)

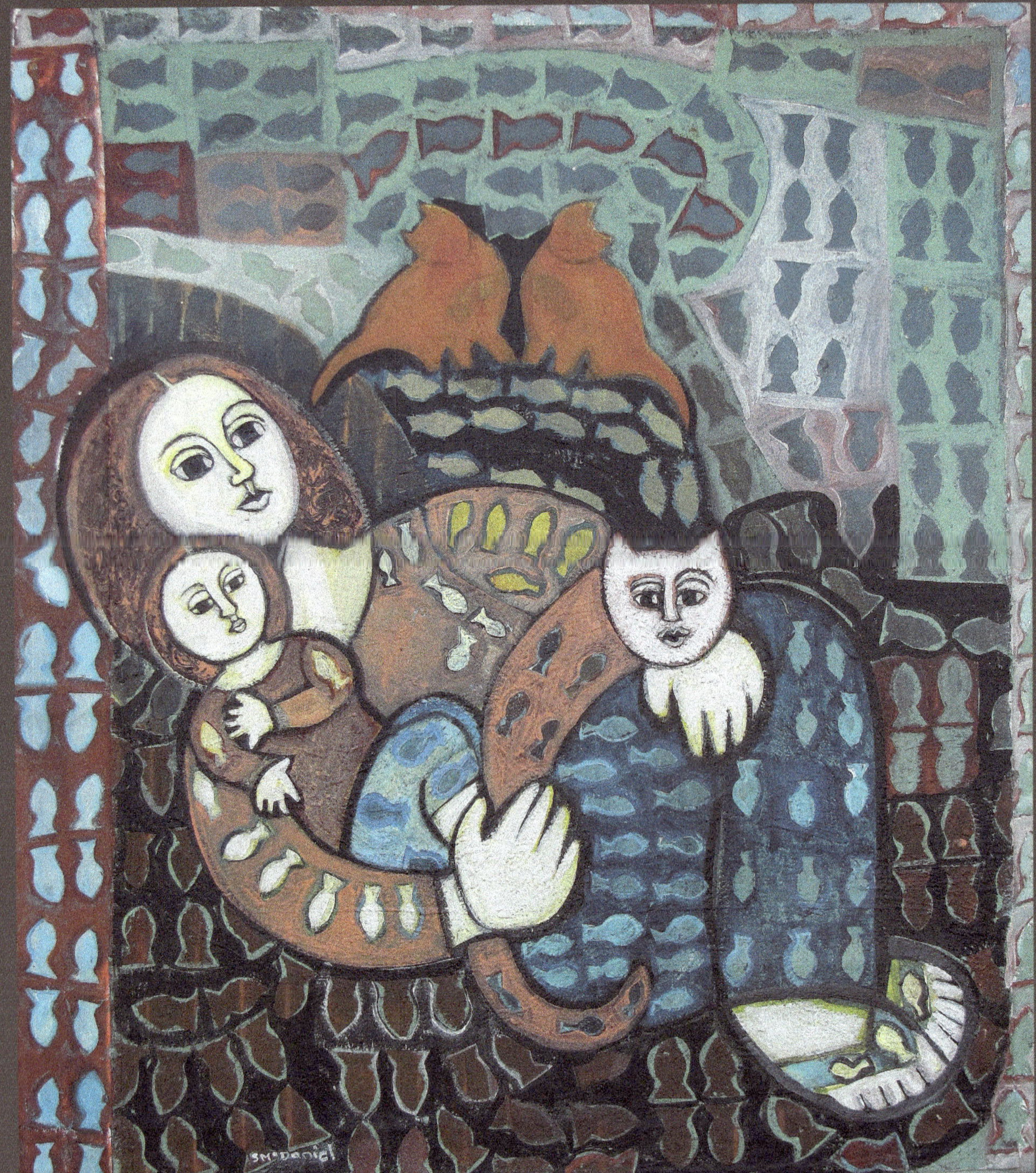

Fish
(80cm x 70cm)

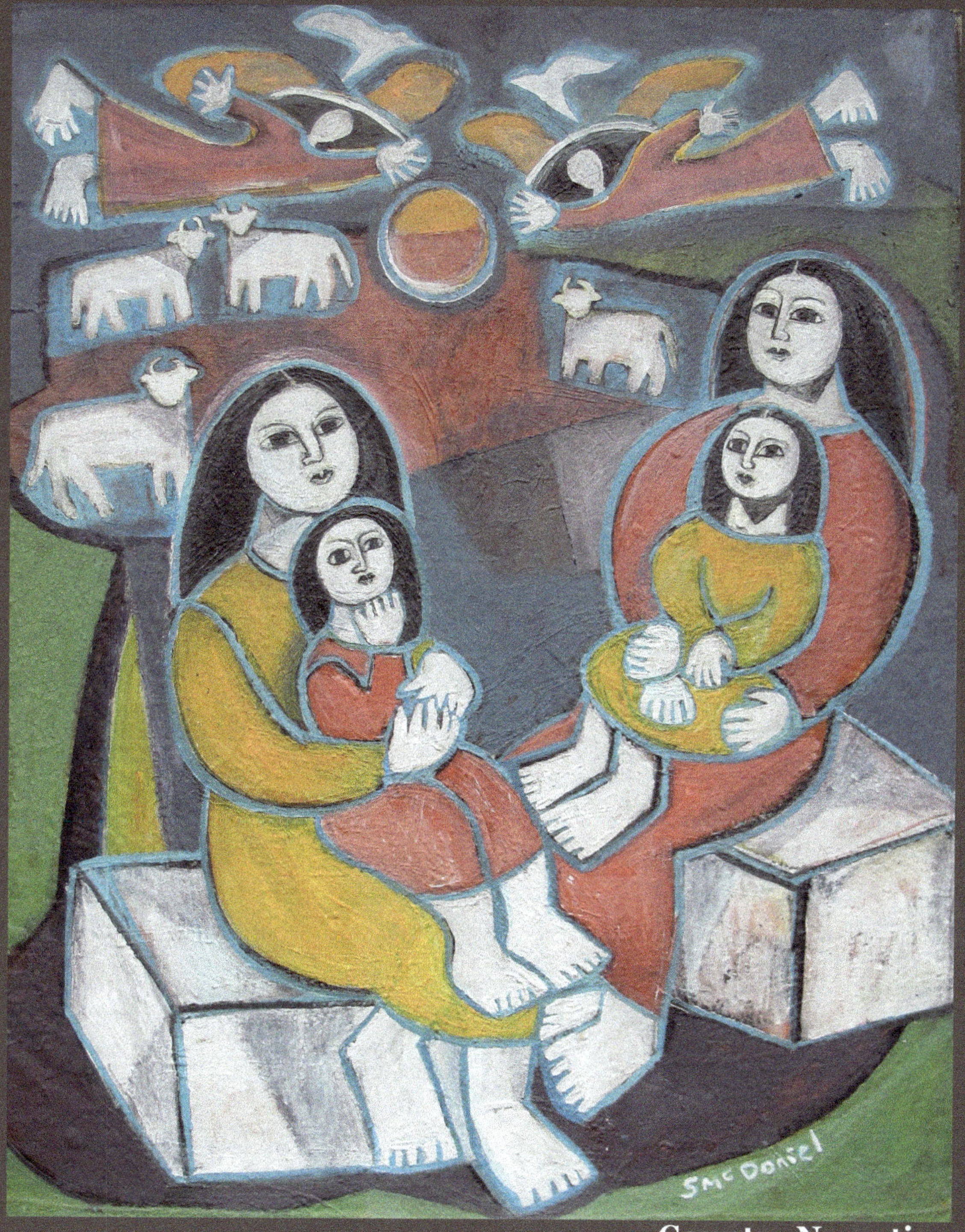

Country Narrative
(70cm x 60cm)

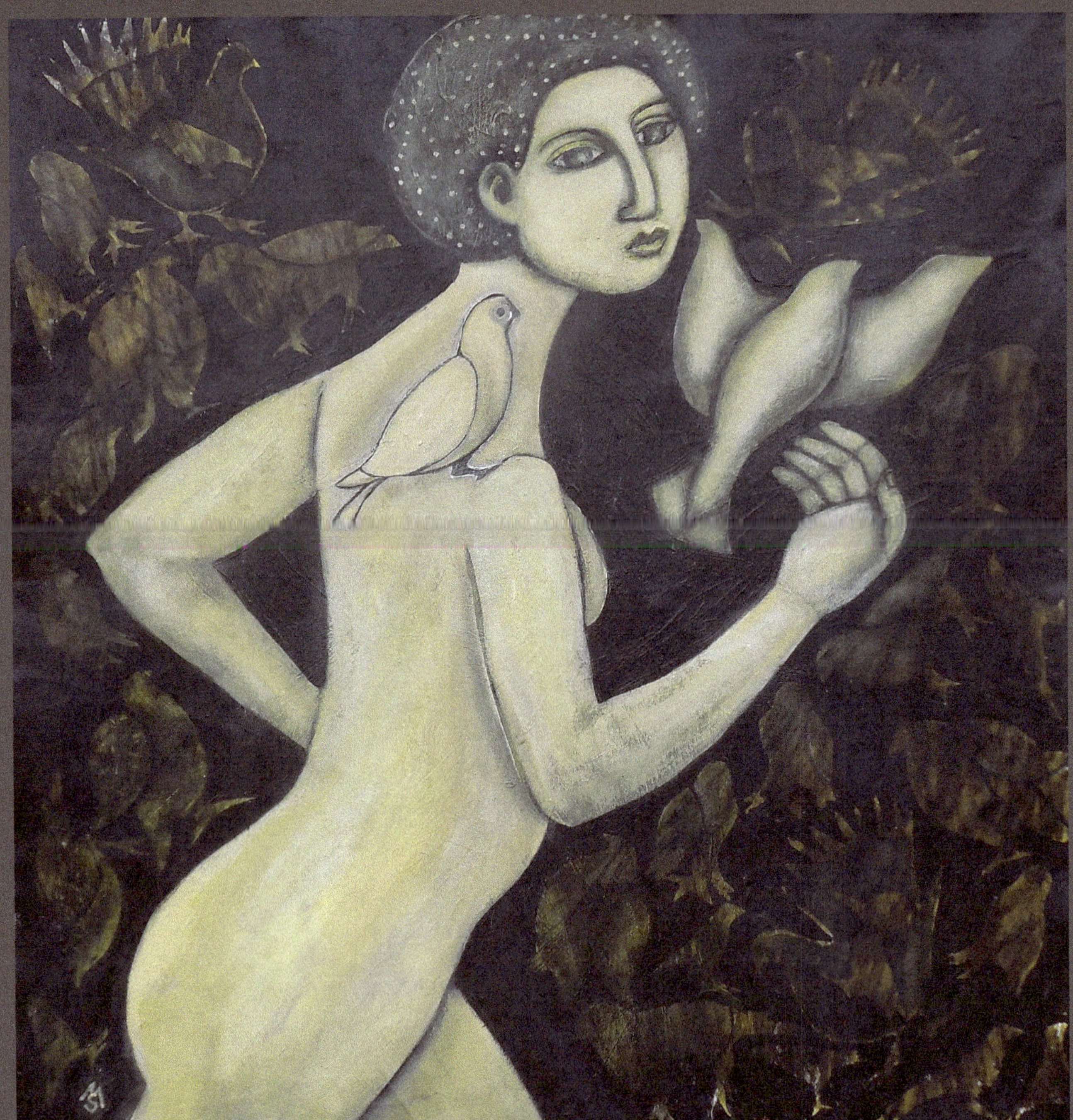

Spangled Coiffure
(79cm x 76cm)

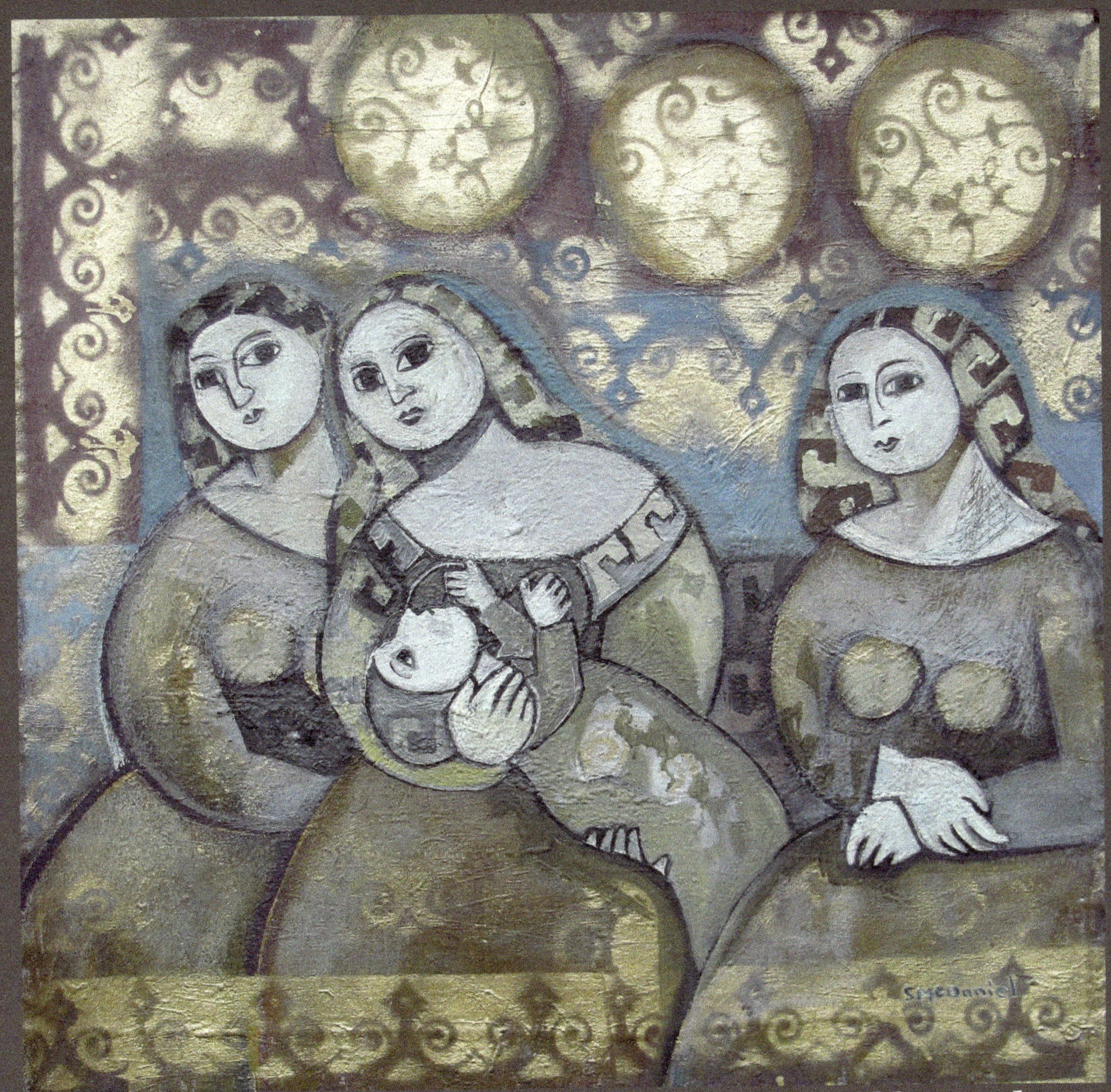

Golden Madonna
(75cm x 75cm)

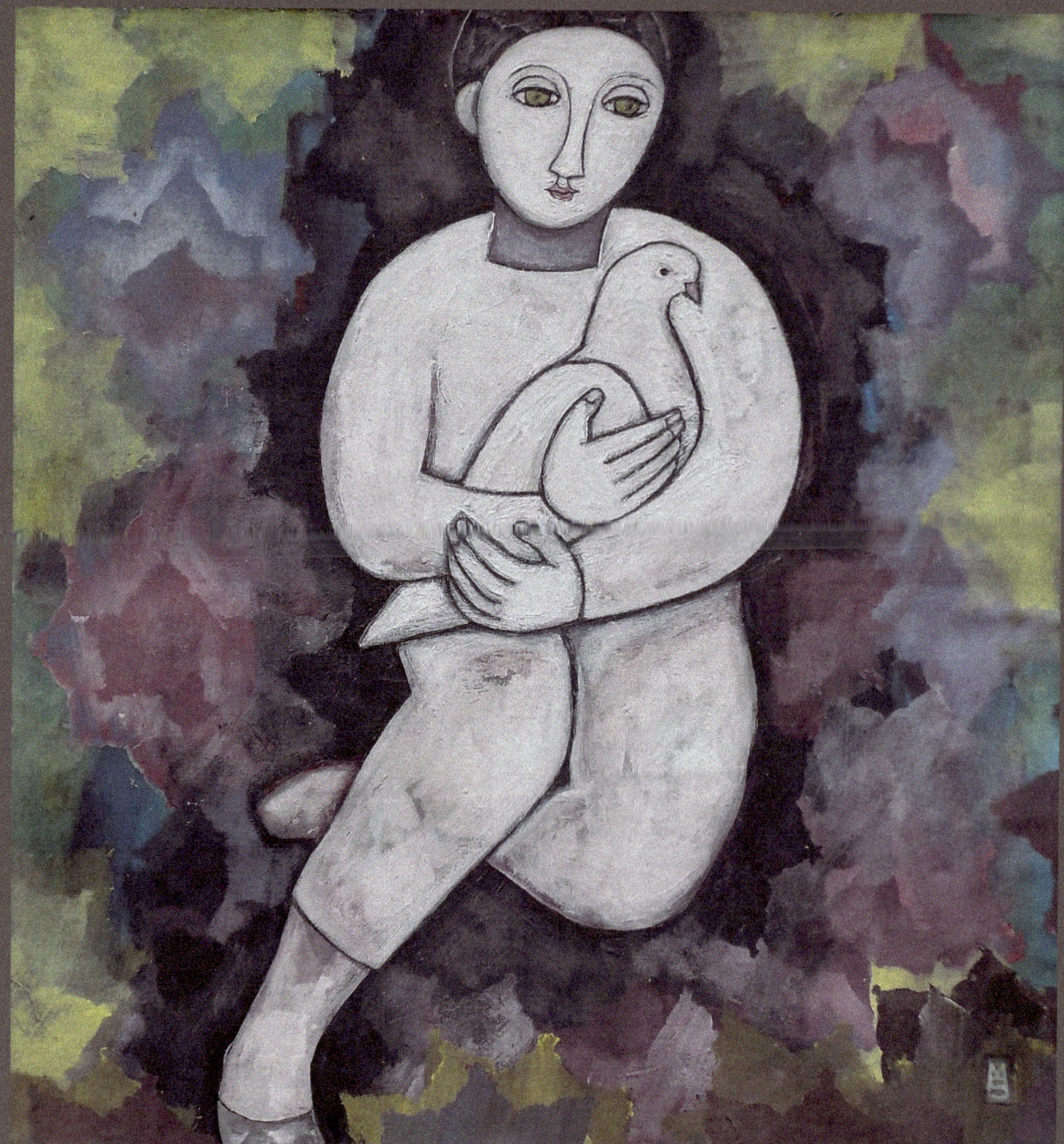

Arabesque
(79cm x 76cm)

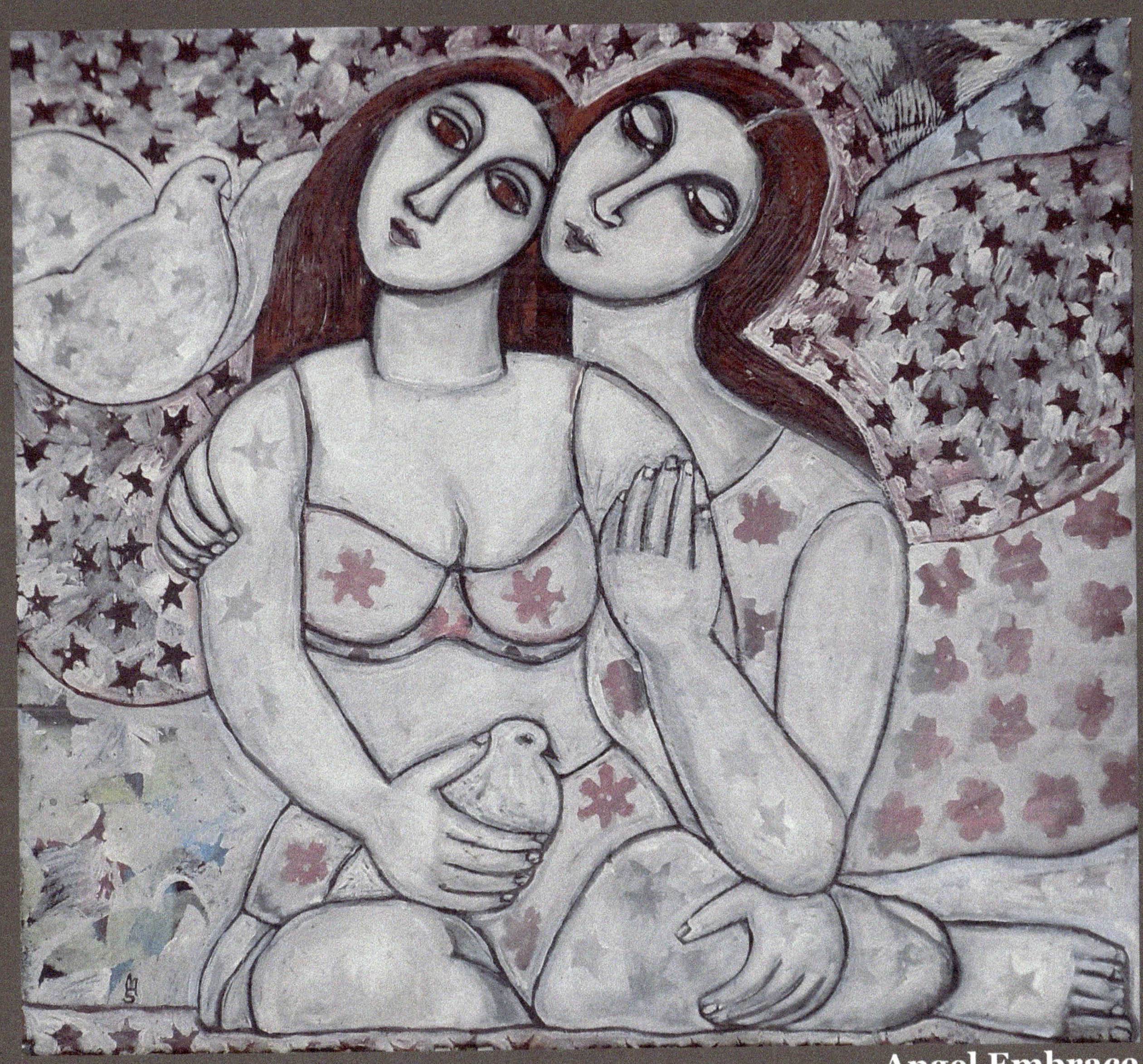

Angel Embrace
(70cm x 79cm)

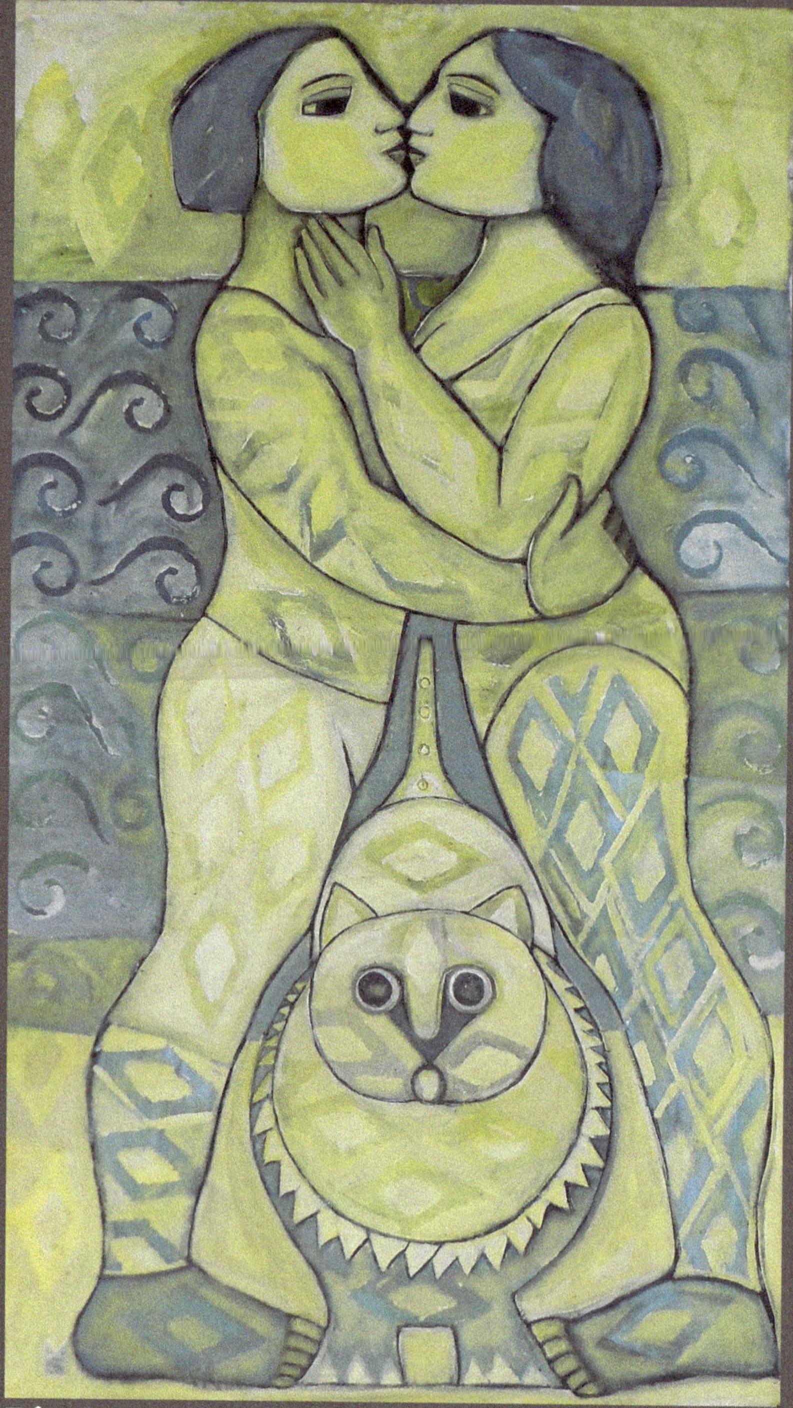

Big Cat
(114cm x 66cm)

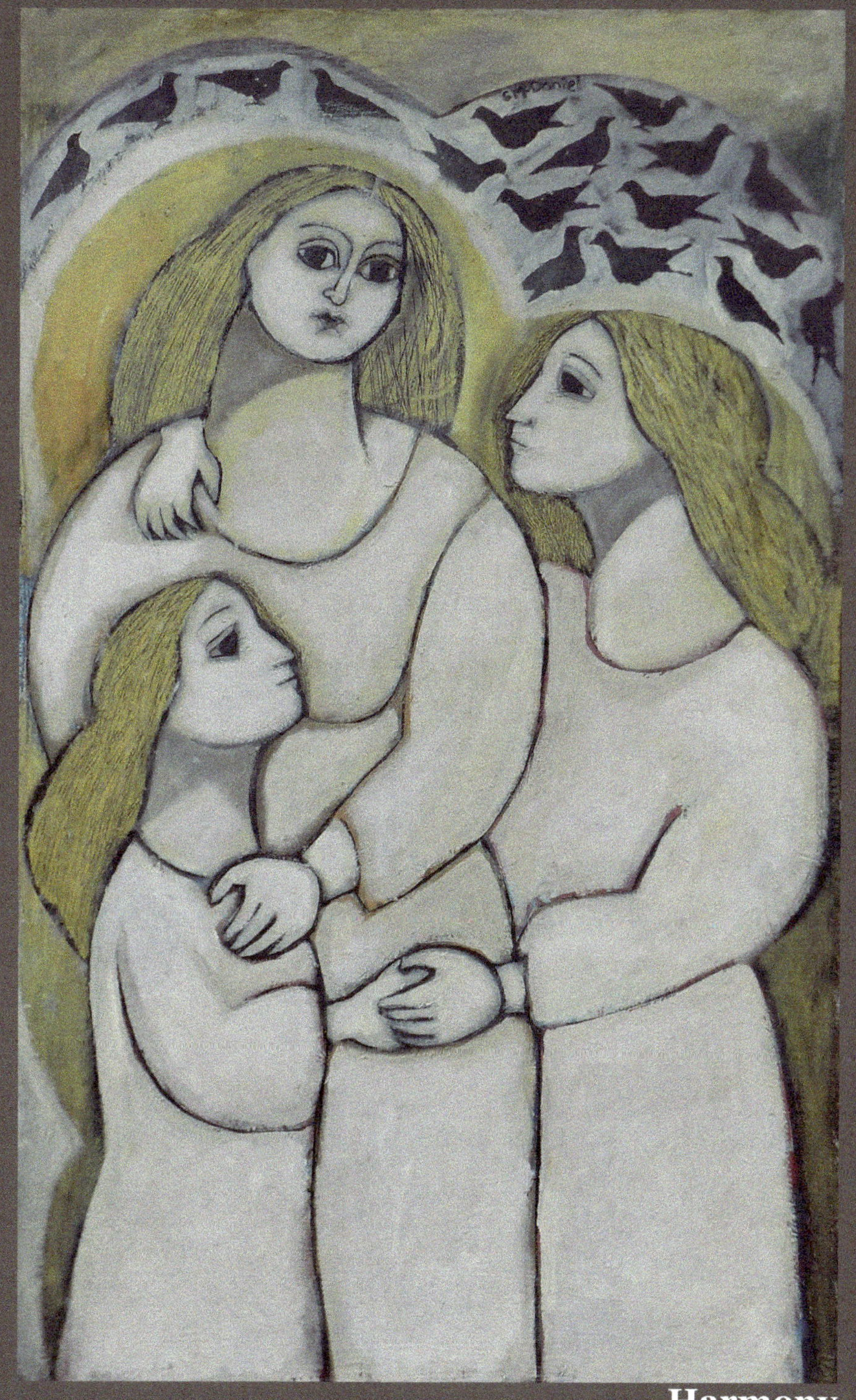

Harmony
(130cm x 80cm)

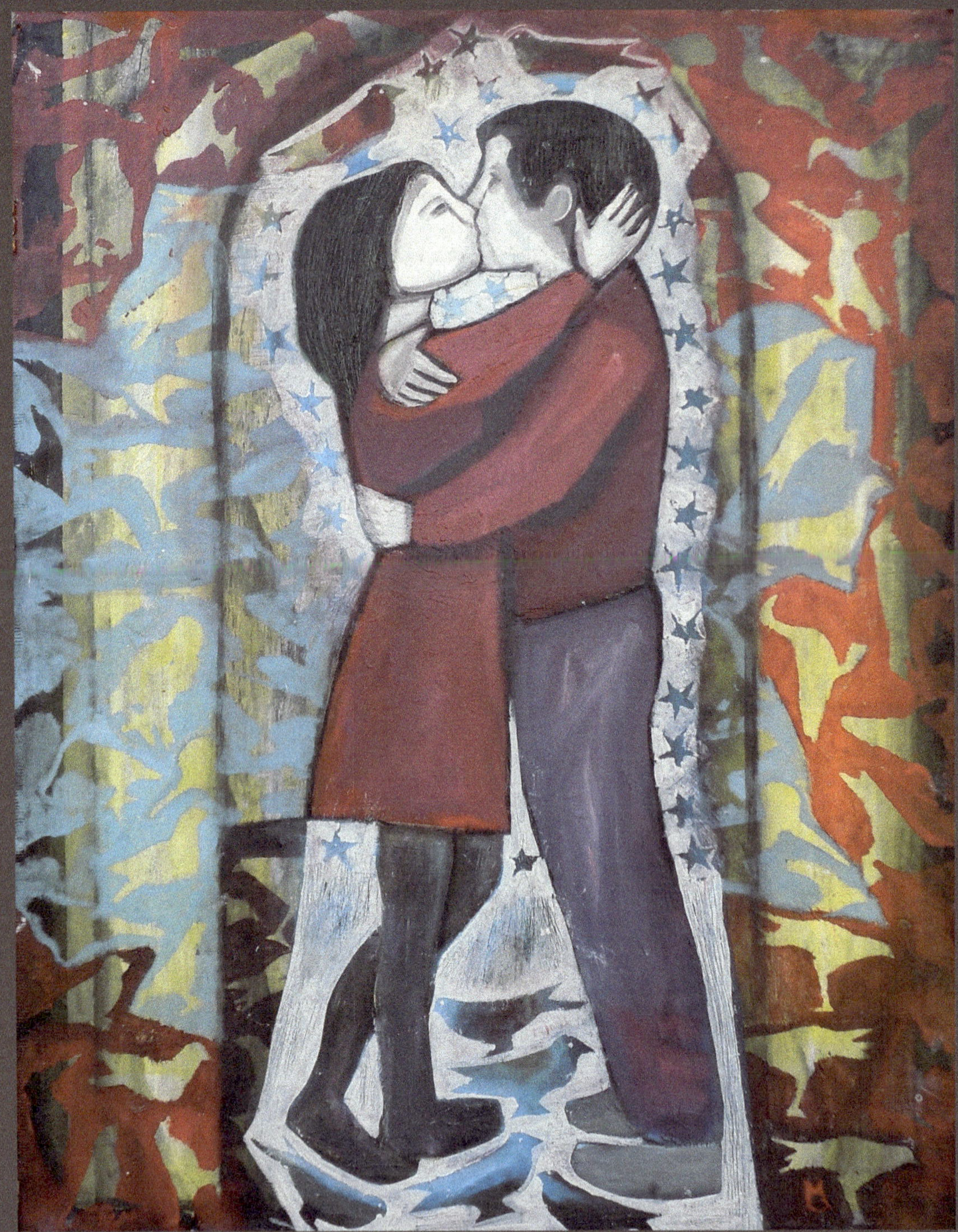

Longing Still
(95cm x 75cm)

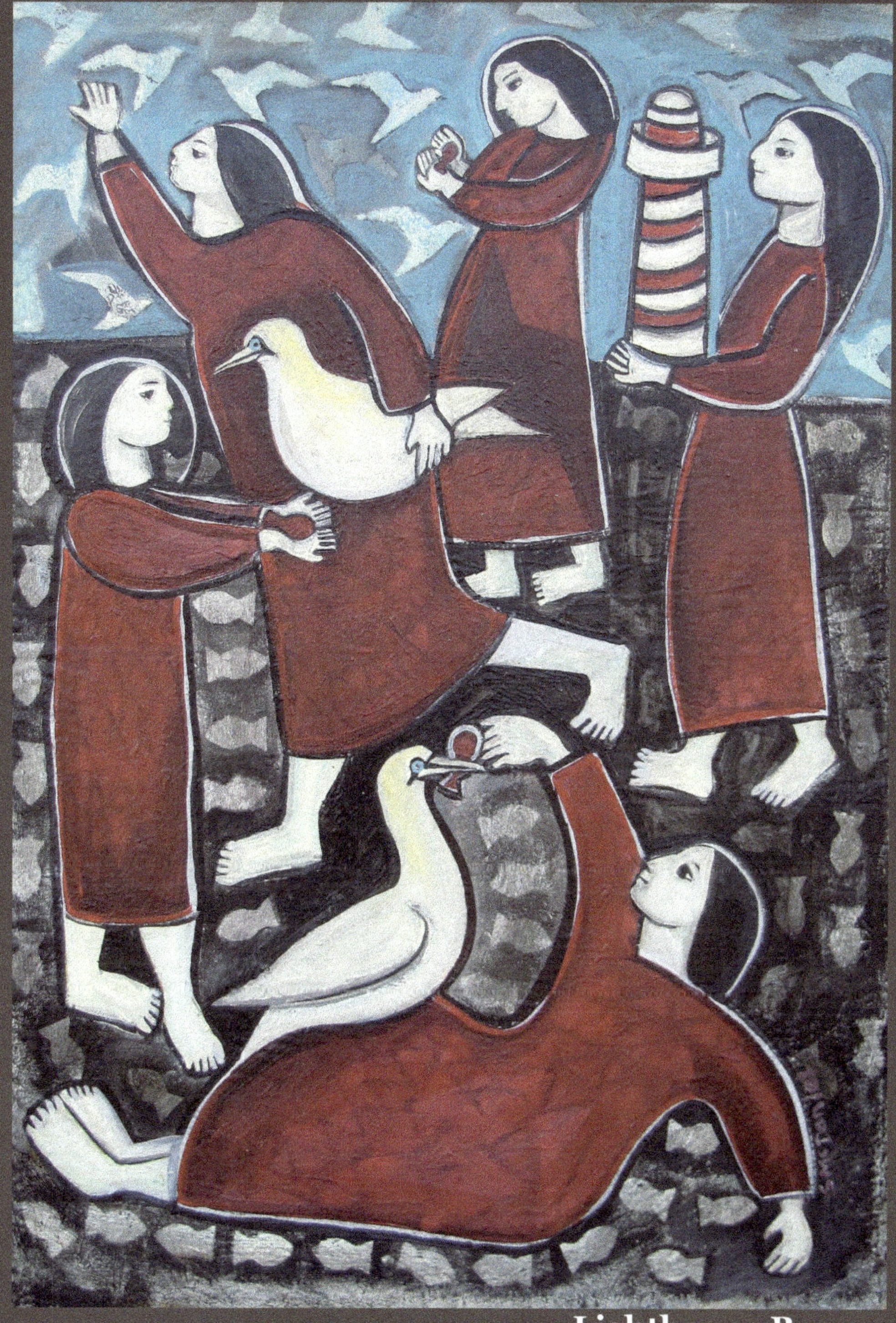

Lighthouse Bearer
(80cm x 55cm)

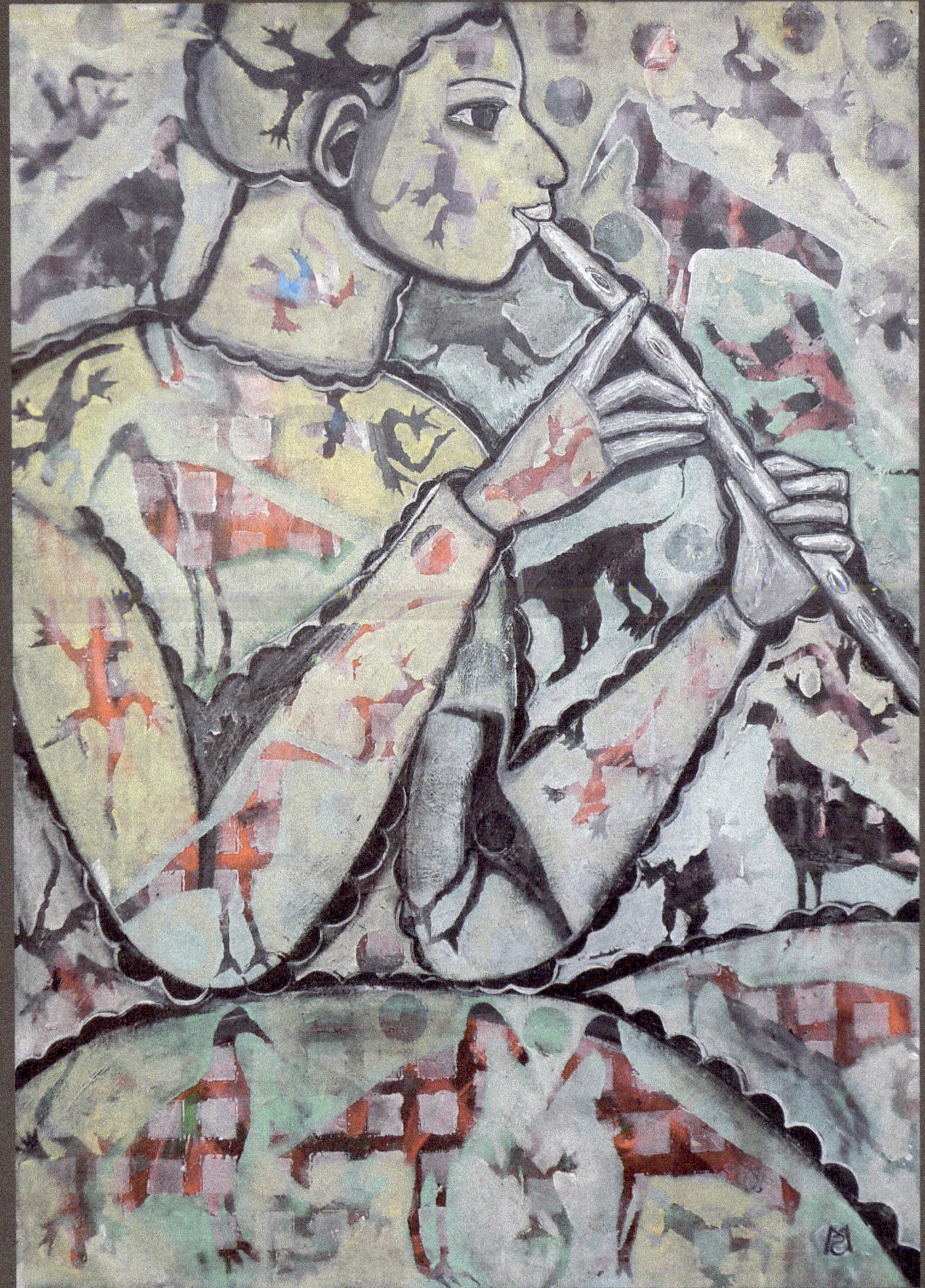

Reverie
(105cm x 75cm)

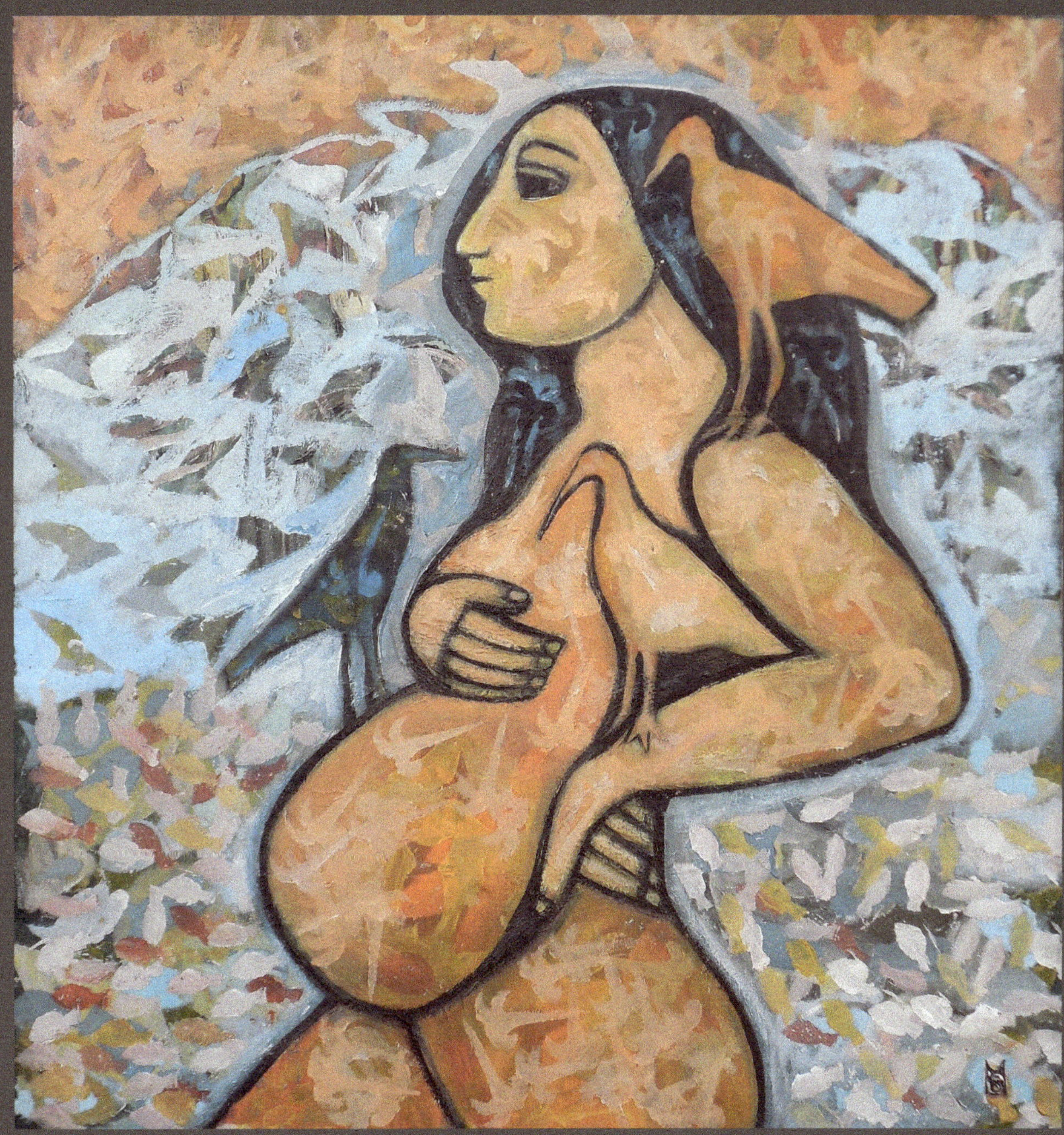

Tenny
(79cm x 76cm)

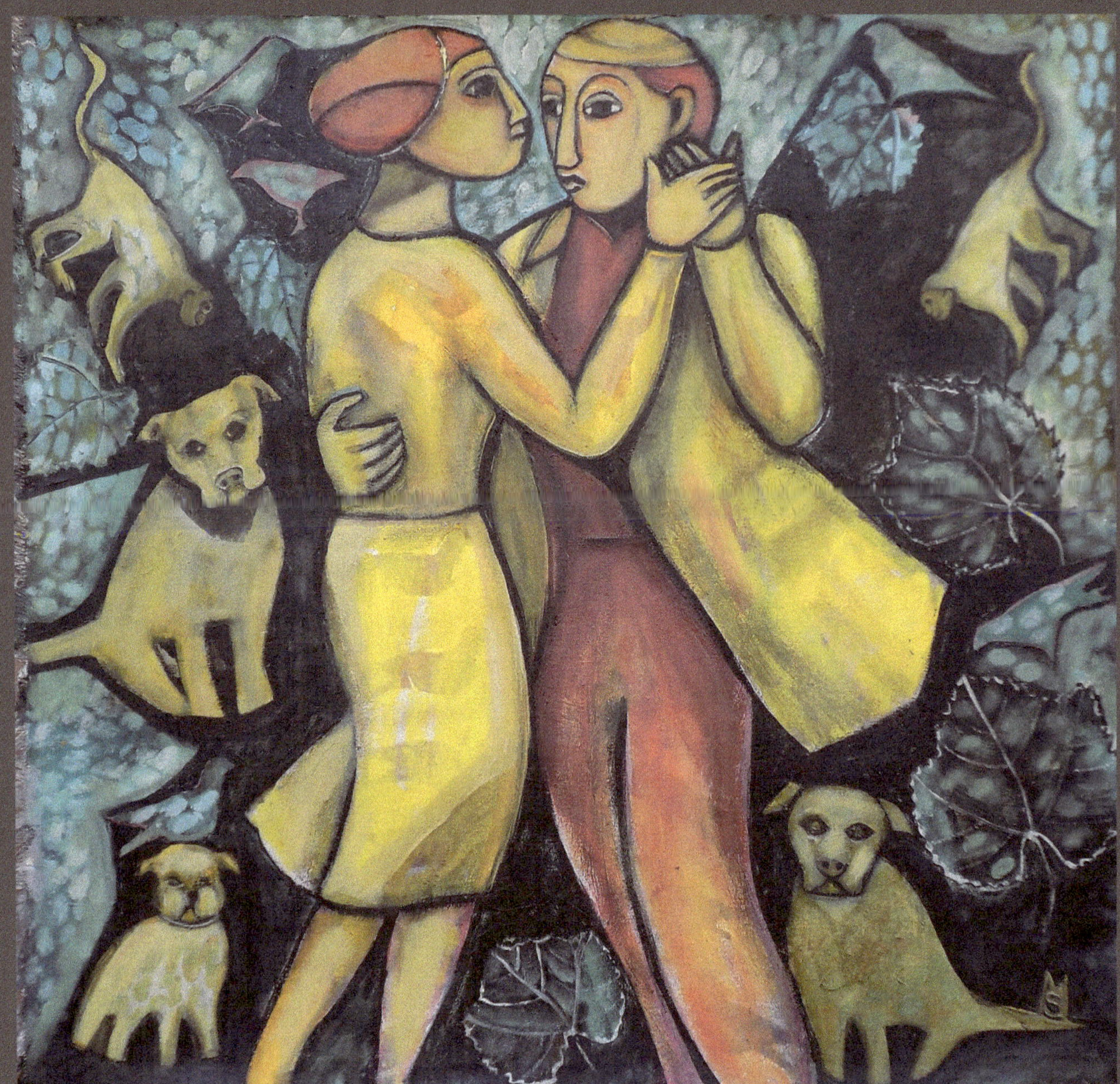

Grape Harvest
(75cm x 79cm)

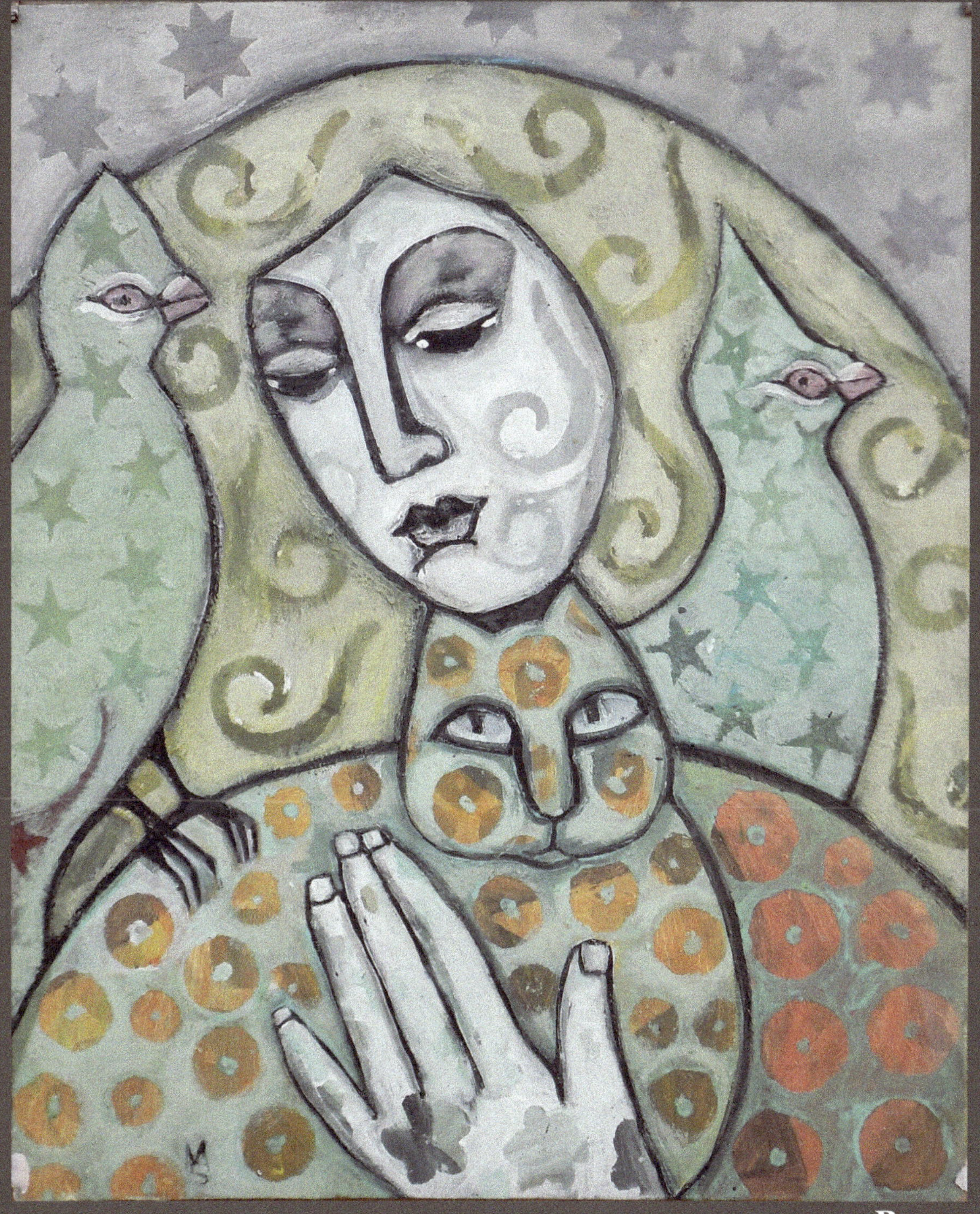

Peace
(61cm x 49cm)

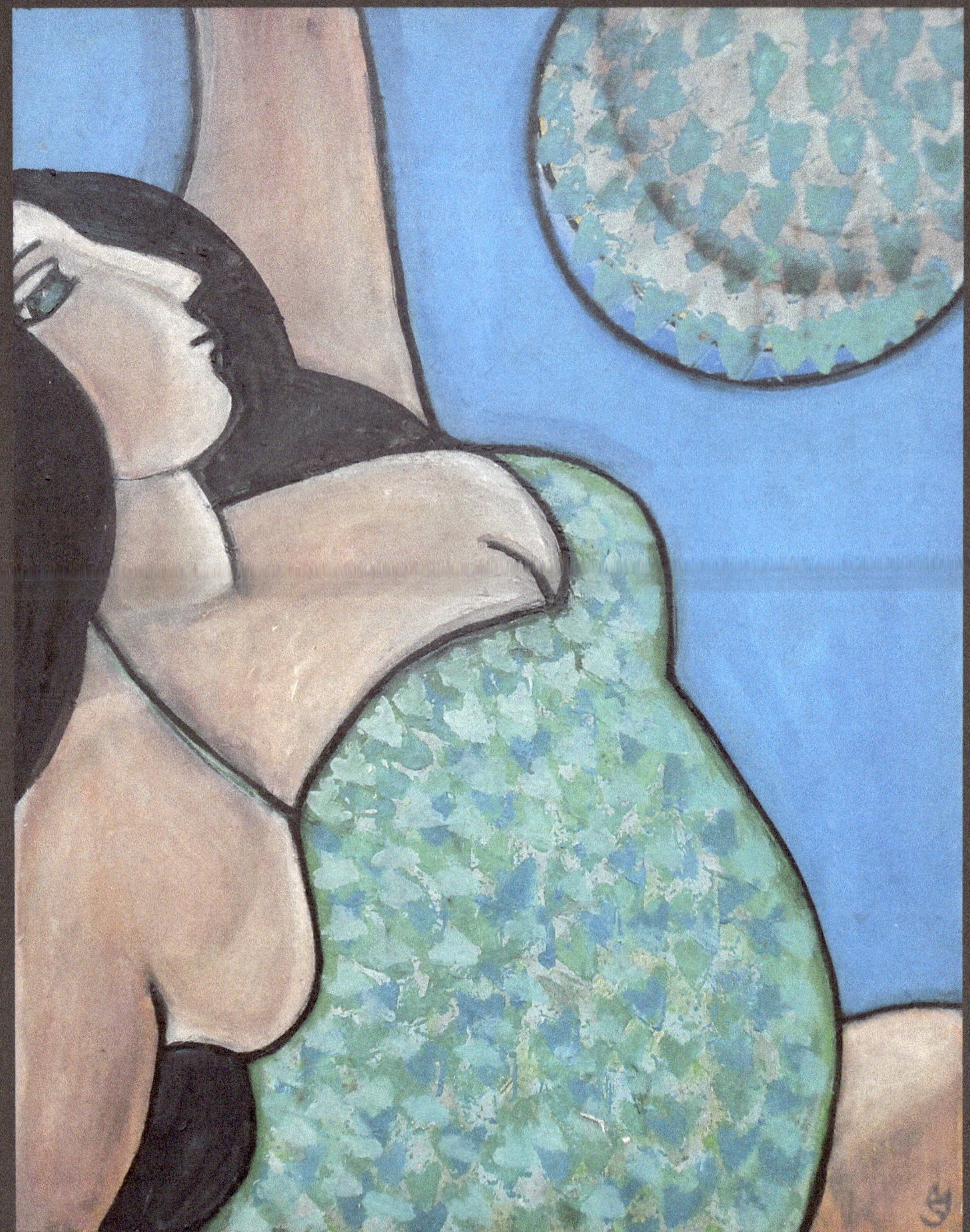

Sylvia
(61cm x 49cm)

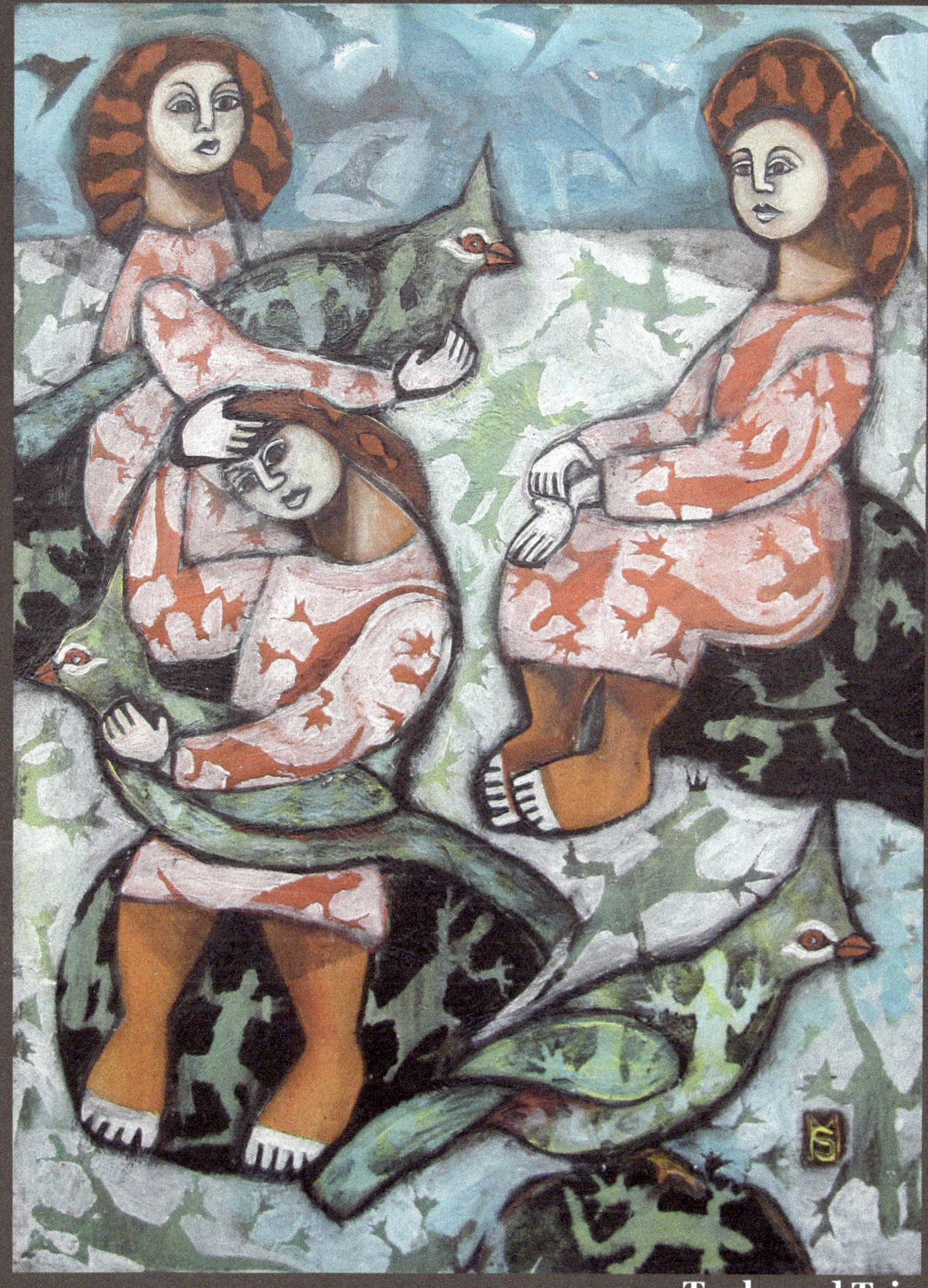

Turbaned Trio
(80cm x 60cm)

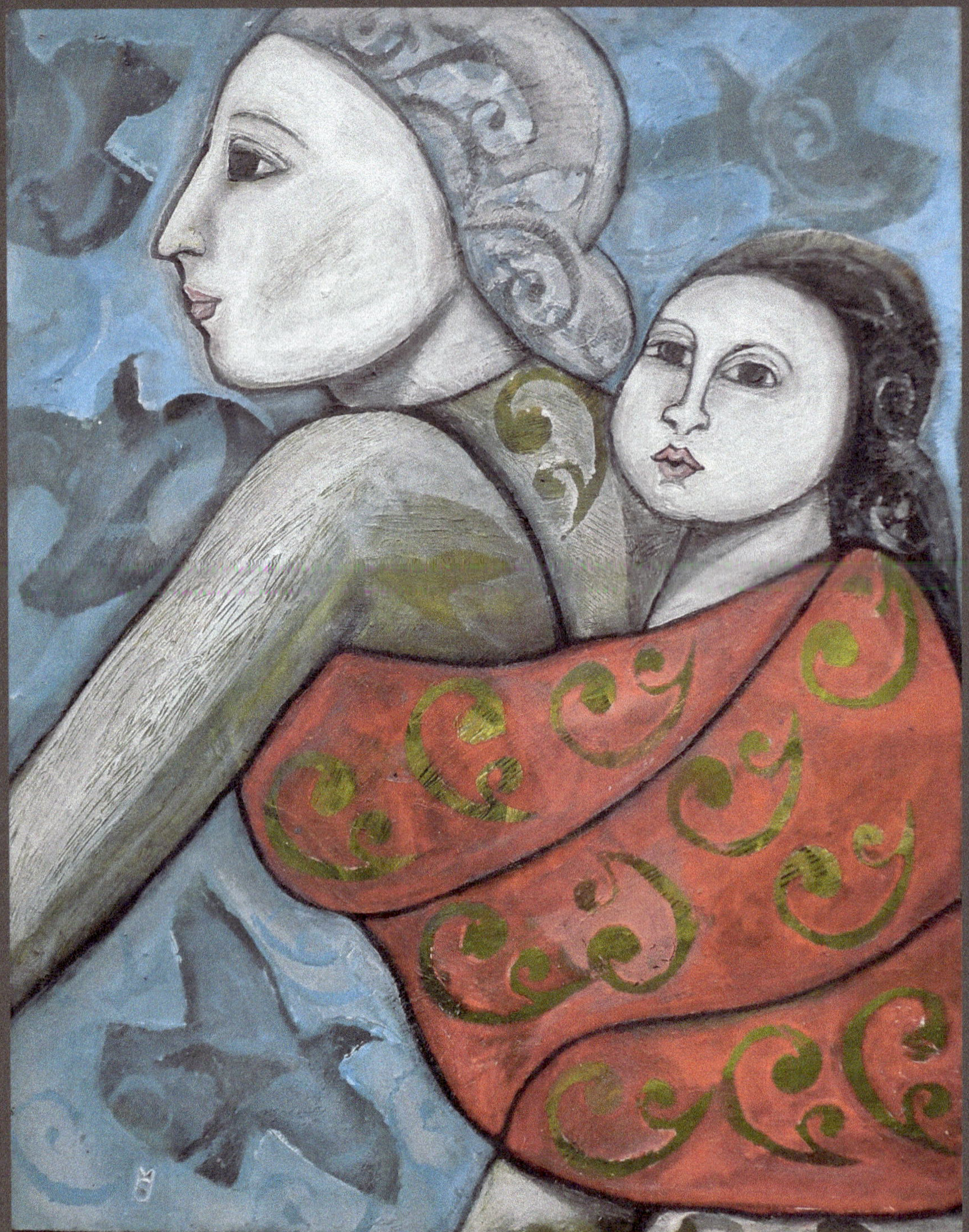

Bird Sky
(61cm x 49cm)

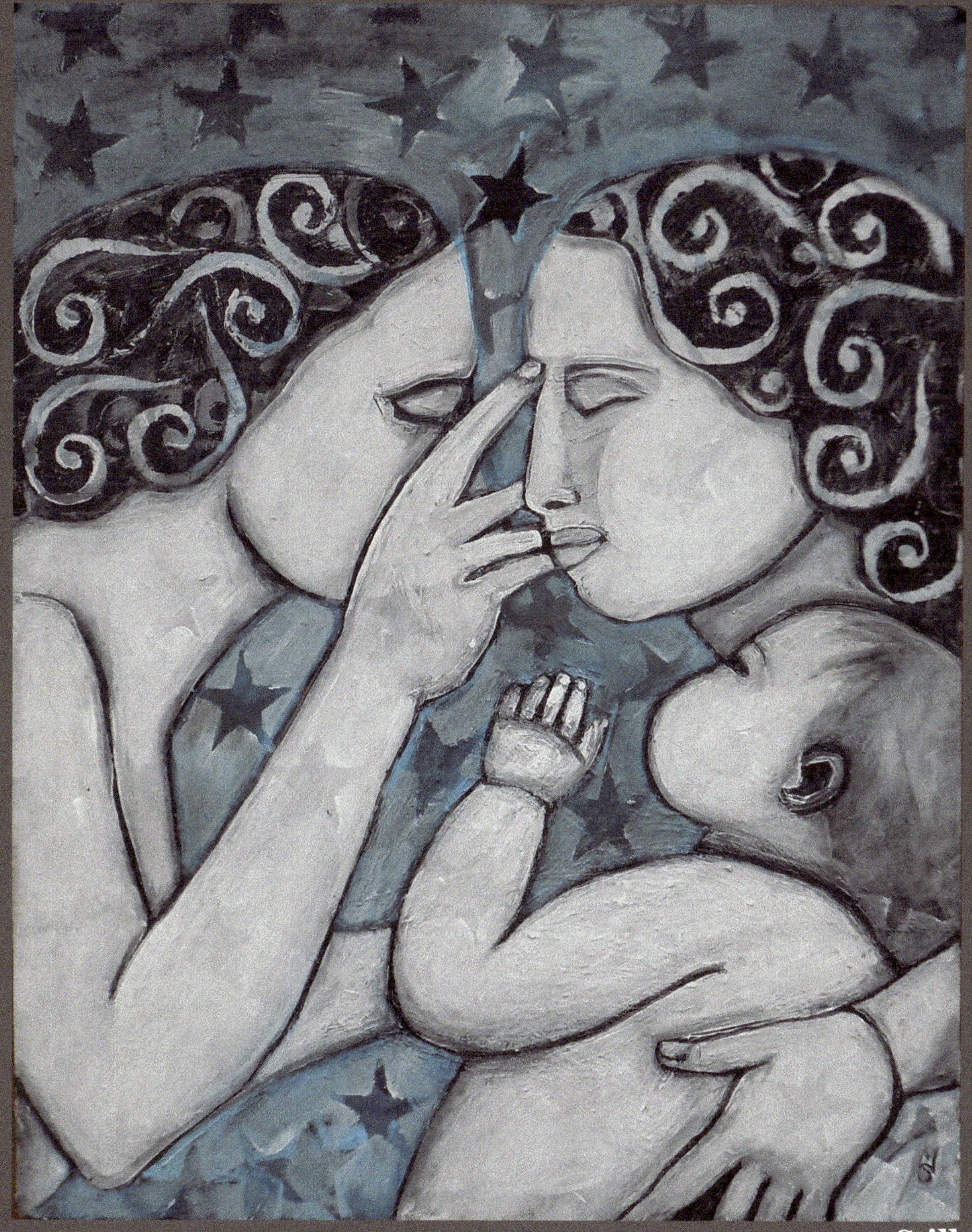

Still
(61cm x 49cm)

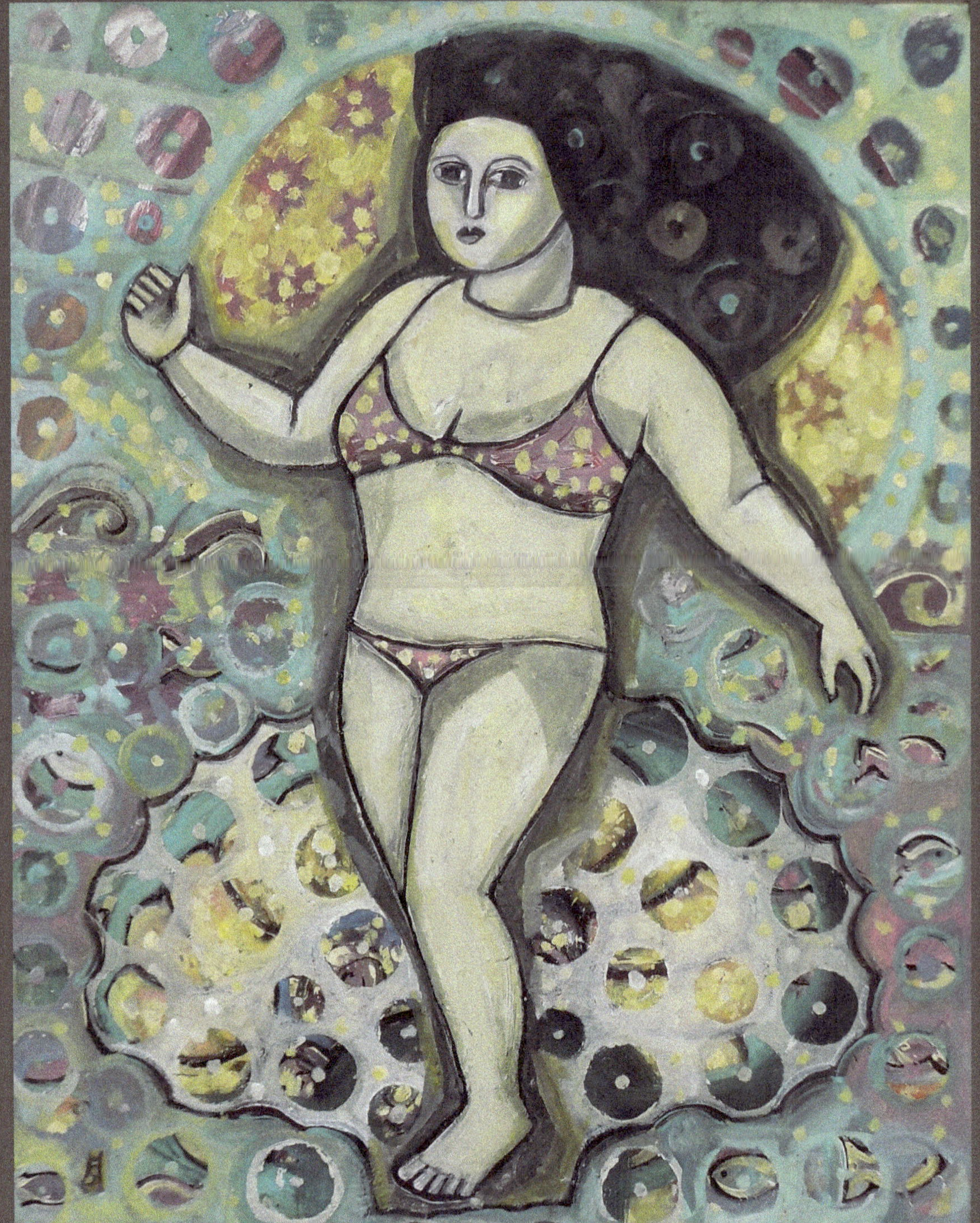

Venus
(75cm x 61cm)

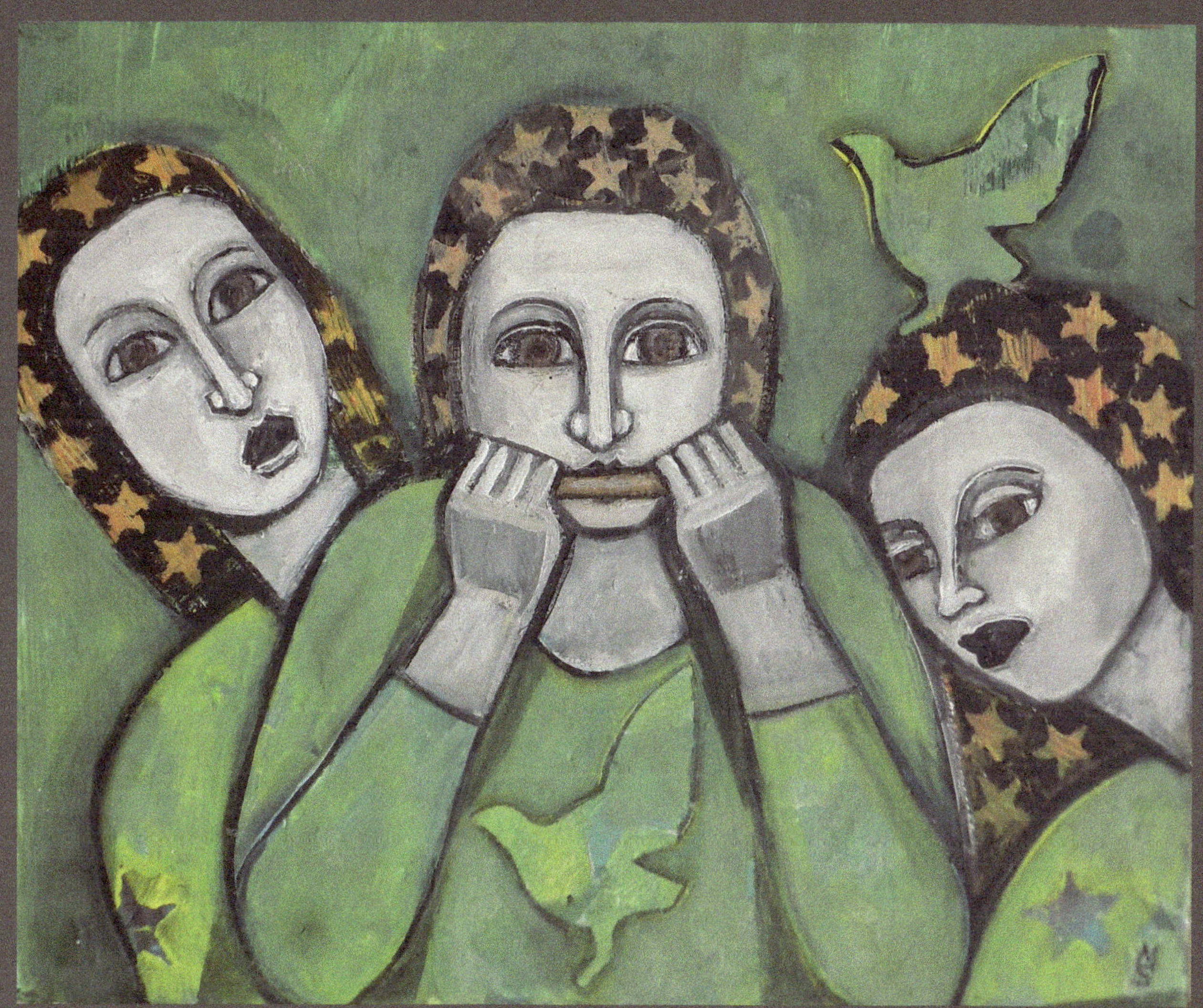

Harmonica Harmonies
(49cm x 61cm)

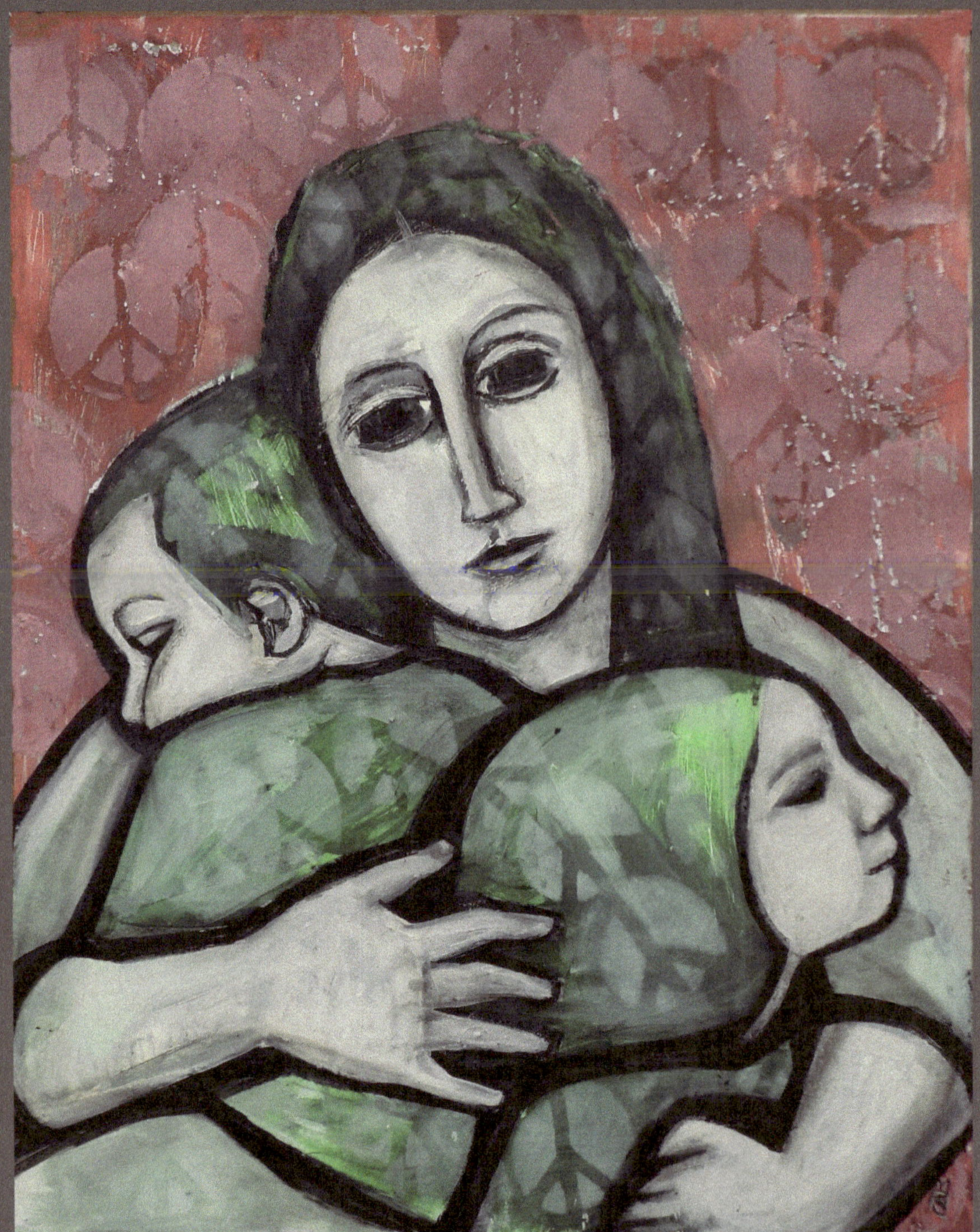

Protection
(61cm x 49cm)

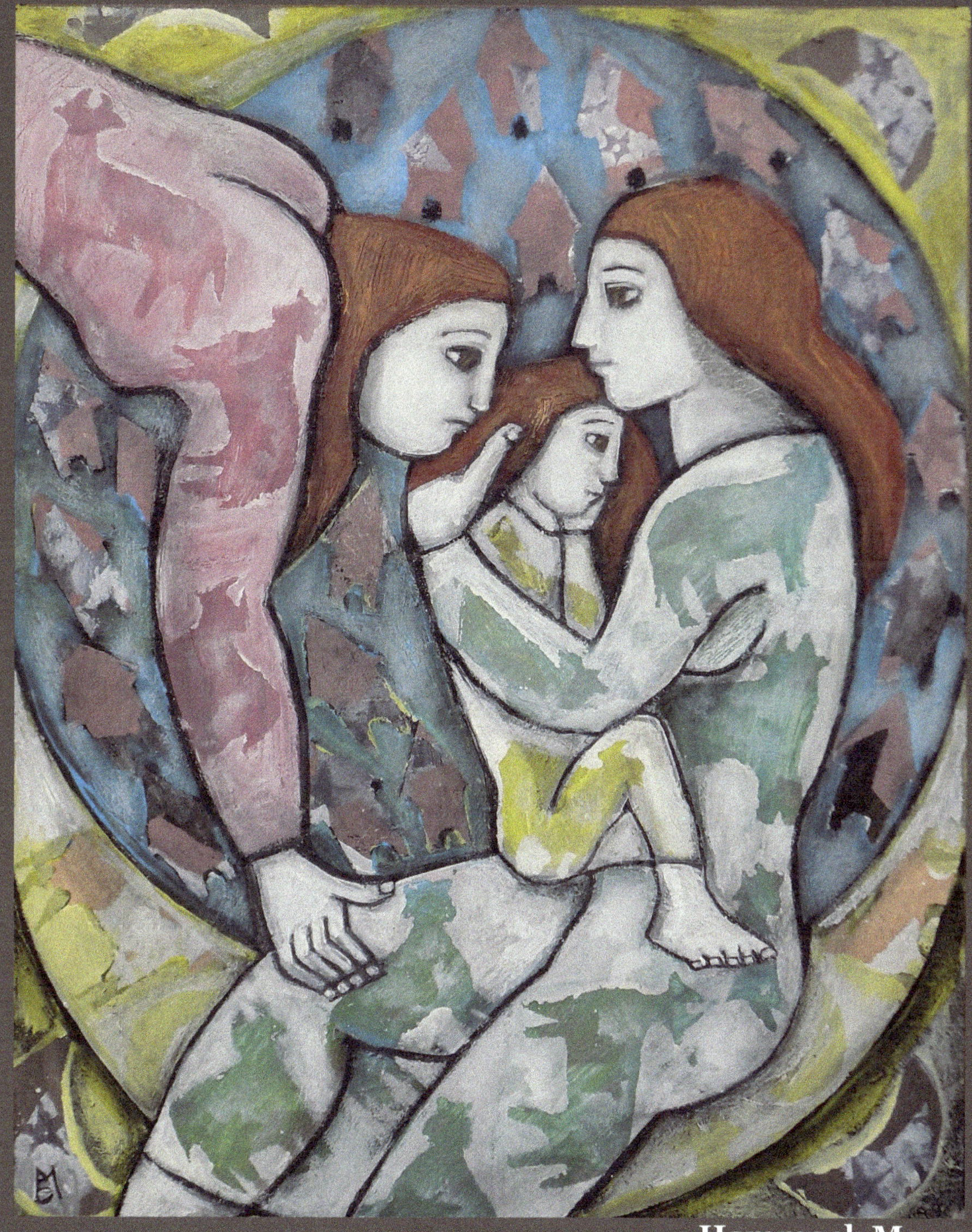

Hammock Moon
(61cm x 49cm)

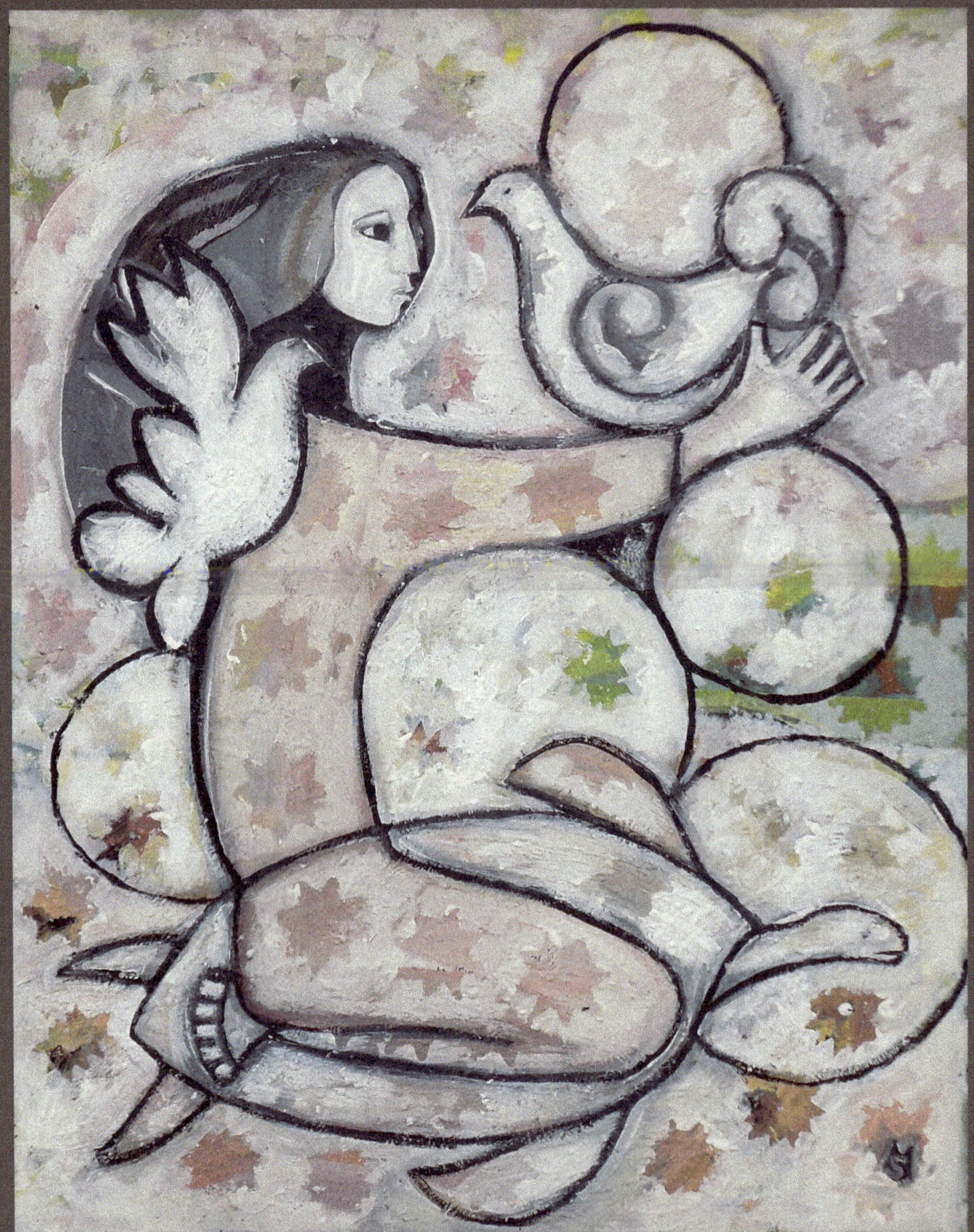

Turtle Travel
(61cm x 49cm)

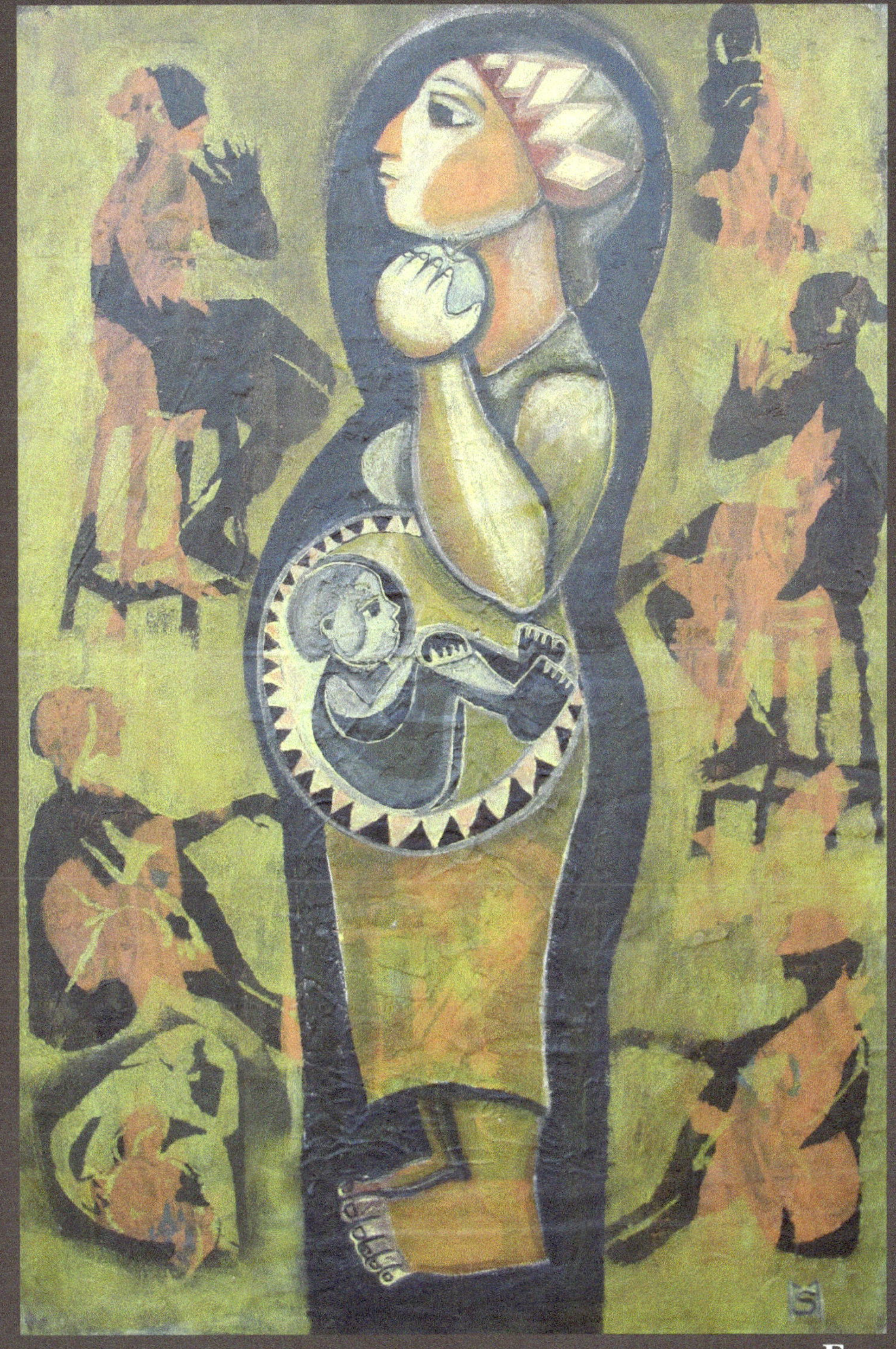

Eva
(95cm x 65cm)

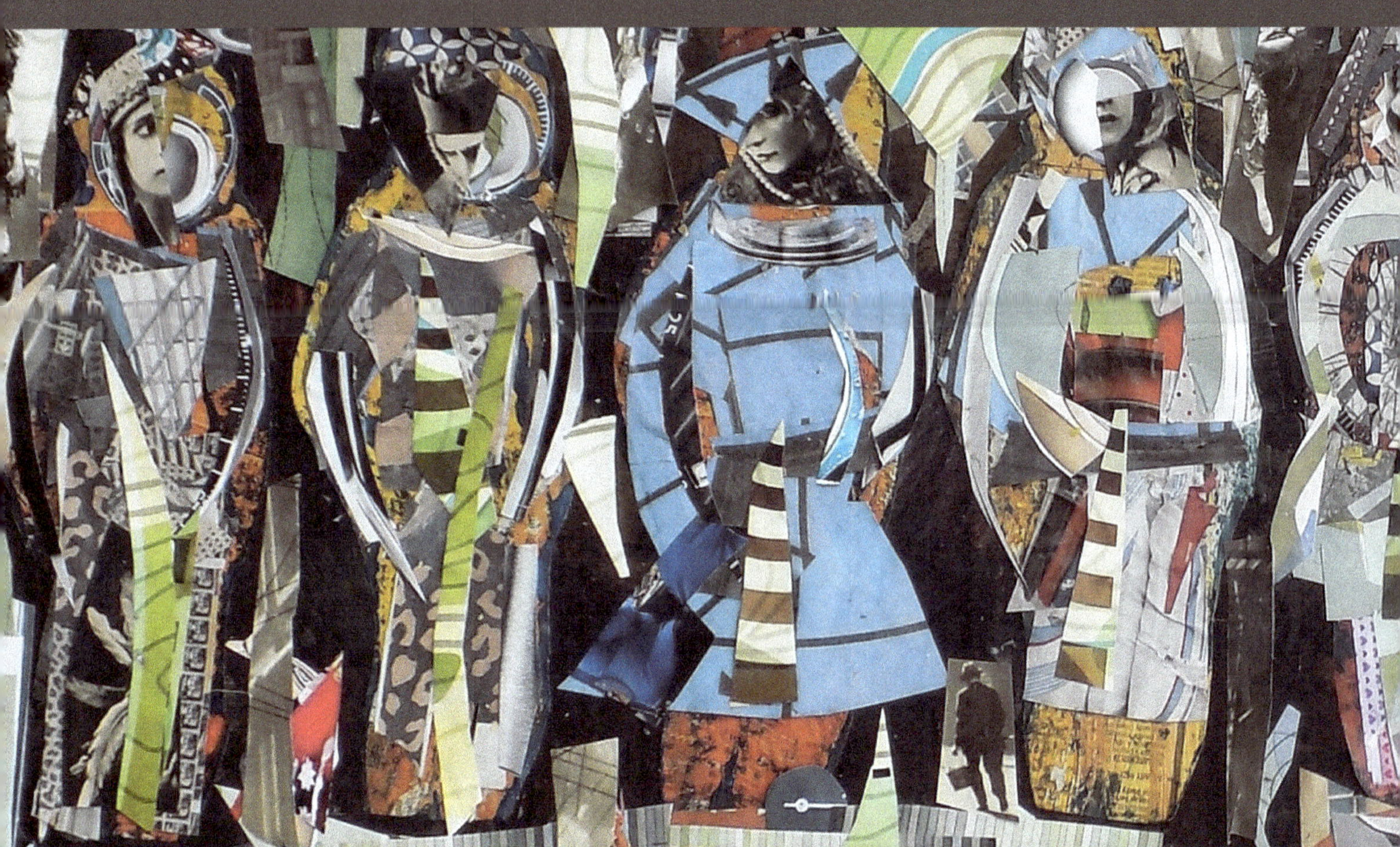

Line Up
(26cm x 83cm)

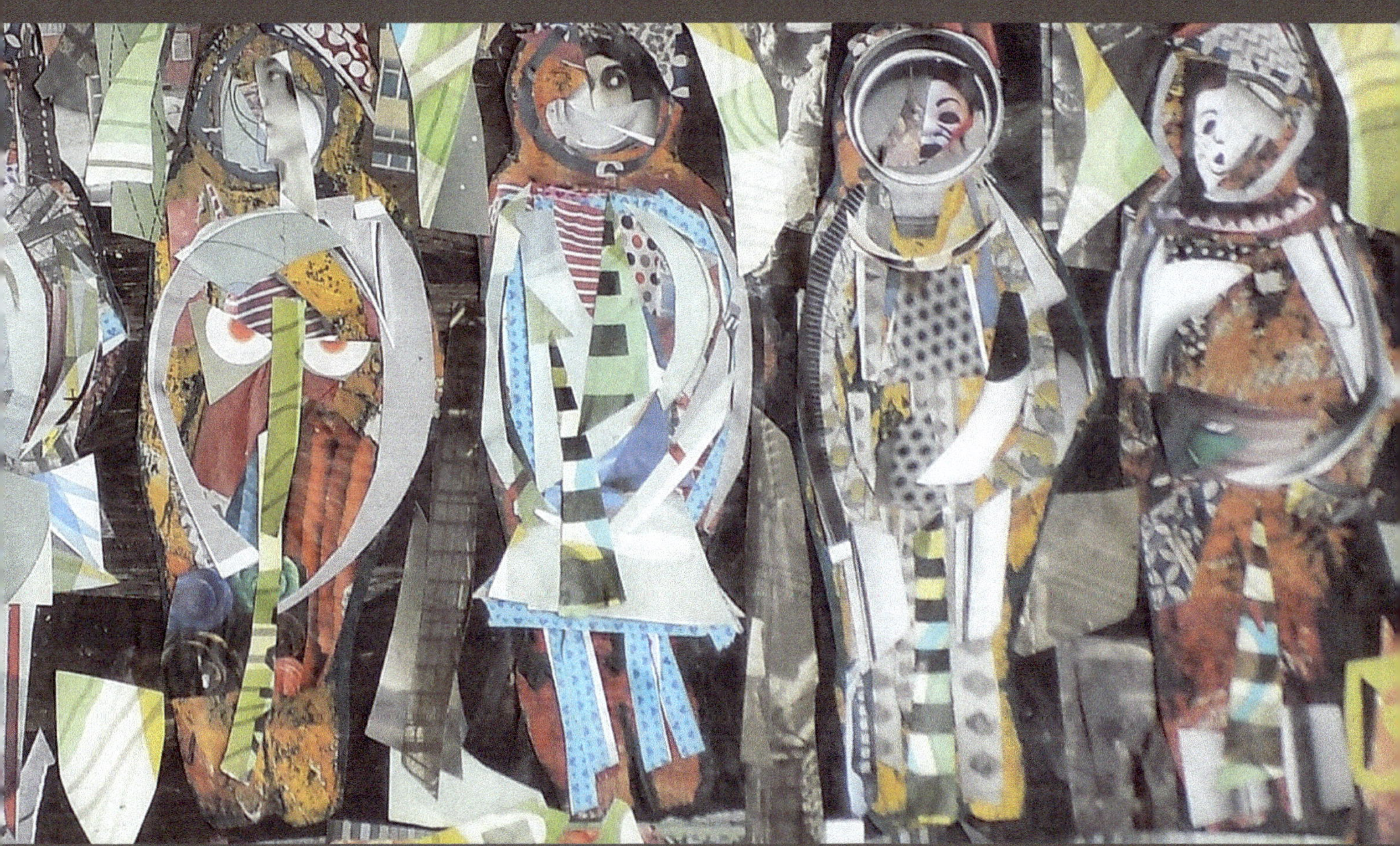

Collage

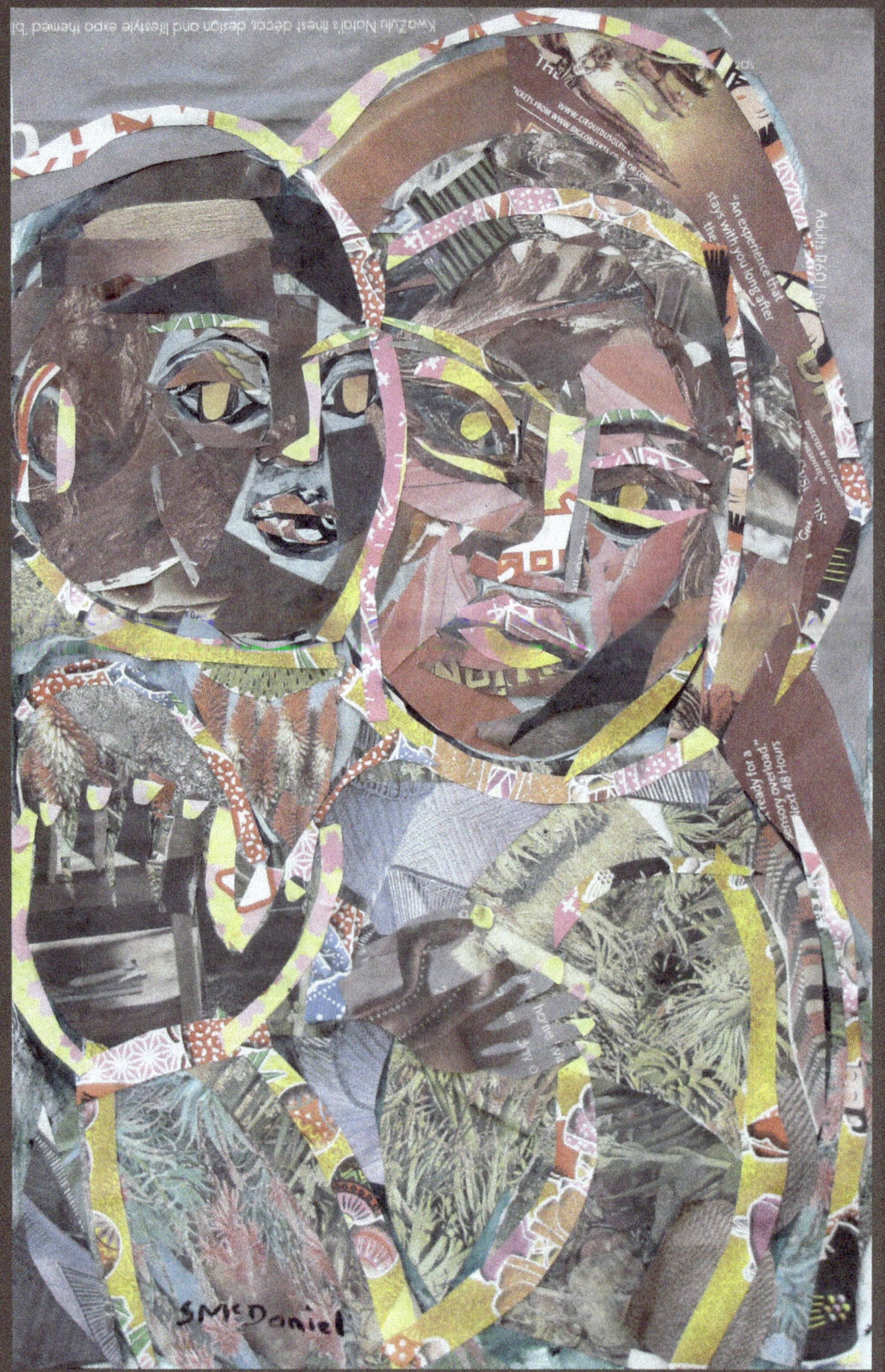

Sensory Overload
(44cm x 28cm)

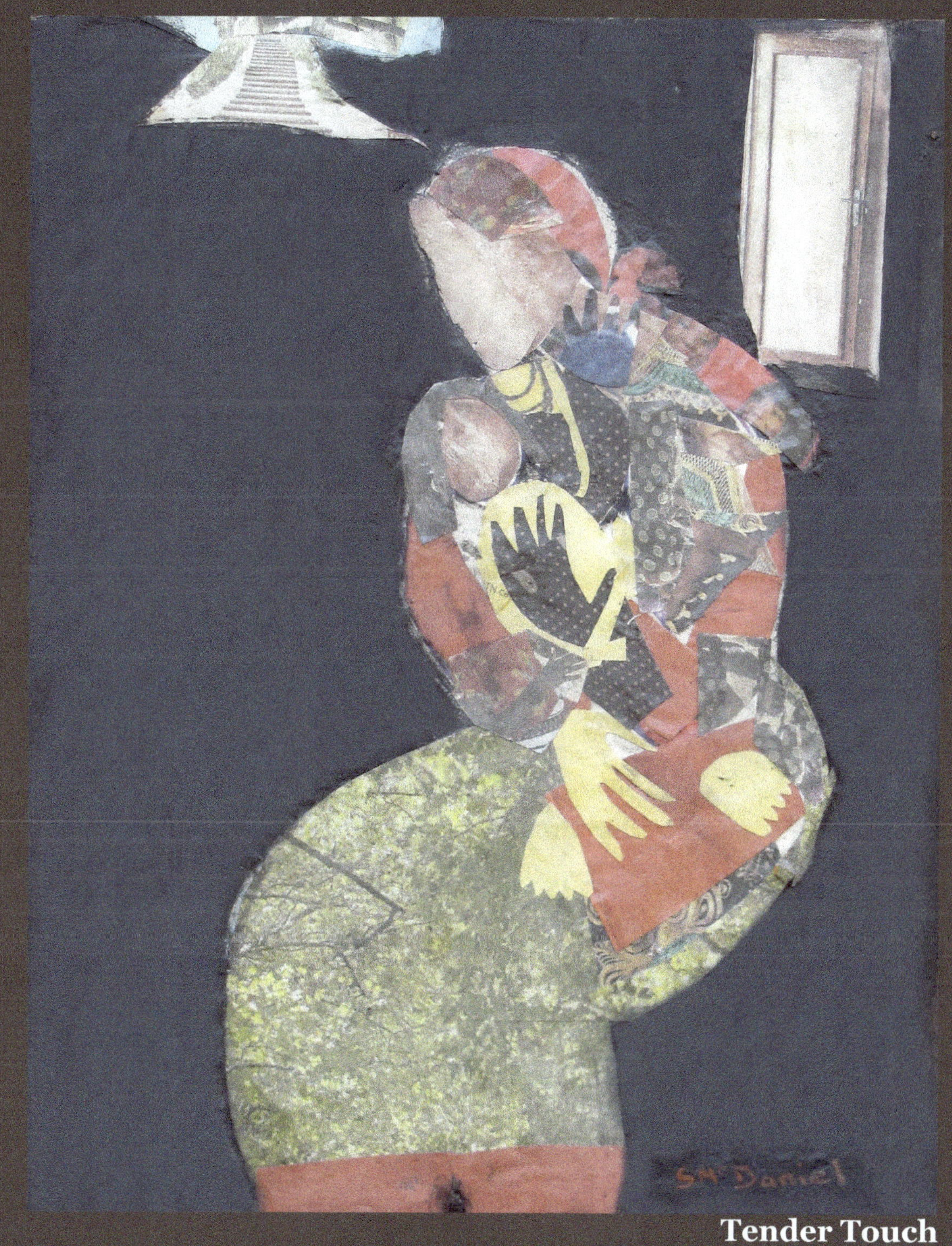

Tender Touch
(39cm x 29cm)
Digital version on pg.220.

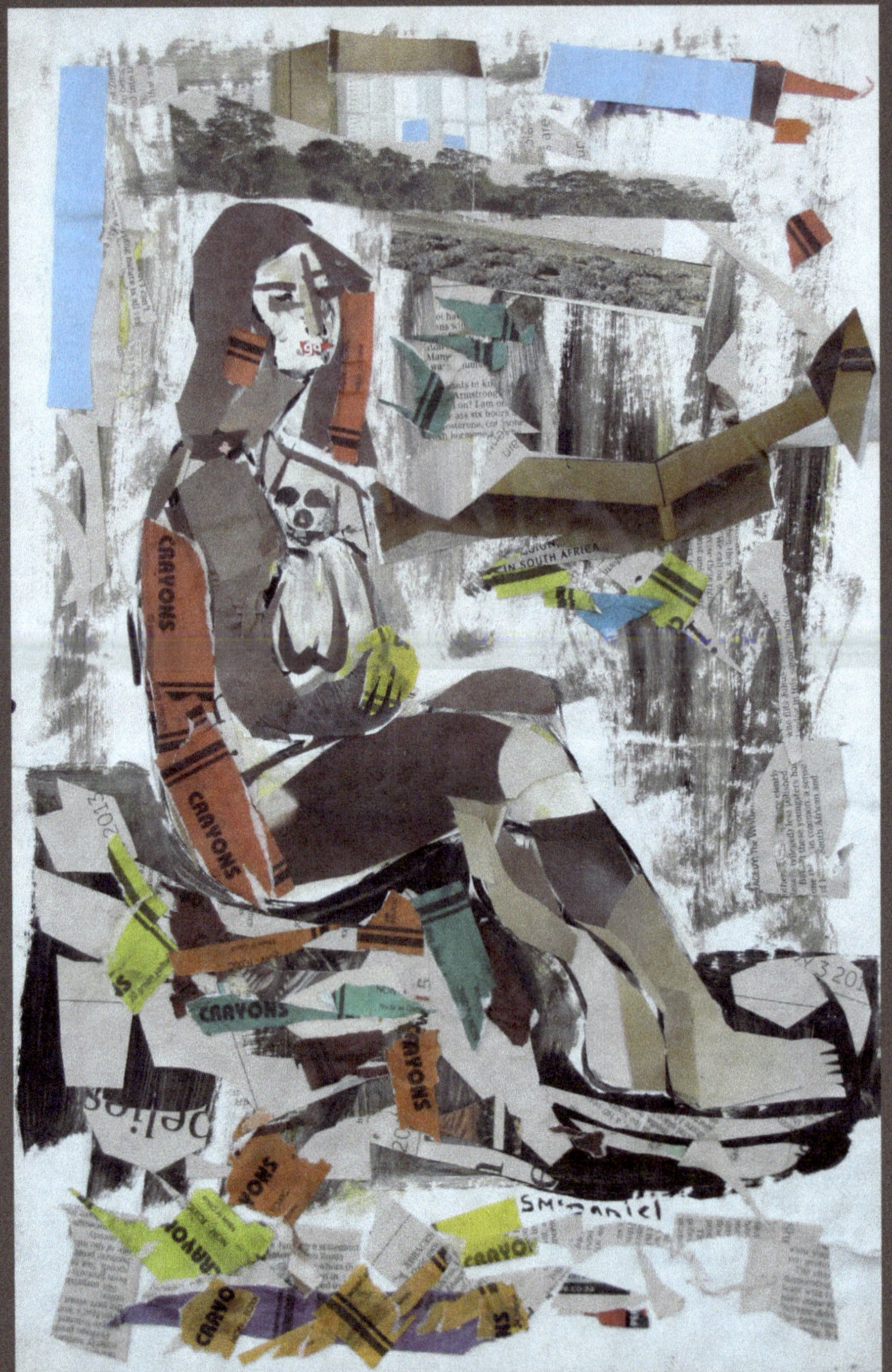

Lap Dog
(42cm x 27cm)
Digital version on pg.187.

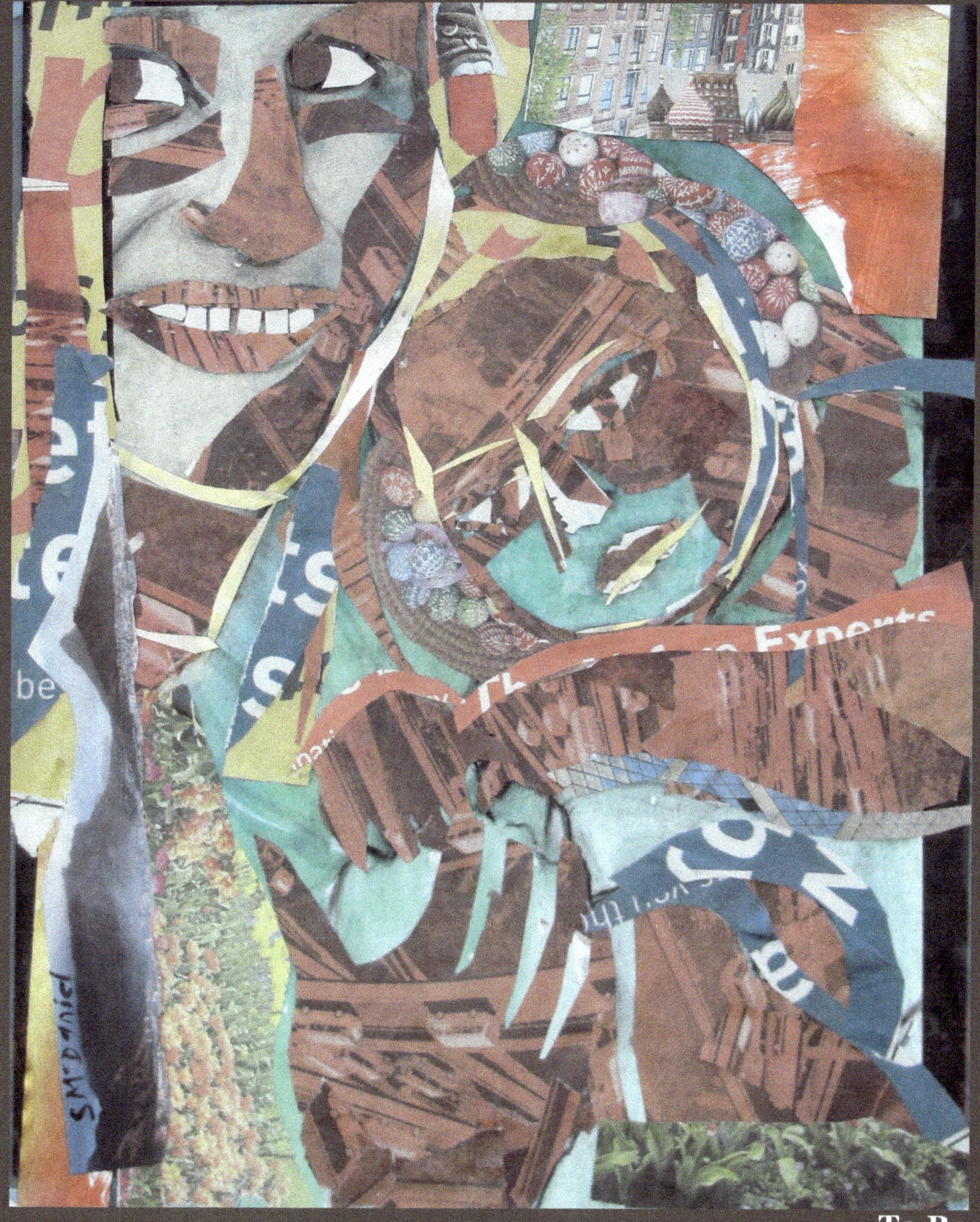

To Be
(42cm x 33cm)

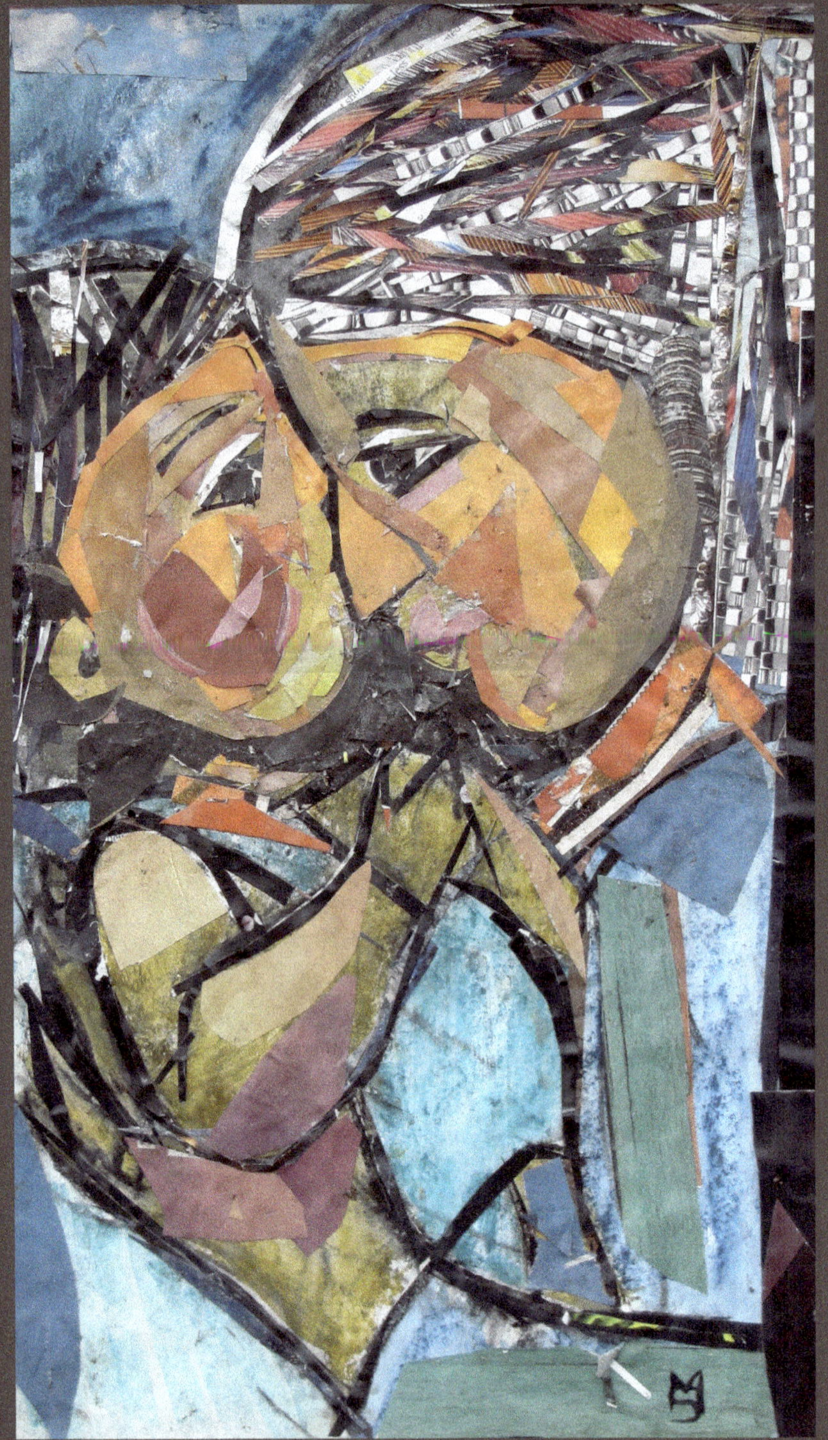

Clasped
(39cm x 22cm)

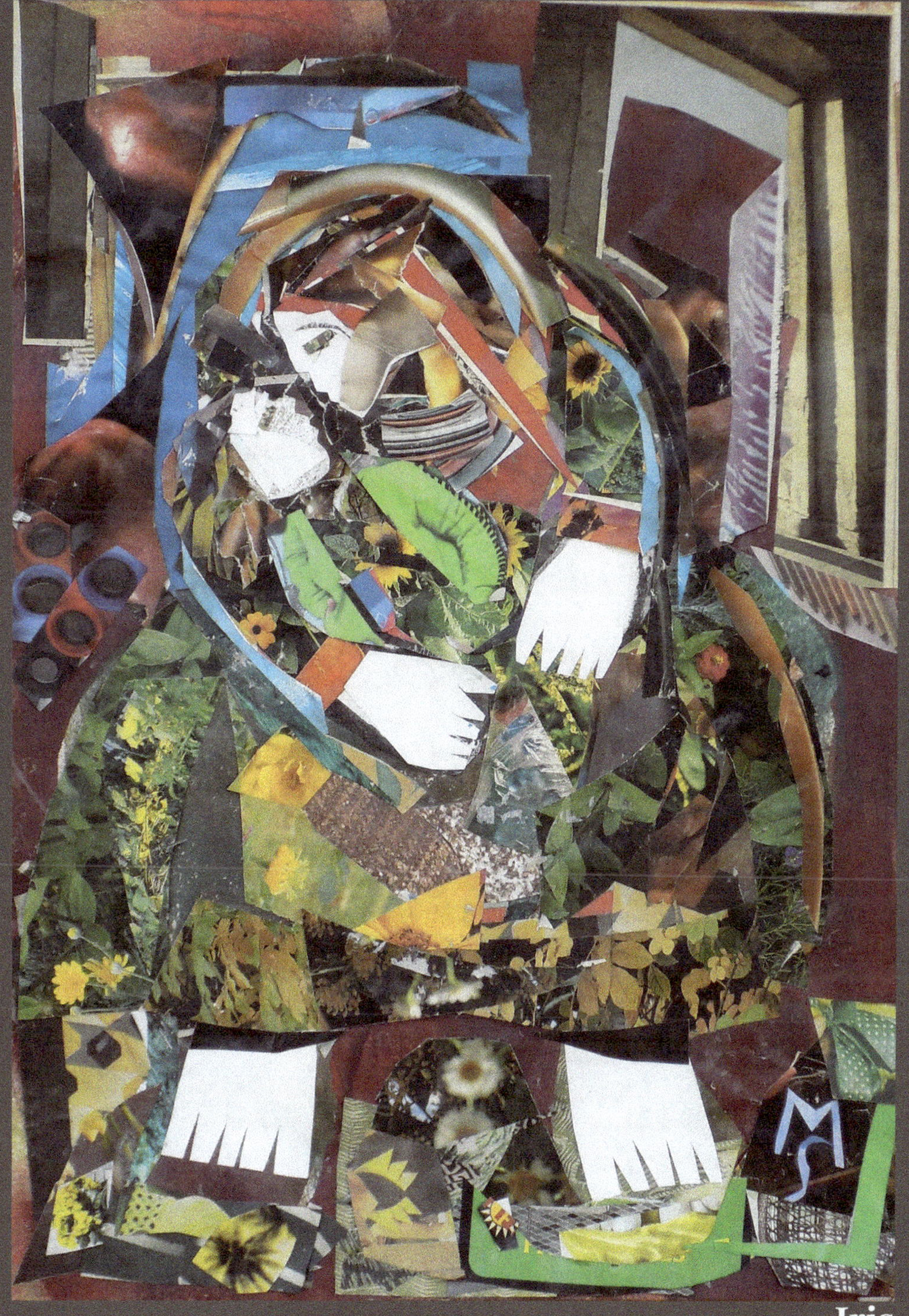

Iris
(41cm x 29cm)

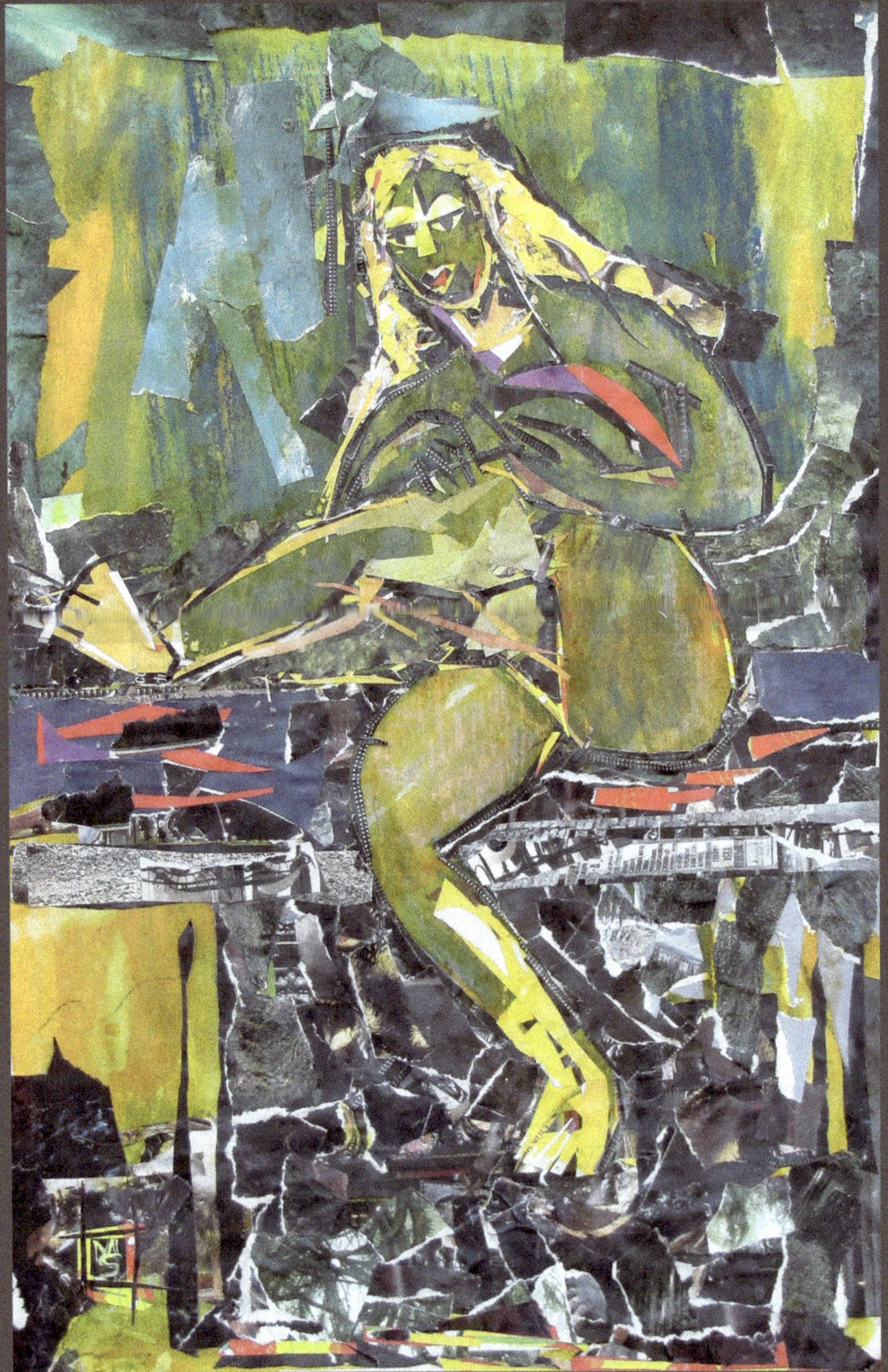

Sweet Silent Thought
(43cm x 29cm)

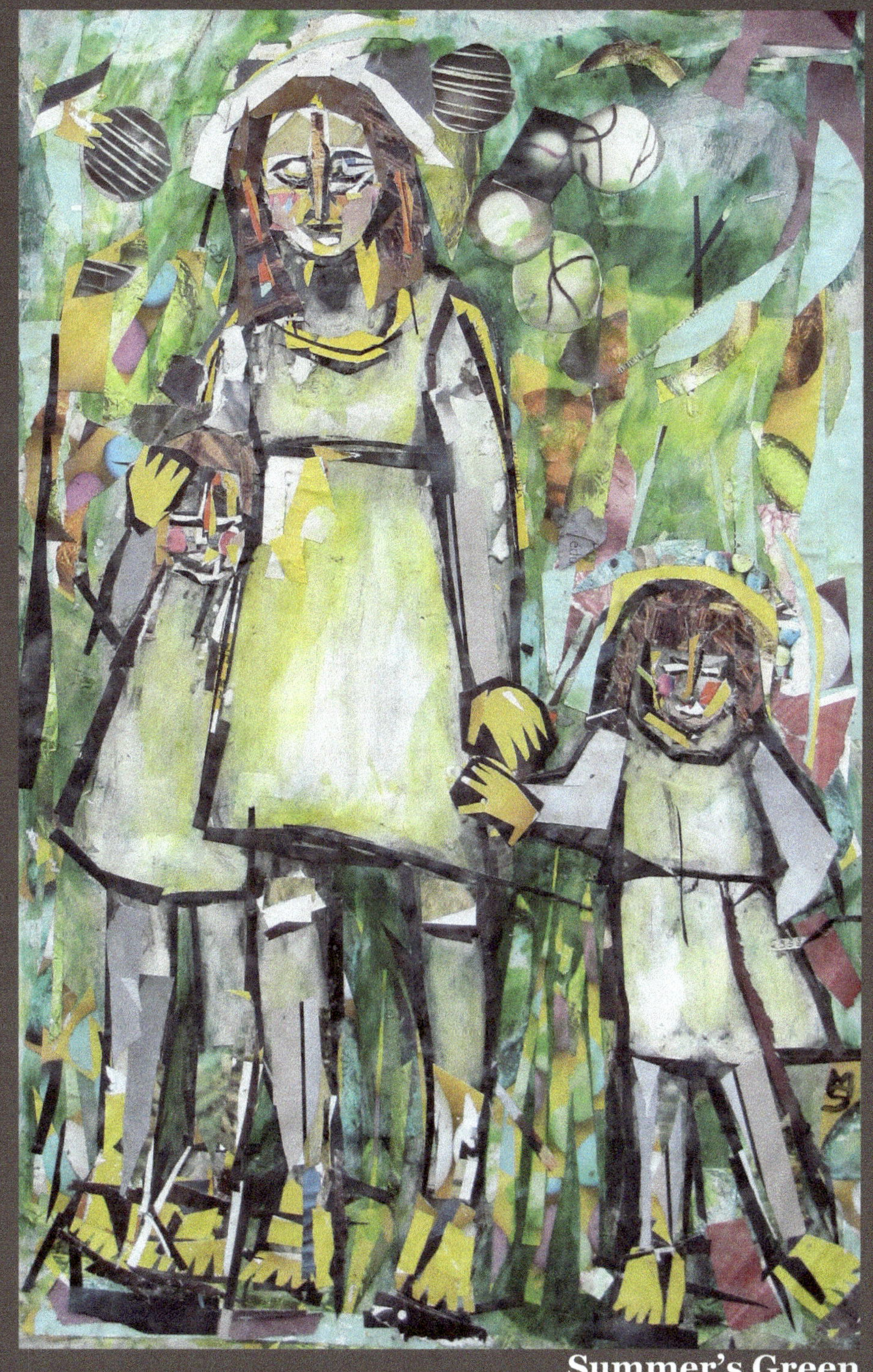

Summer's Green
(43cm x 28cm)

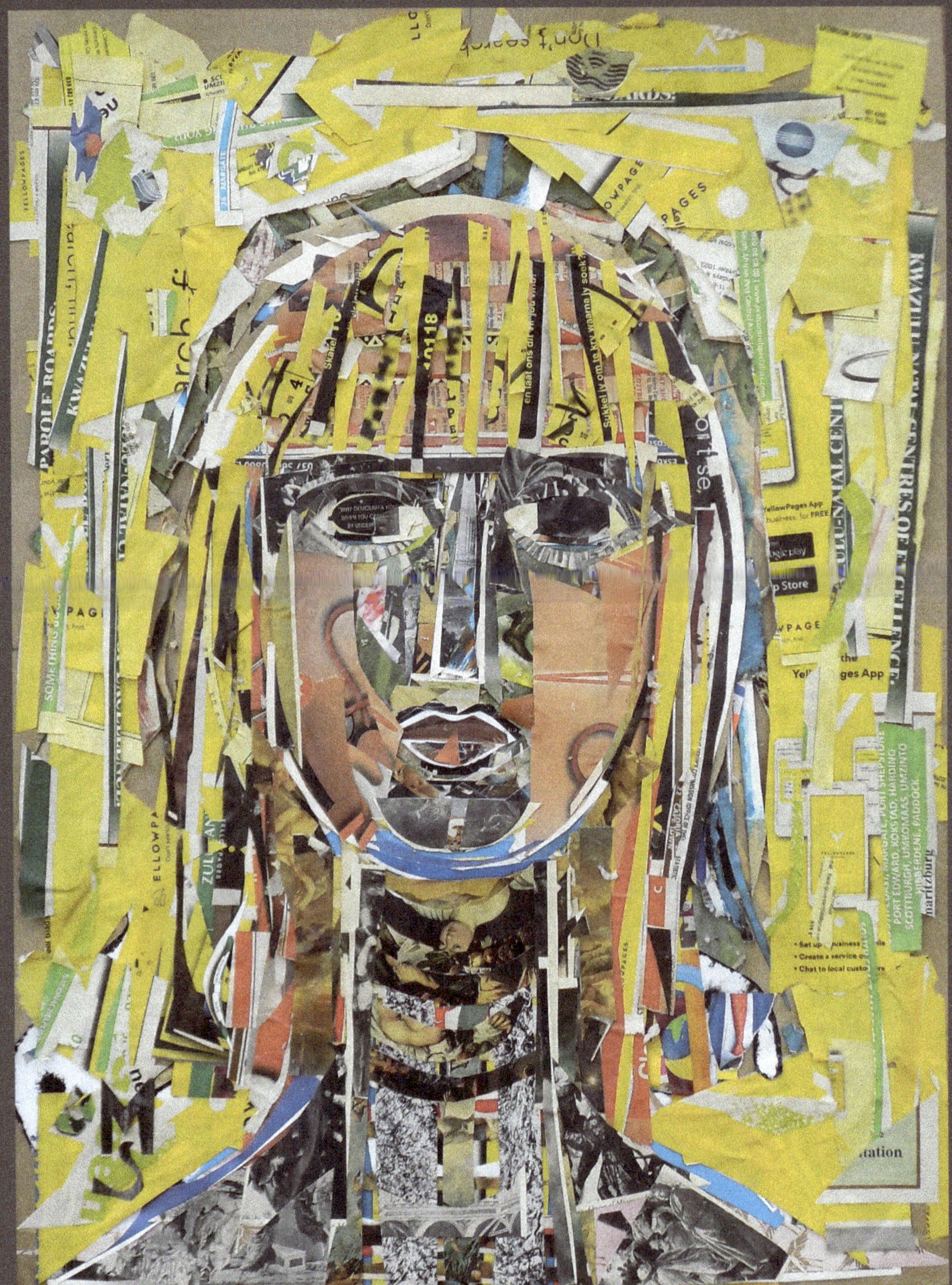

Georgiana
(50cm x 38cm)

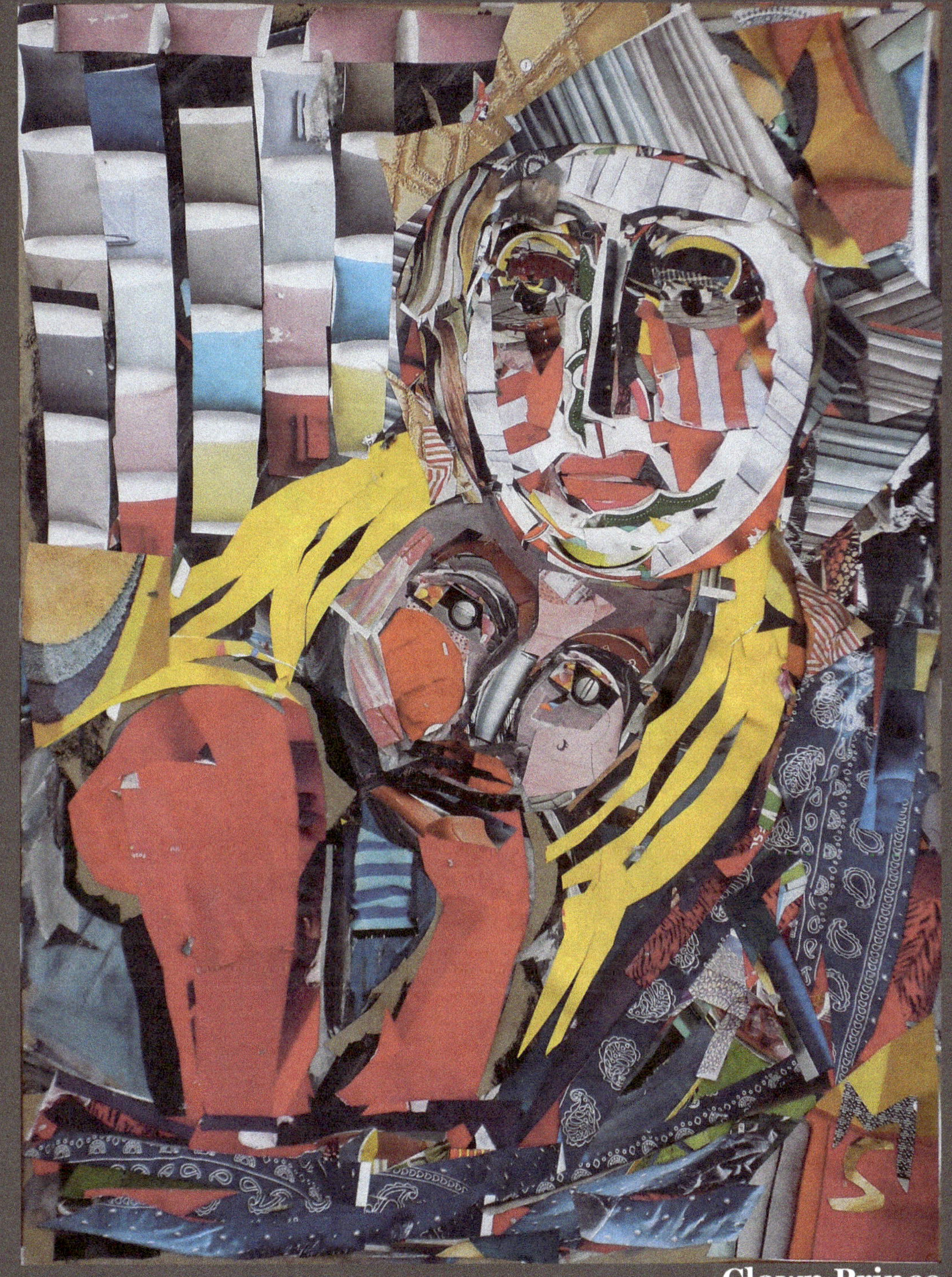

Clown Prince
(51cm x 38cm)

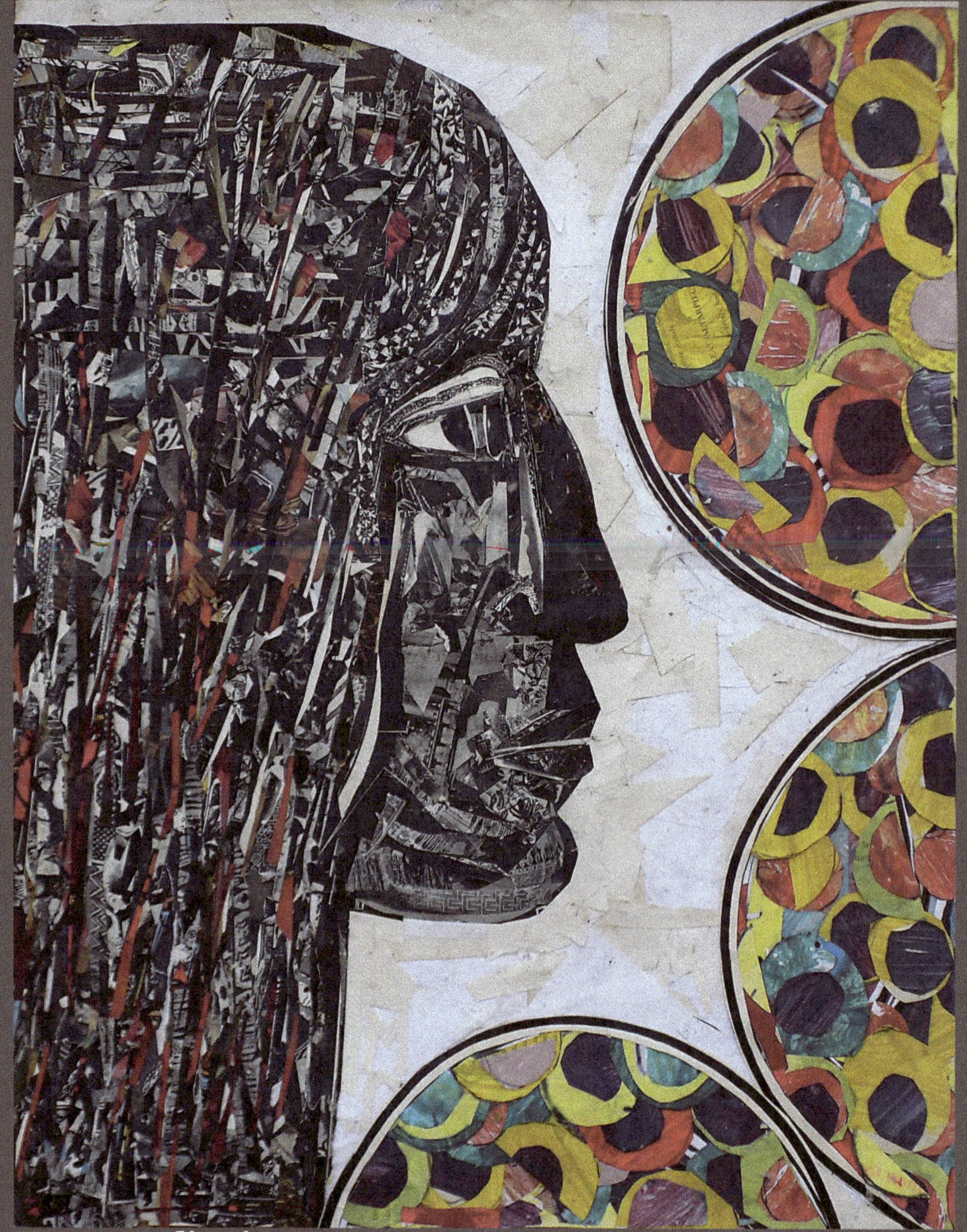

Moon Meditation
(50cm x 40cm)

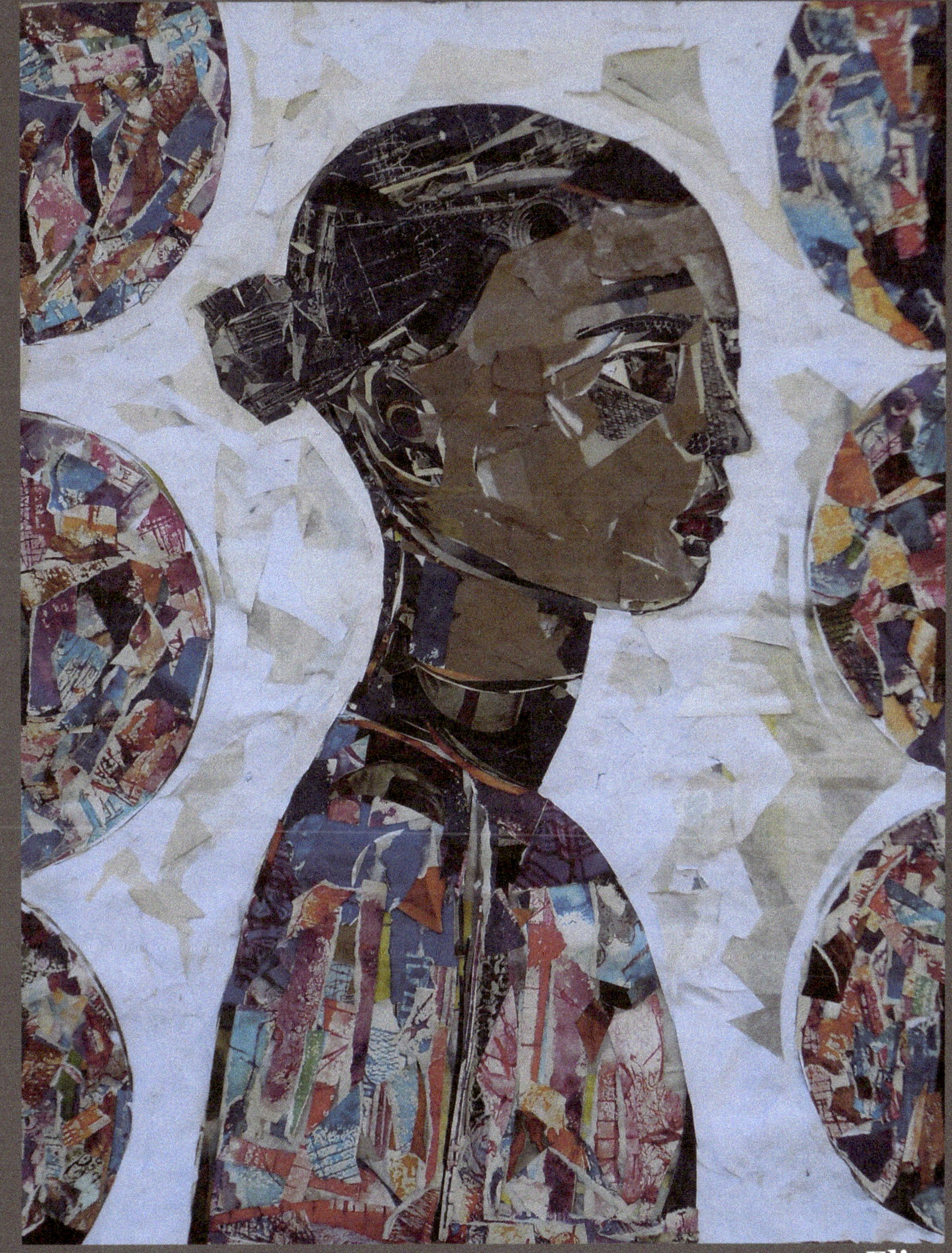

Elise
(69cm x 53cm)

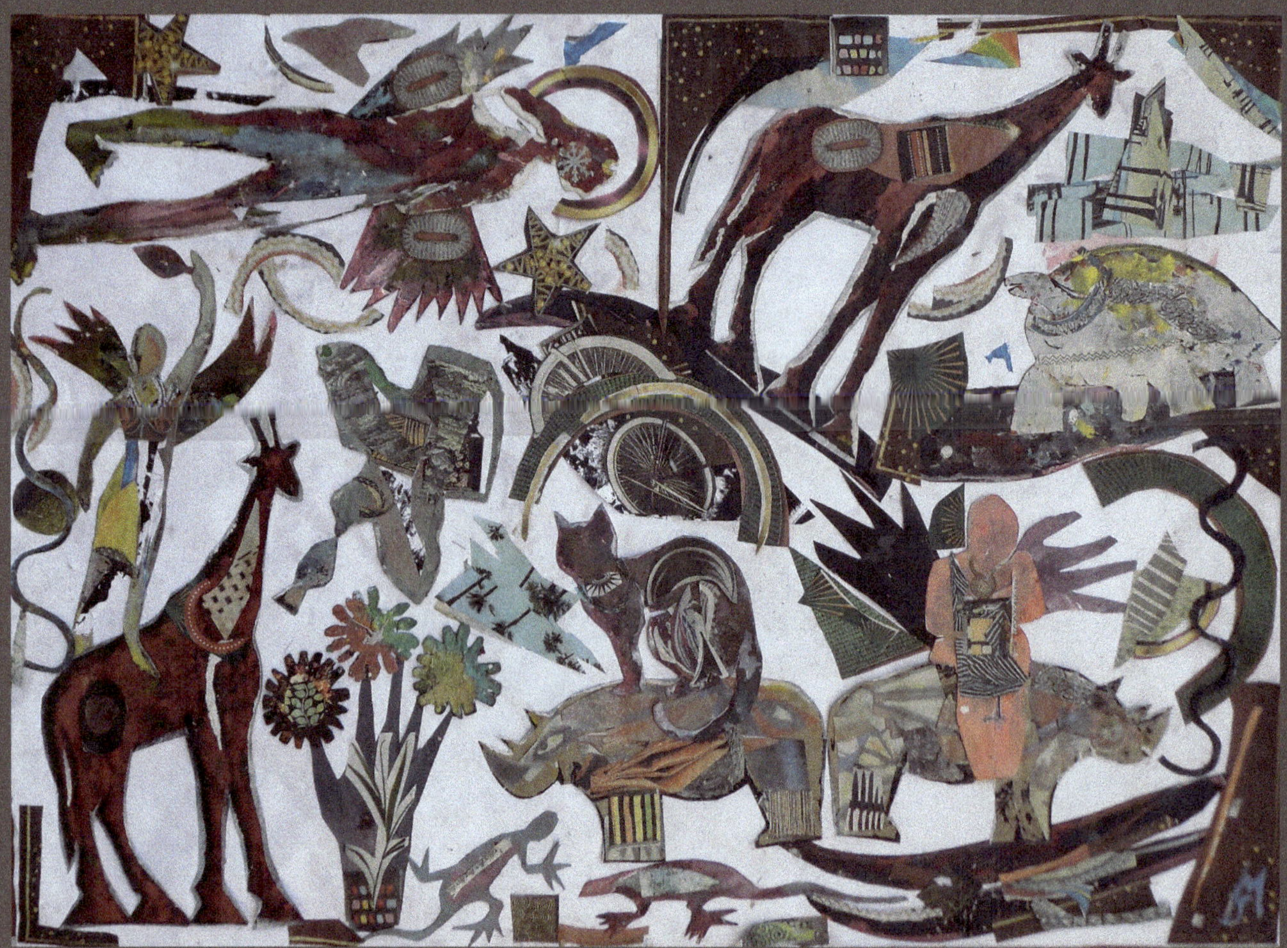

Ark Angels
(60cm x 85cm)

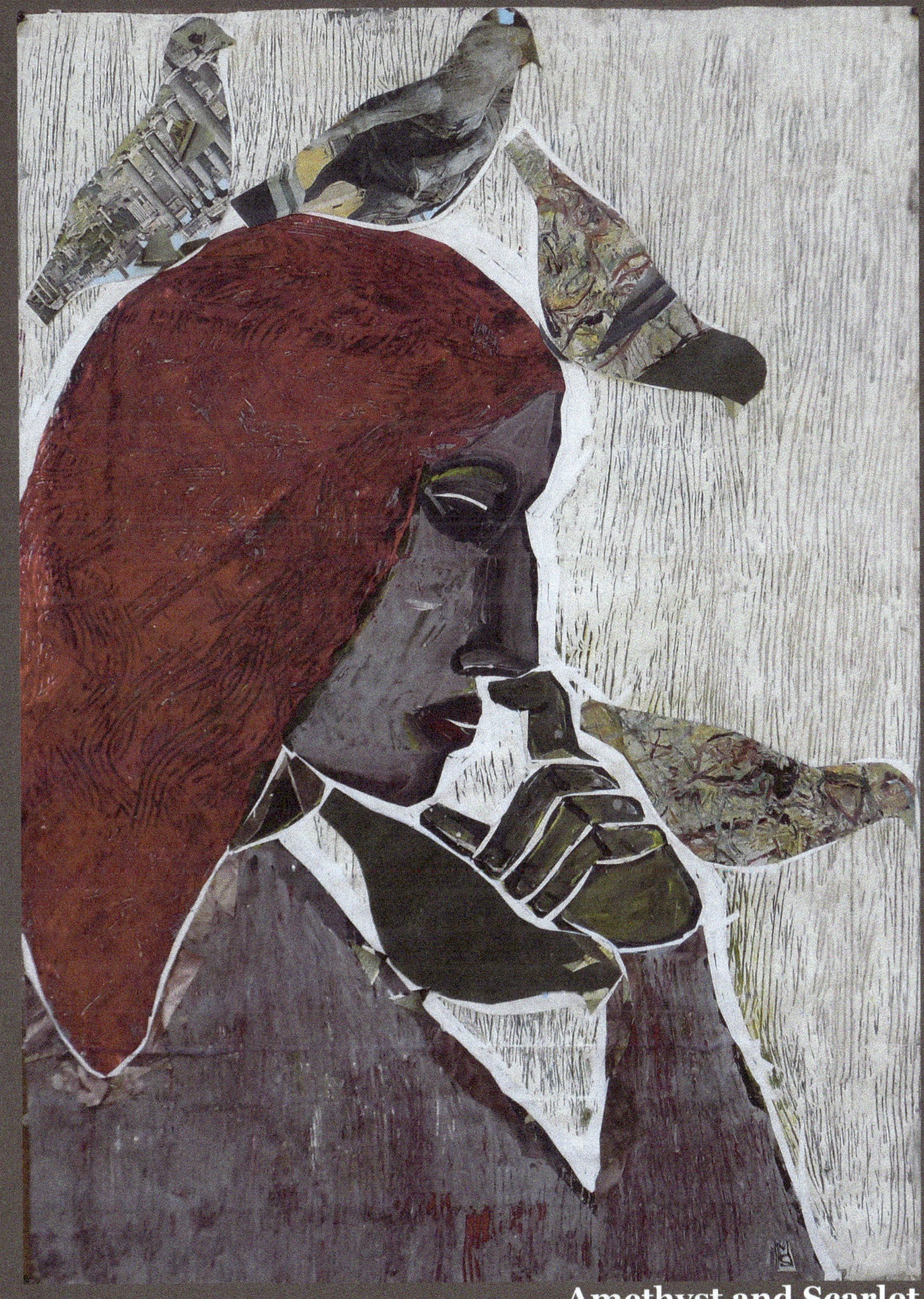

Amethyst and Scarlet
(76cm x 54cm)

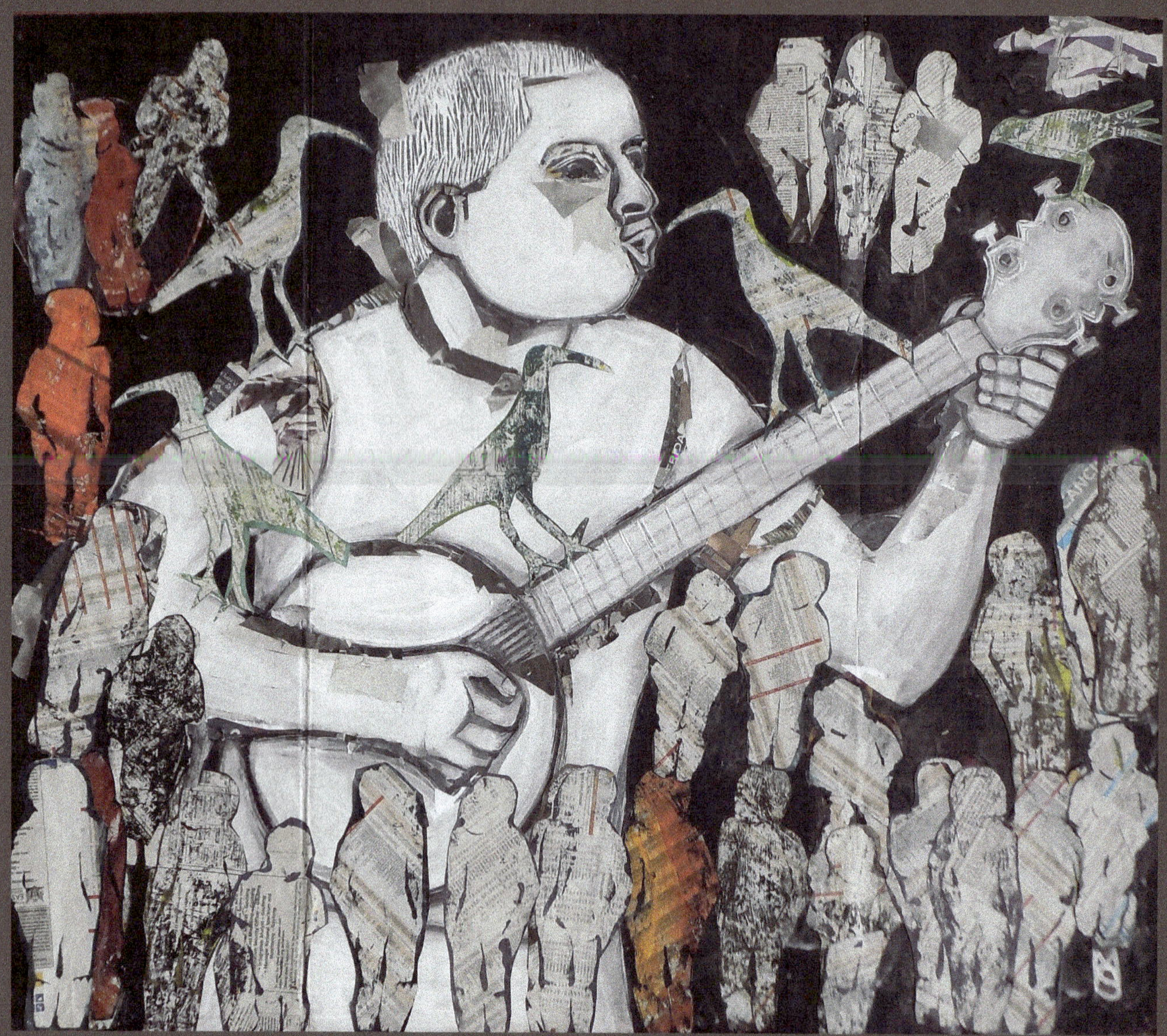

Antique Song
(83cm x 97cm)

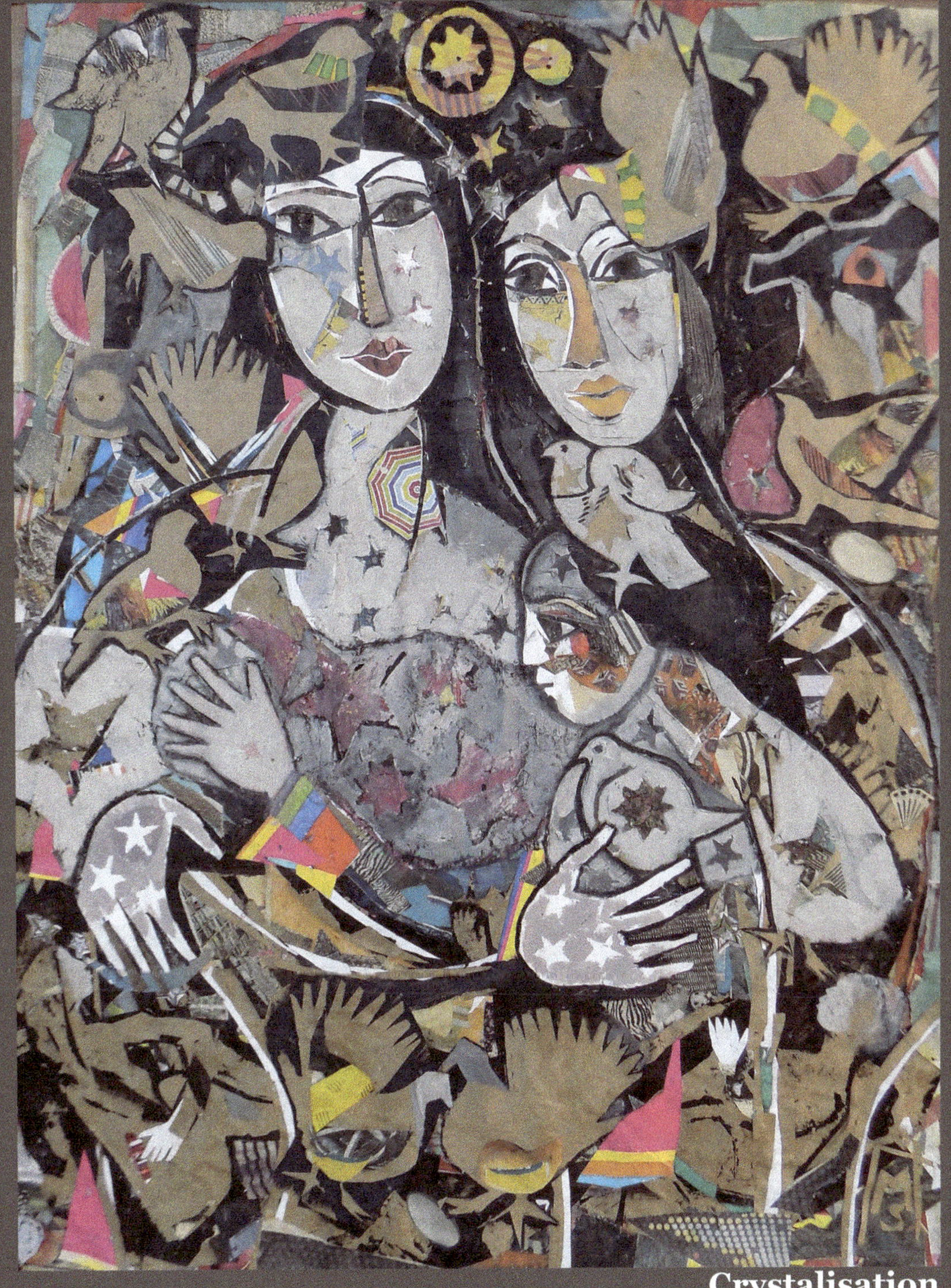

Crystalisation
(103cm x 79cm)

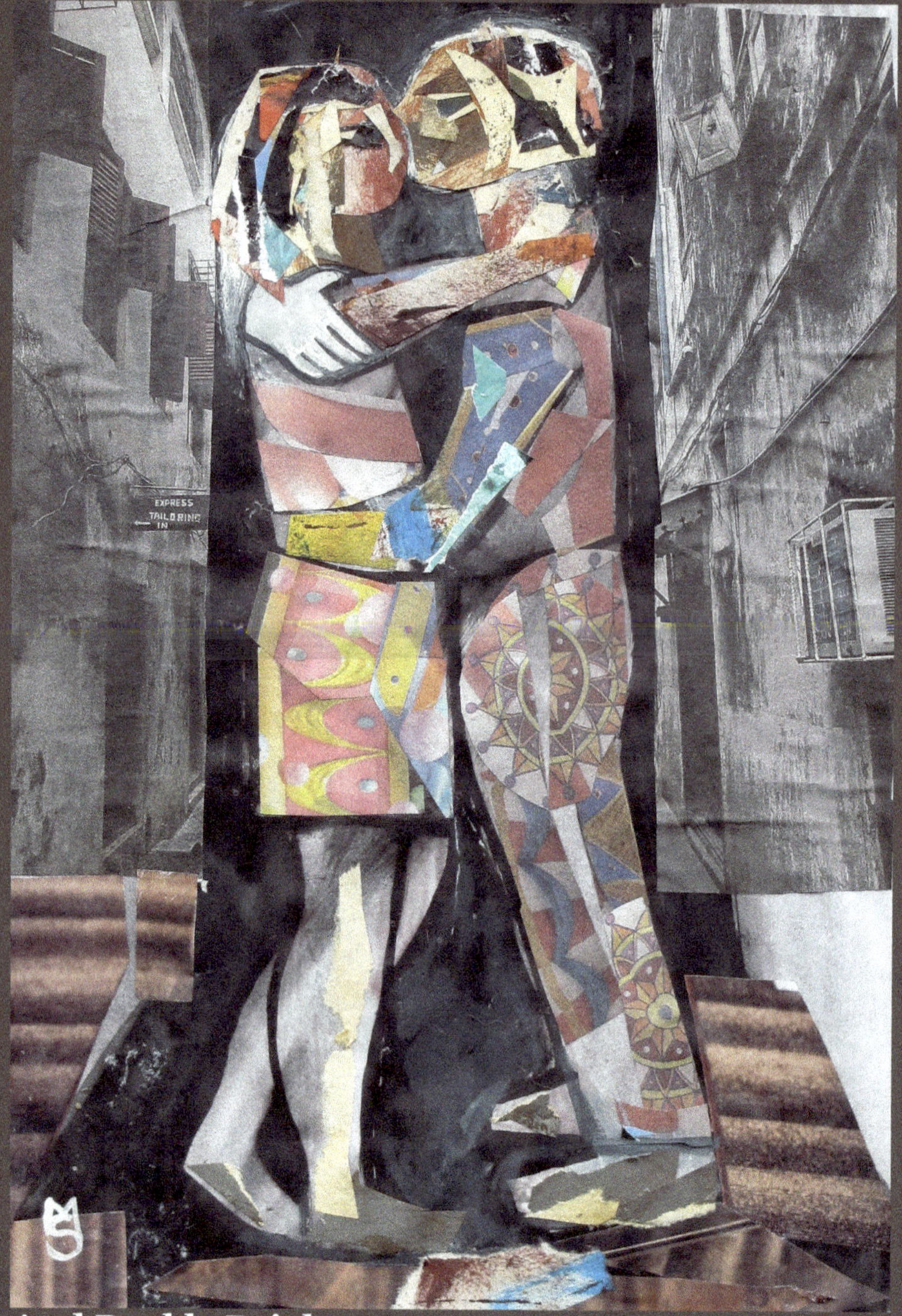

And Darkly Bright
(28cm x 20cm)

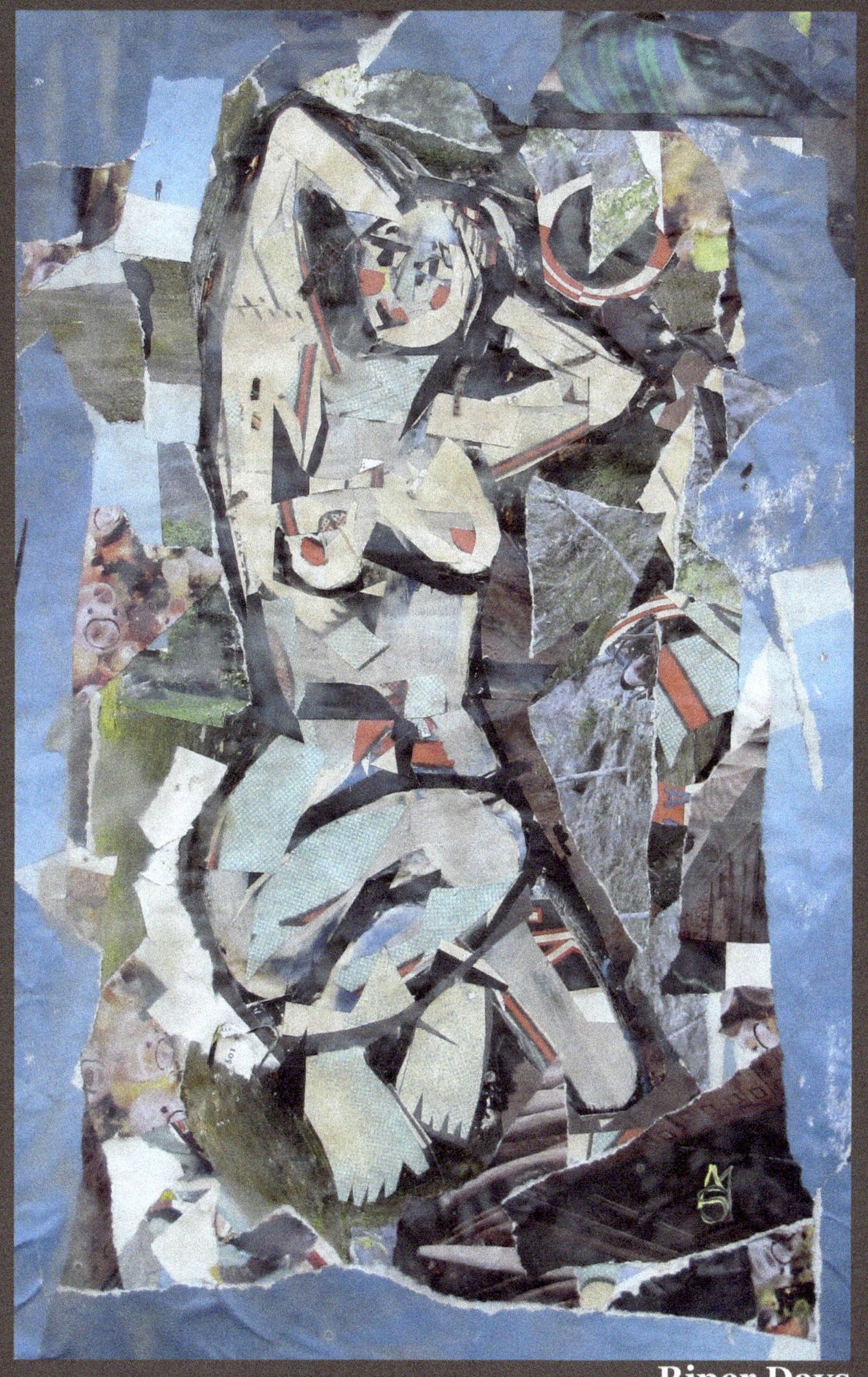

Riper Days
(43cm x 28cm)

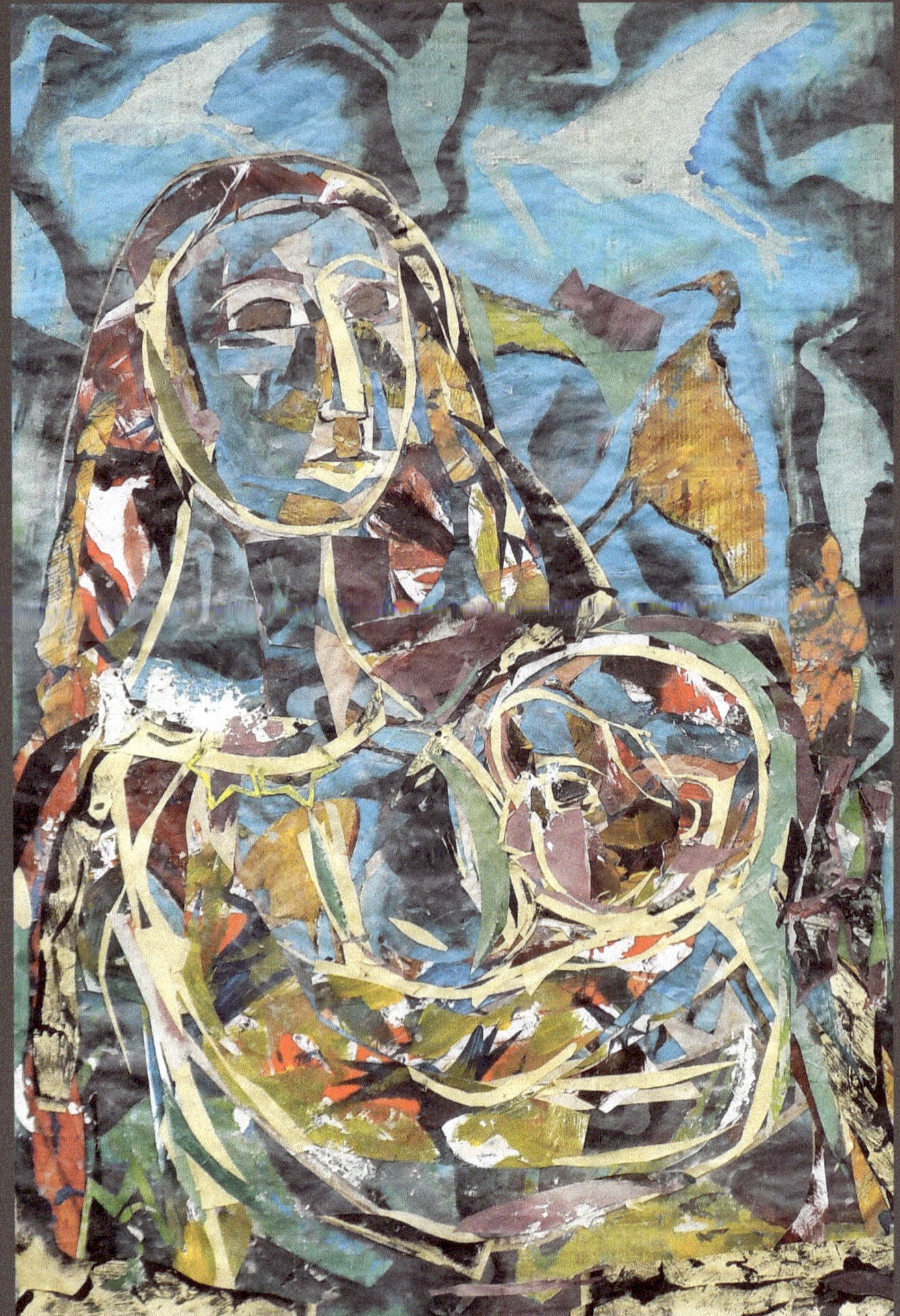

Realisation
(80cm x 56cm)
Digital version on pg.201.

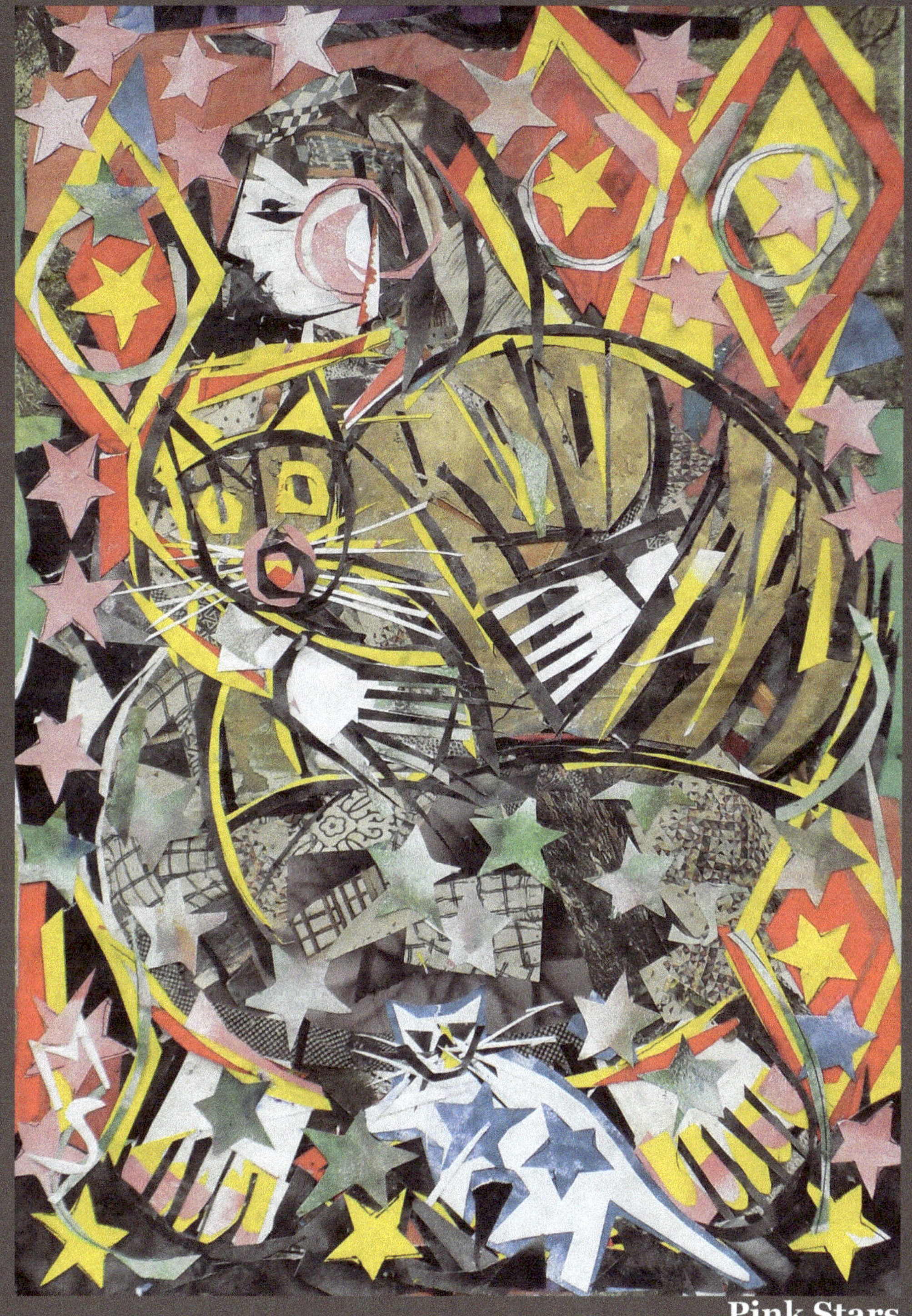

Pink Stars
(40cm x 28cm)

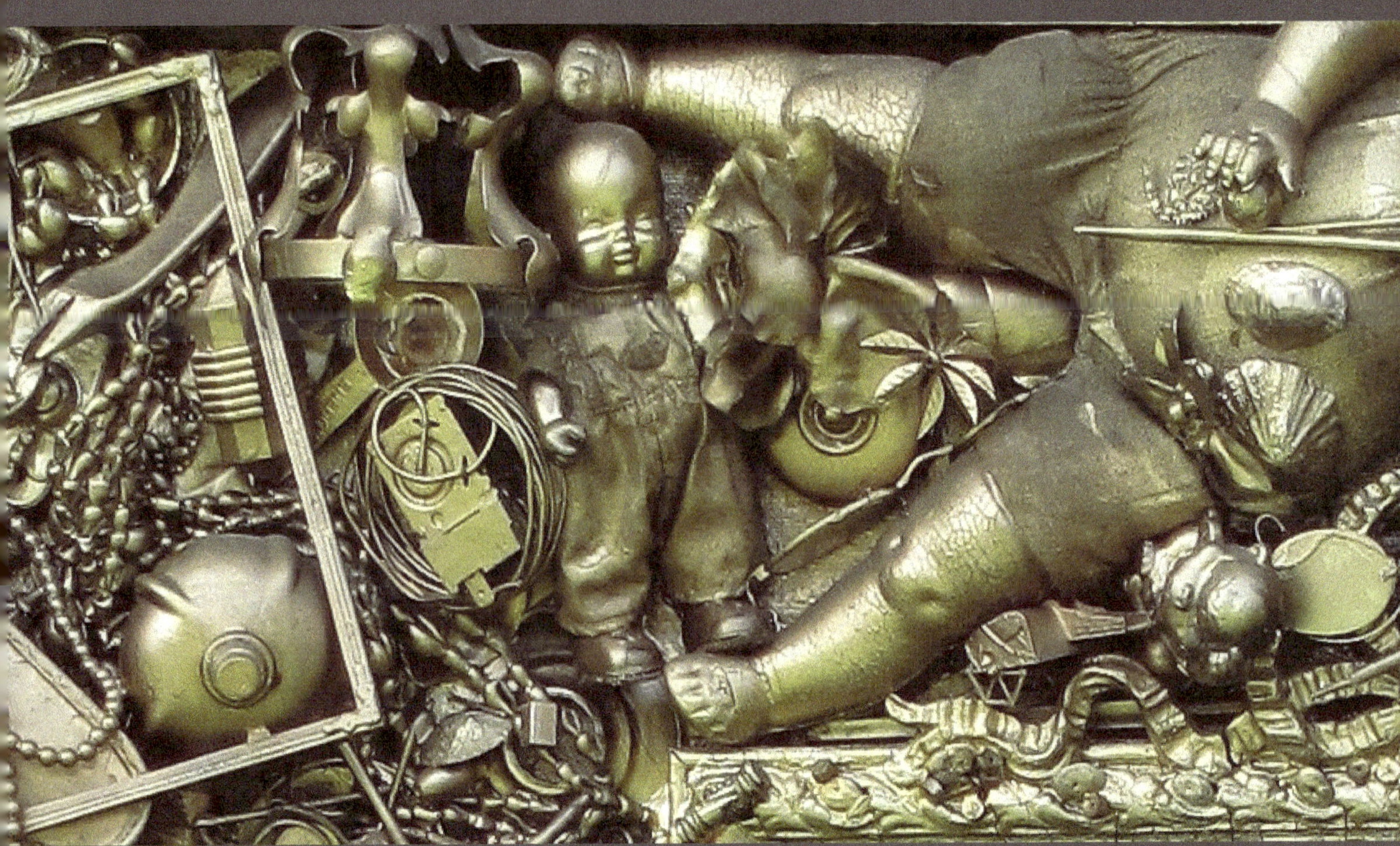

Suzie
(110cm x 110cm)

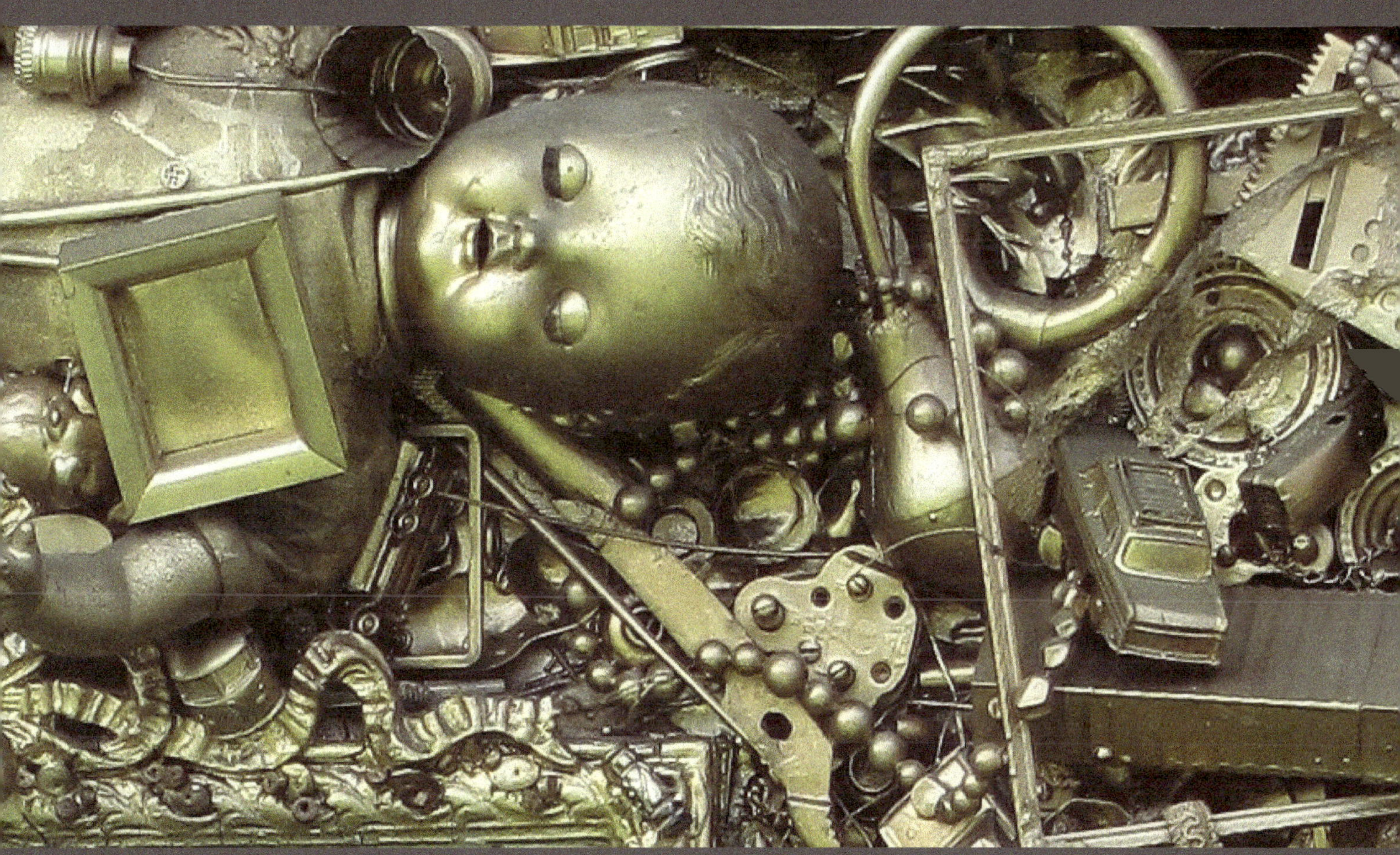

Found Objects - *Transformed*

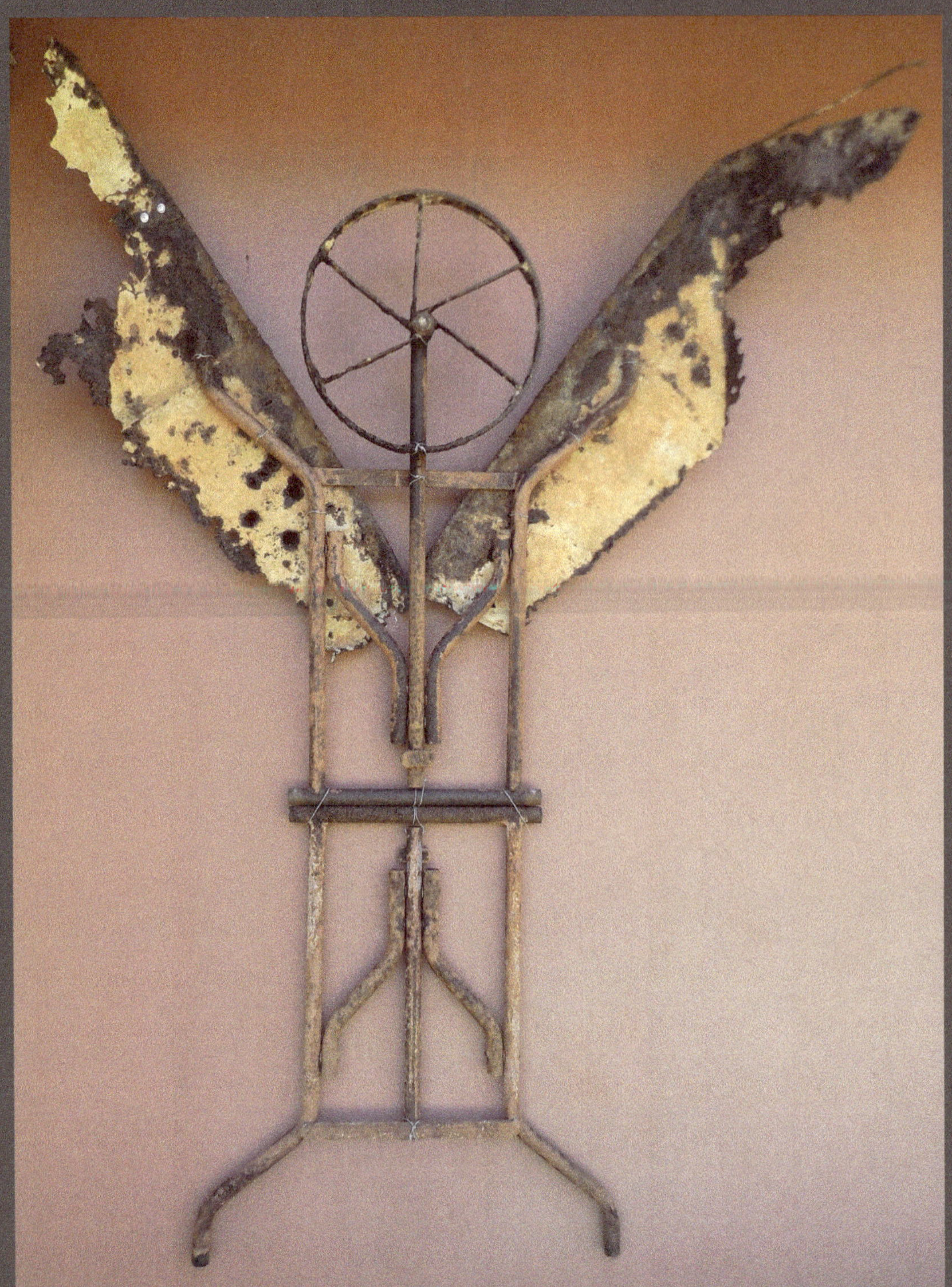

Jan's Angel
(180cm x 125cm)

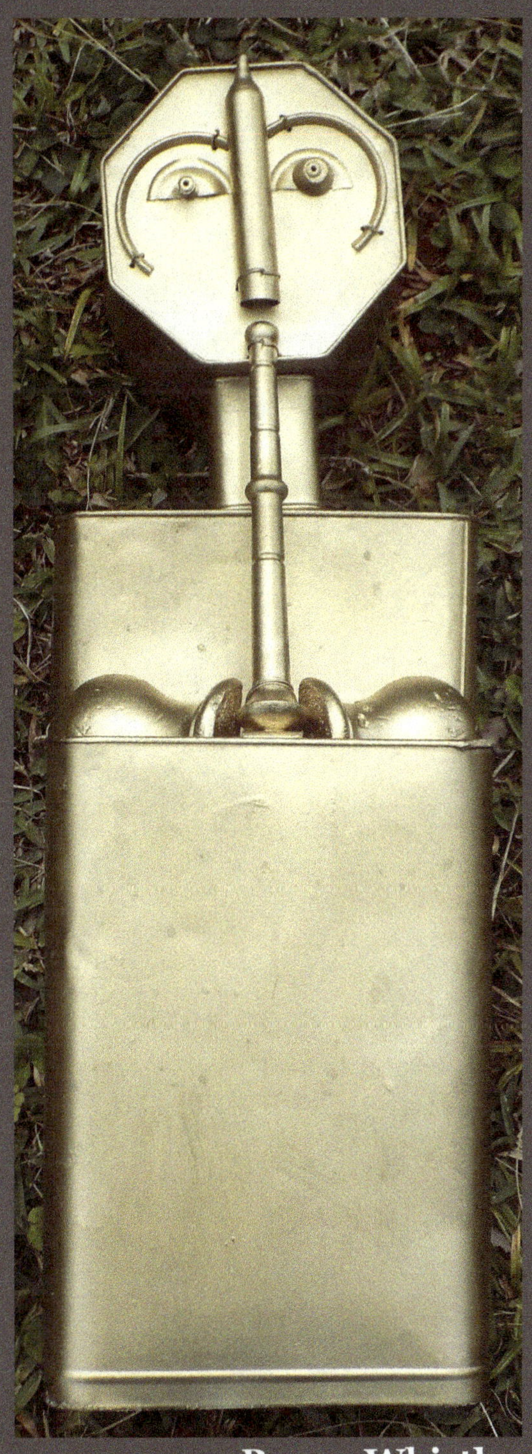

Penny Whistler
(51cm x 17cm)

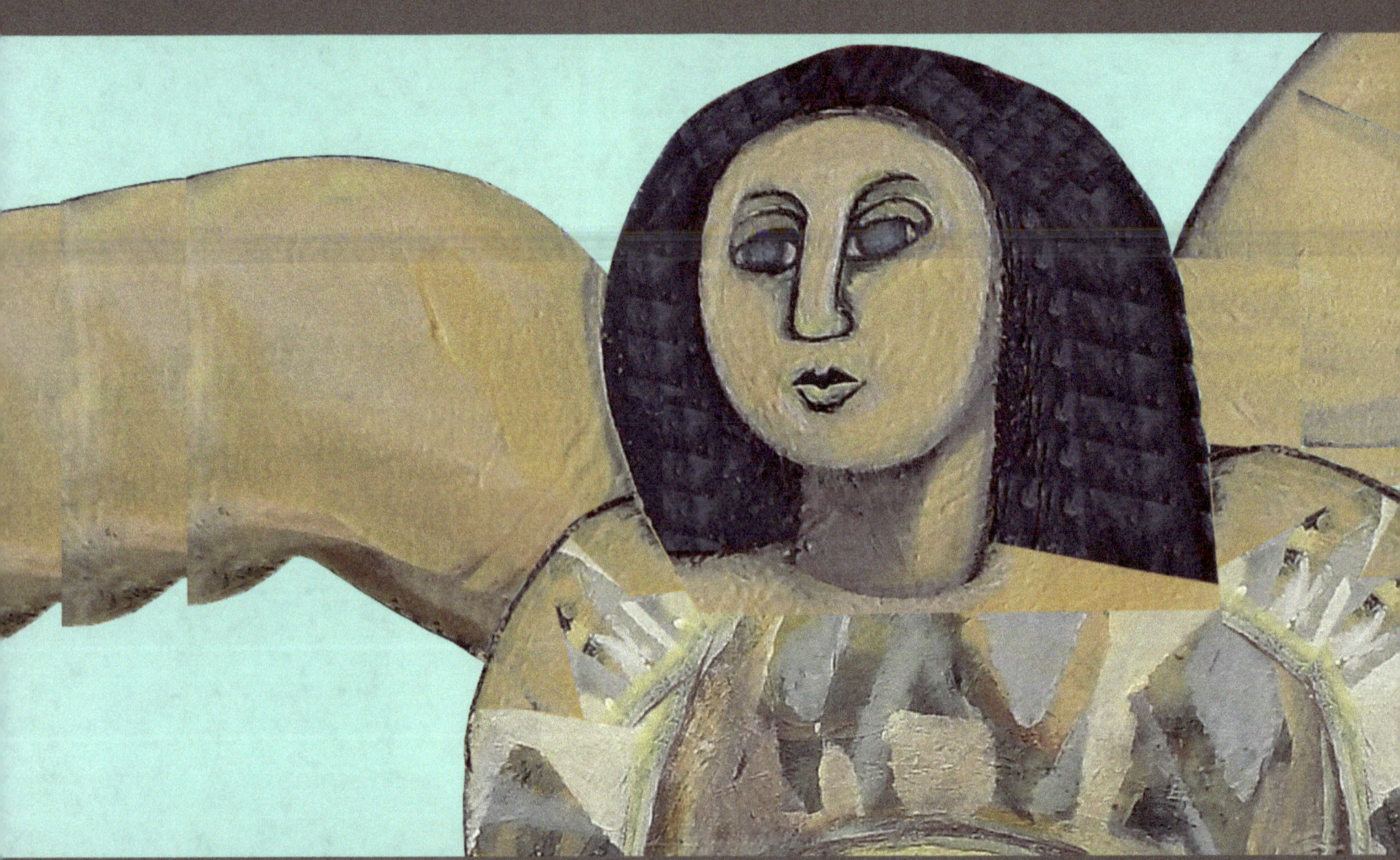

Angelica
(60cm x 110cm)
Full image on pg.202.

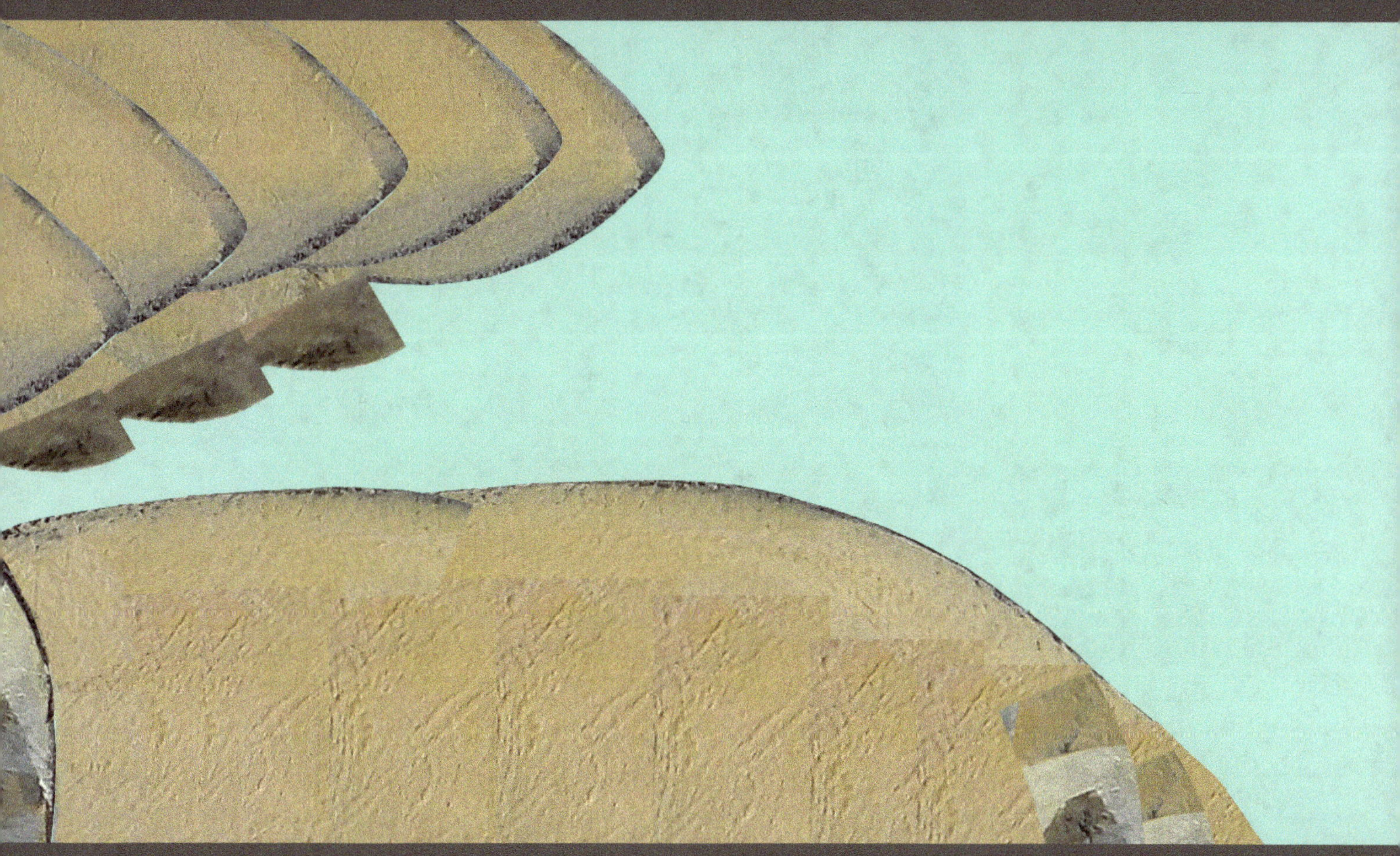

Digital

Digital Art - Merging, connecting re-imagining

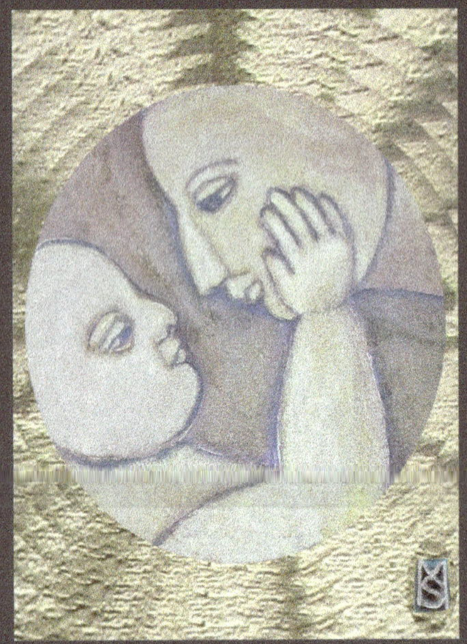

Digital art for me is a combining and connecting of past paintings into a newly-merged form . . . a redoing in part, a new harmonizing . . . into digital painting . . . to fuse and blend . . . a re-seeing . . . integration. . . from a new perspective . . .

Sepia Madonna
(130cm x 75cm)

A wounded finger frustratingly prevented me temporarily from completing a painting. My husband Barry responded by generously offering to photograph this painting and to "experimentally"- complete it - (as an interim solution!) in a digital format. We used a freely distributed open-source programme, called GIMP, offering many possibilities, a process which immediately prompted a beckoning response in me - an alternative mode of picture-making , discovering new ways to design and combine. With Barry's Gimp-guidance this became a "digital dueting" - a collaborative recycling, digitally adapting images from my original art -pieces - thus re-inventing - re-evaluating - a re-appraising and re-examining- a serendipitous stumble down this exciting and inspiring digital Rabbit-hole.

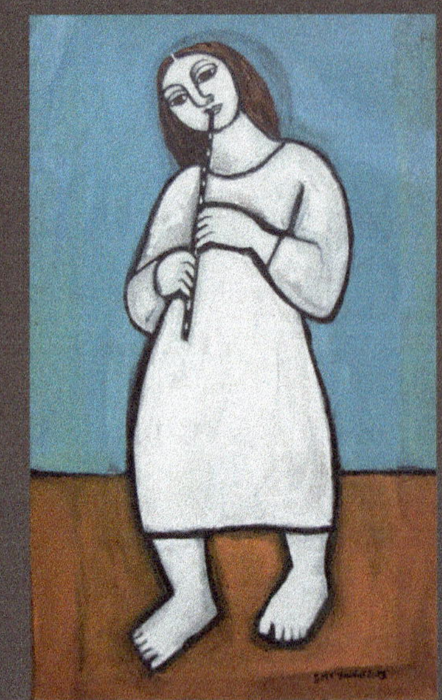

Music Maker
(125cm x 75cm)
Original painting used for digital art on next page.

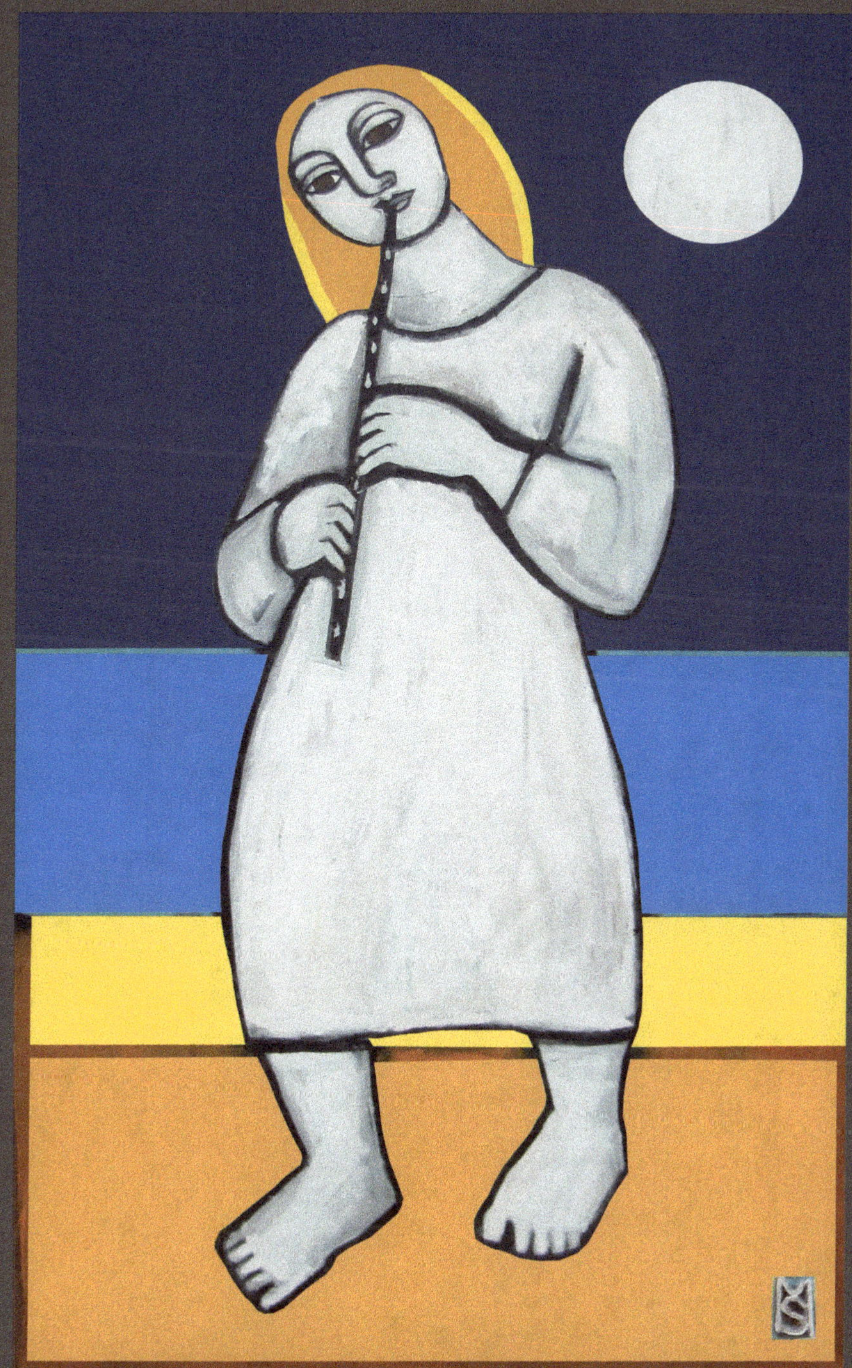

Music Maker
(125cm x 75cm)
Digital version created from original painting on previous page.

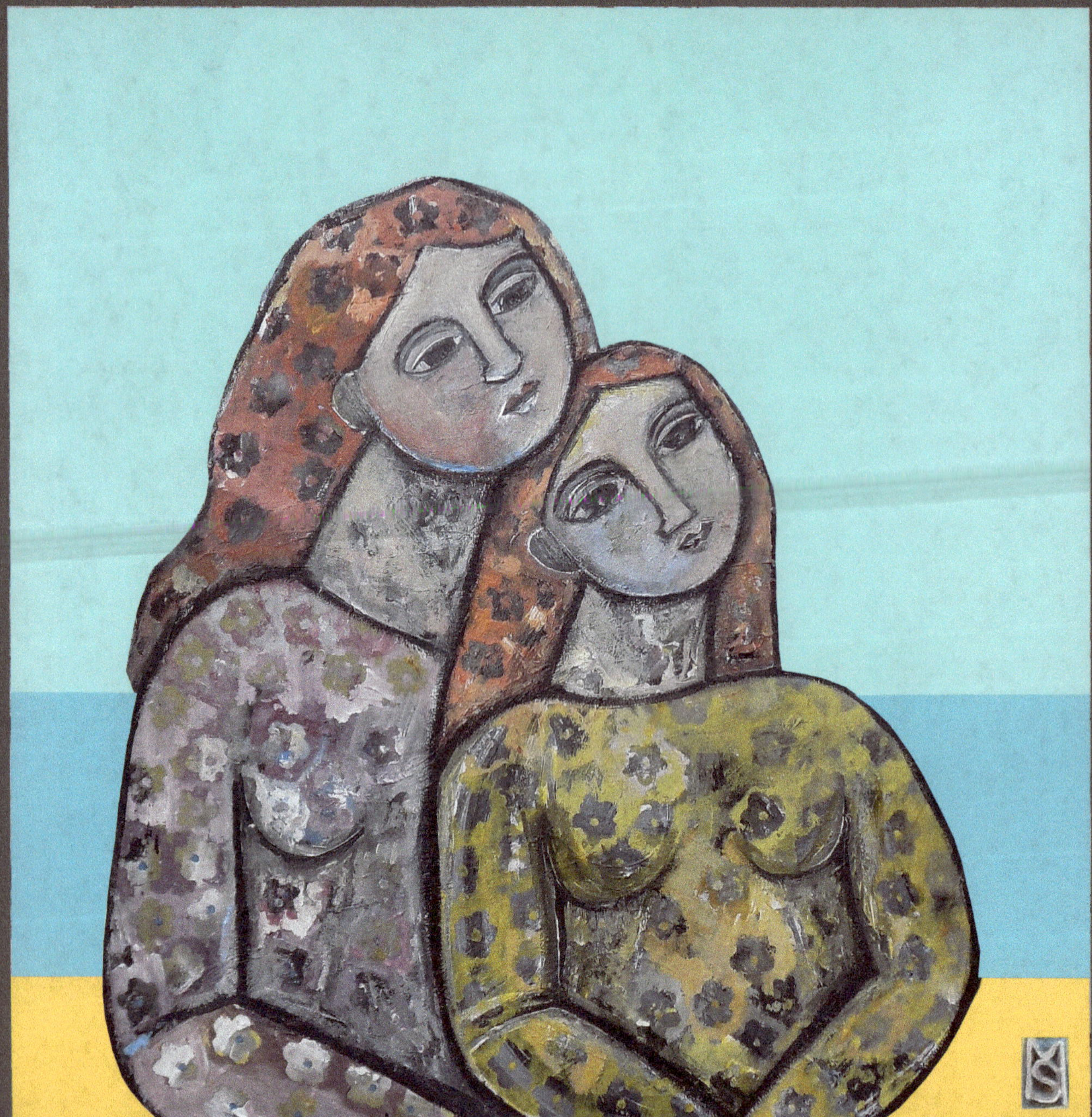

Flower Girls
(78cm x 78cm)

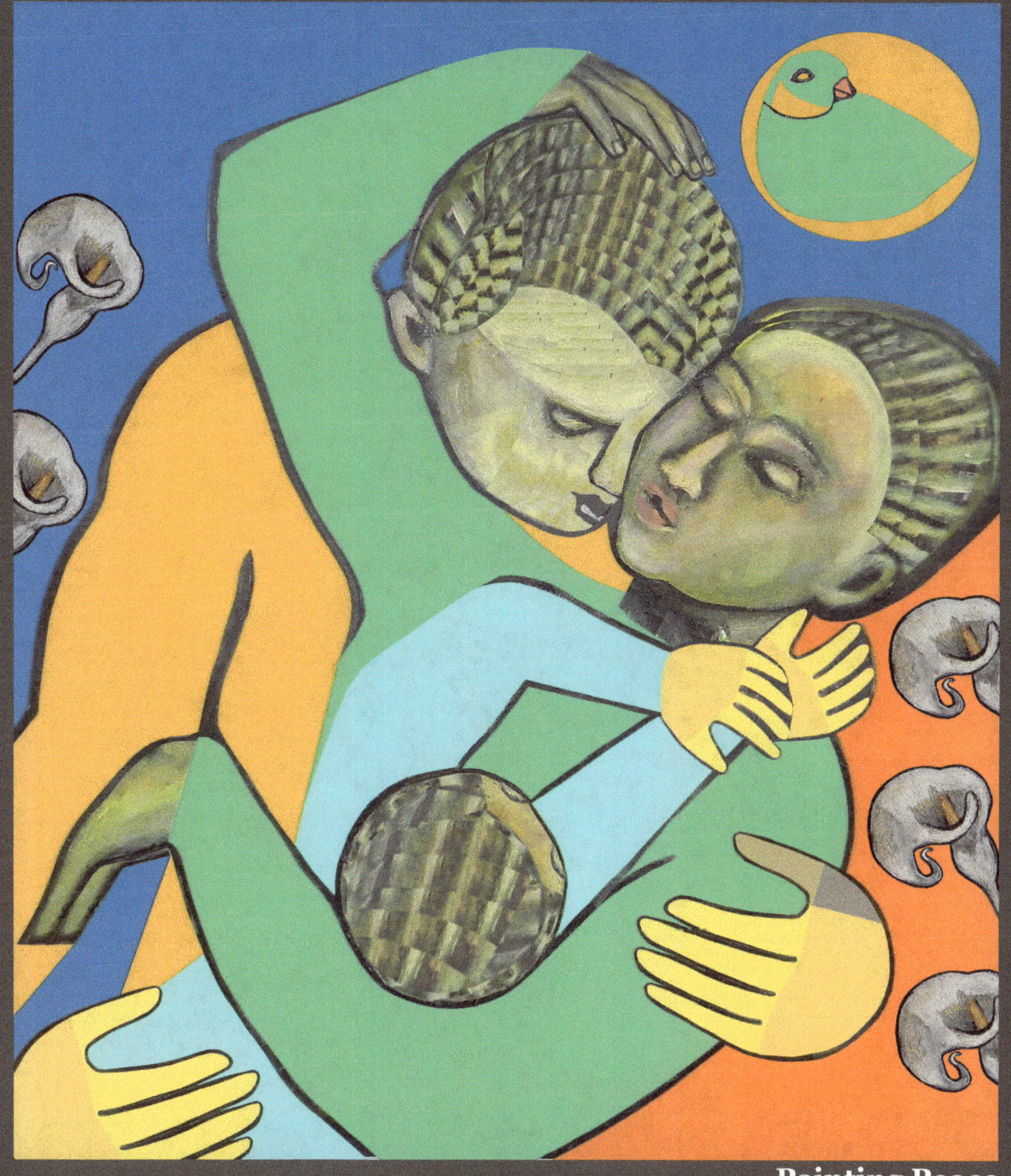

Painting Peace
(79cm x 70cm)

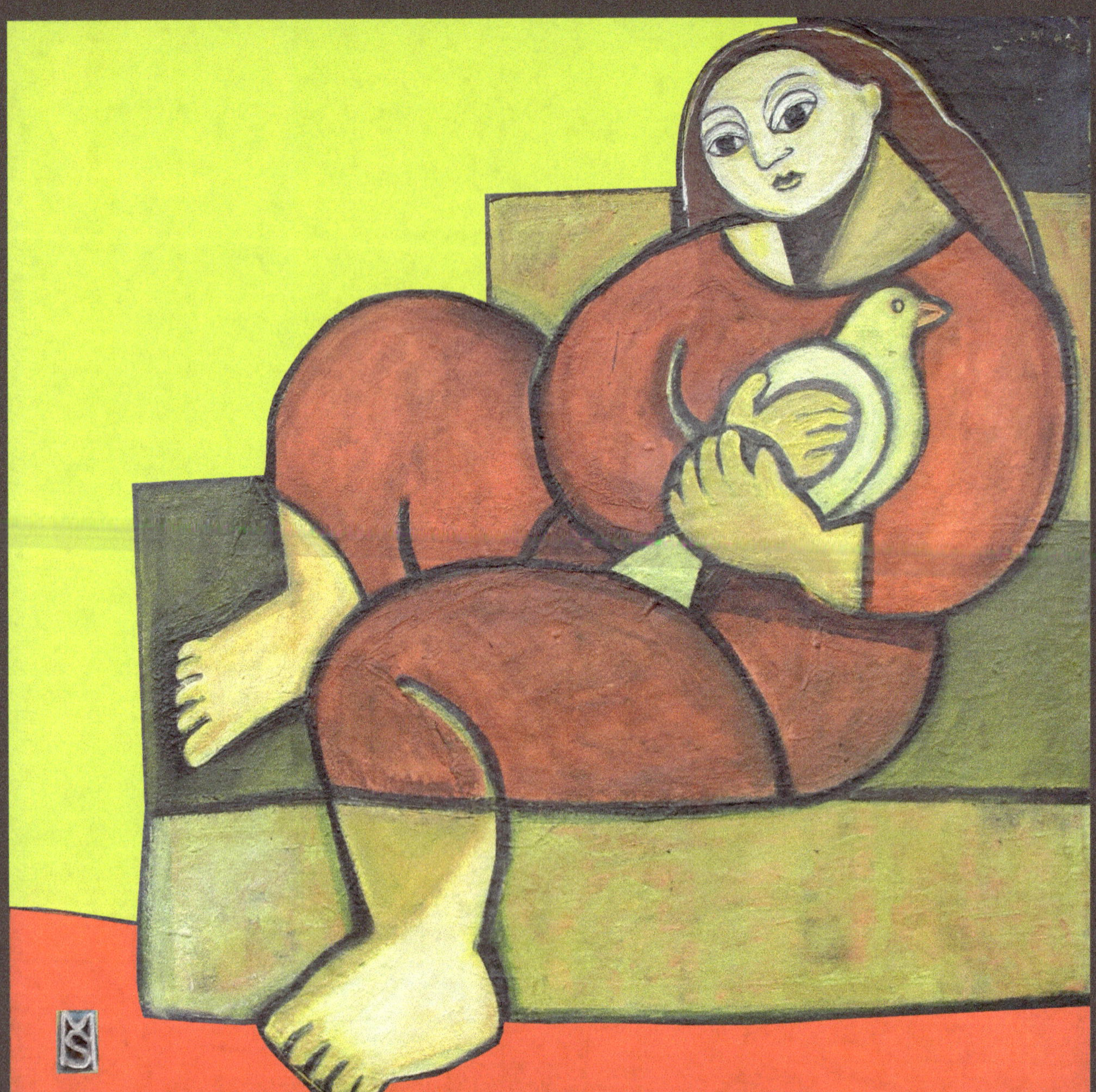

Gentle Genesis
(70cm x 70cm)
Original painting on pg.78.

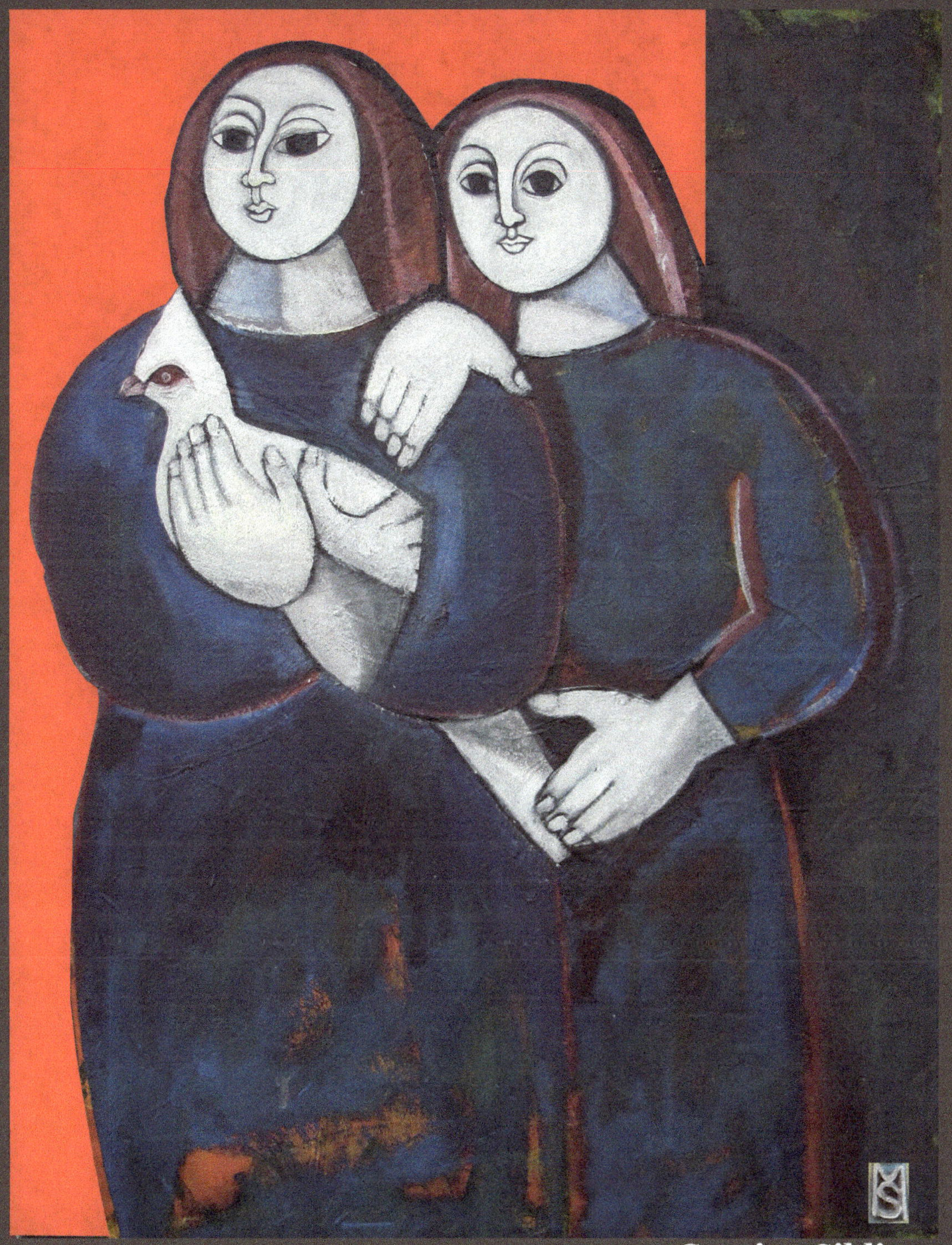

Gentian Siblings
(95cm x 75cm)
Original painting on pg.36.

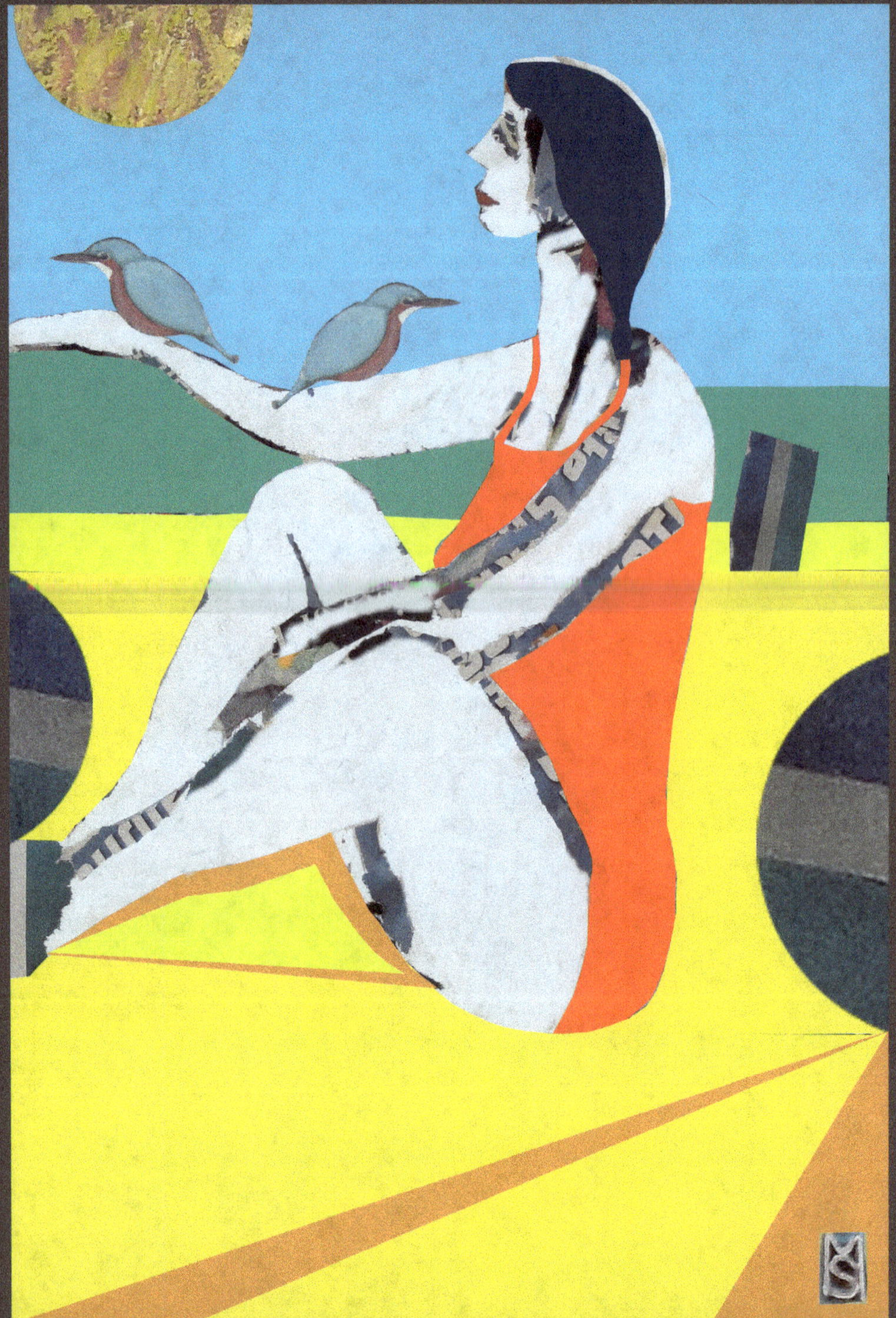

Red Lipped Lady
(40cm x 25cm)

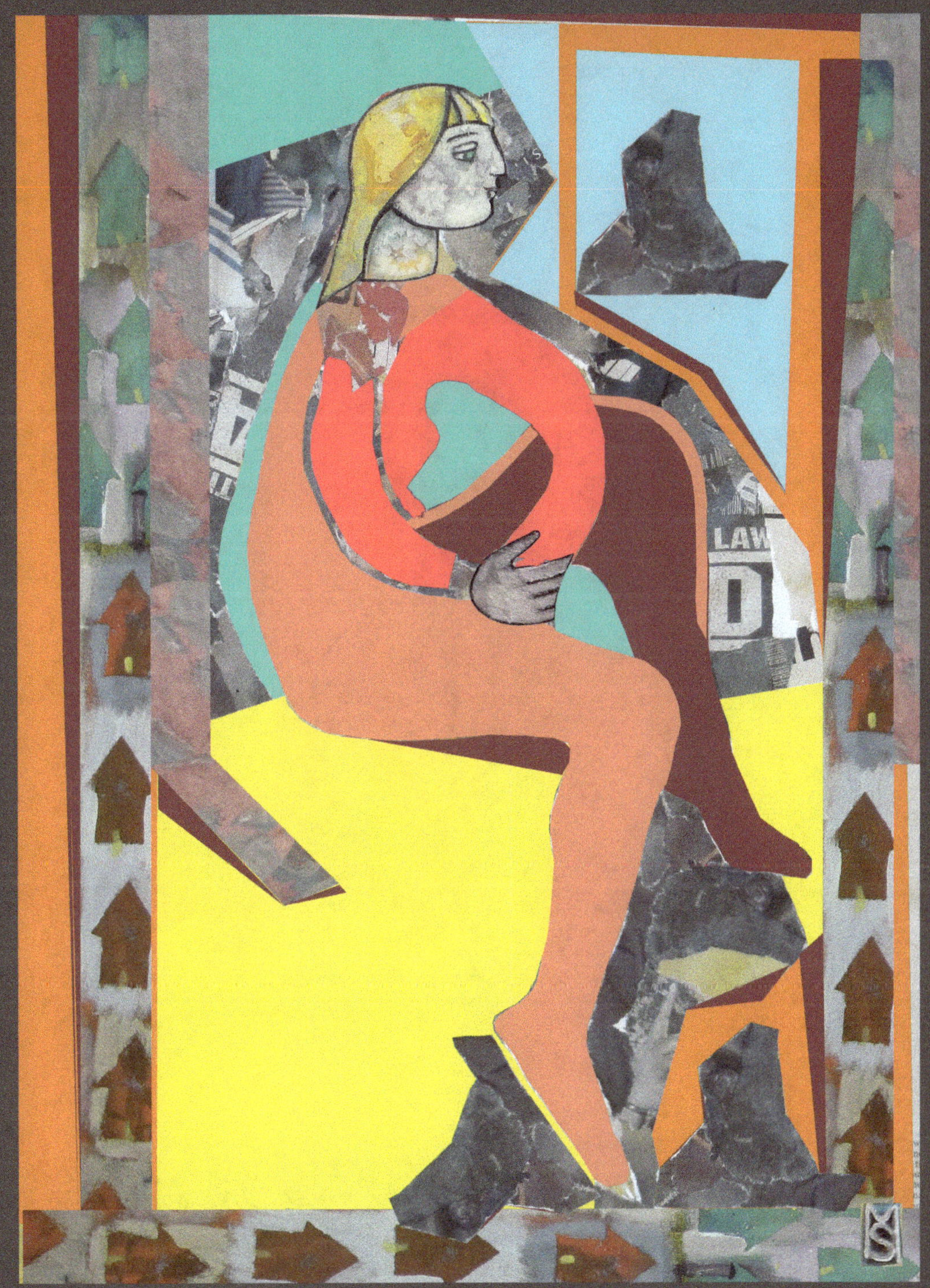

Yellow Lady
(40cm x 25cm)

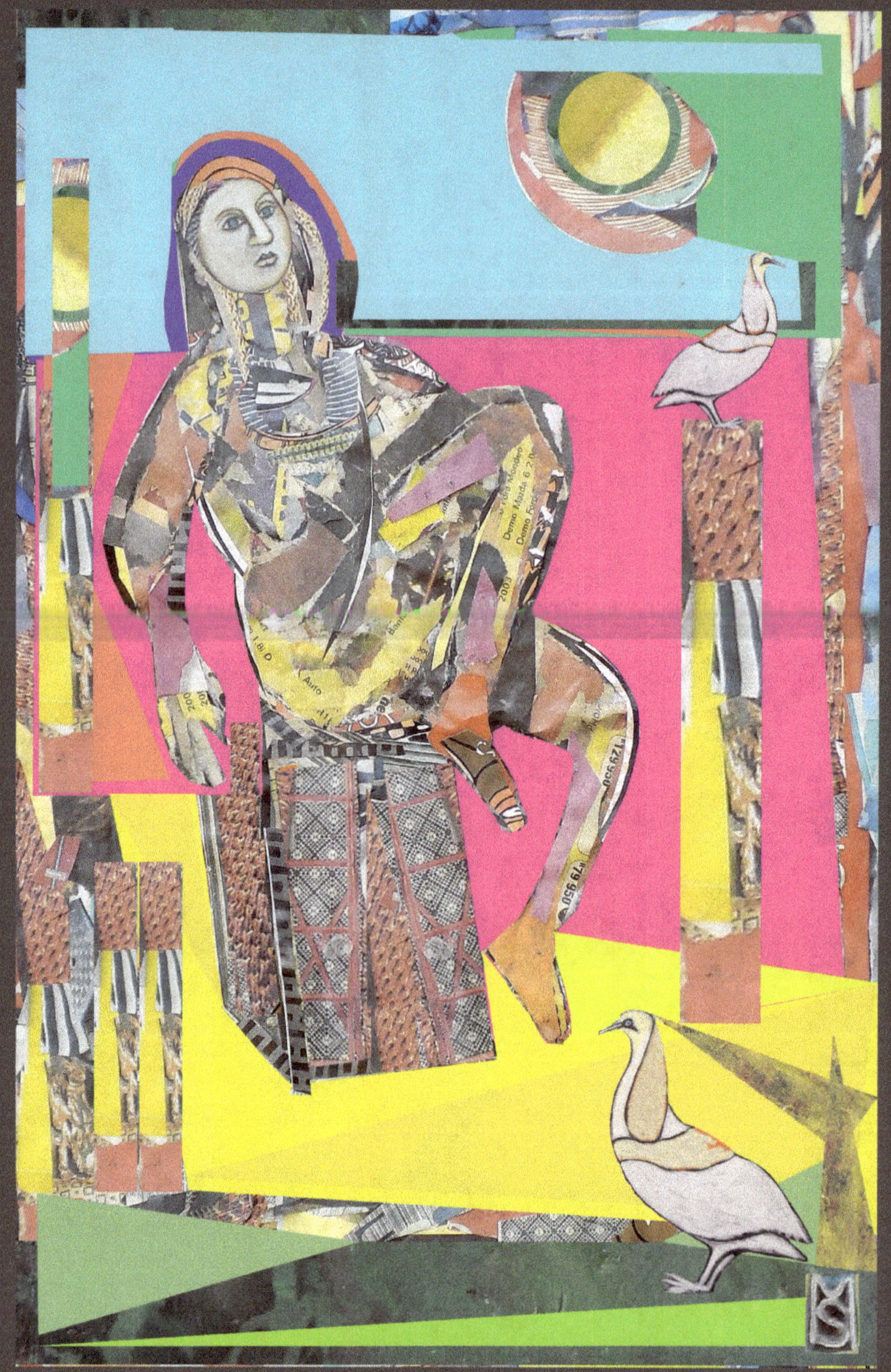

Liz Collage
(45cm x 30cm)

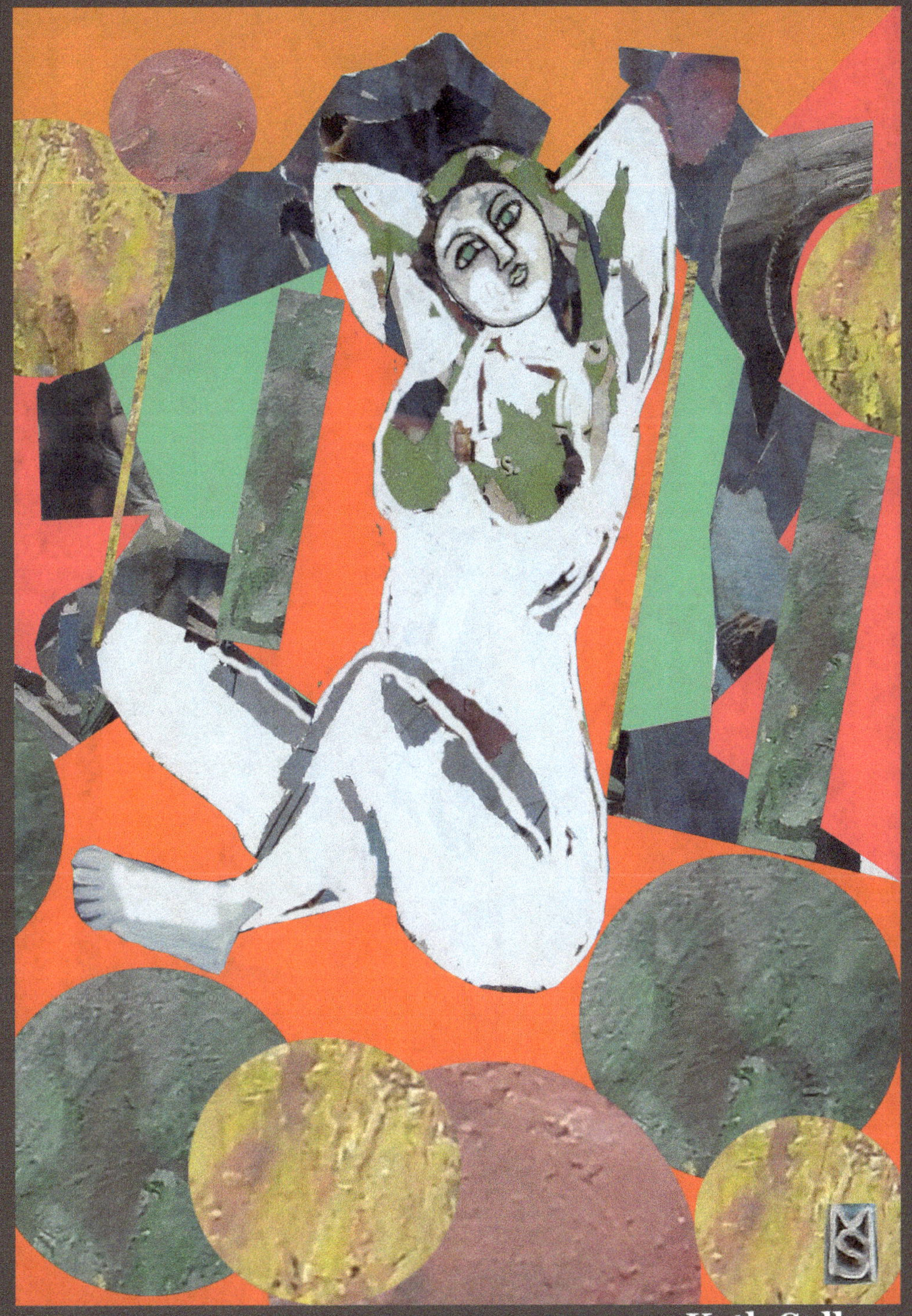

Kath Collage
(45cm x 30cm)

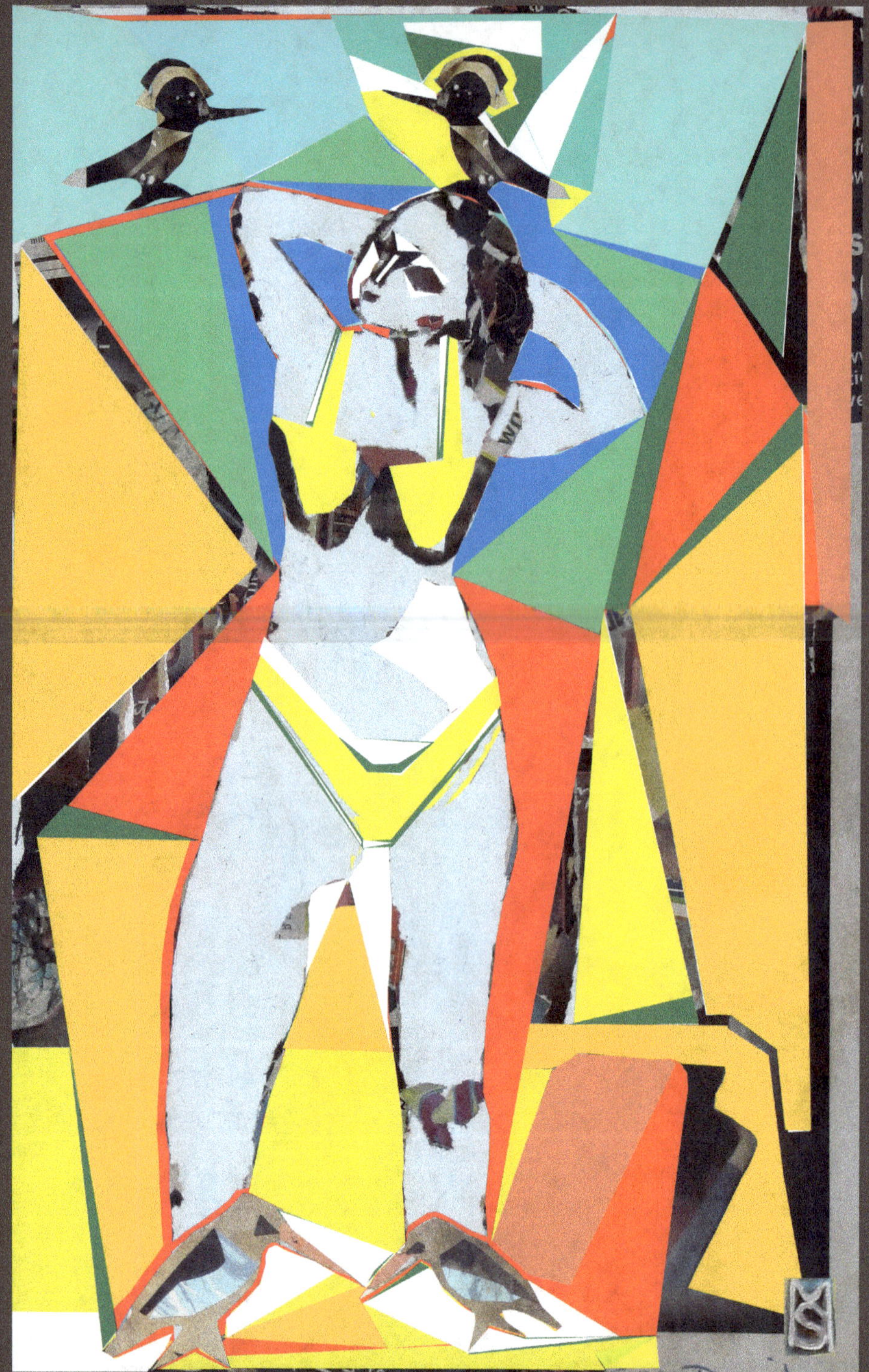

Kirsten
(40cm x 25cm)

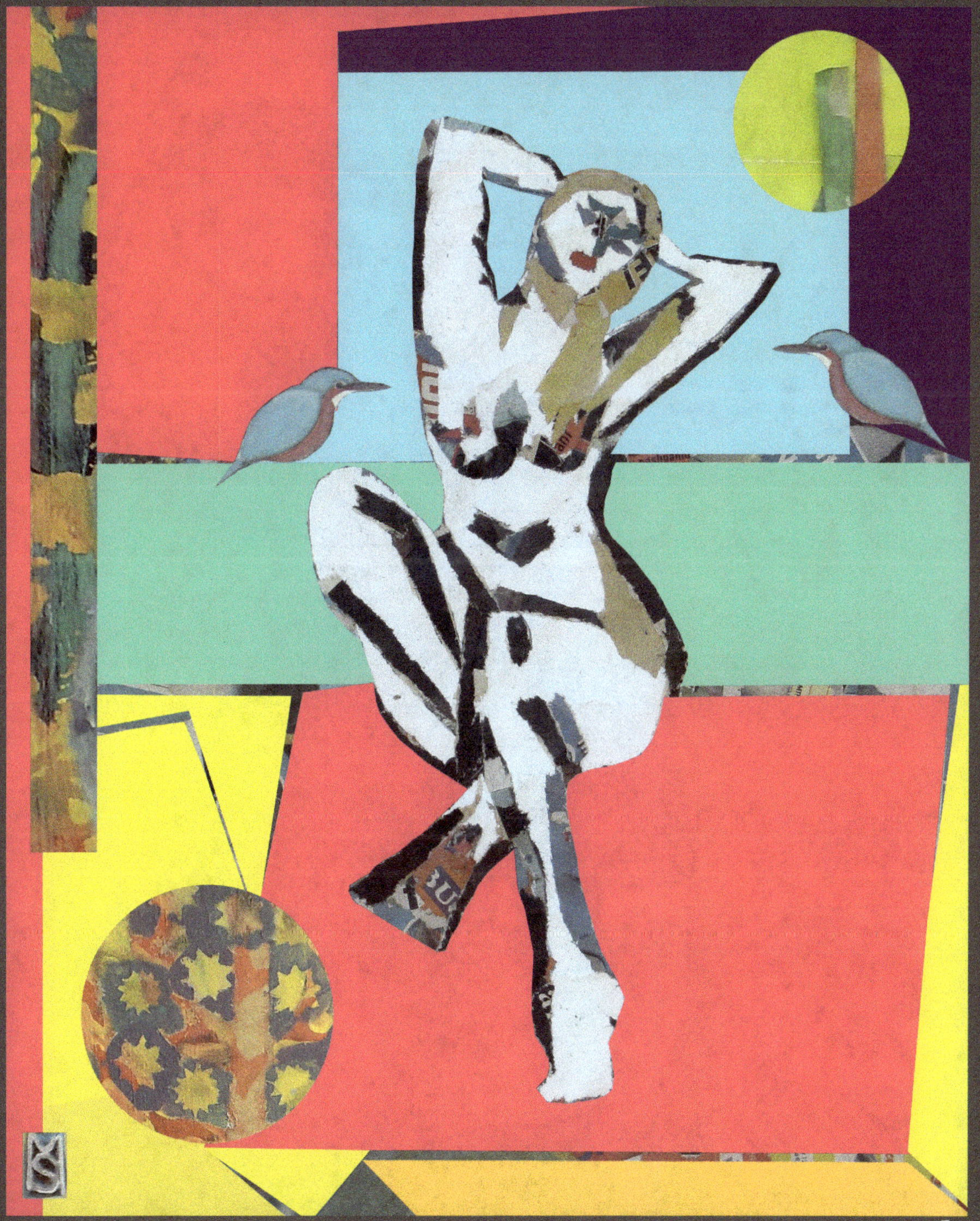

Intro Nude
(40cm x 25cm)

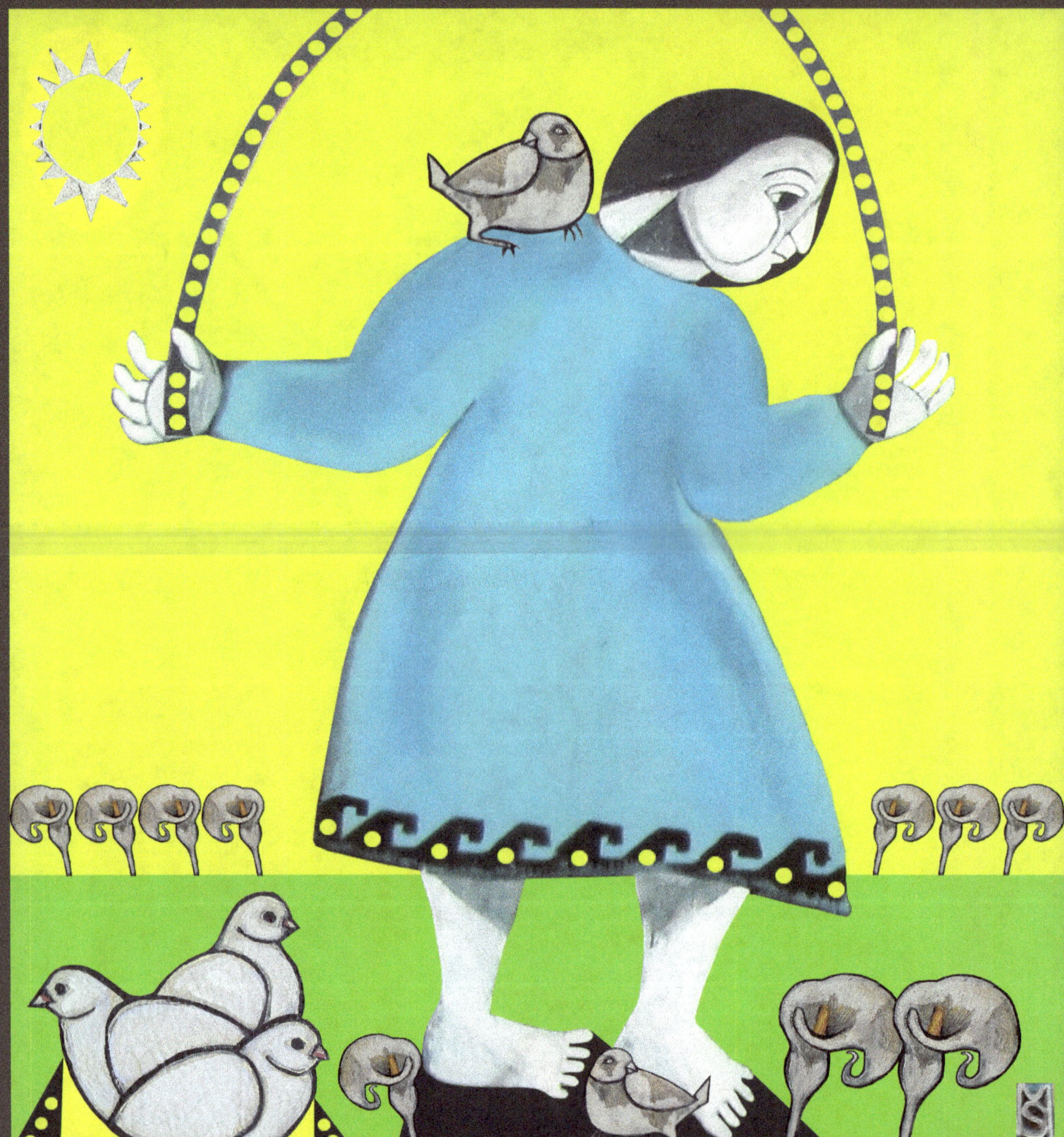

Turquoise Tunic 1
(40cm x 37cm)
Extraction from original painting on pp.7-8.

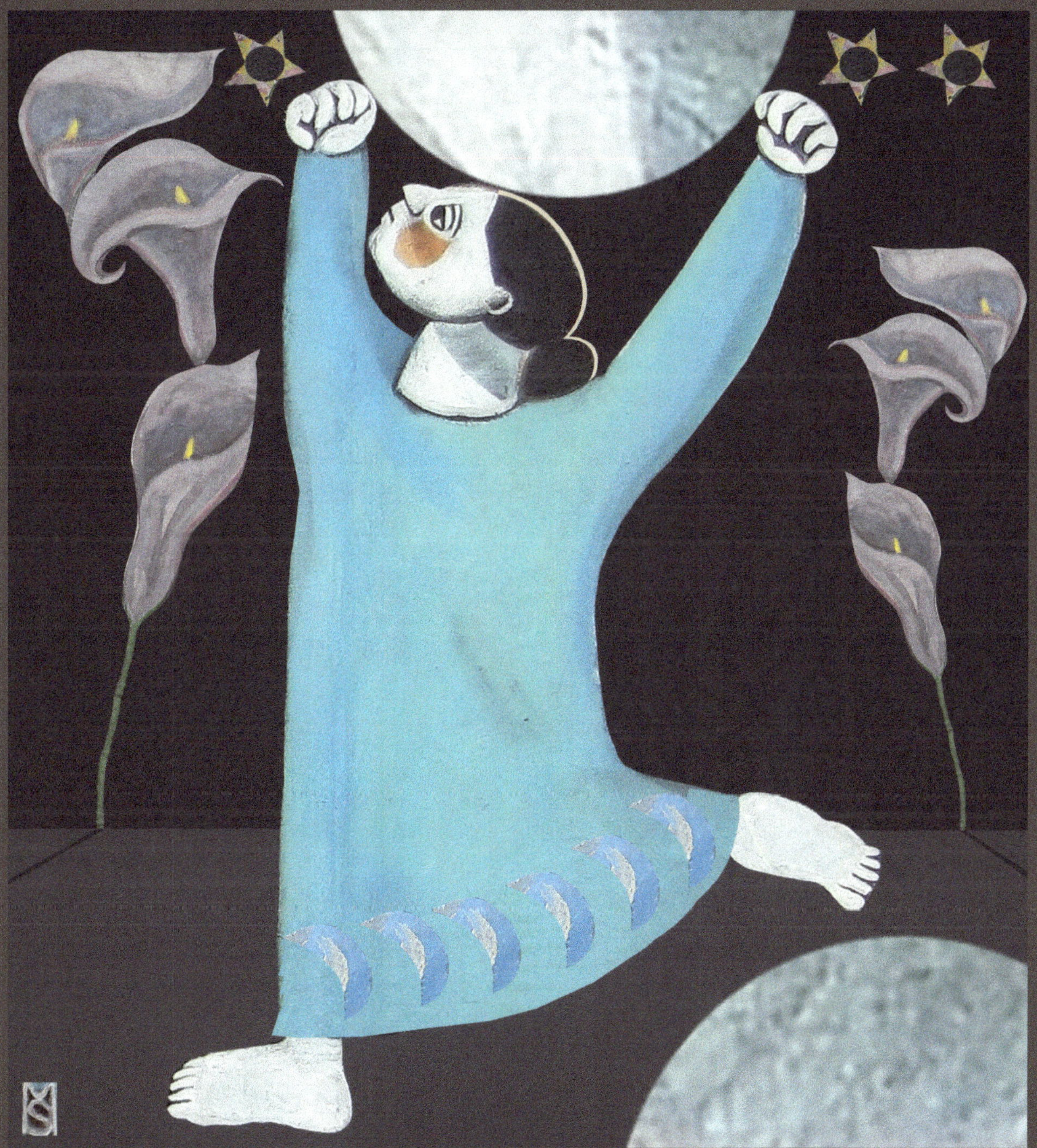

Turquoise Tunic 2
(40cm x 37cm)
Extraction from original painting on pp.7-8.

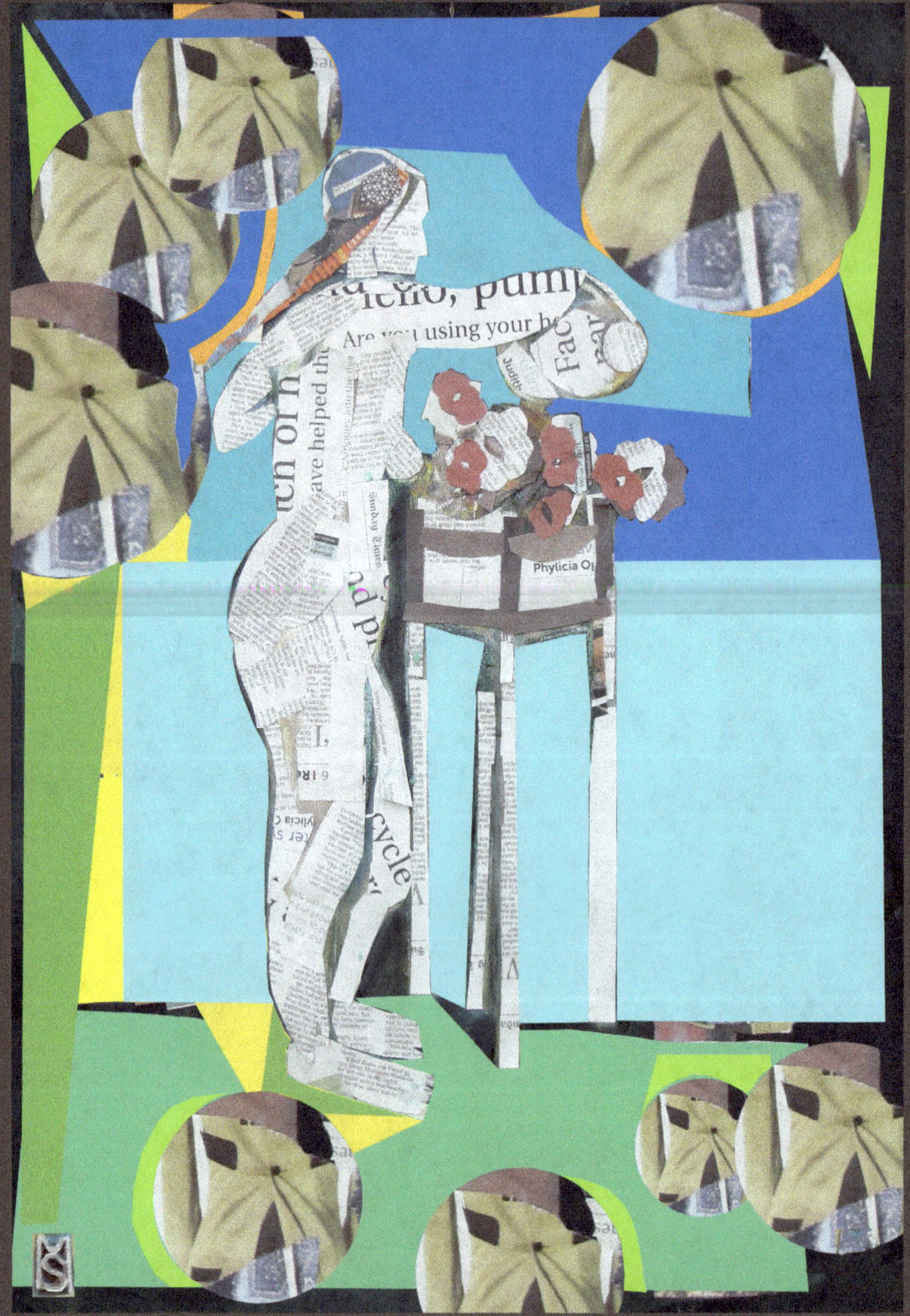

Cycles
(65cm x 45cm)

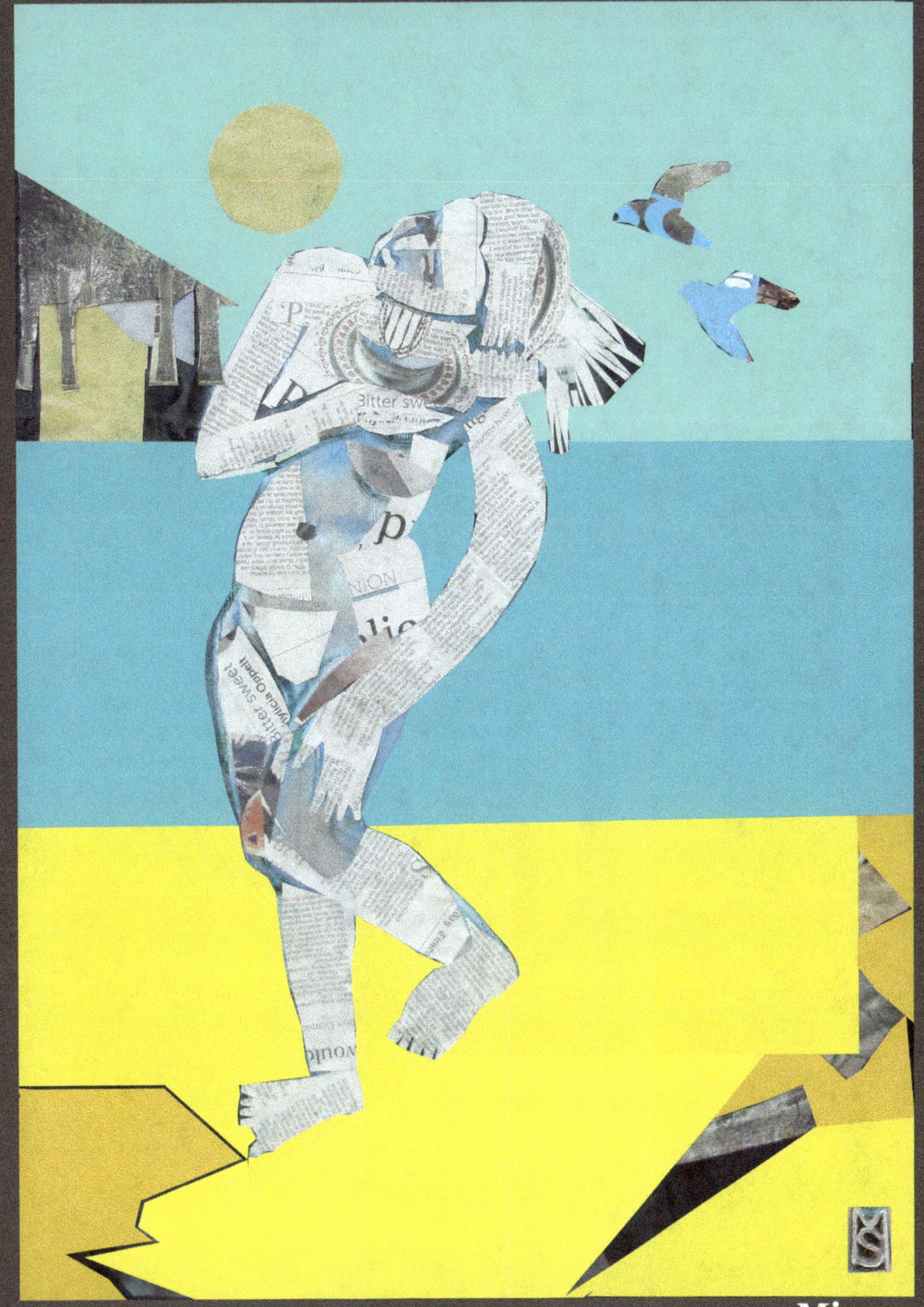

Mirage
(66cm x 46cm)

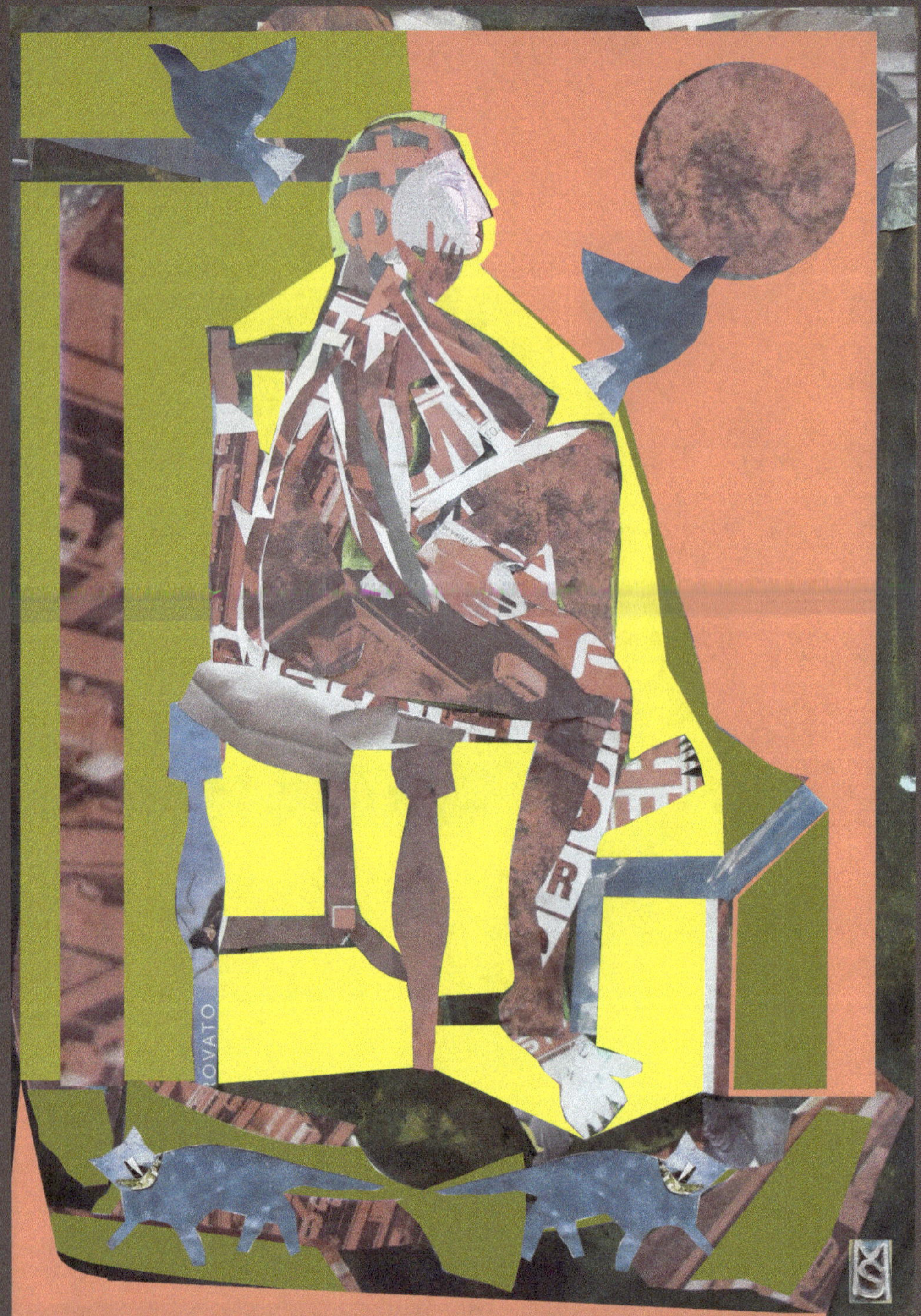

Valid
(65cm x 45cm)

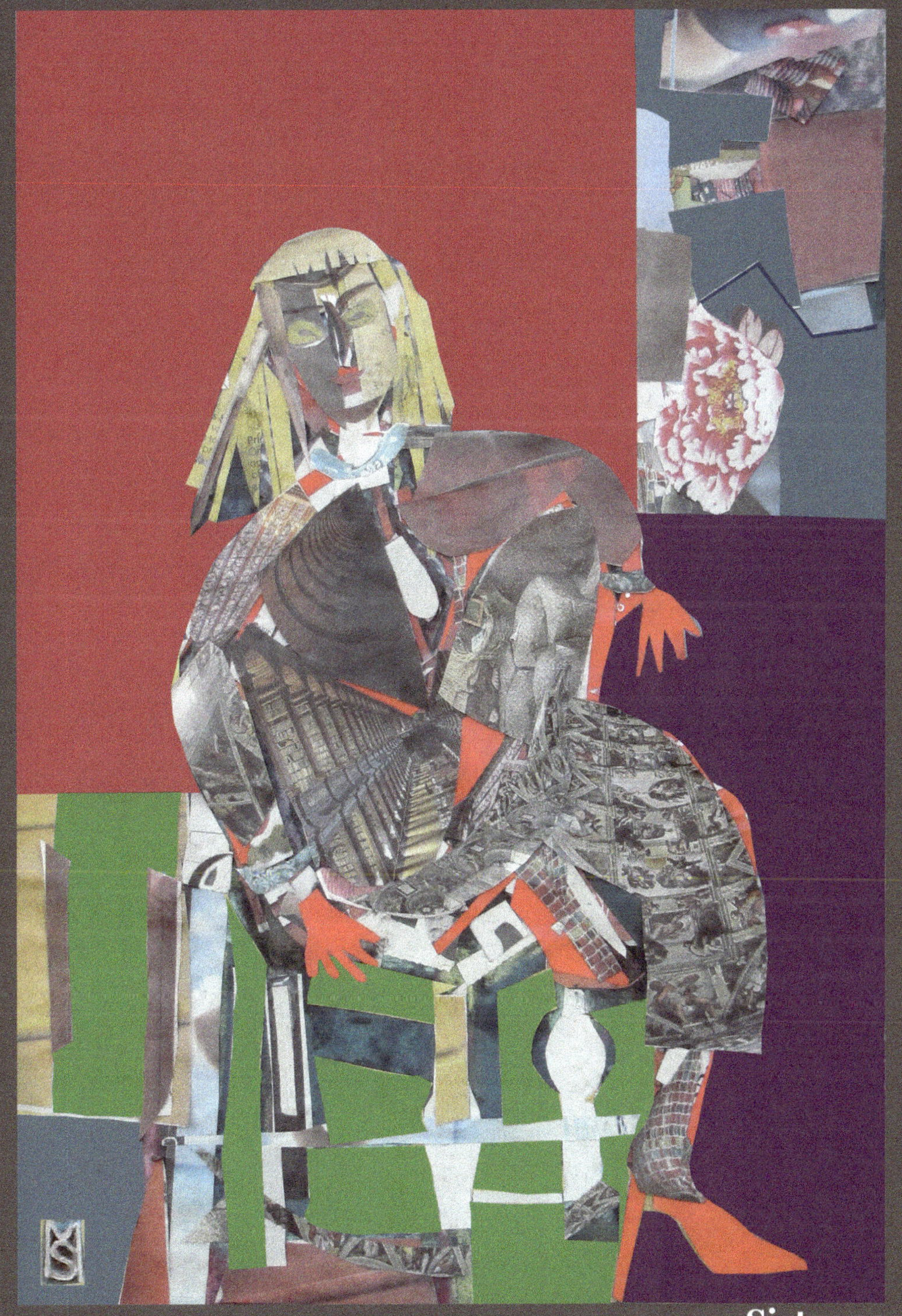

Sisteena
(48cm x 34cm)

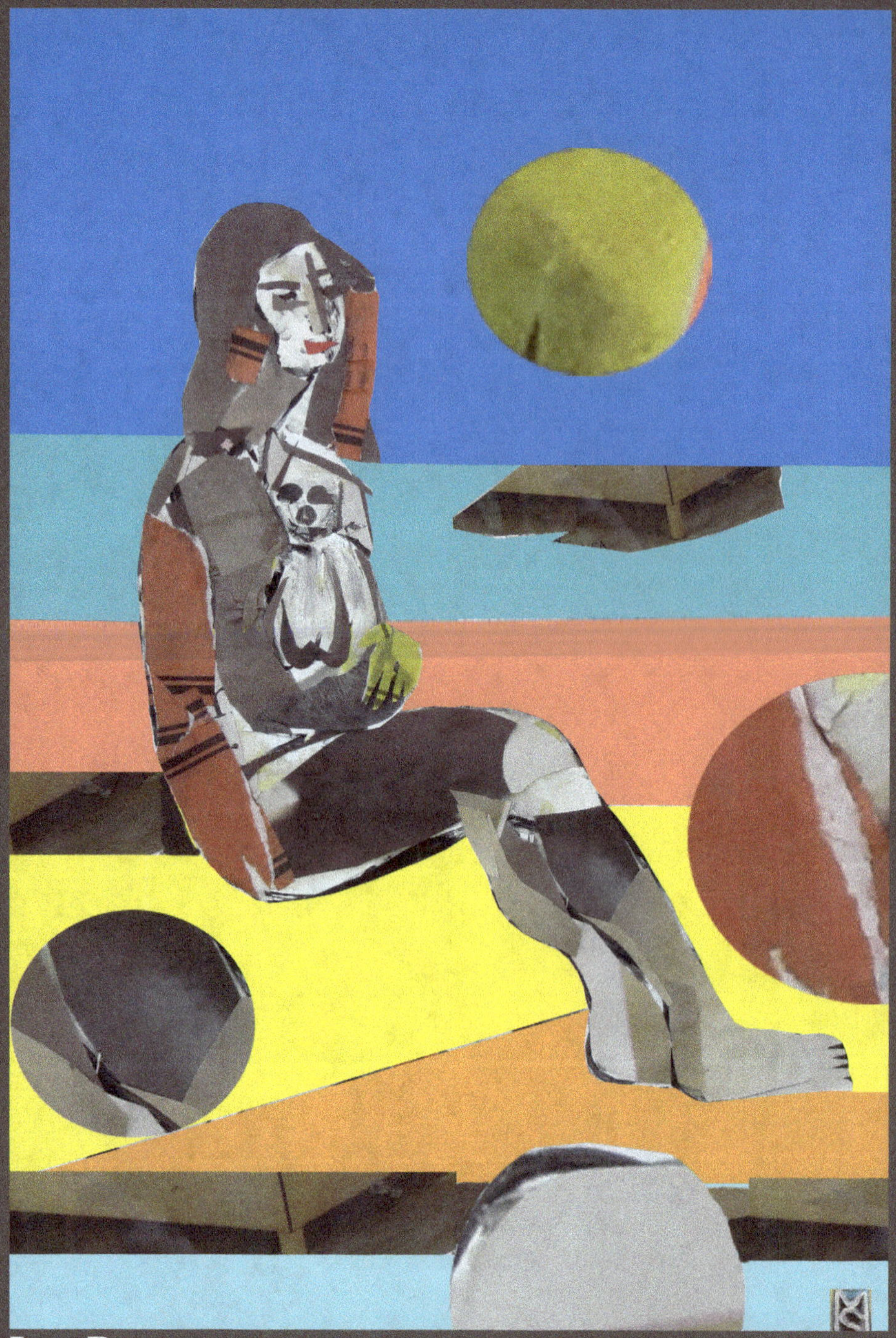

Lap Dog
(42cm x 27cm)
Original collage on pg.145.

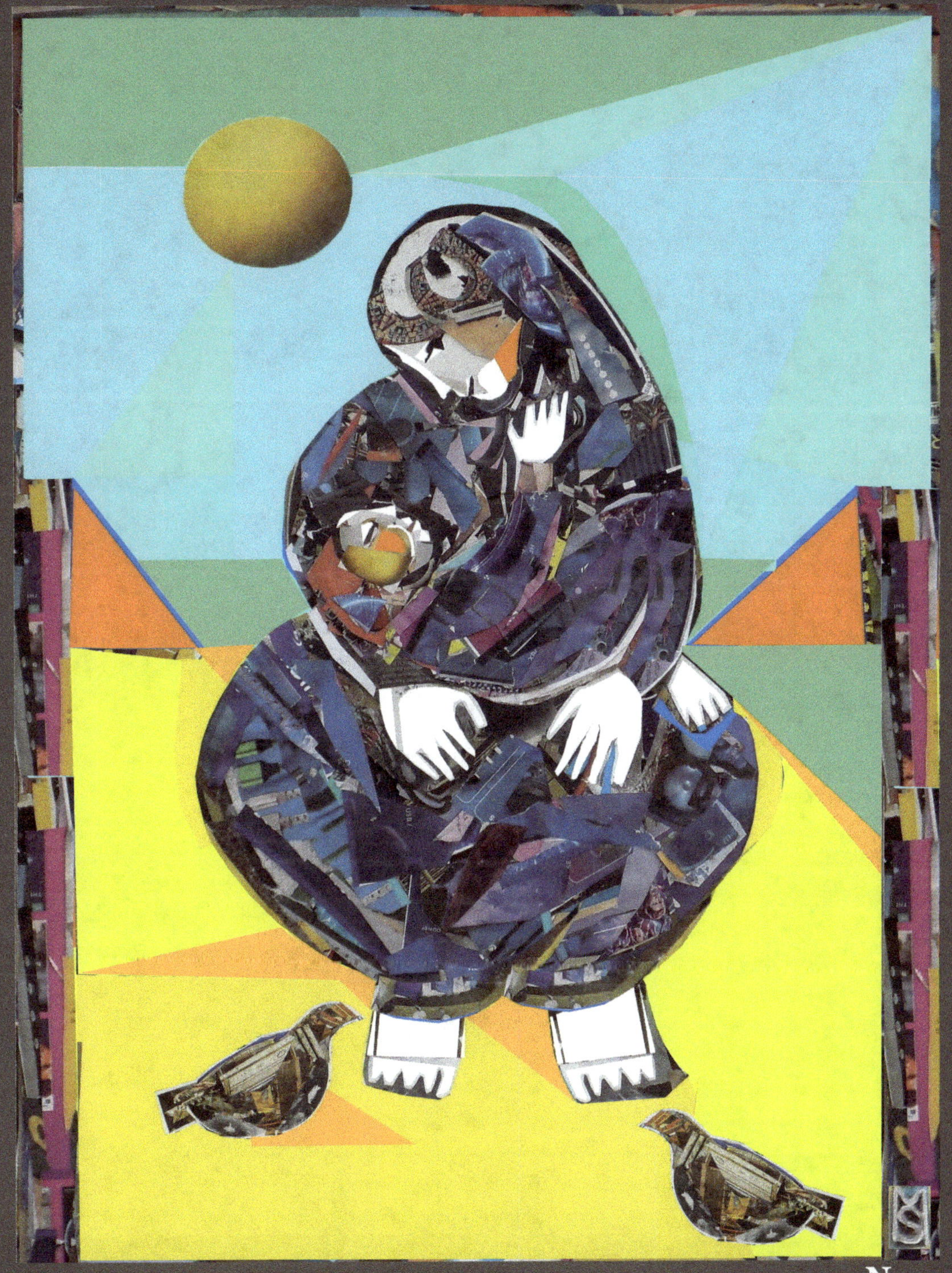

New

(50cm x 38cm)

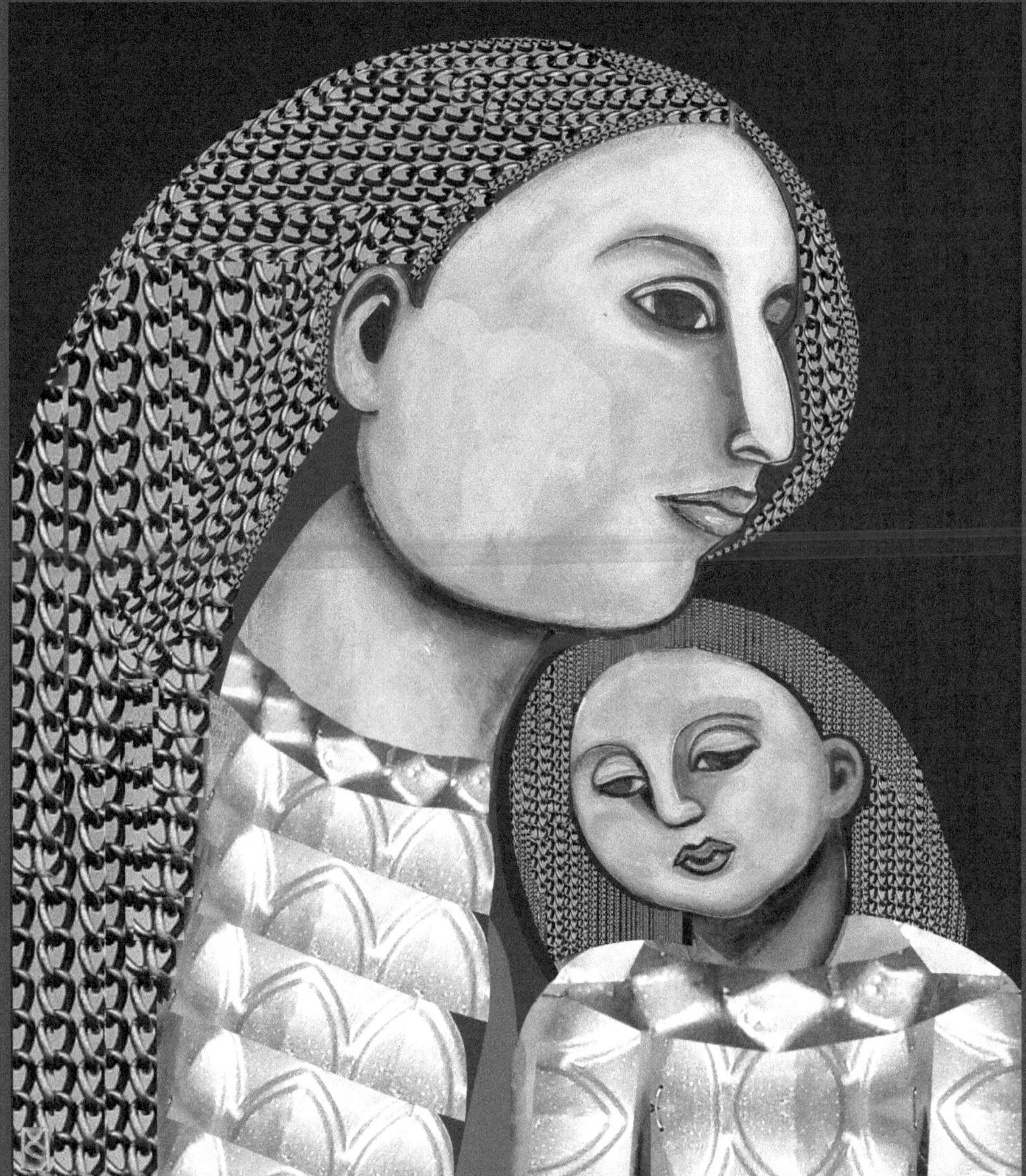

Inherent Harmony
(95cm x 75cm)
Original painting on pg.47.

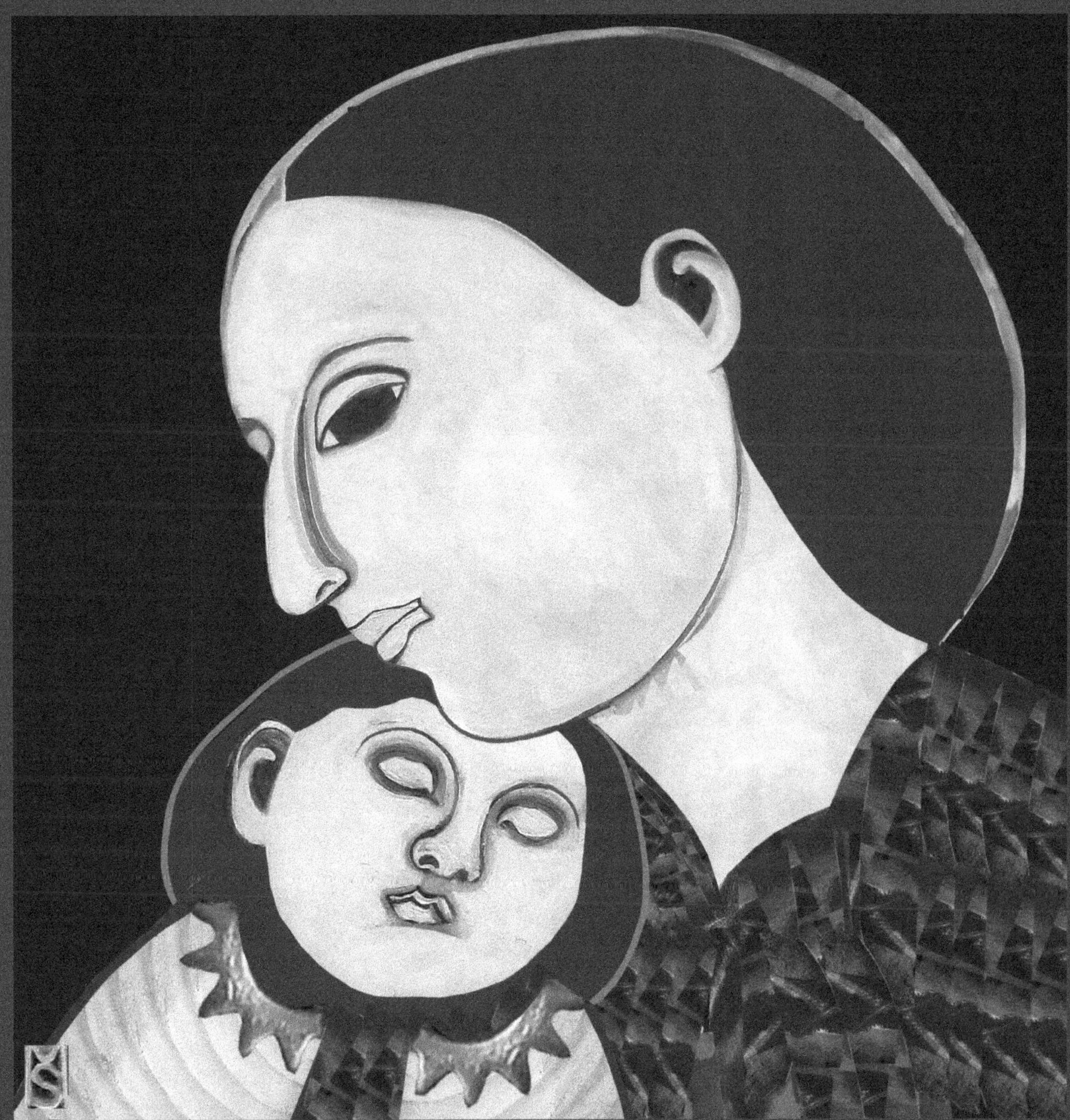

Global Eyes
(75cm x 70cm)
Original painting on pg.48.

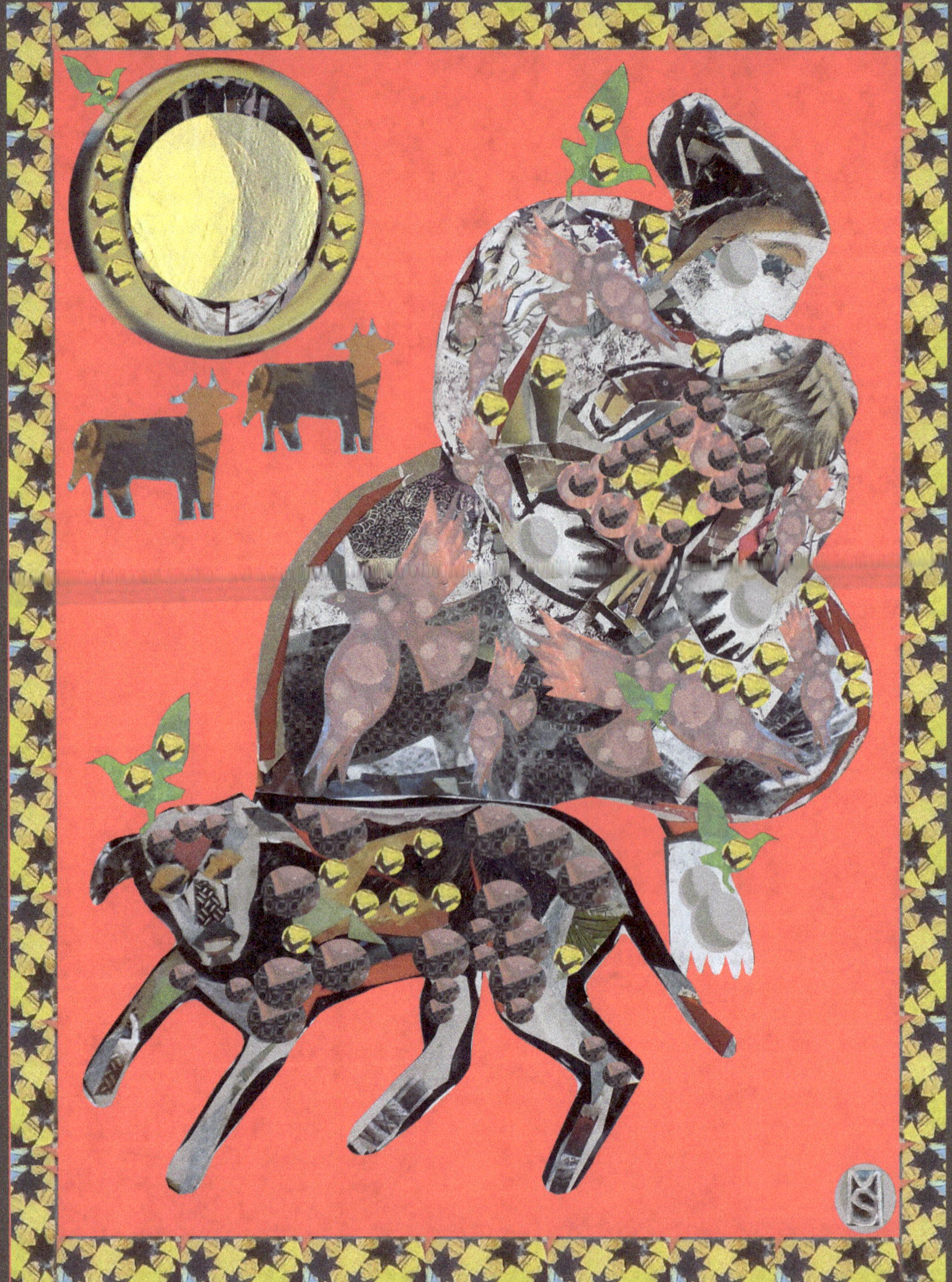

Caritas
(41cm x 28cm)

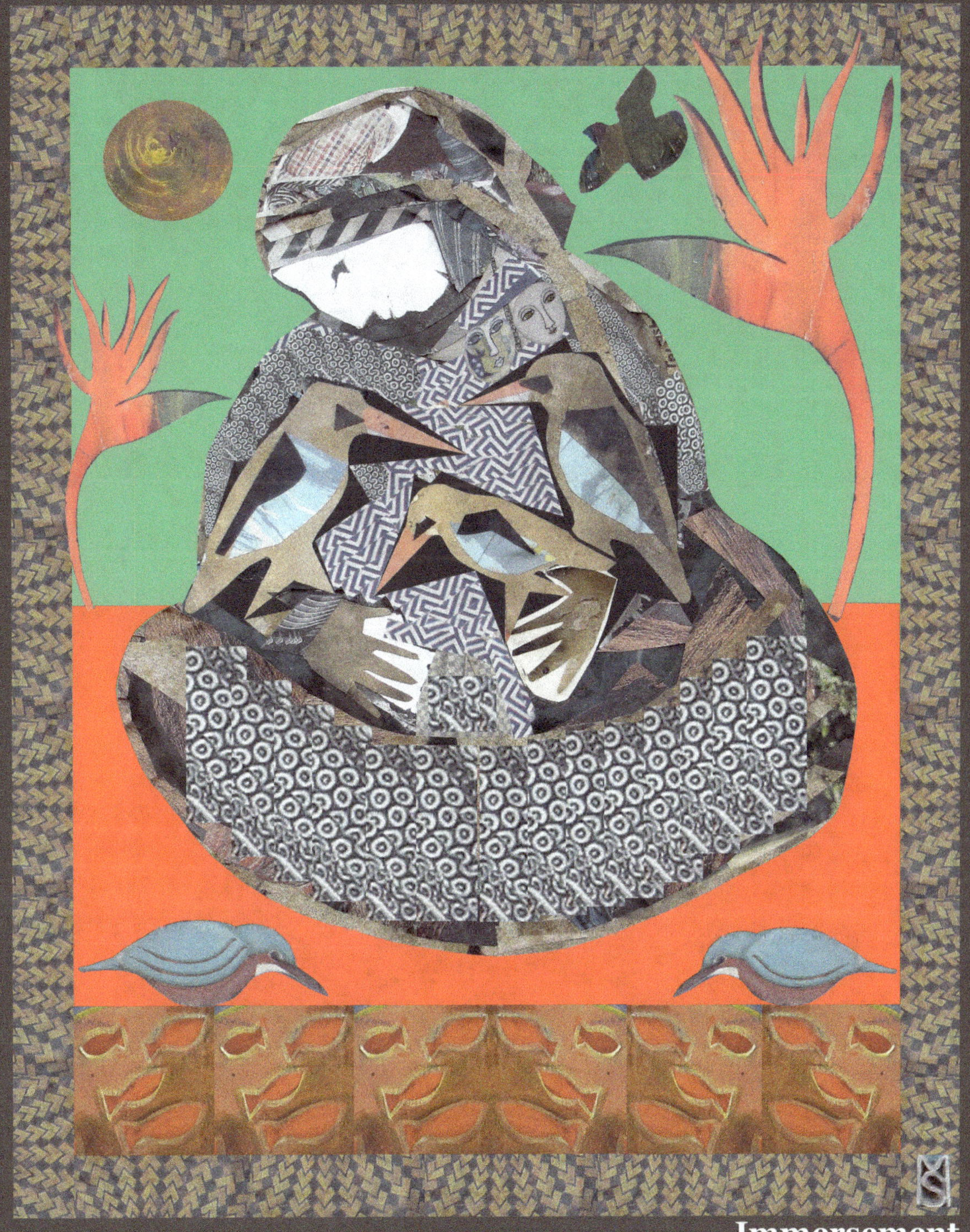

Immersement
(42cm x 34cm)

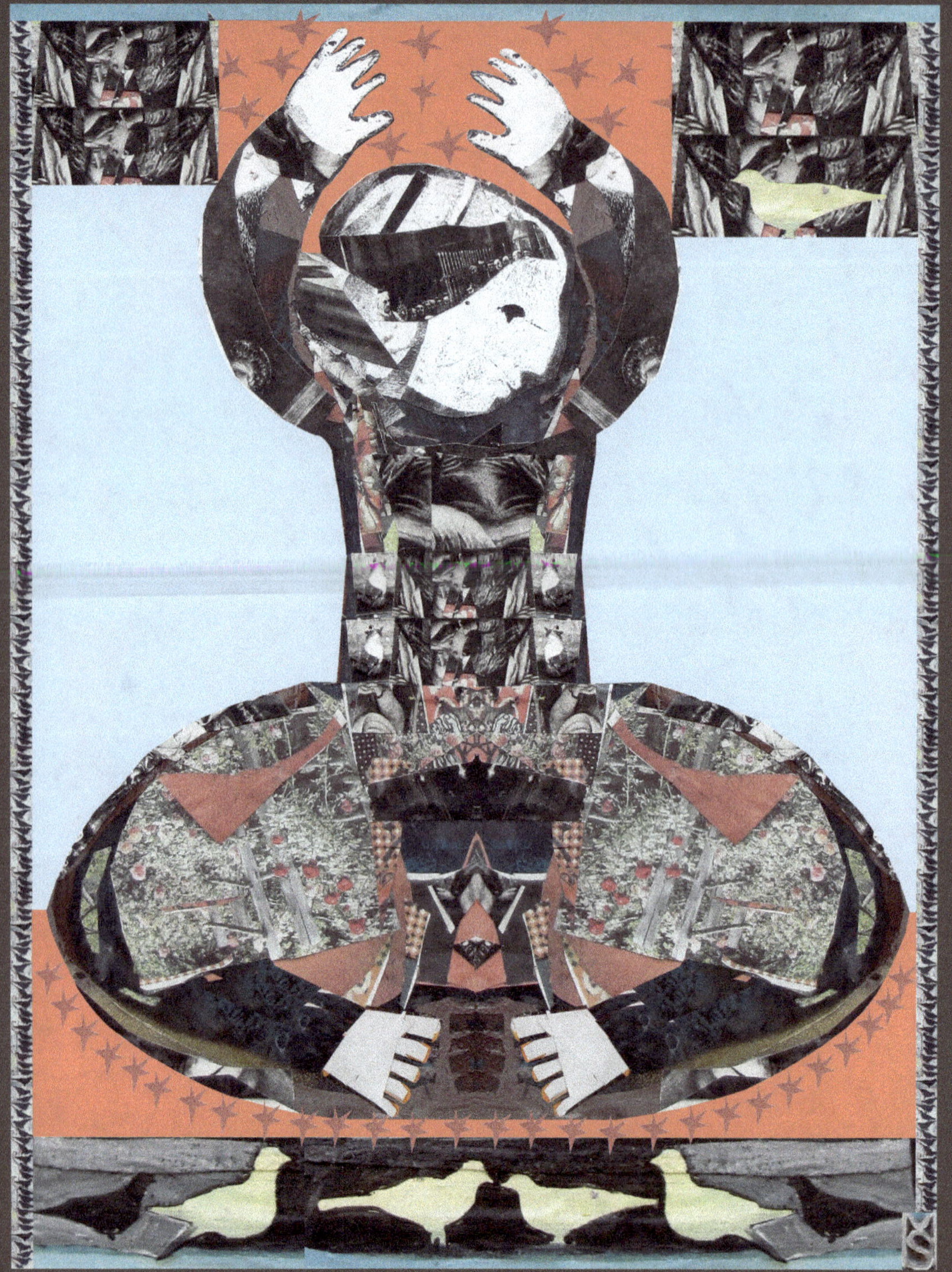

Memories
(42cm x 34cm)

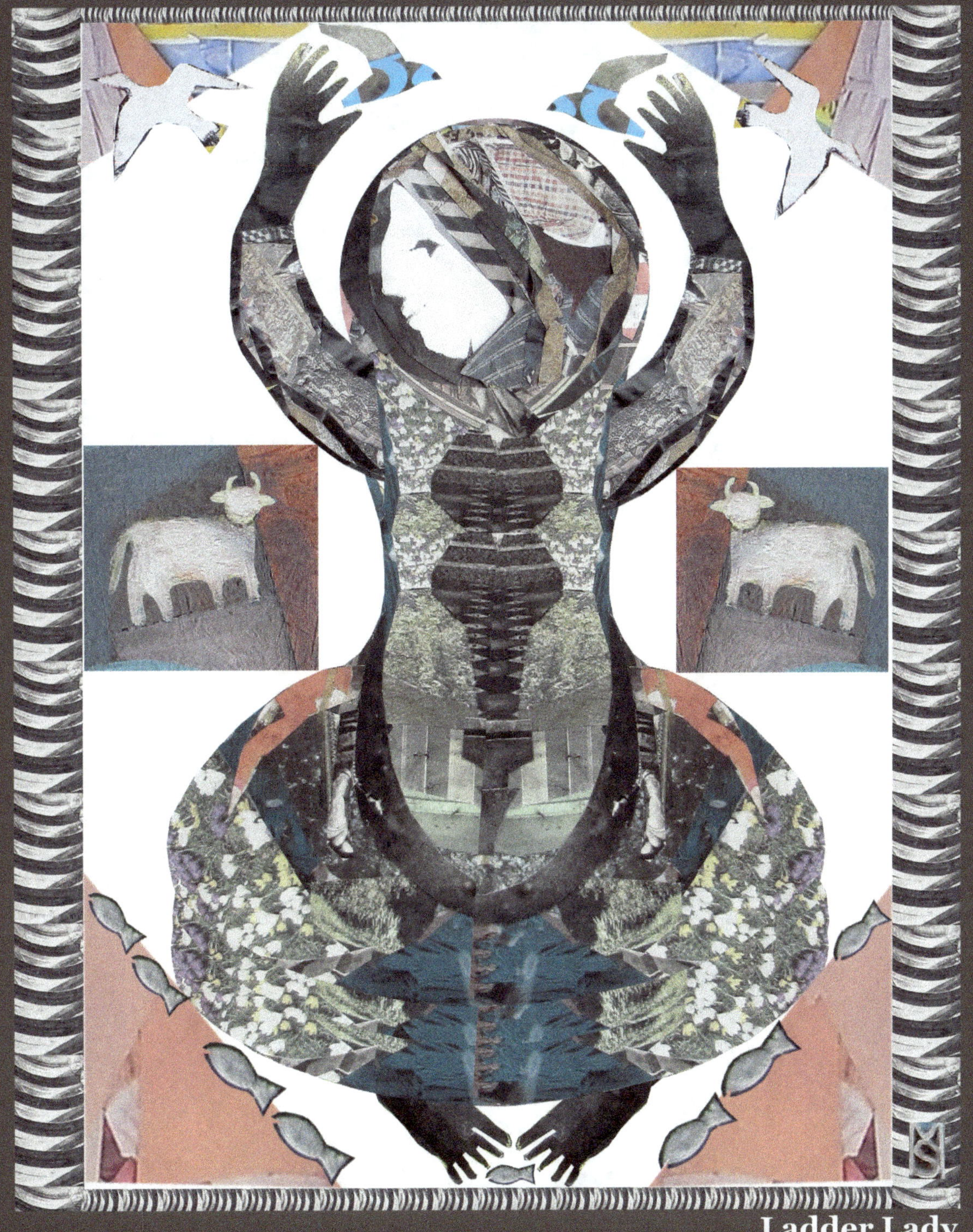

Ladder Lady
(42cm x 34cm)

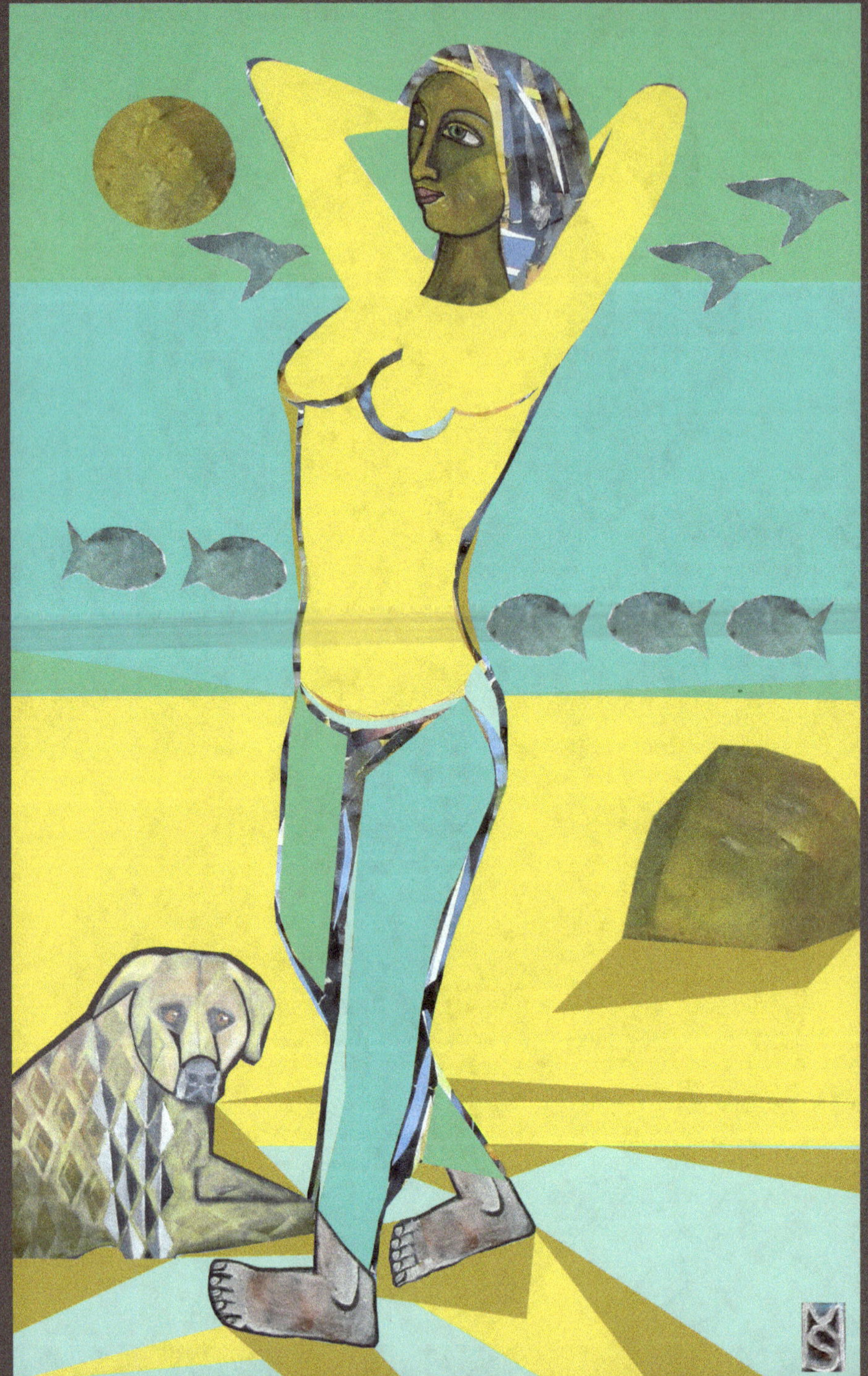

Lilli
(43cm x 28cm)

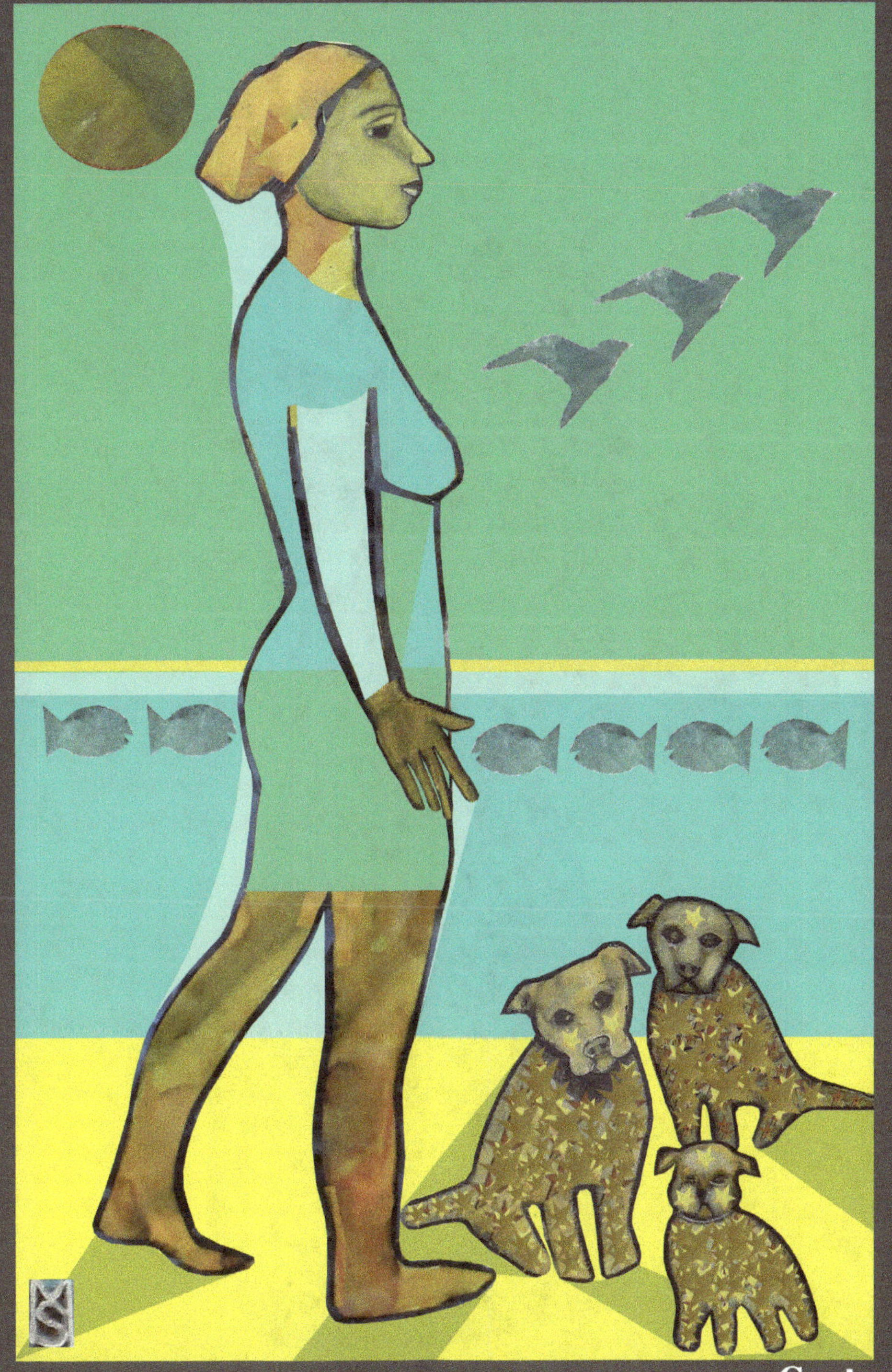

Greta
(43cm x 28cm)

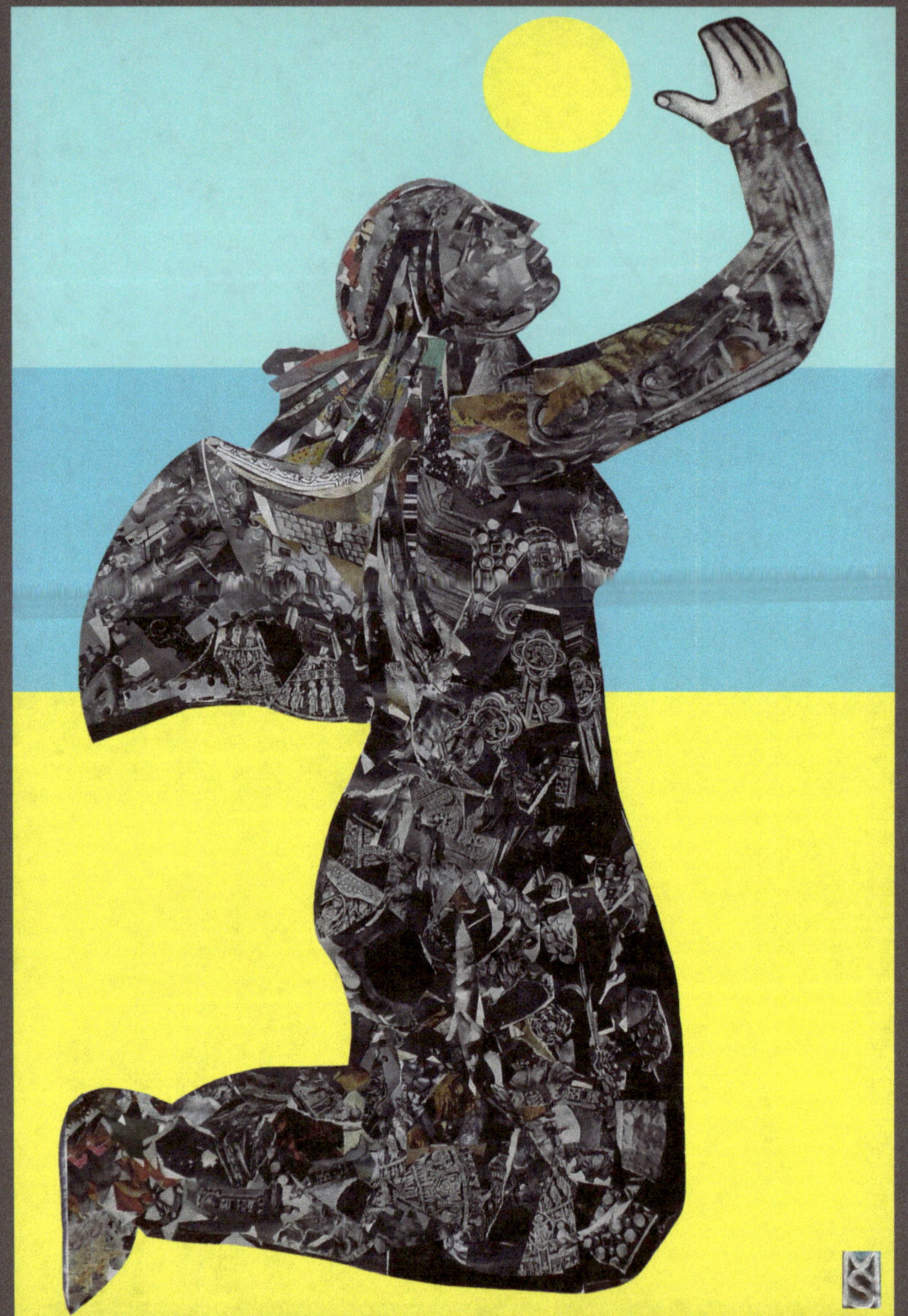

Beach Angel
(75cm x 52cm)

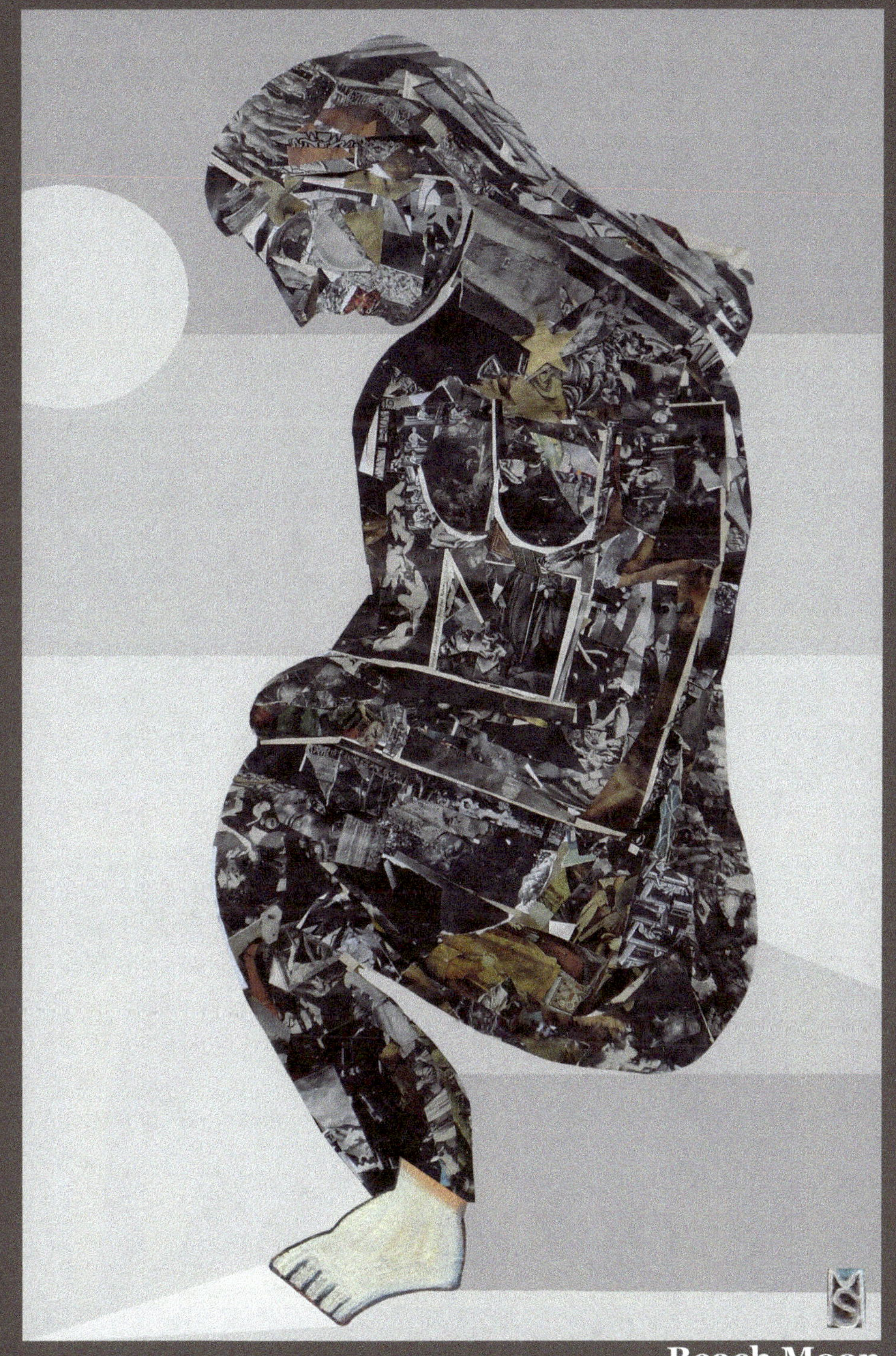

Beach Moon
(75cm x 50cm)

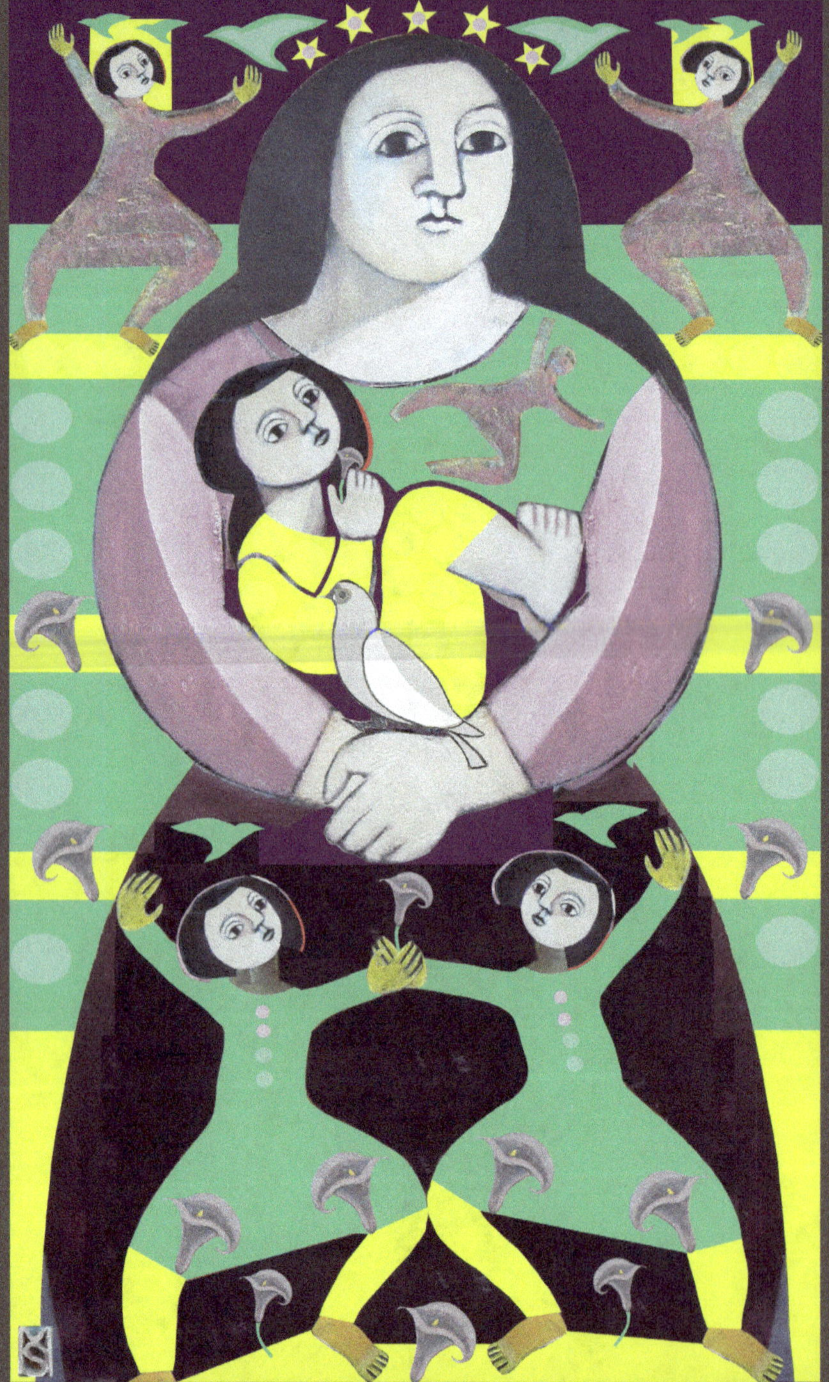

Harmonious
(130cm x 75cm)
Original painting on pg.88.

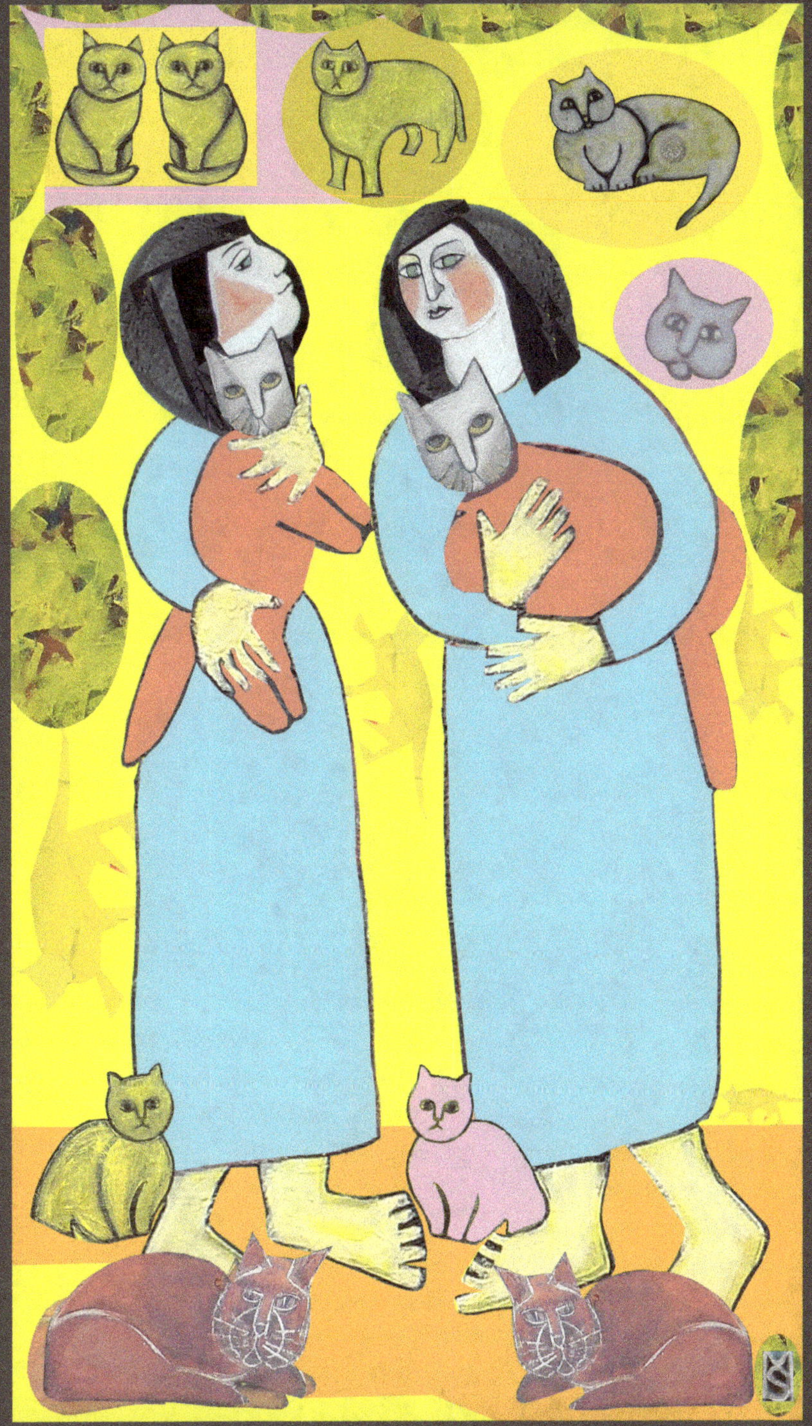

Cats
(130cm x 75cm)

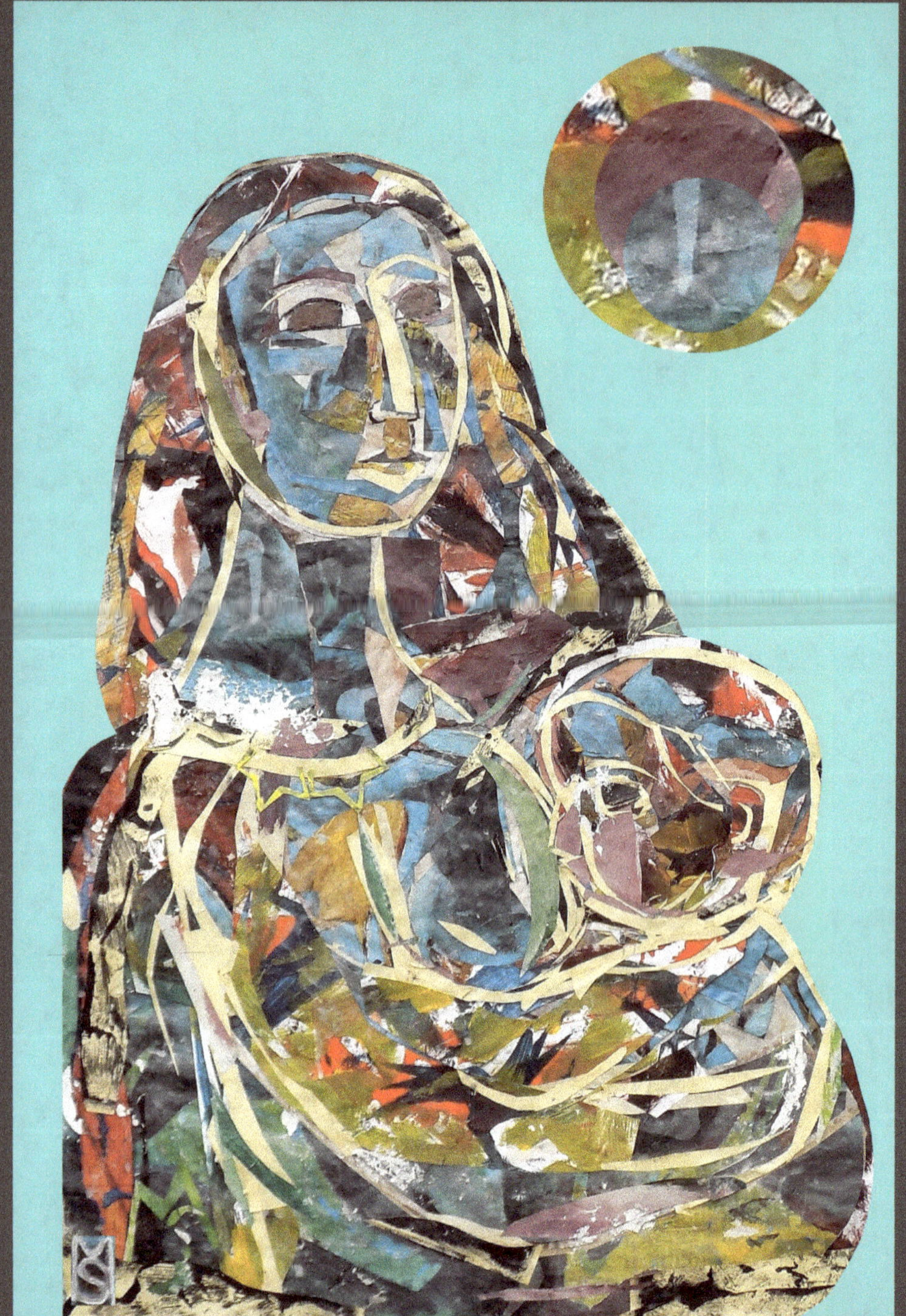

Realisation
(80cm x 56cm)
Original collage on pg.161.

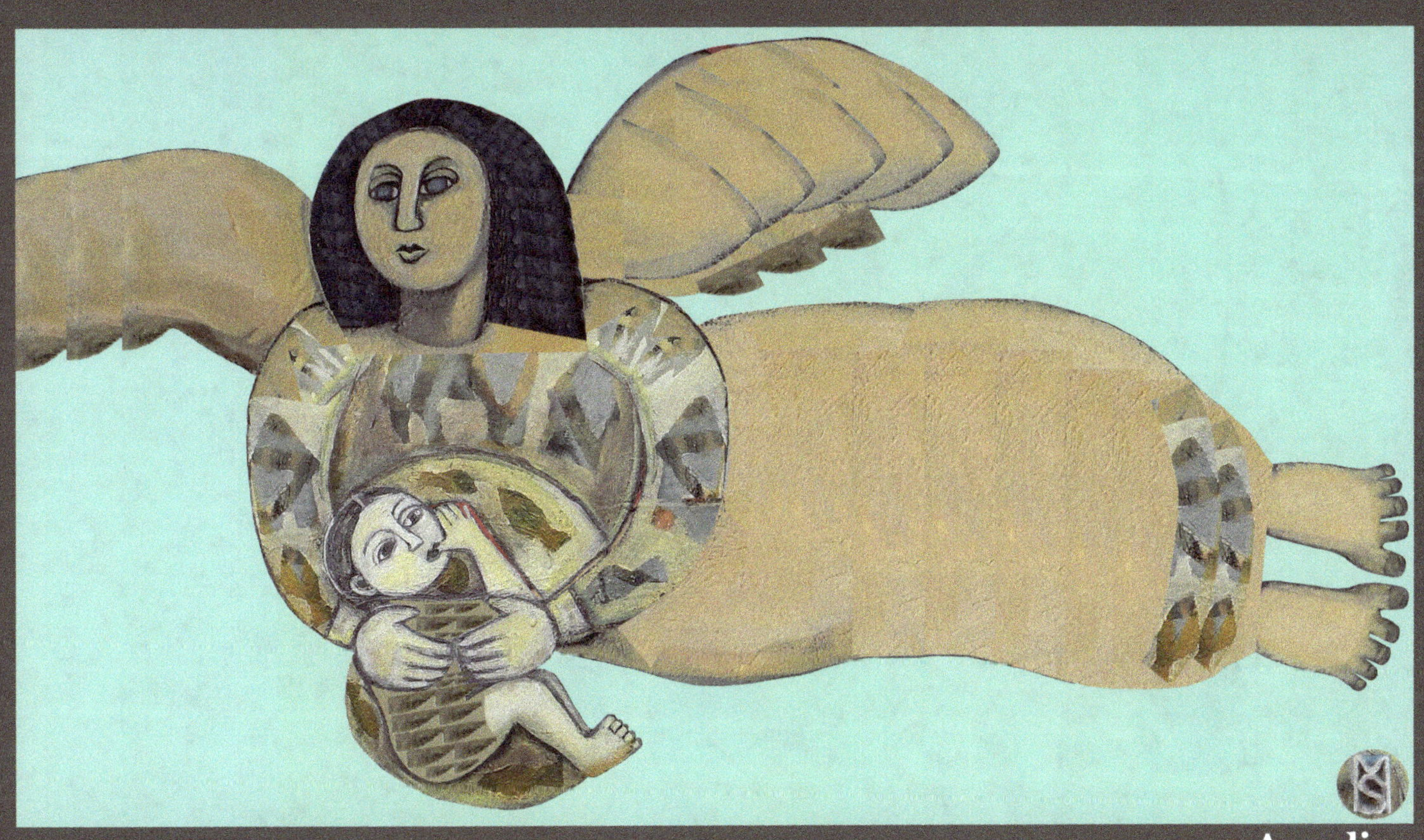

Angelica
(60cm x 110cm)
Partial image on pg.167.

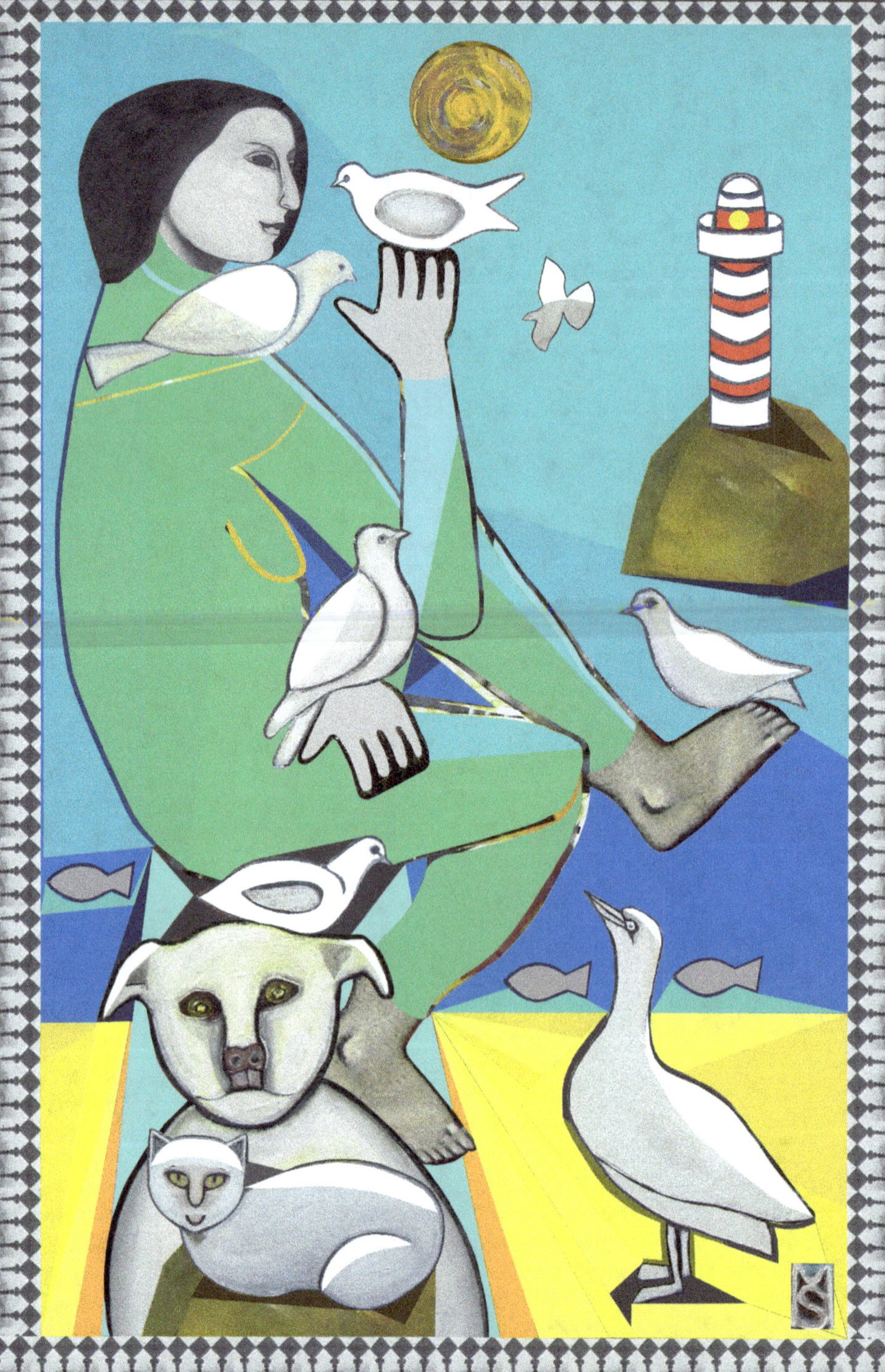

Yvonne
(43cm x 28cm)

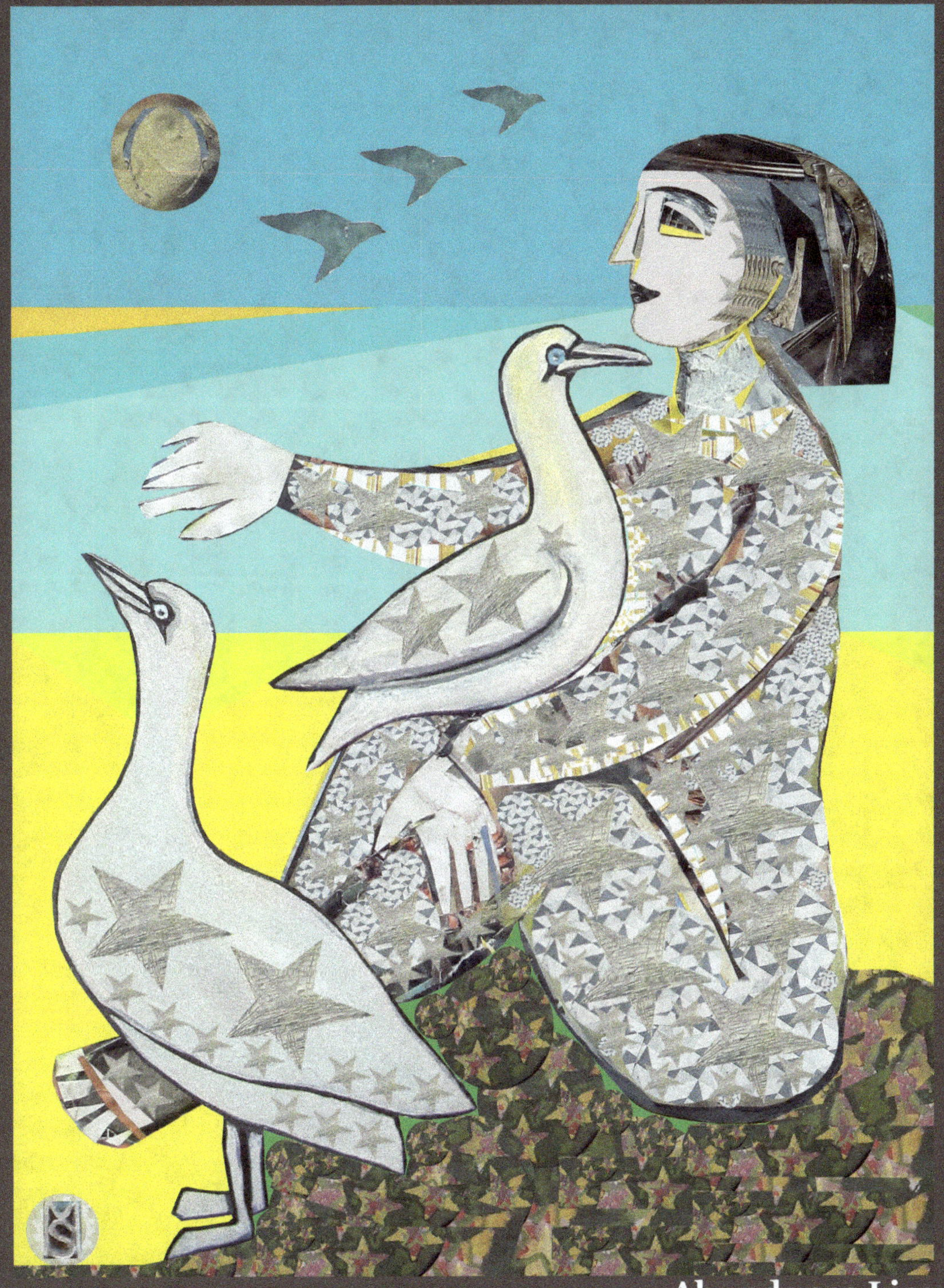

Abundance Lies
(44cm x 34cm)

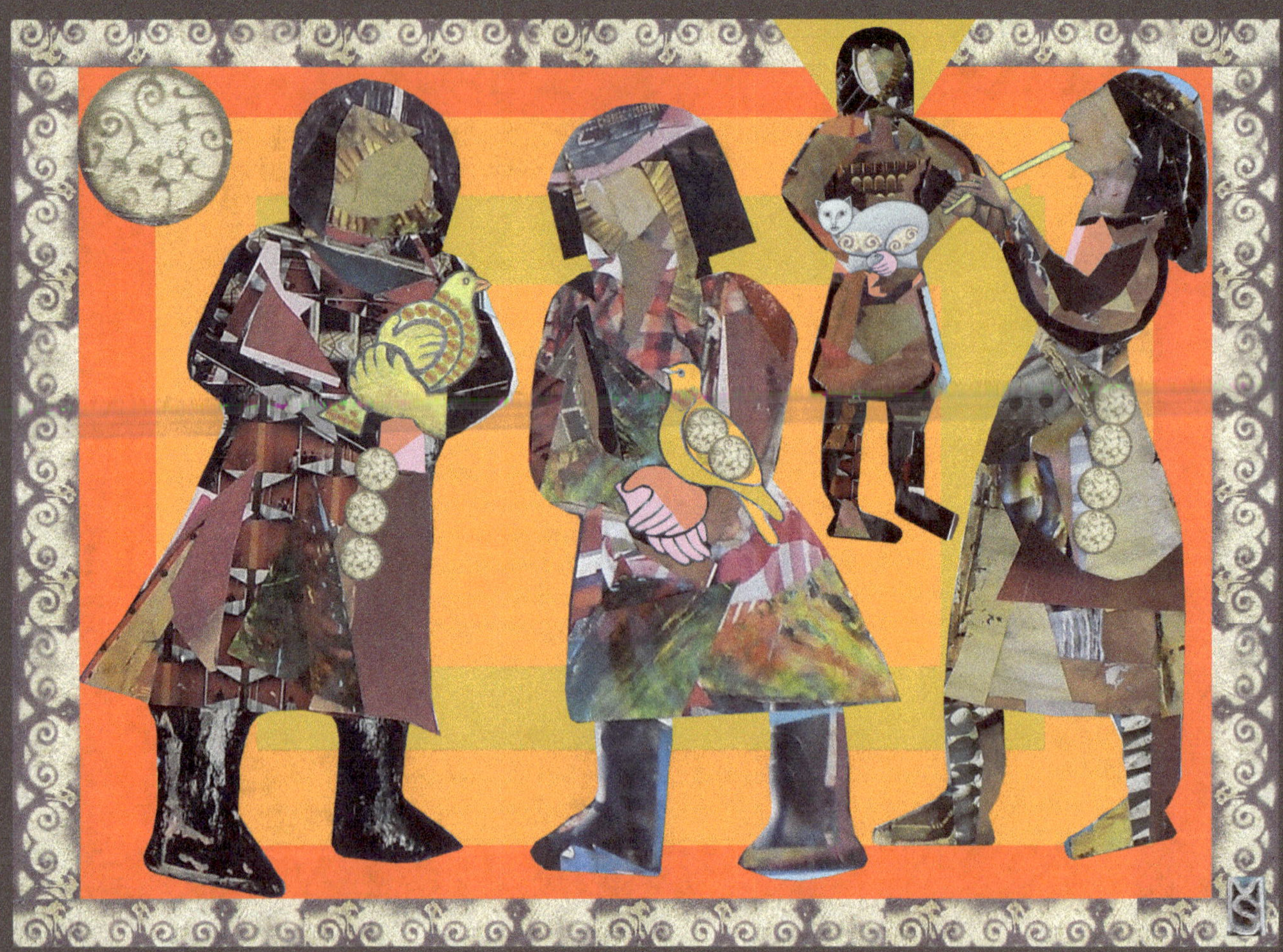

Antique Song
(34cm x 48cm)

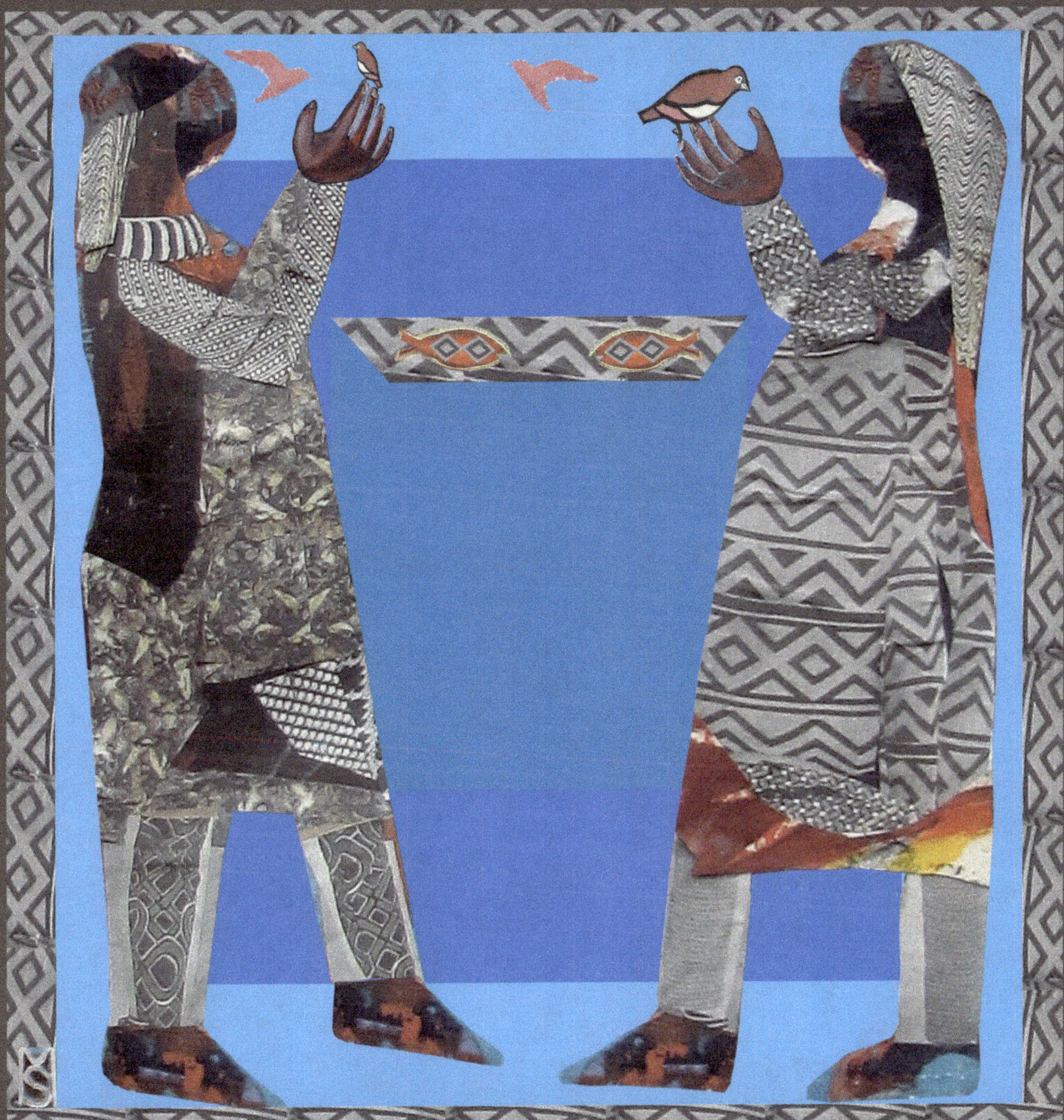

And Nights Bright Days
(55cm x 55cm)

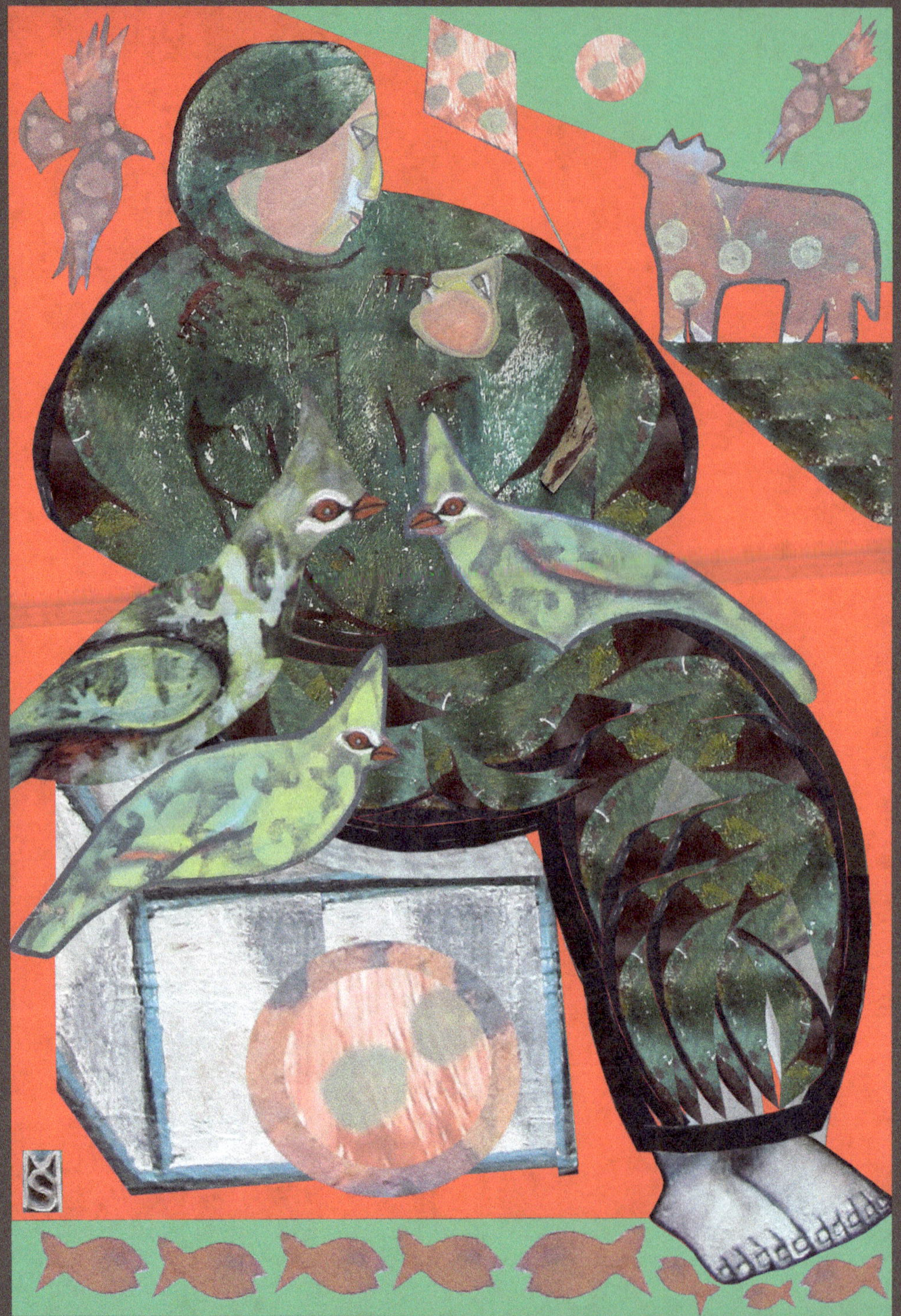

Moss Mother
(41cm x 29cm)

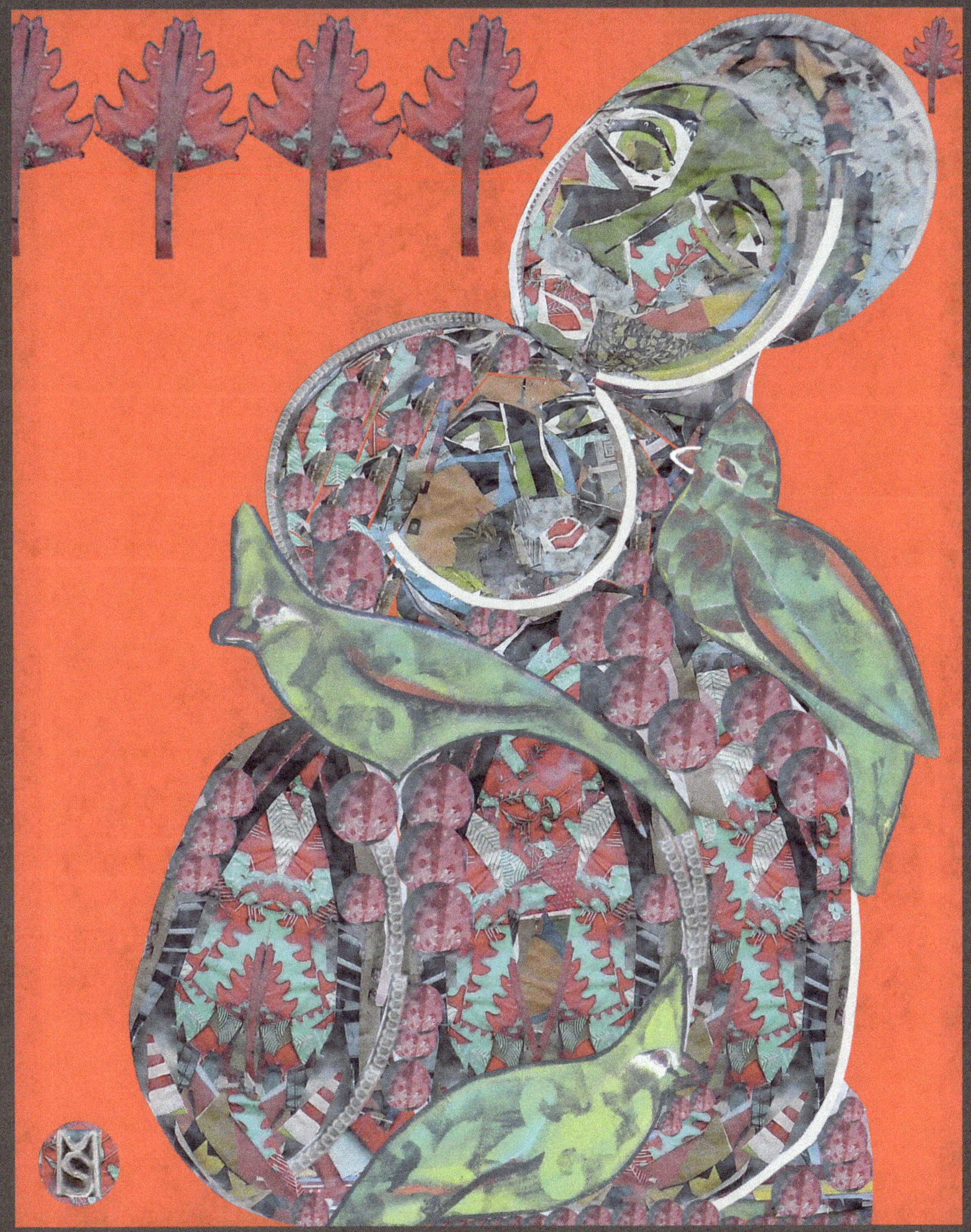

Unwavering
(74cm x 50cm)

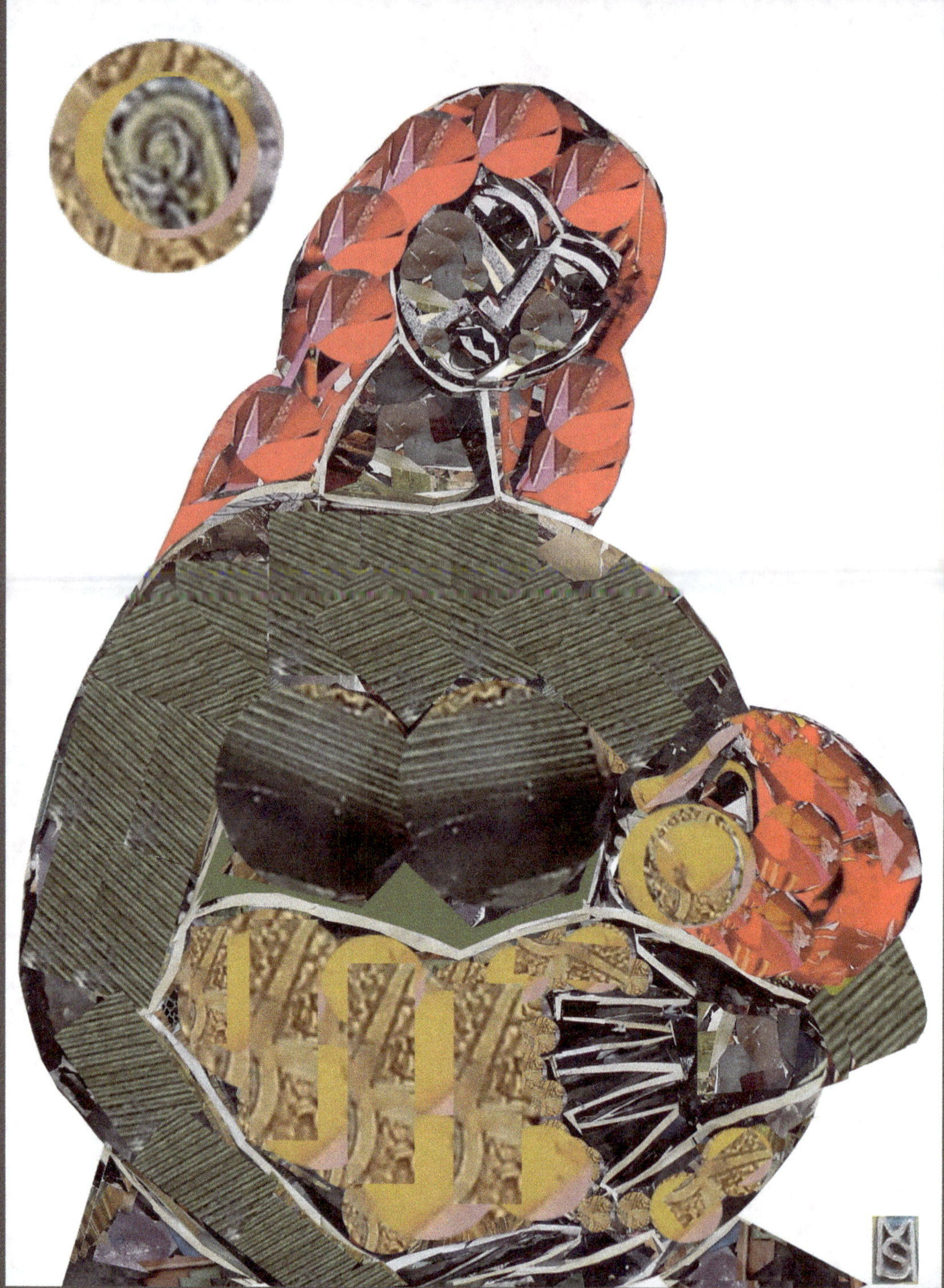

Red Hair
(76cm x 56cm)

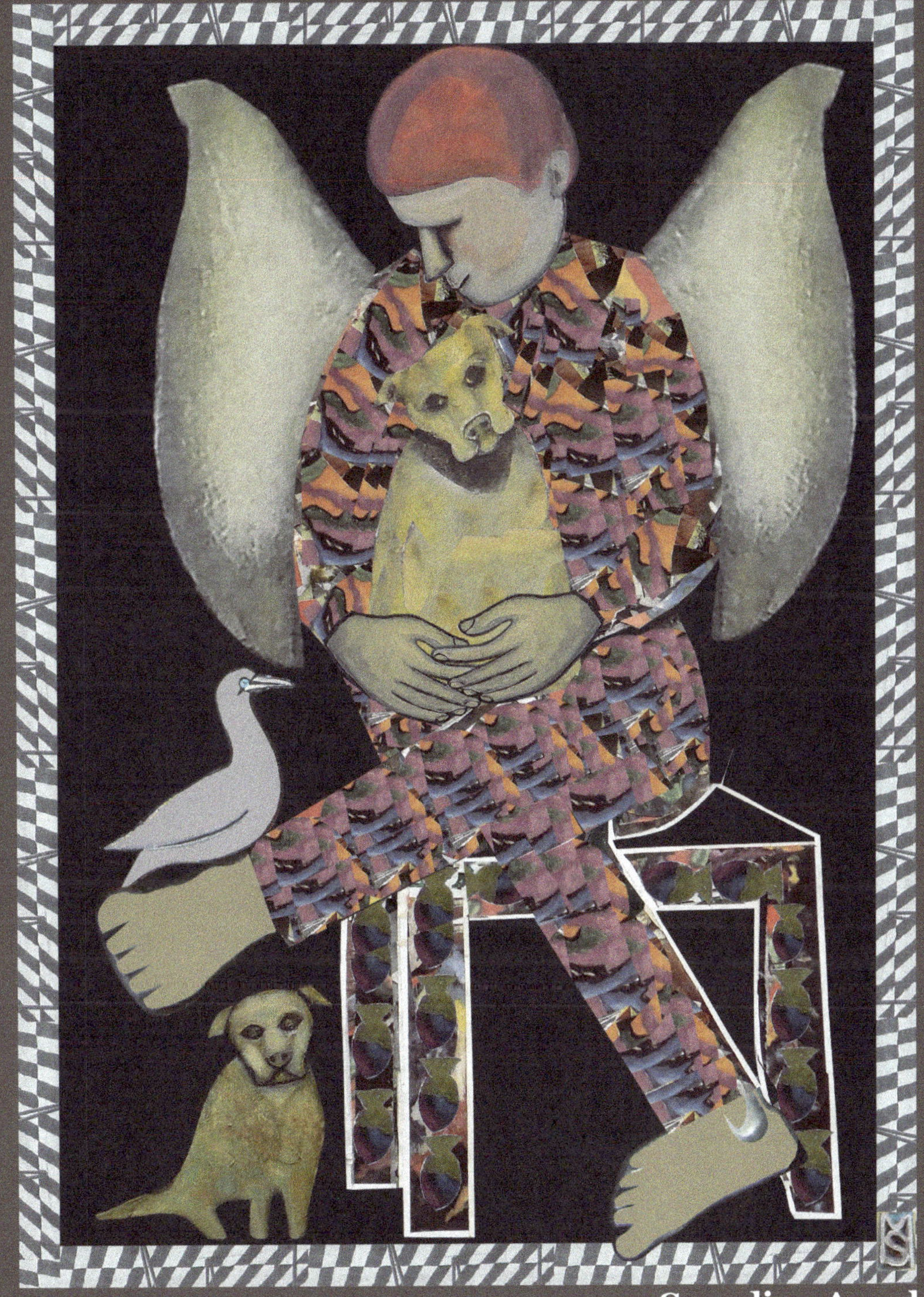

Guardian Angel
(71cm x 52cm)

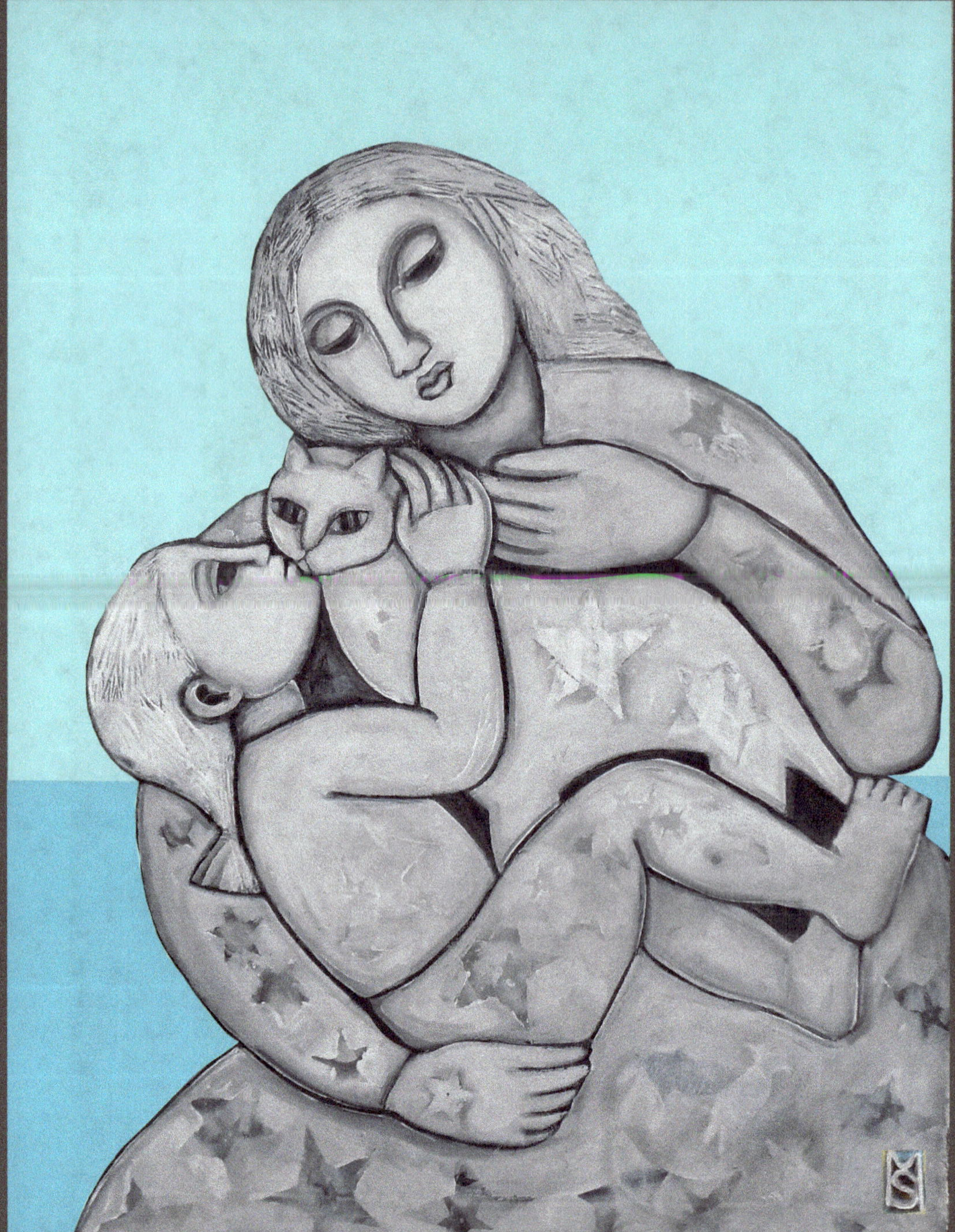

Cat Caress
(92cm x 72cm)
Original painting on pg.95.

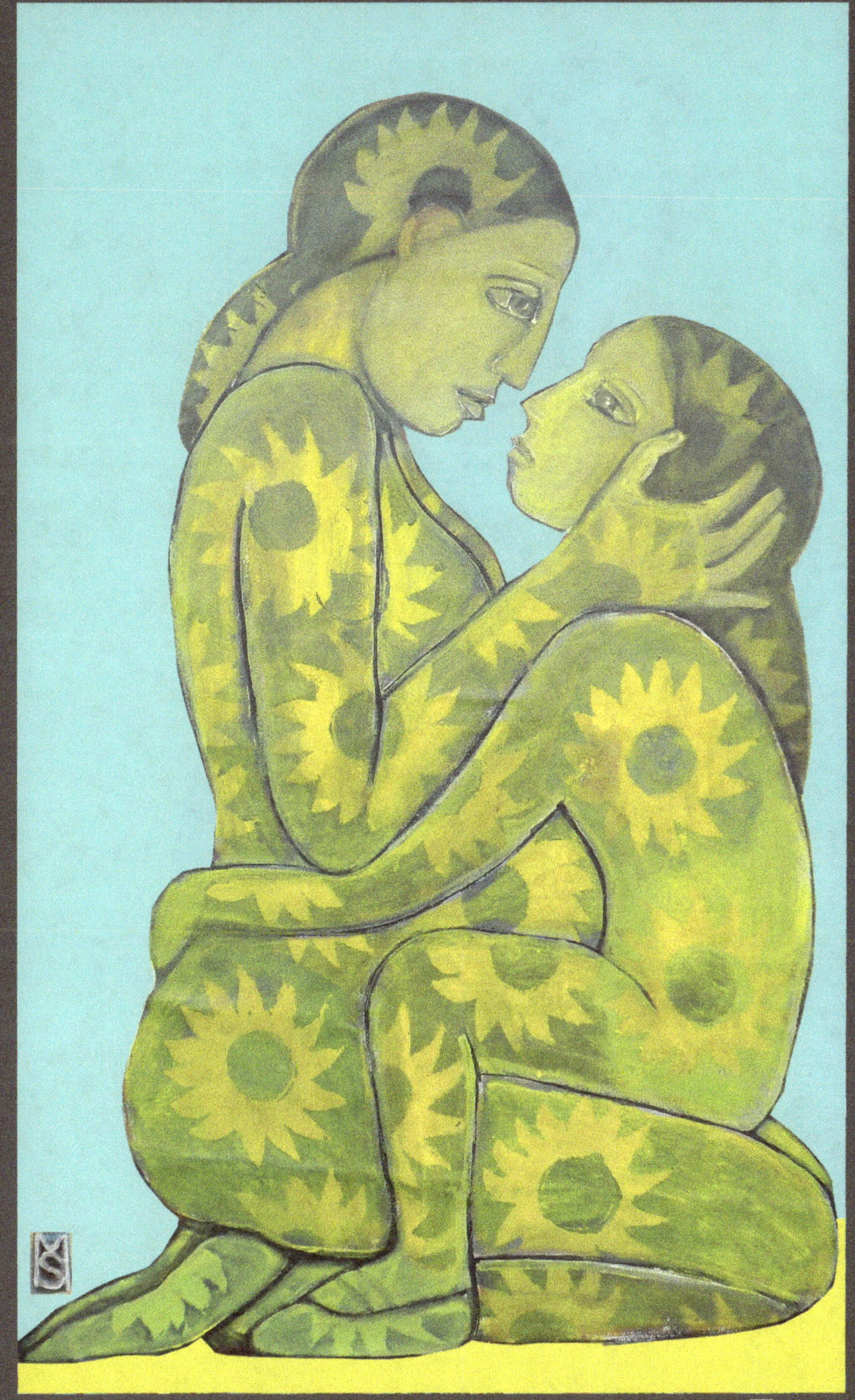

Trust
(103cm x 63cm)

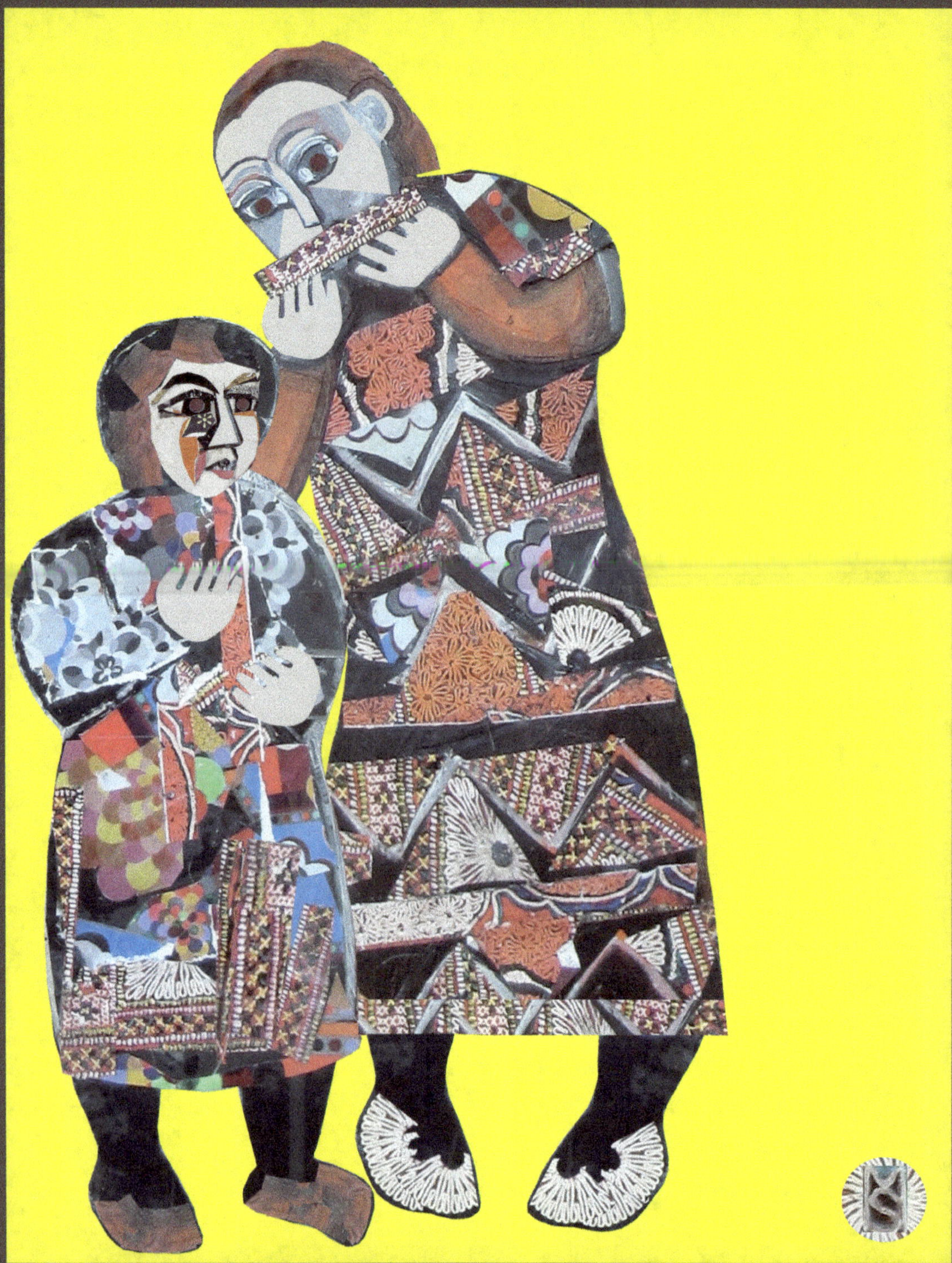

Musicians
(45cm x 35cm)

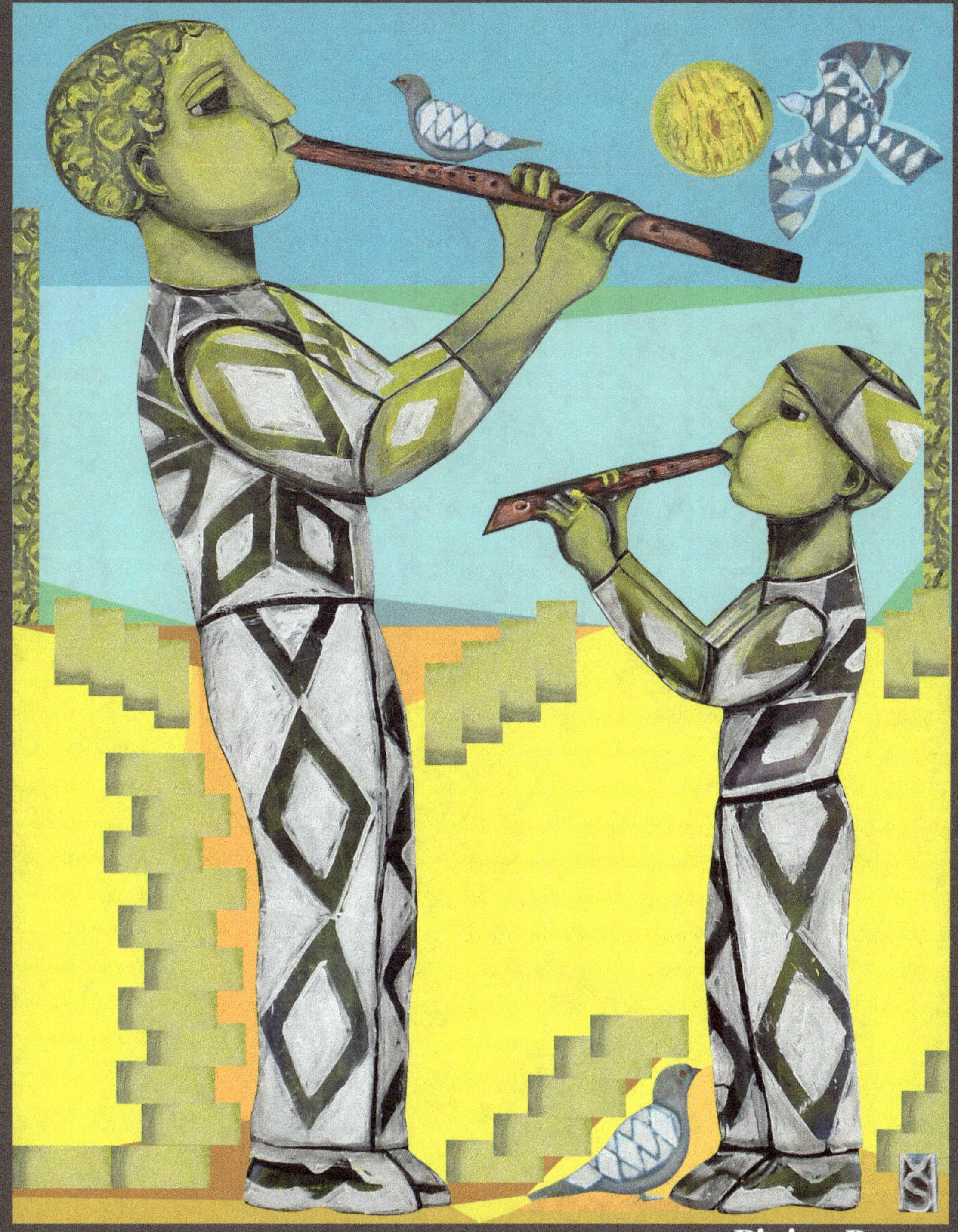

Piping Poems
(95cm x 75cm)

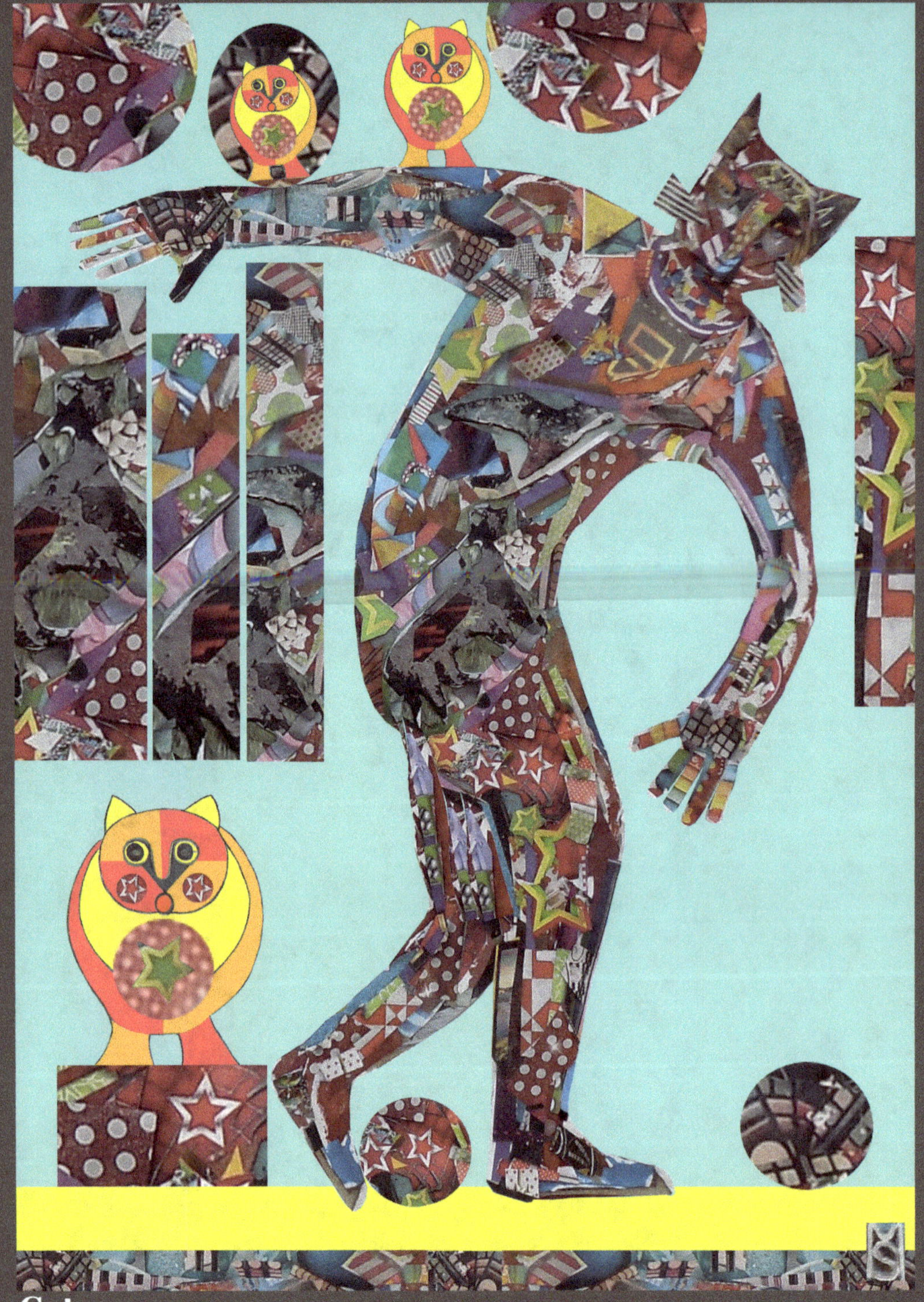

Catman
(75cm x 54cm)

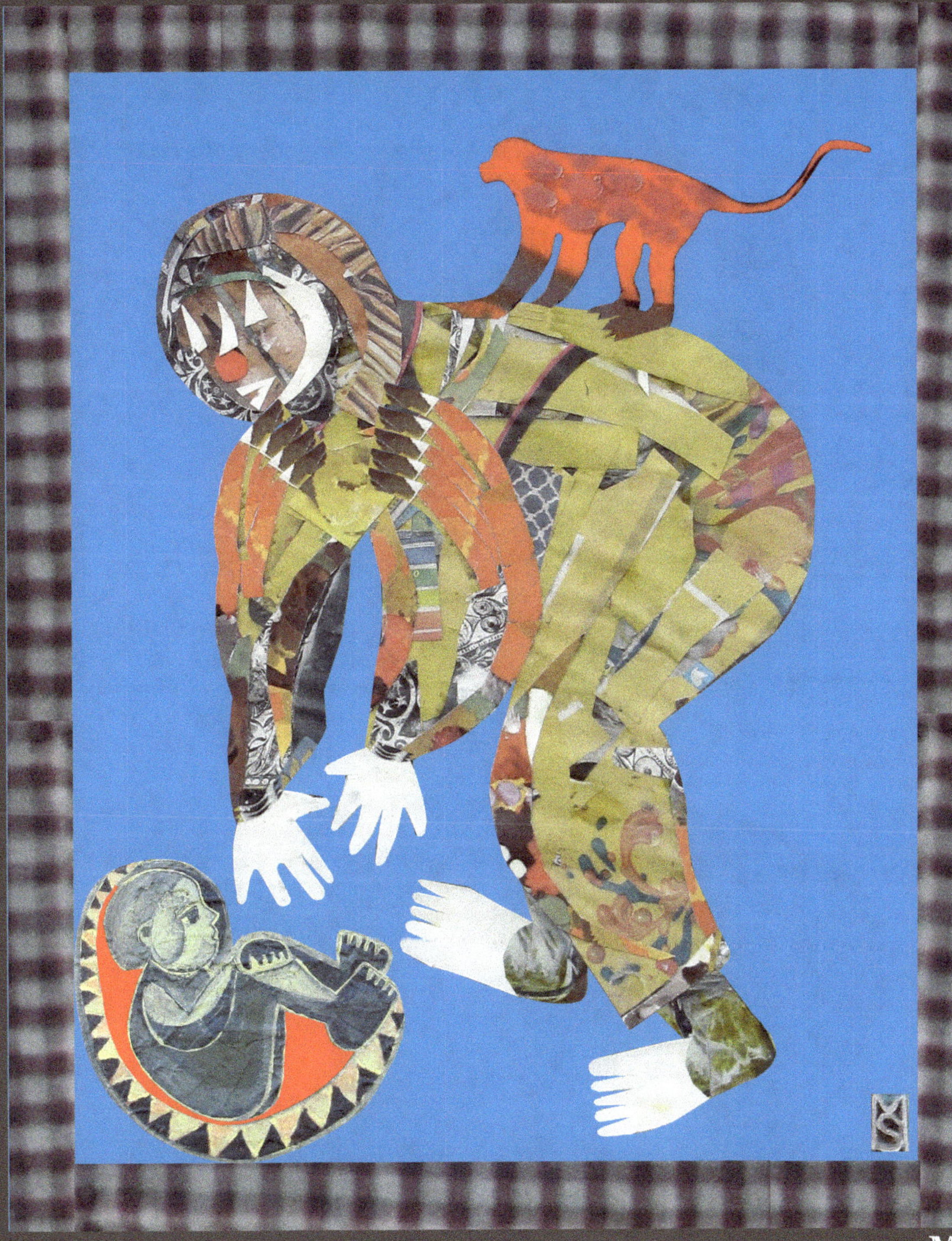

Mo
(40cm x 33cm)

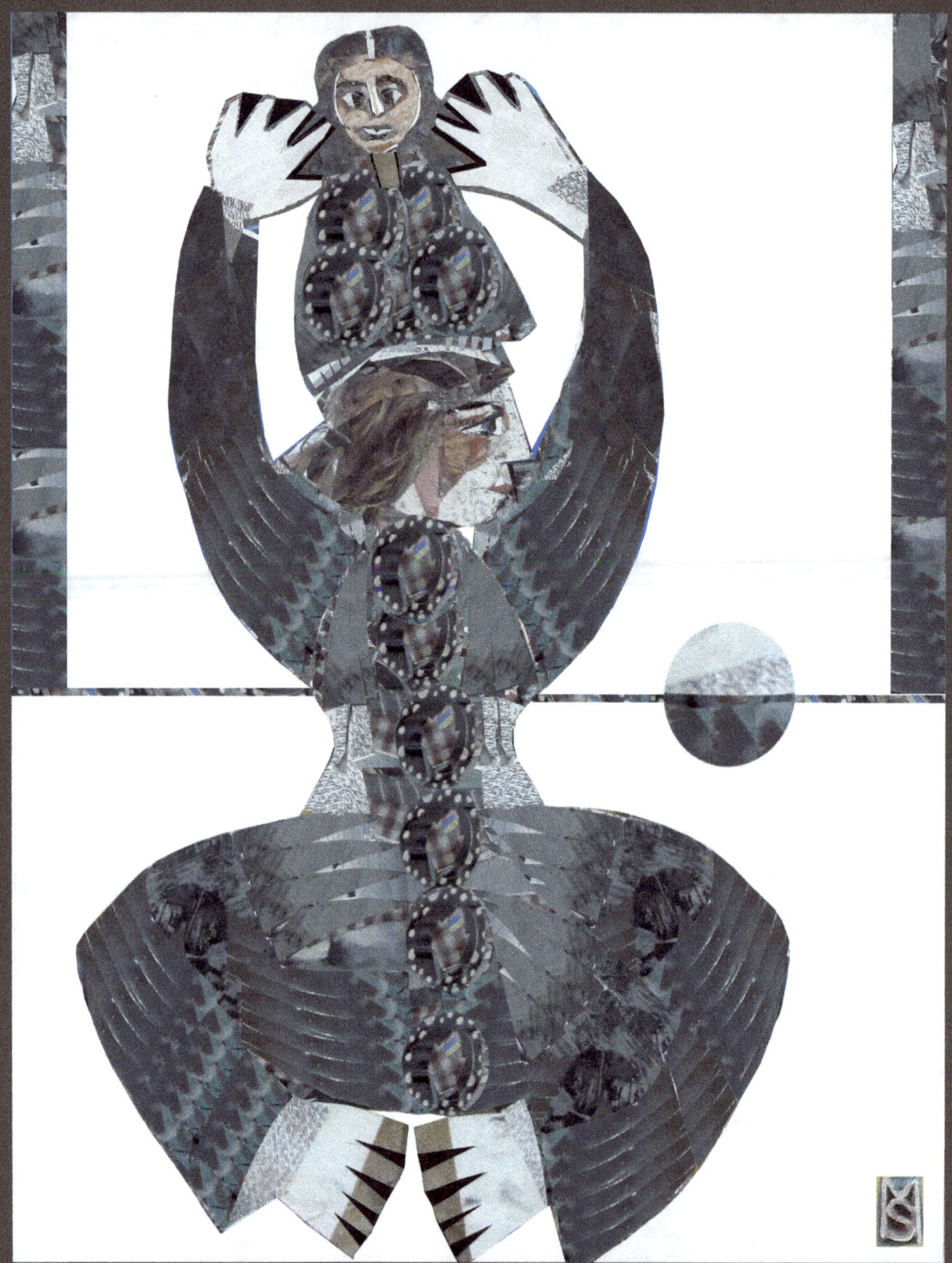

Old Gold
(42cm x 34cm)

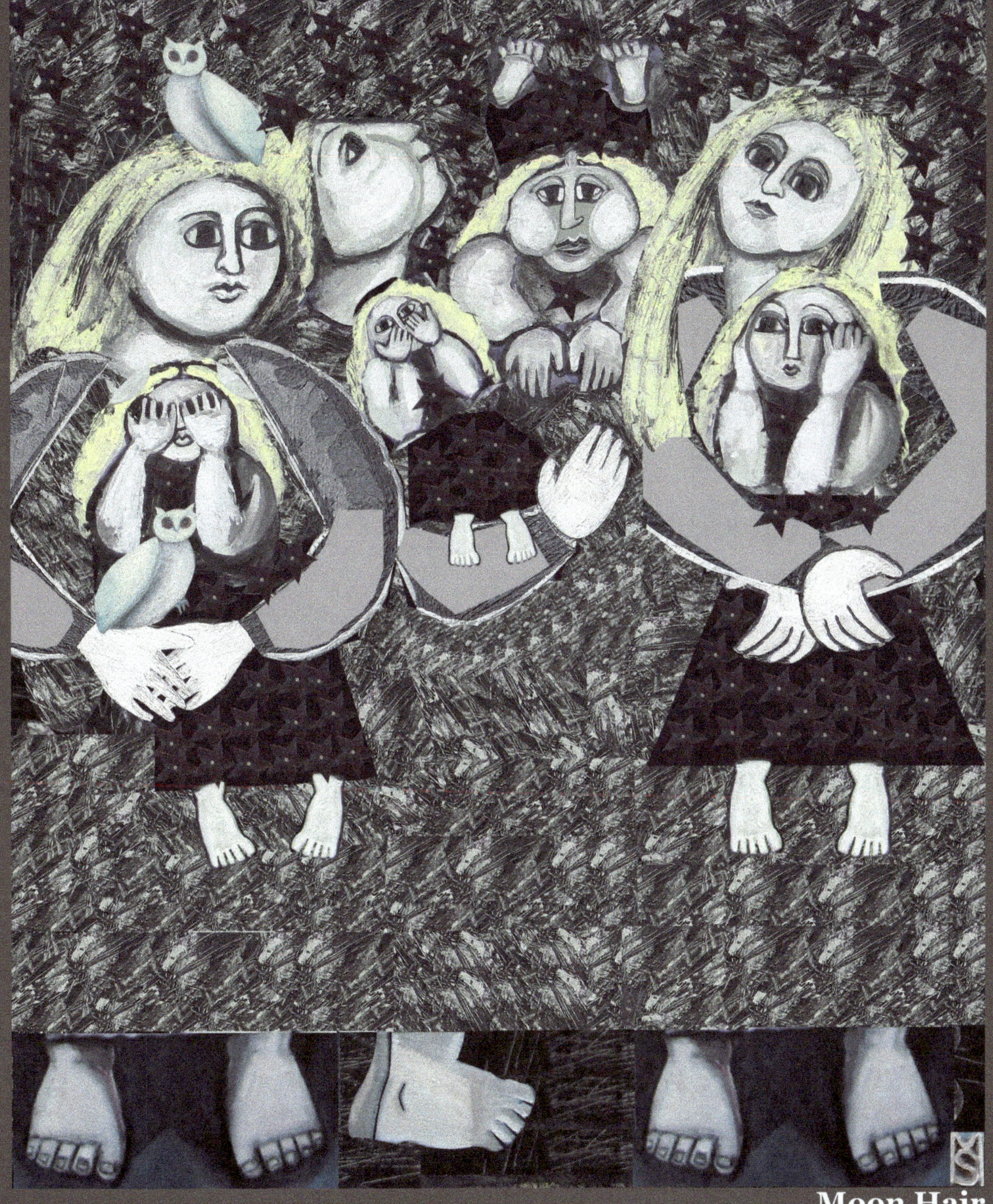

Moon Hair
(70cm x 60cm)

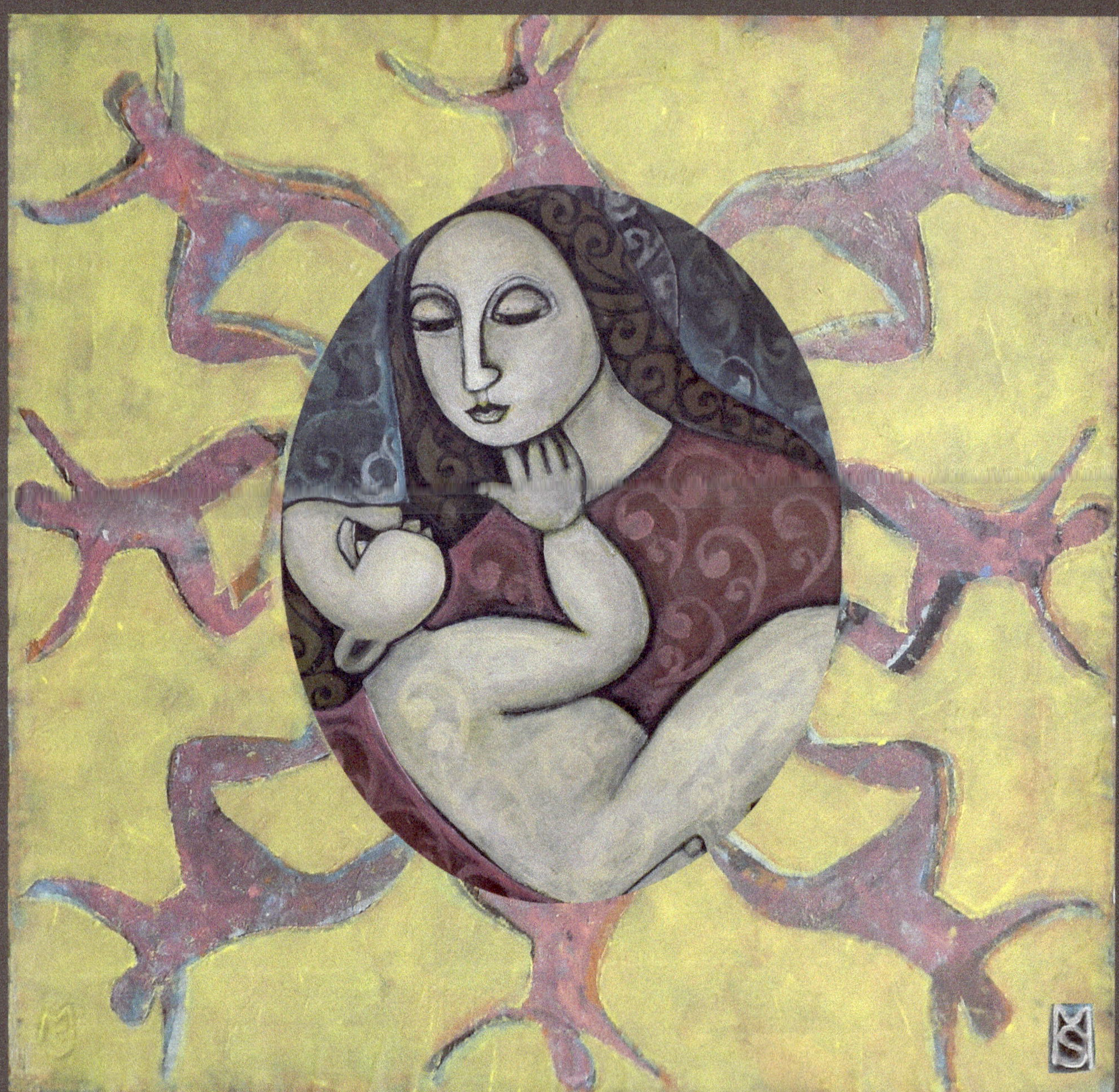

Revering Matisse
(90cm x 95cm)

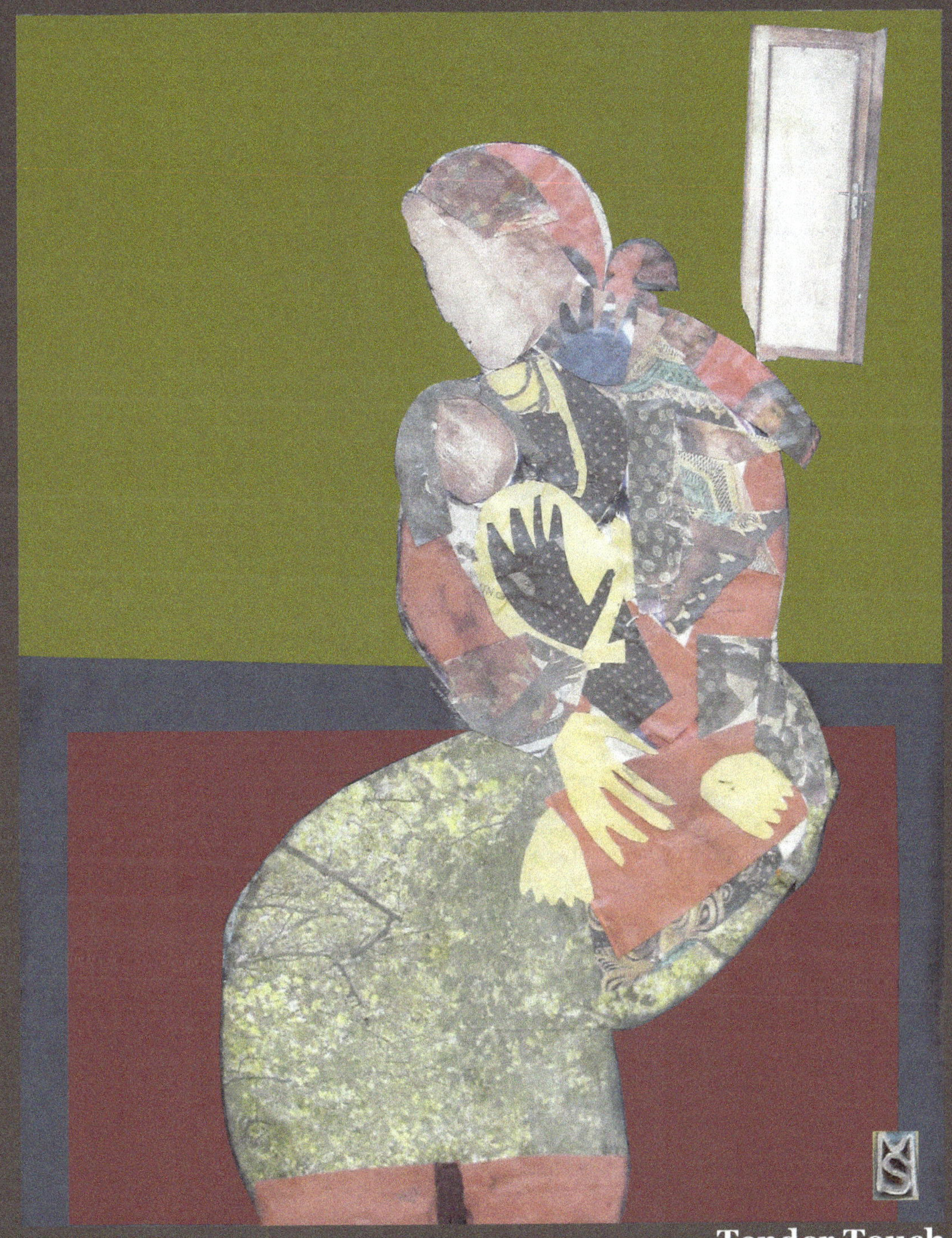

Tender Touch
(39cm x 29cm)
Original collage on pg.144.

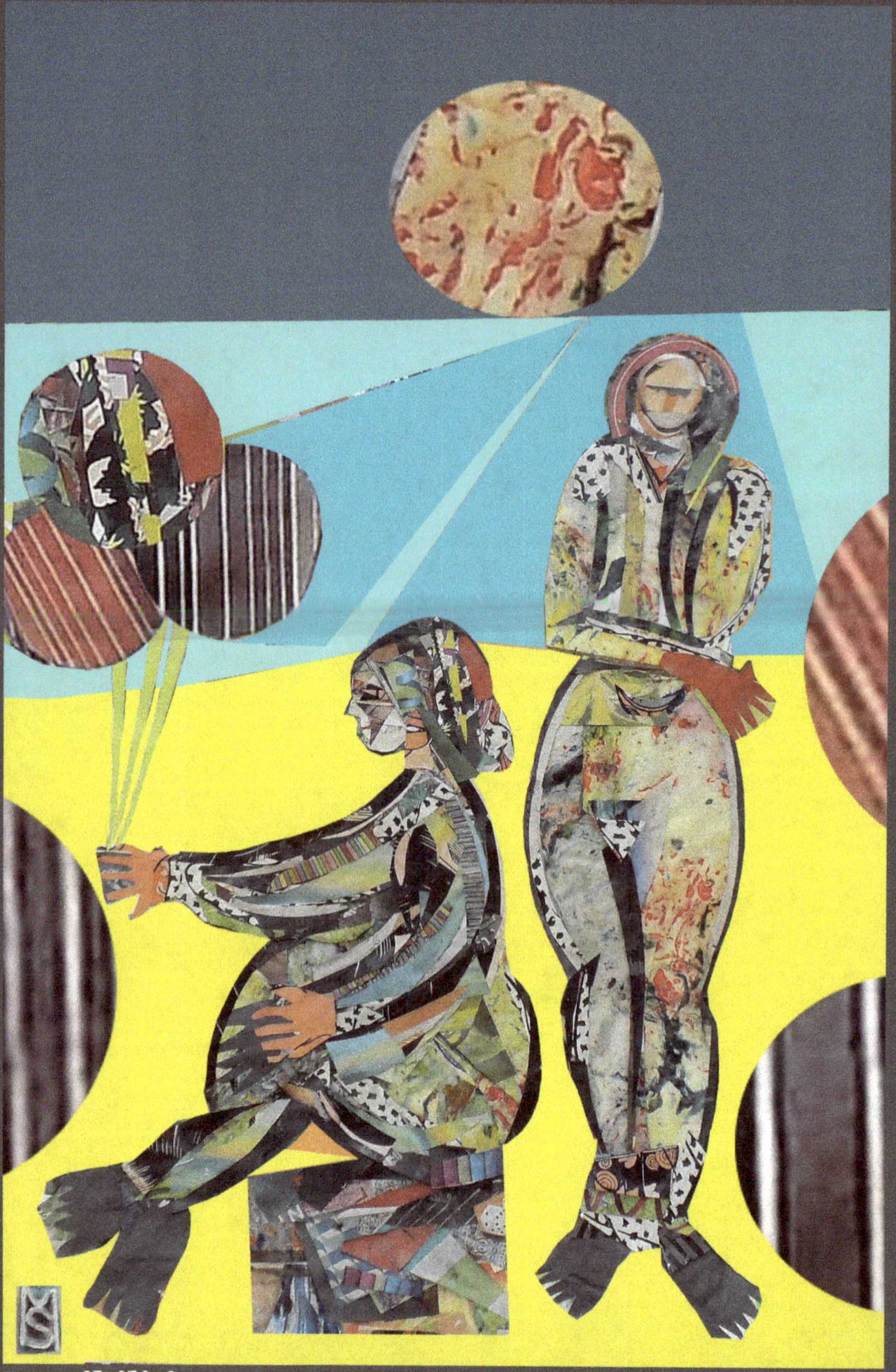

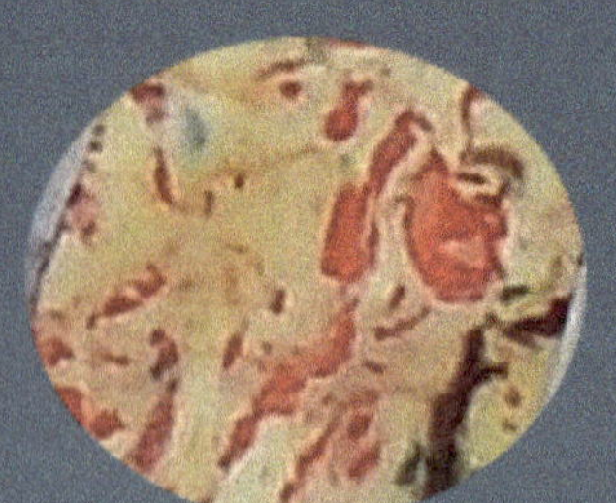

Possibilities
(57cm x 39cm)

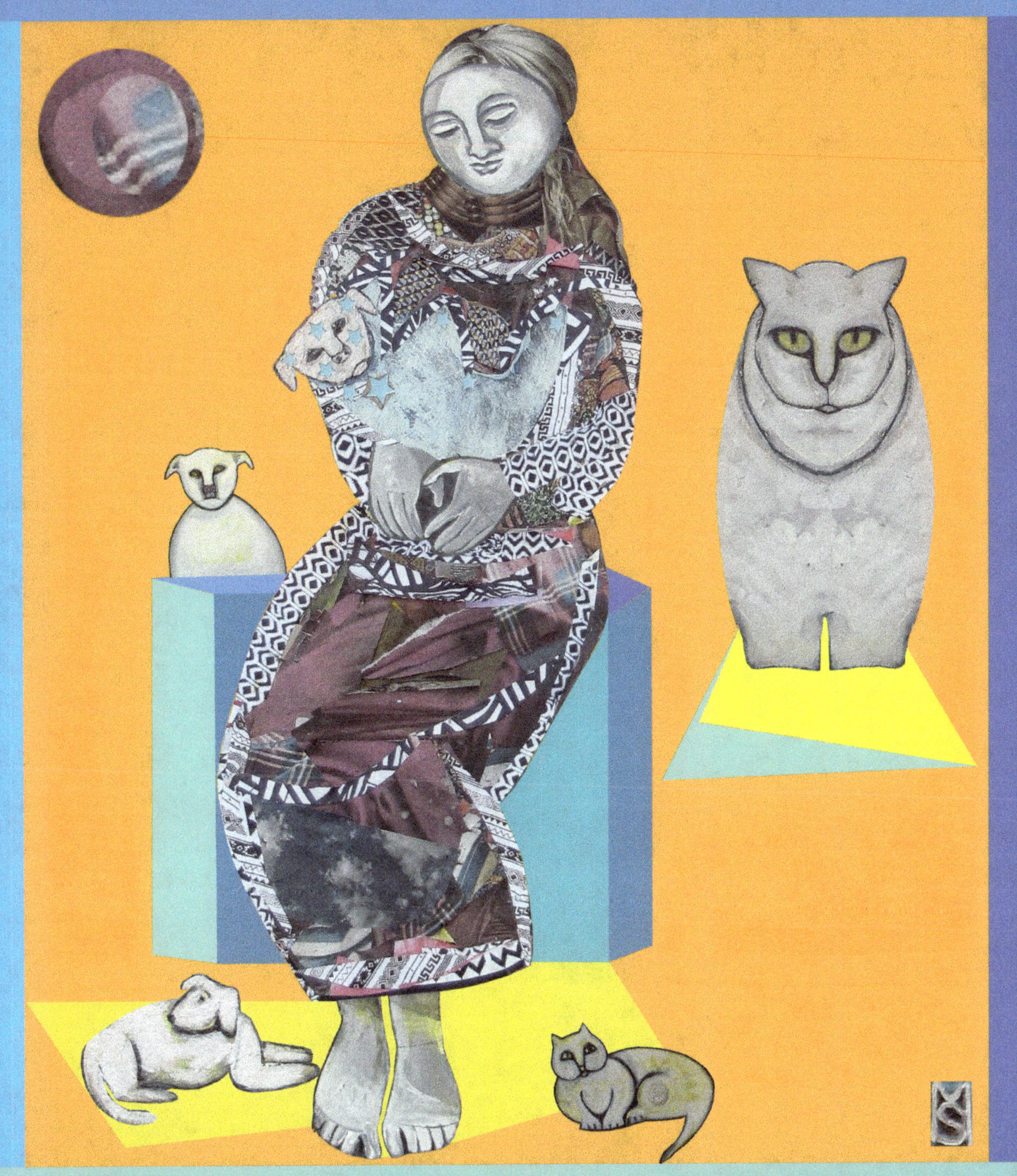

Tenderness
(39cm x 29cm)

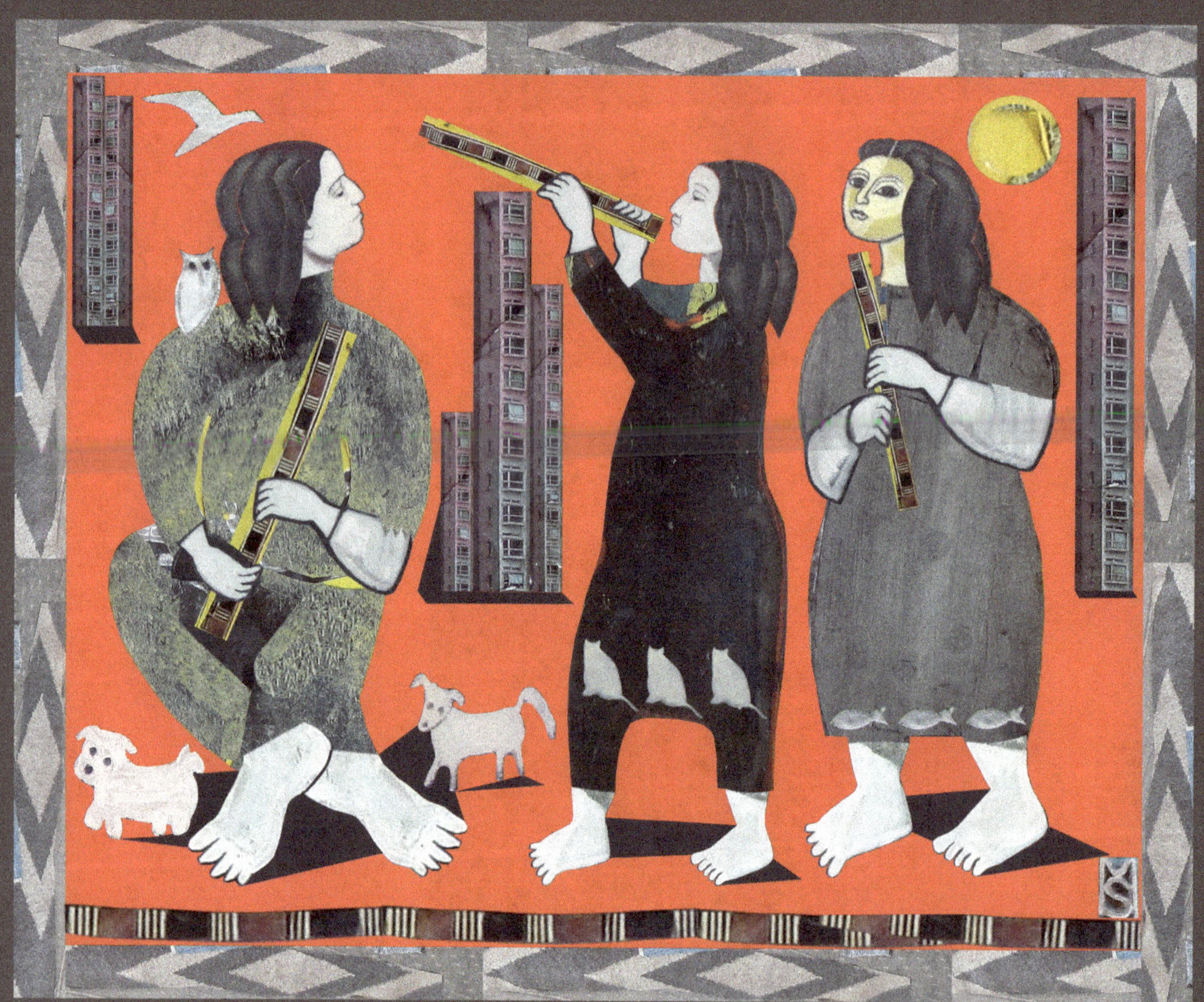

Zuggadee
(34cm x 42cm)

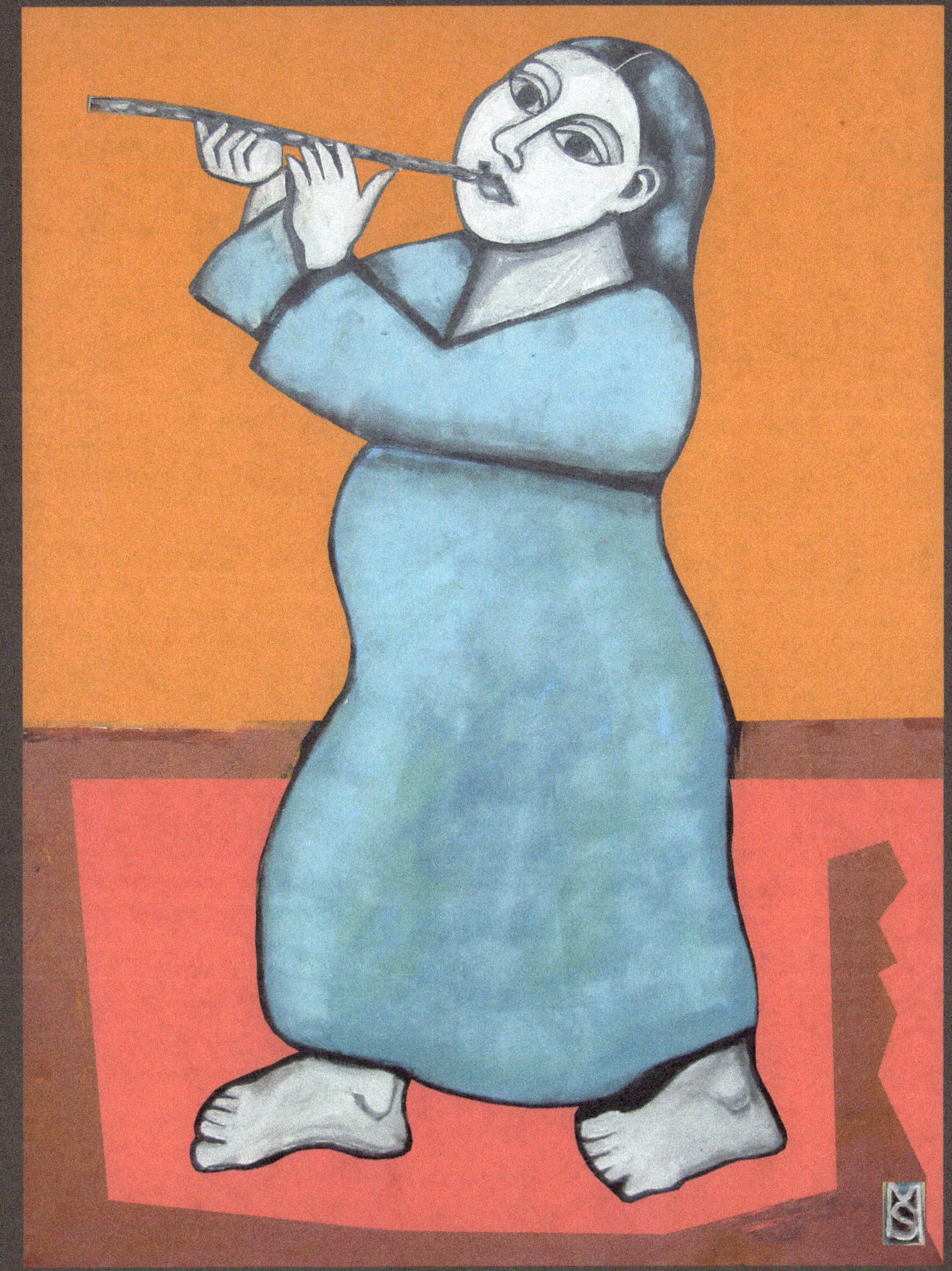

Musician
(100cm x 75cm)

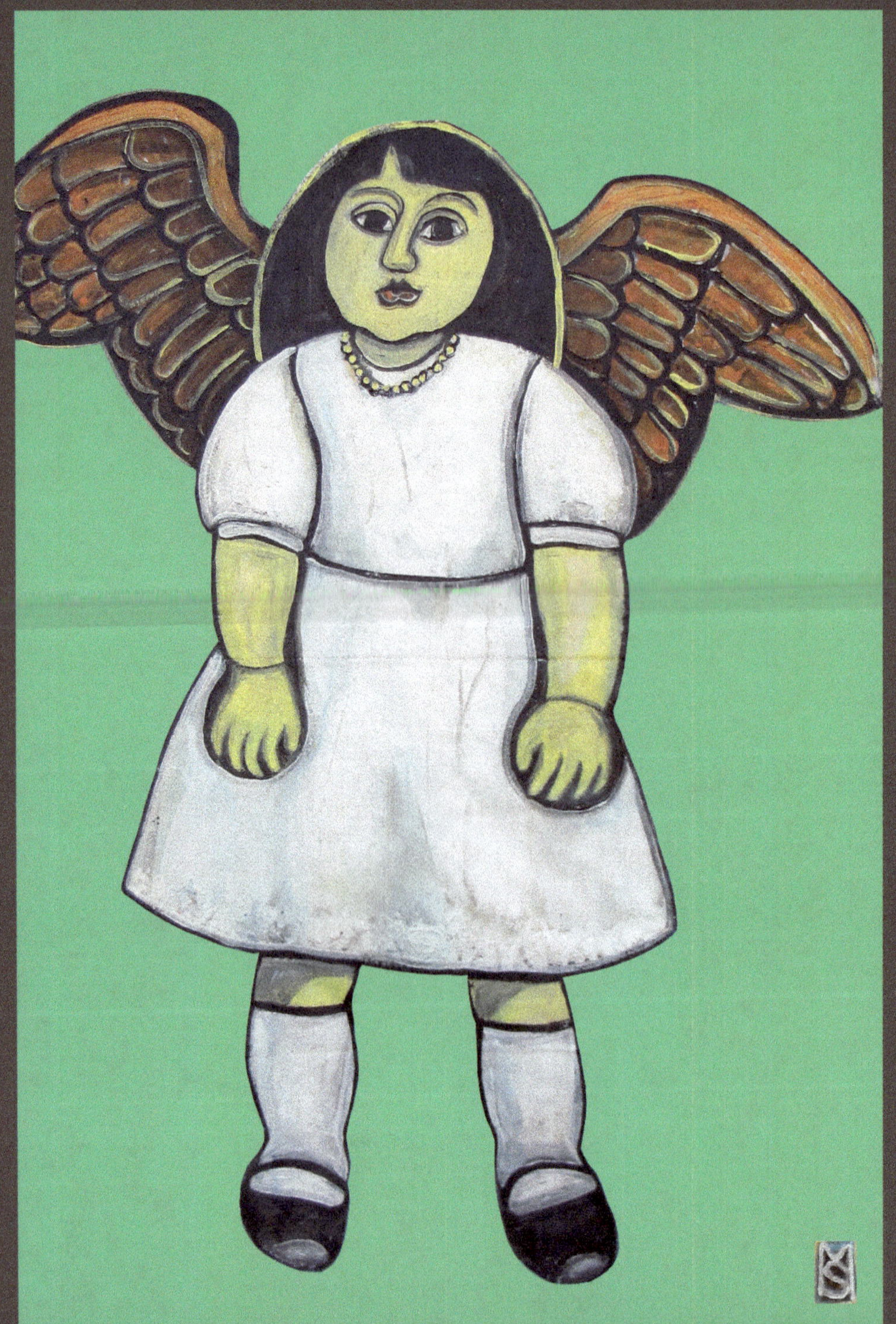

Rosa
(95cm x 65cm)

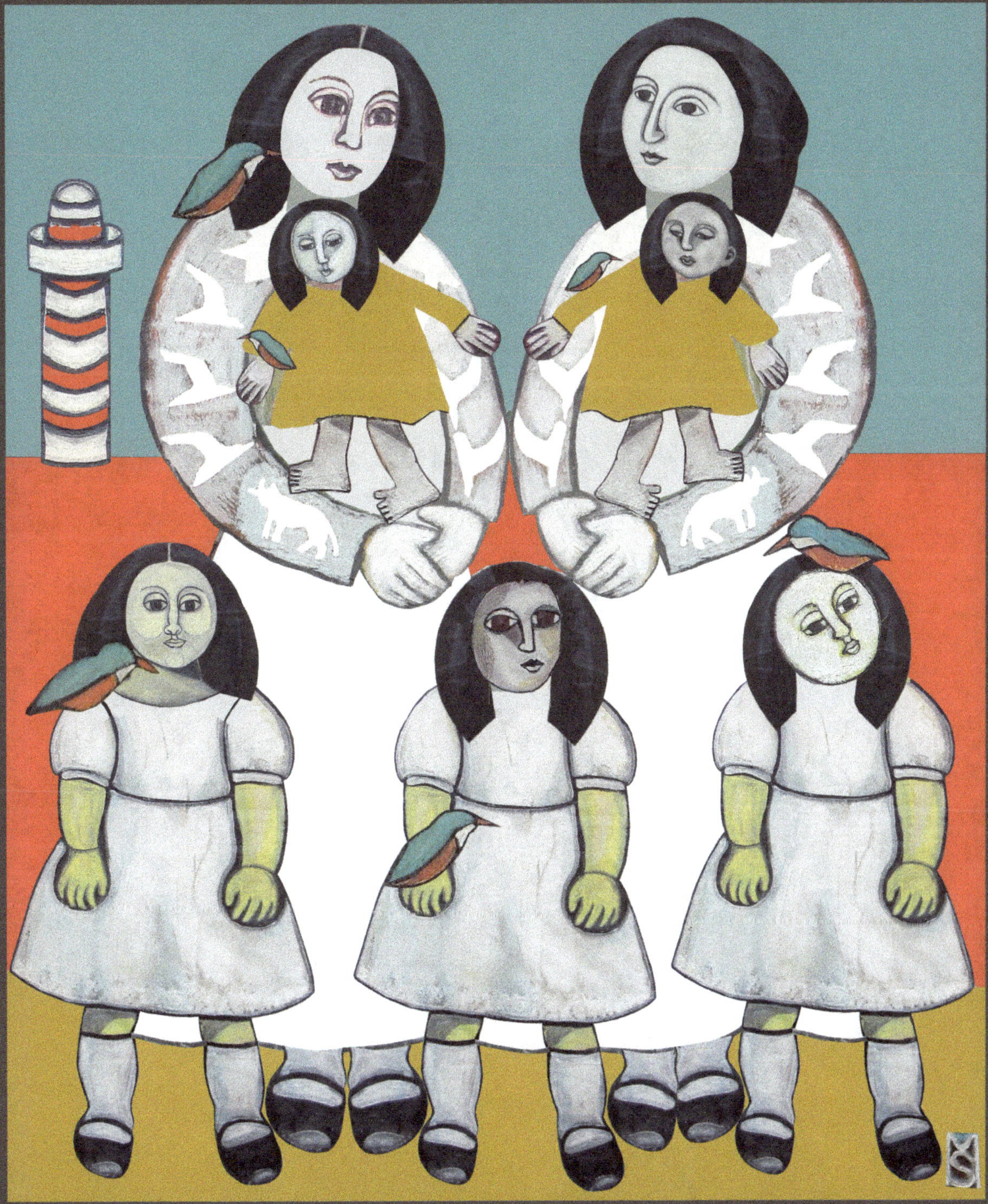

Grouped
(70cm x 60cm)

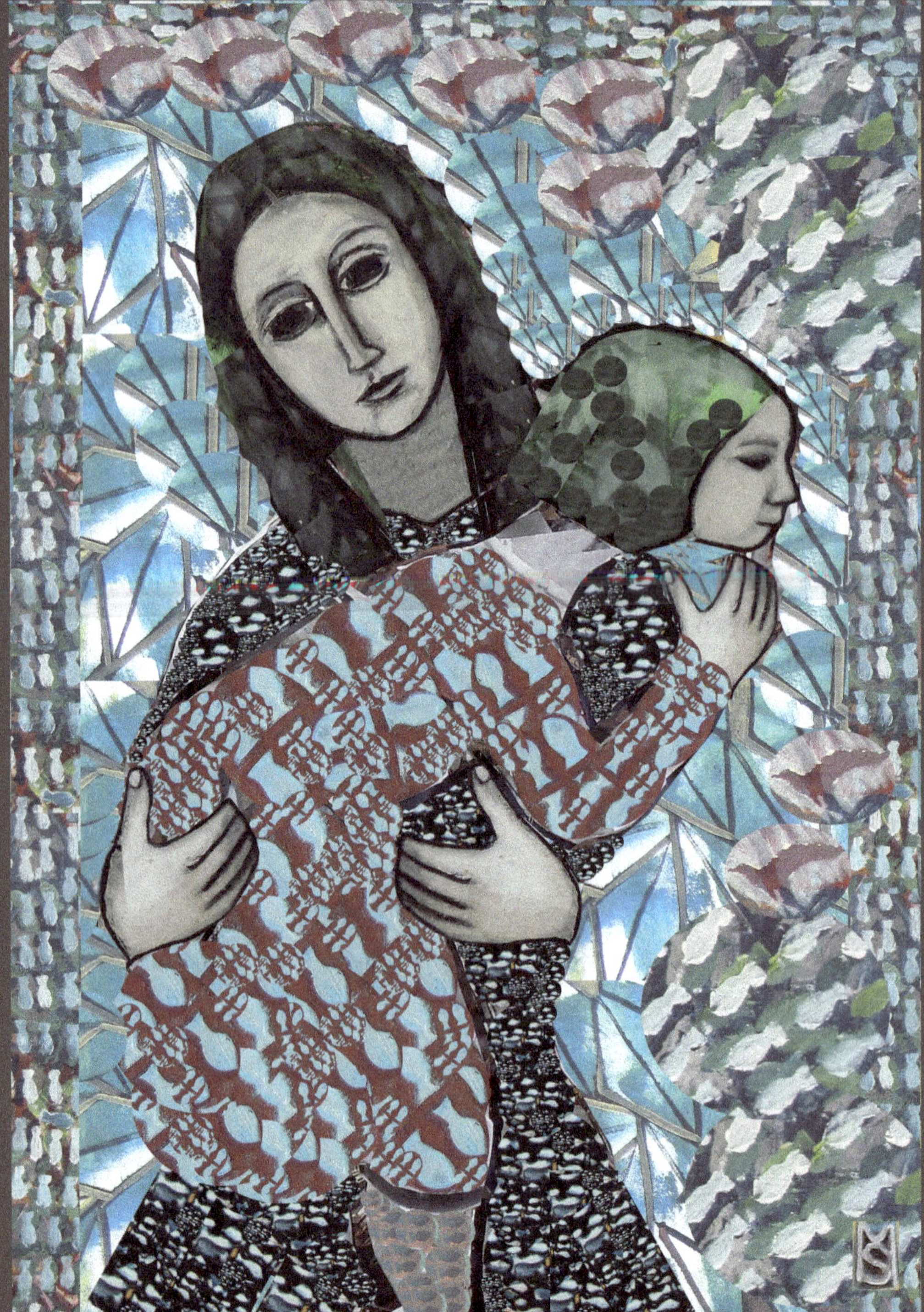

Reposar
(75cm x 54cm)

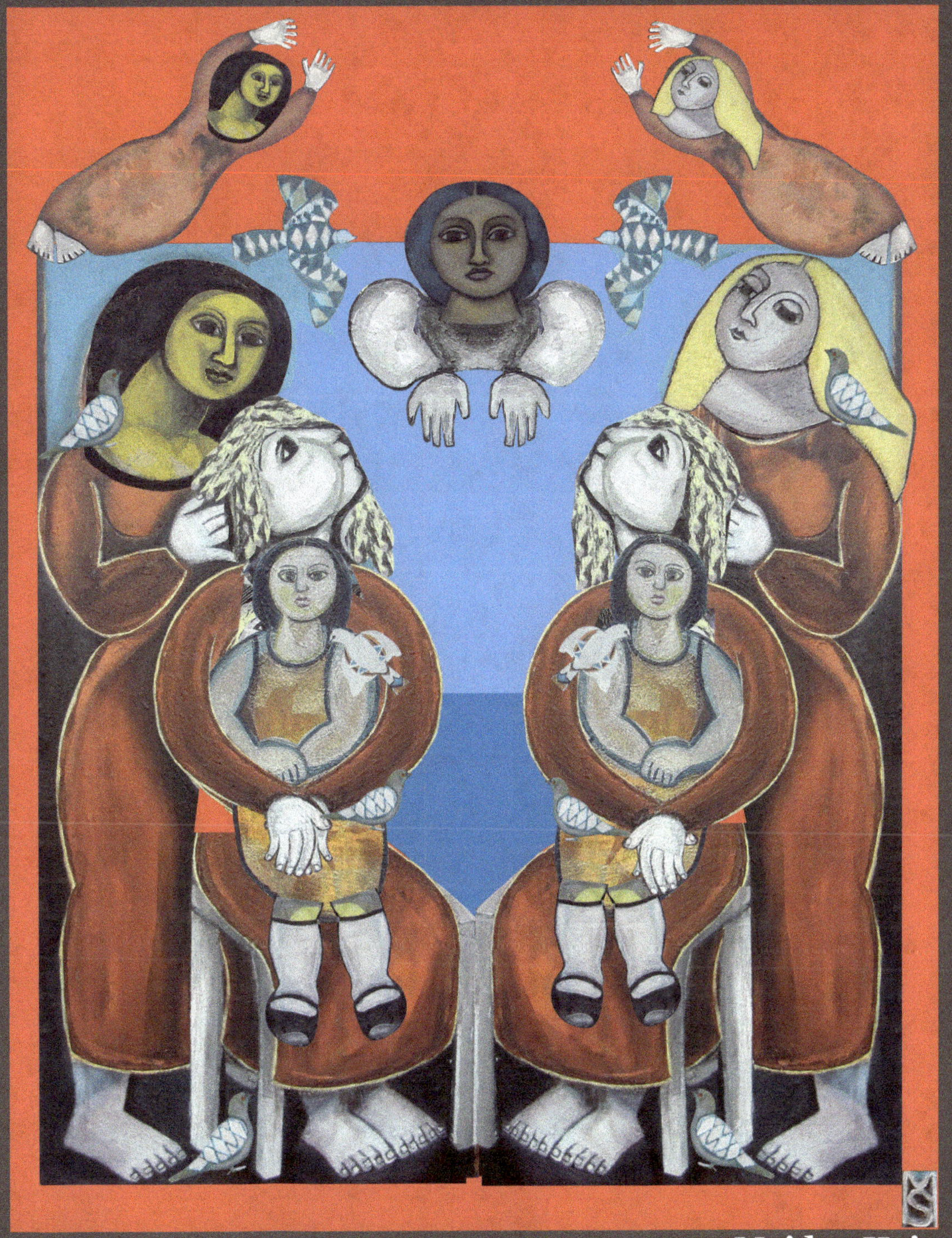

Maiden Hair
(70cm x 60cm)

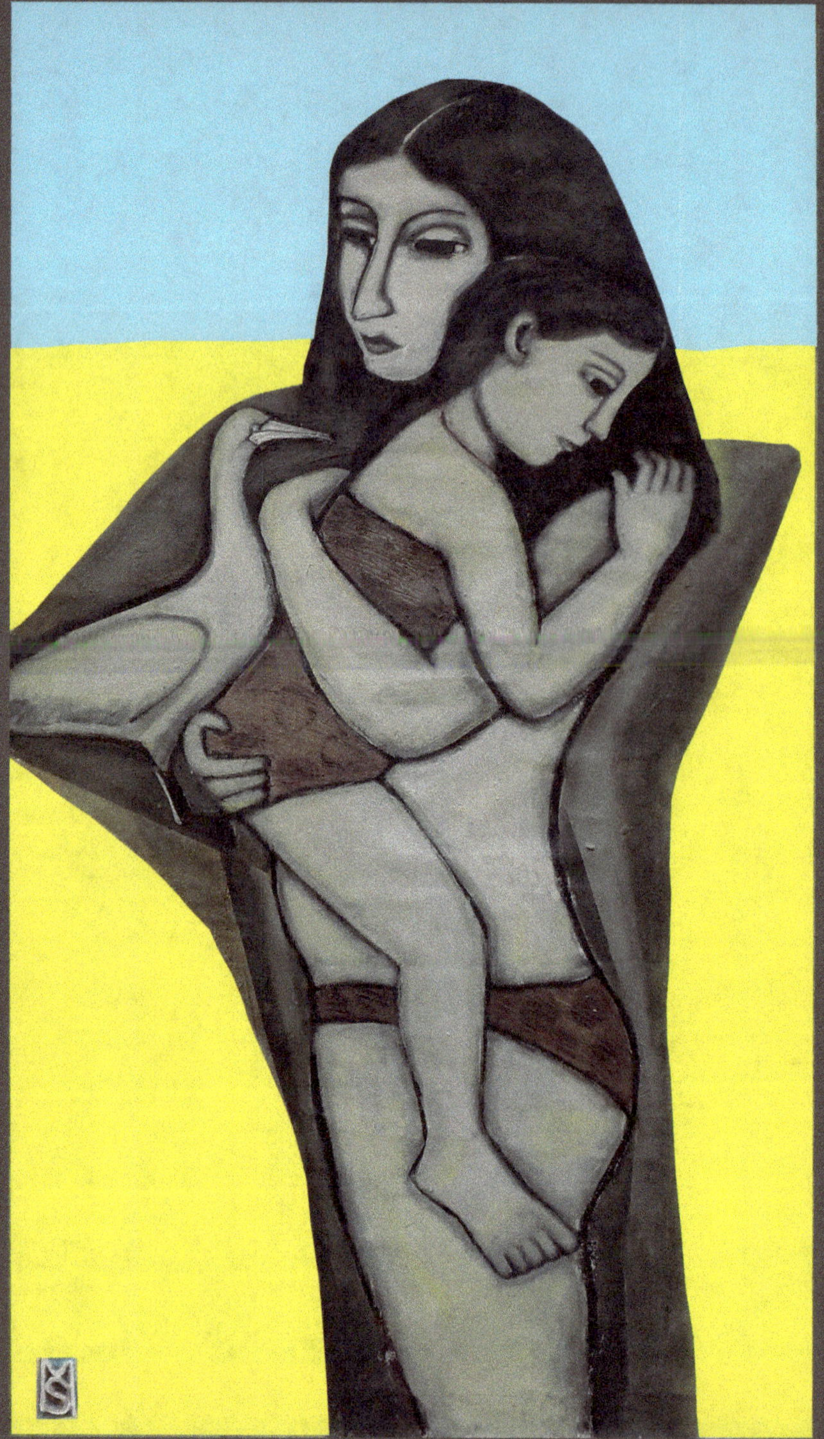

Gannet Beach
(114cm x 66cm)

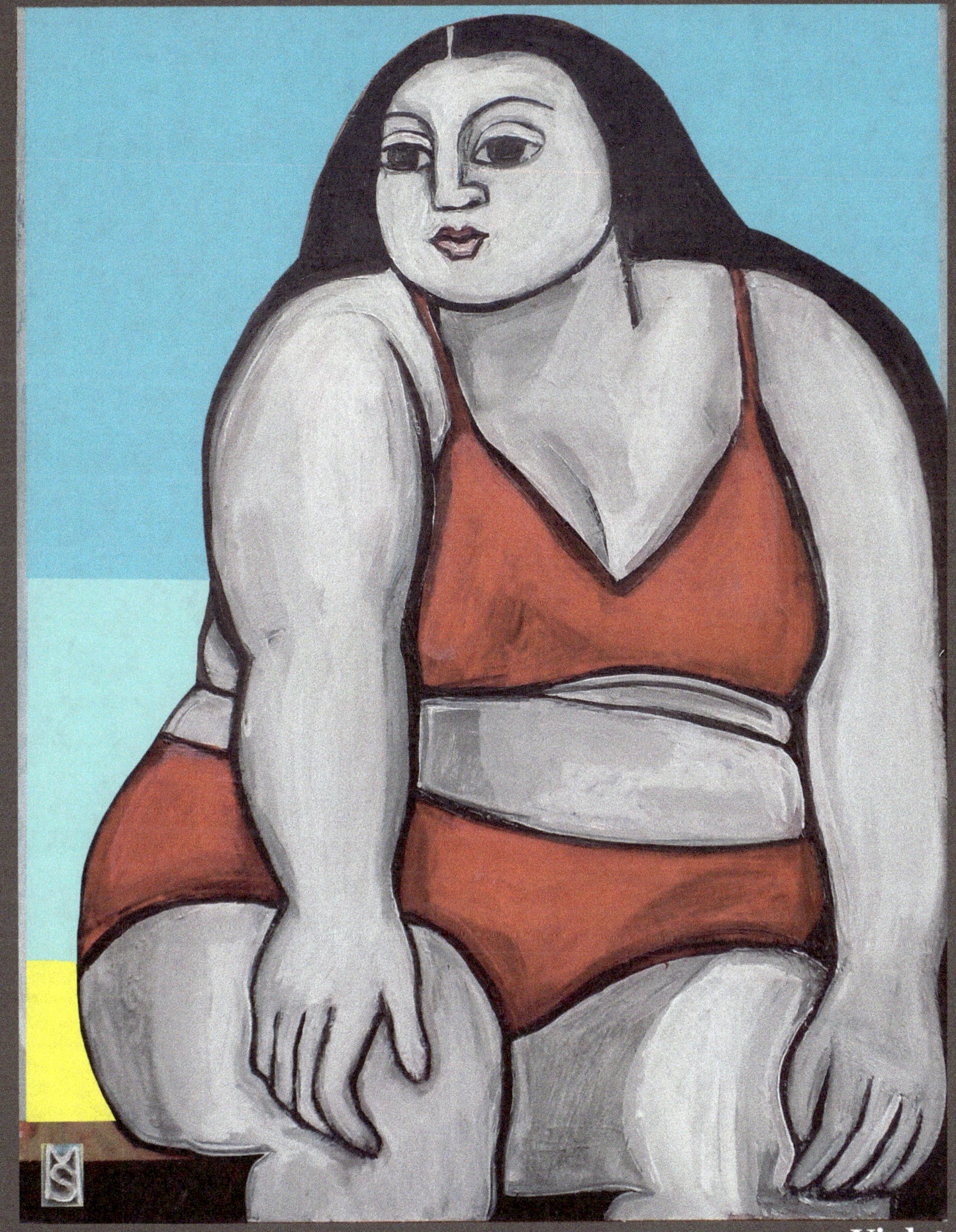

Violet
(61cm x 49cm)
Original painting on pg.70.

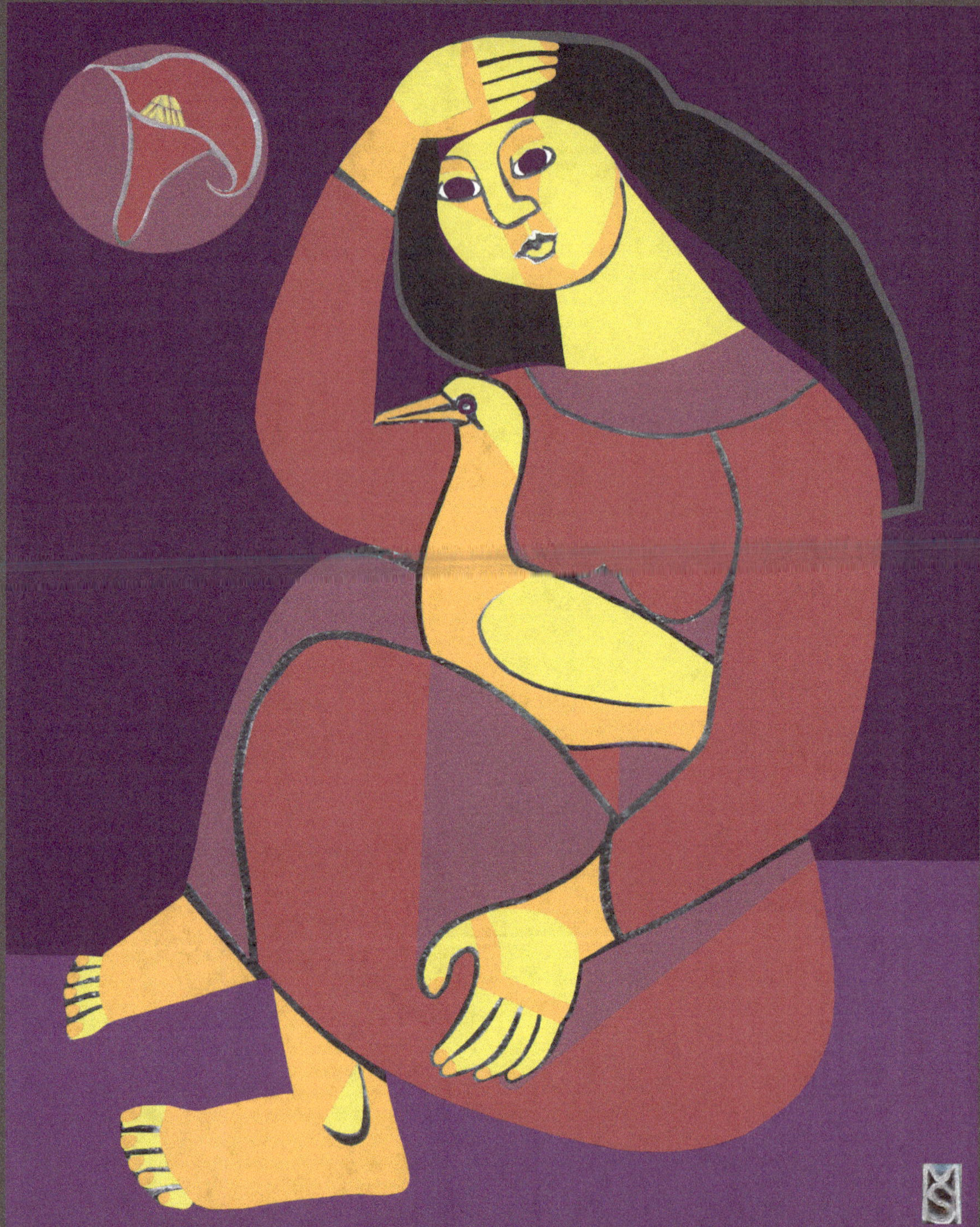

Sage Femme
(70cm x 55cm)

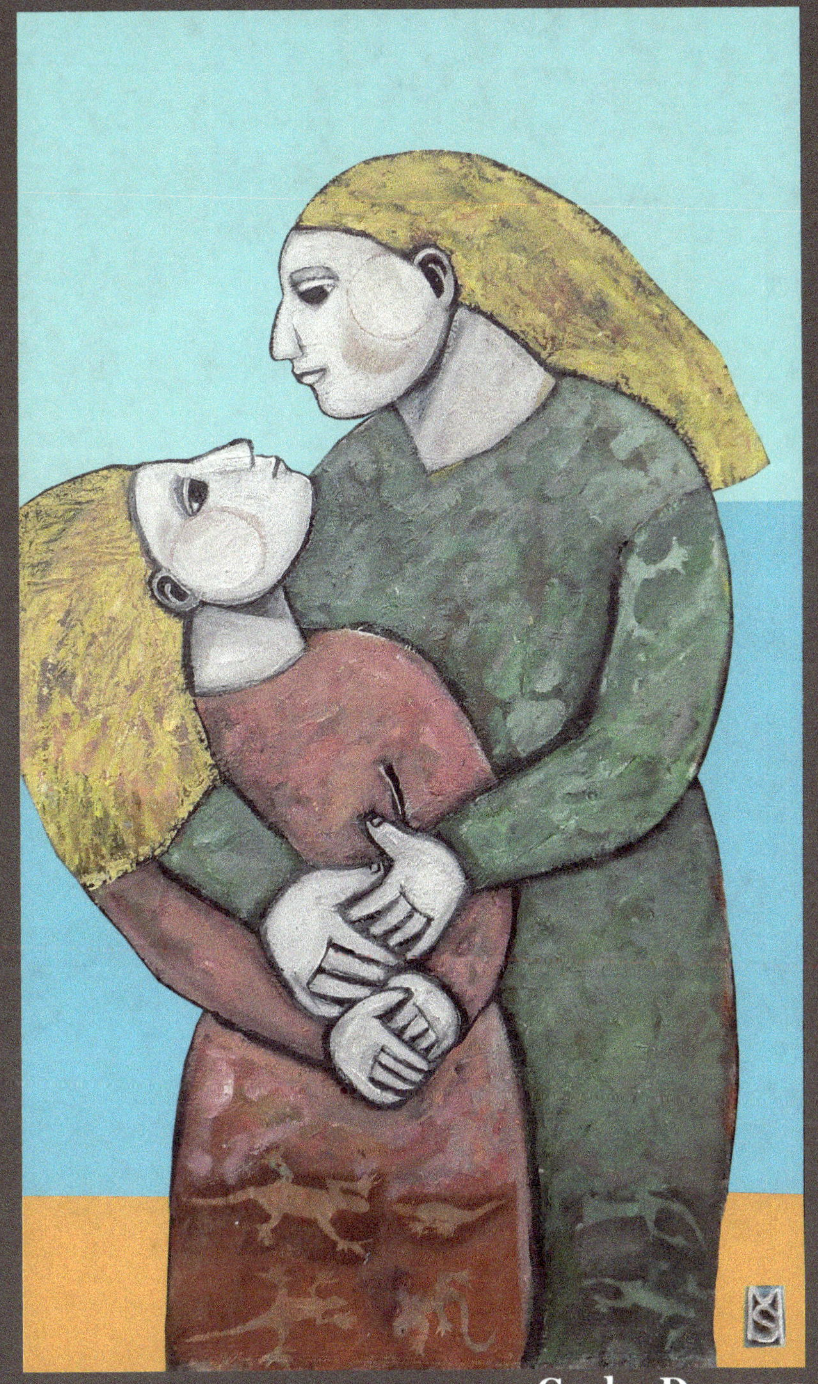

Gecko Dresses
(130cm x 80cm)
Original painting on pg.112.

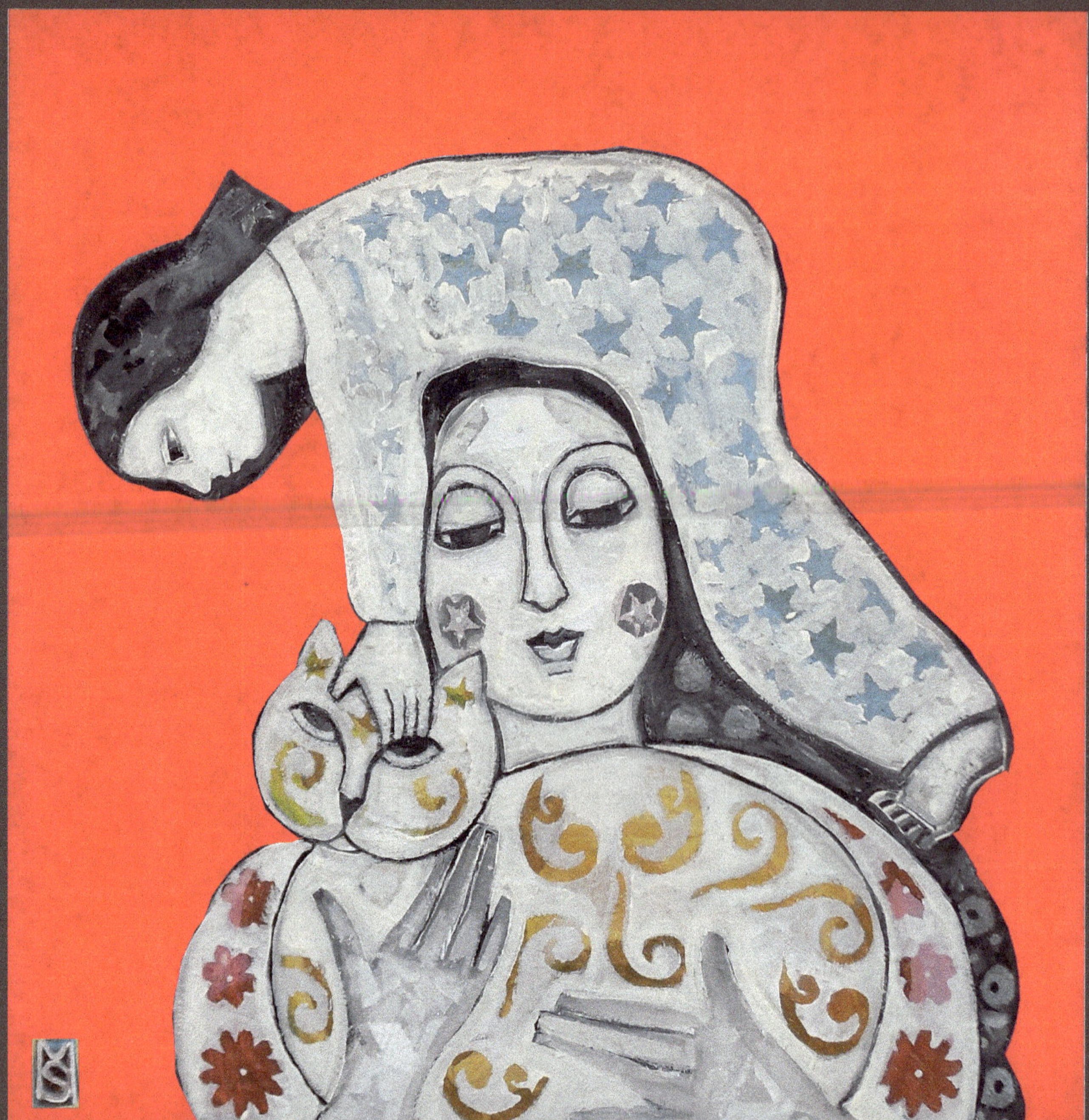

Amico
(85cm x 85cm)

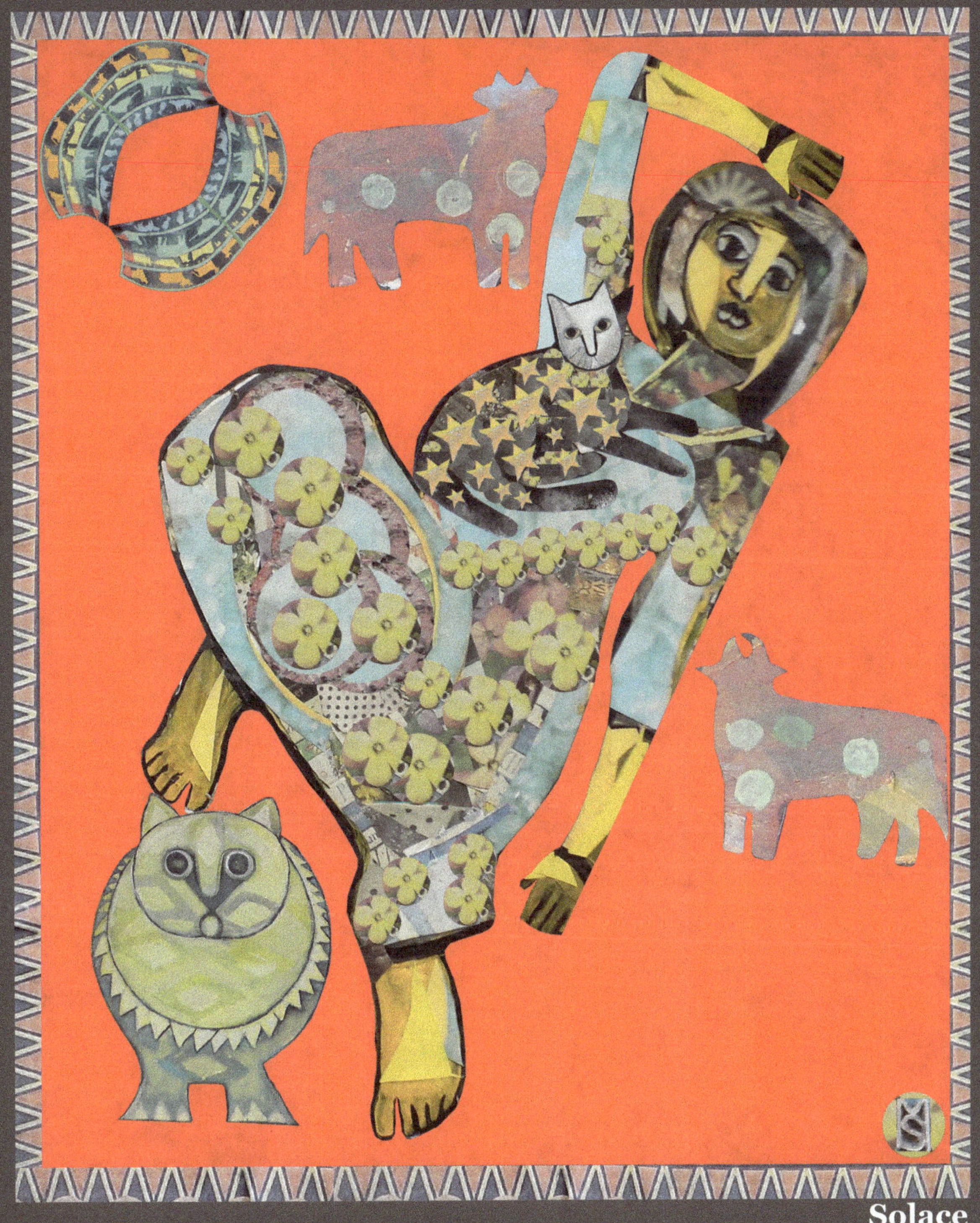

Solace
(42cm x 35cm)

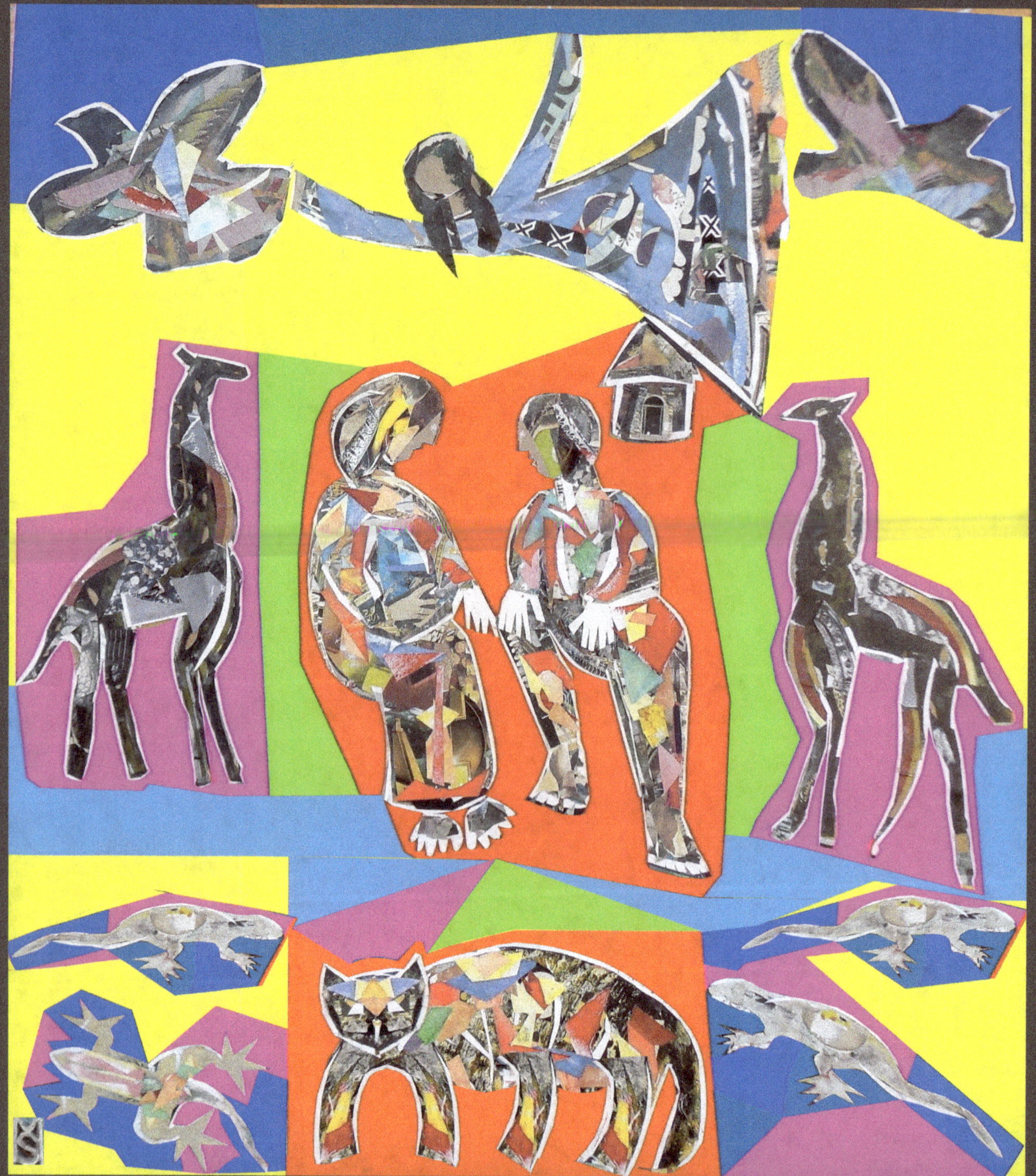

Neon Orange
(67cm x 60cm)

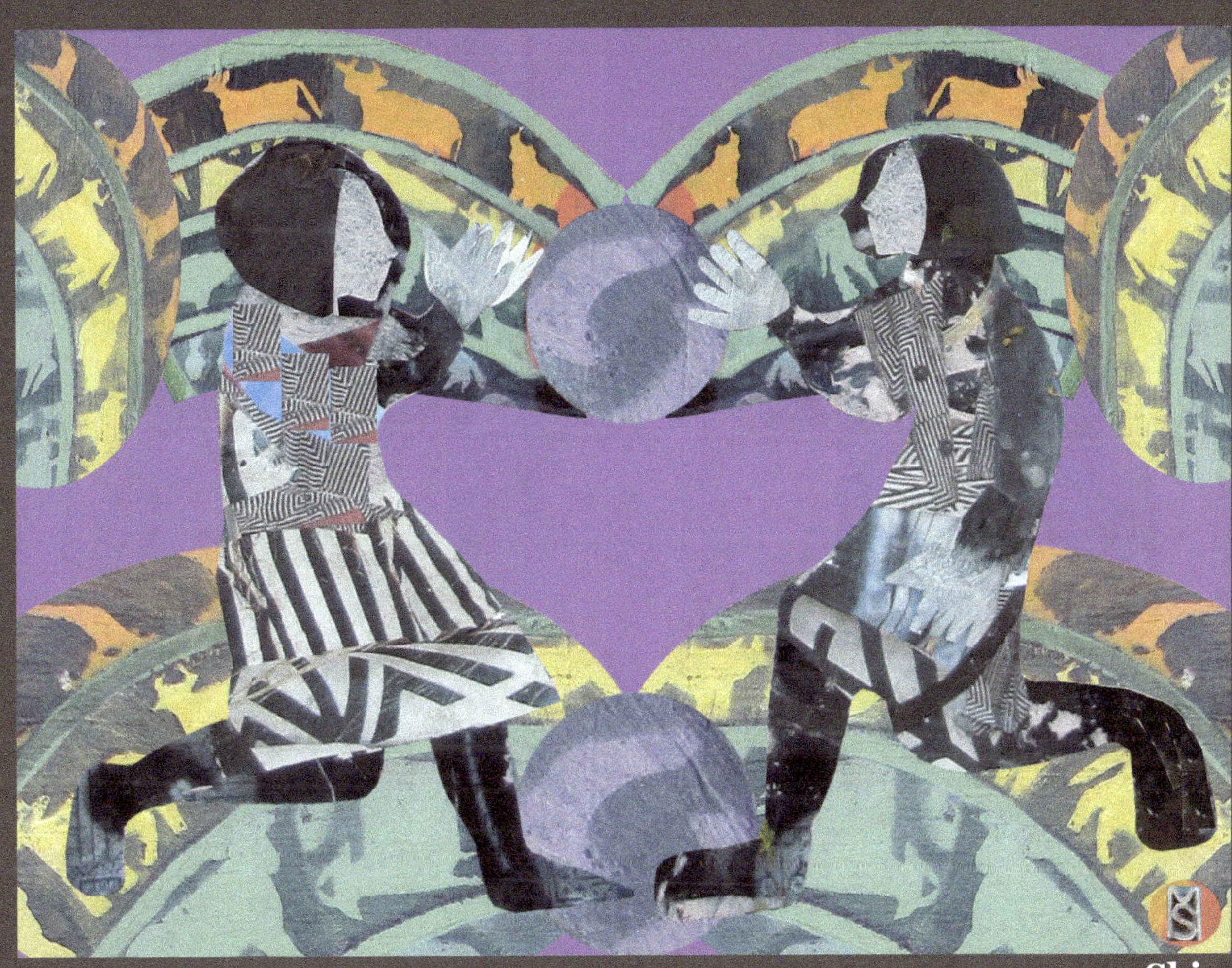

Skip
(42cm x 57cm)

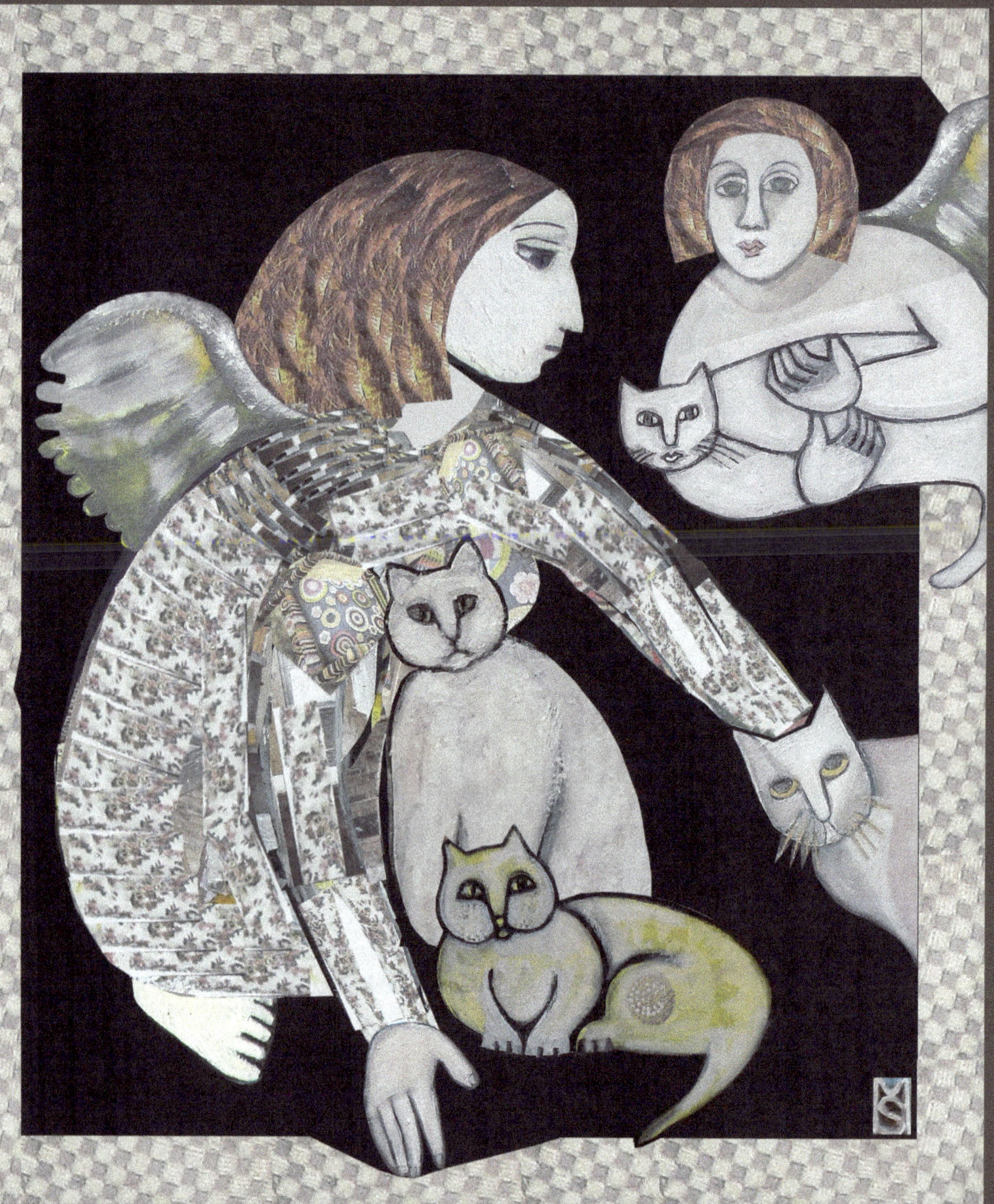

Someone Cared
(42cm x 38cm)

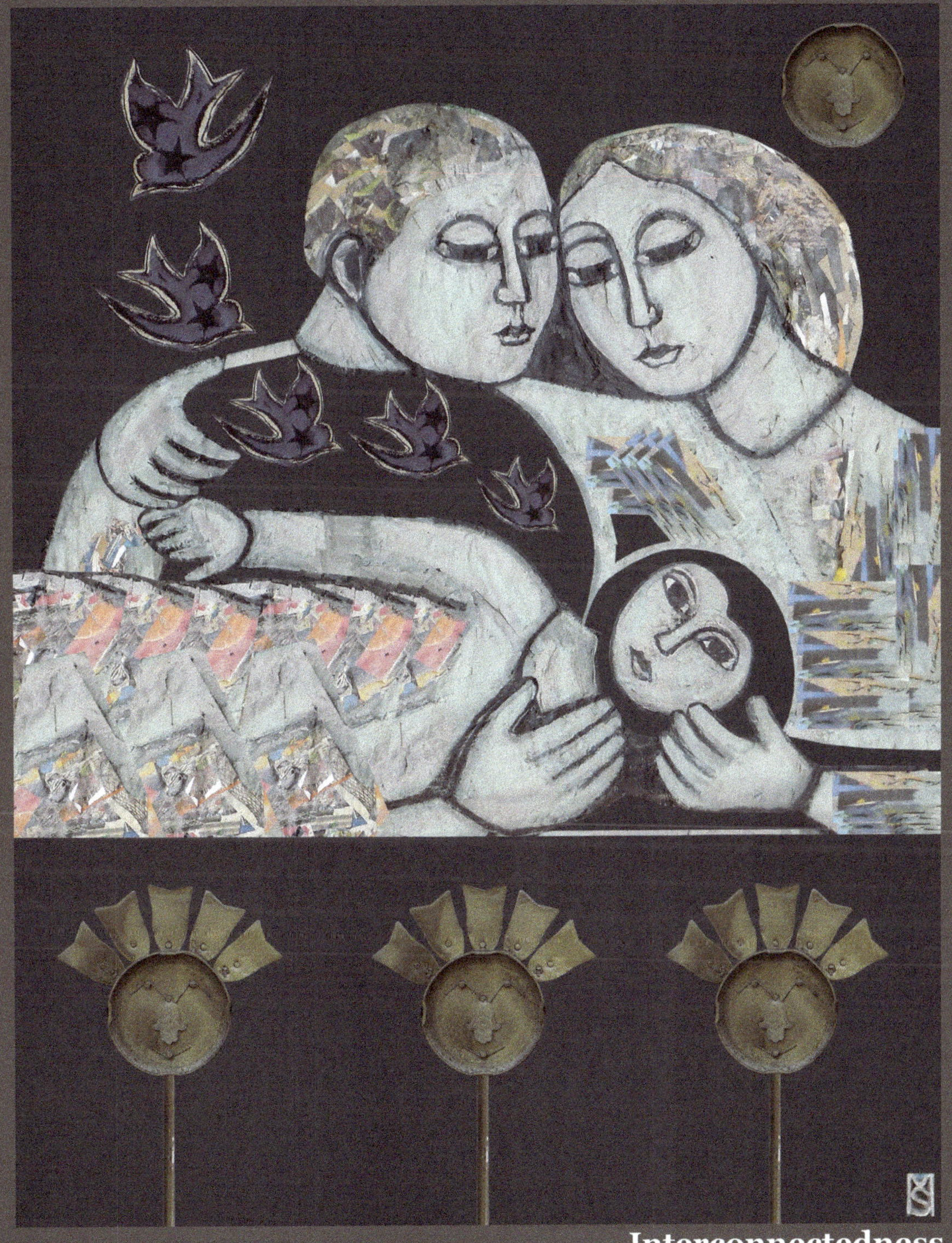

Interconnectedness
(99cm x 76cm)

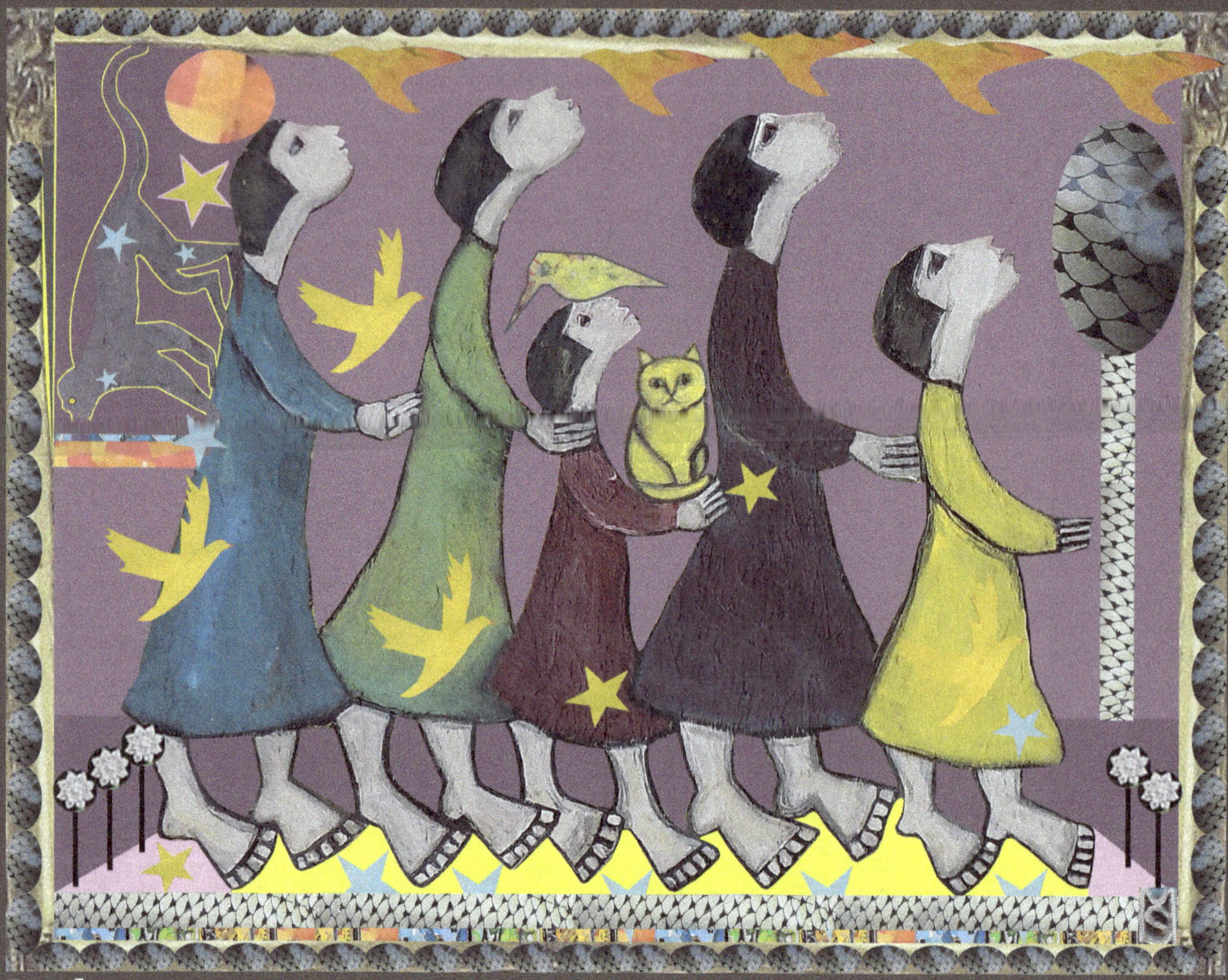

Look
(78cm x 103cm)

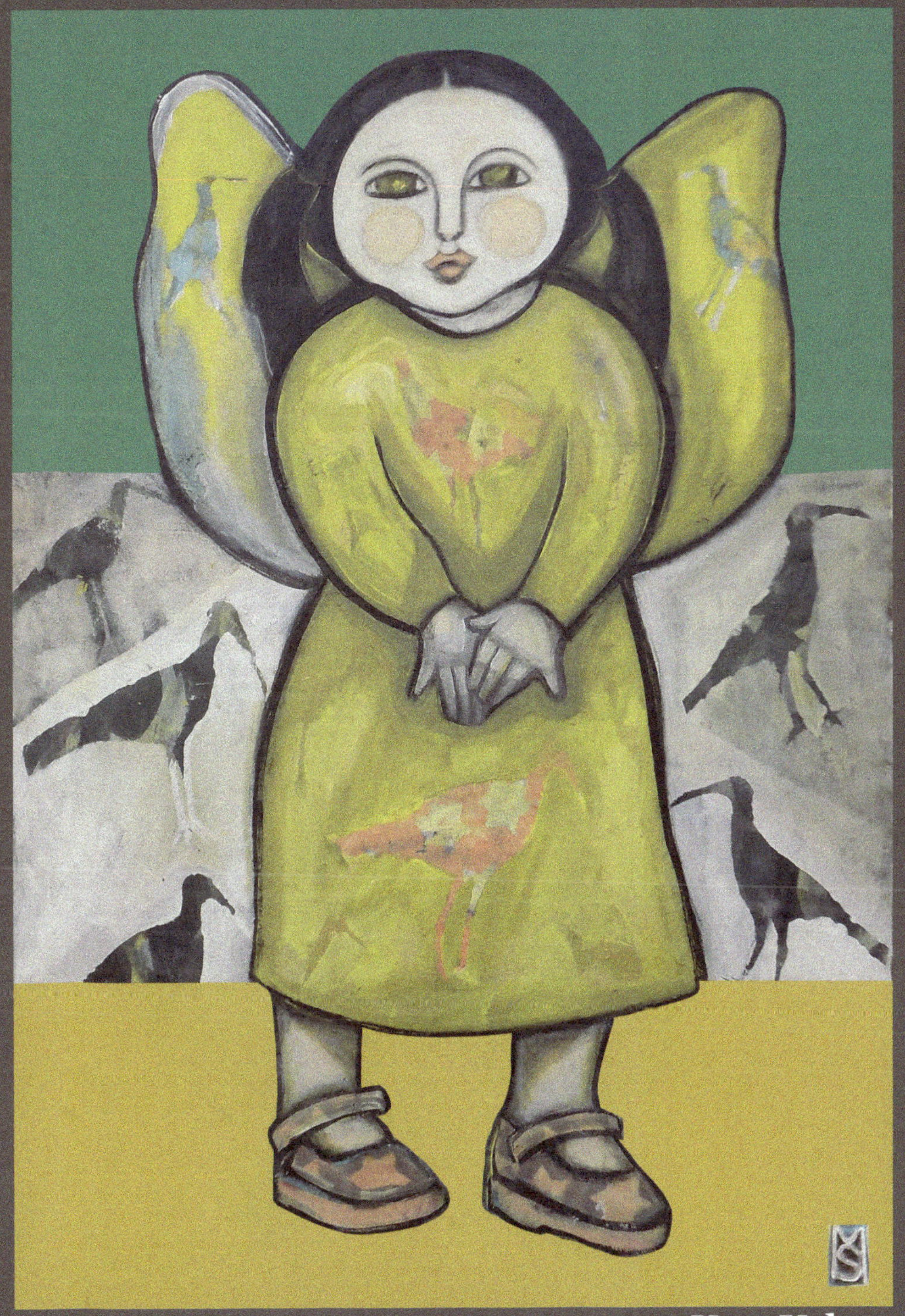

Vera Velcro
(110cm x 75cm)

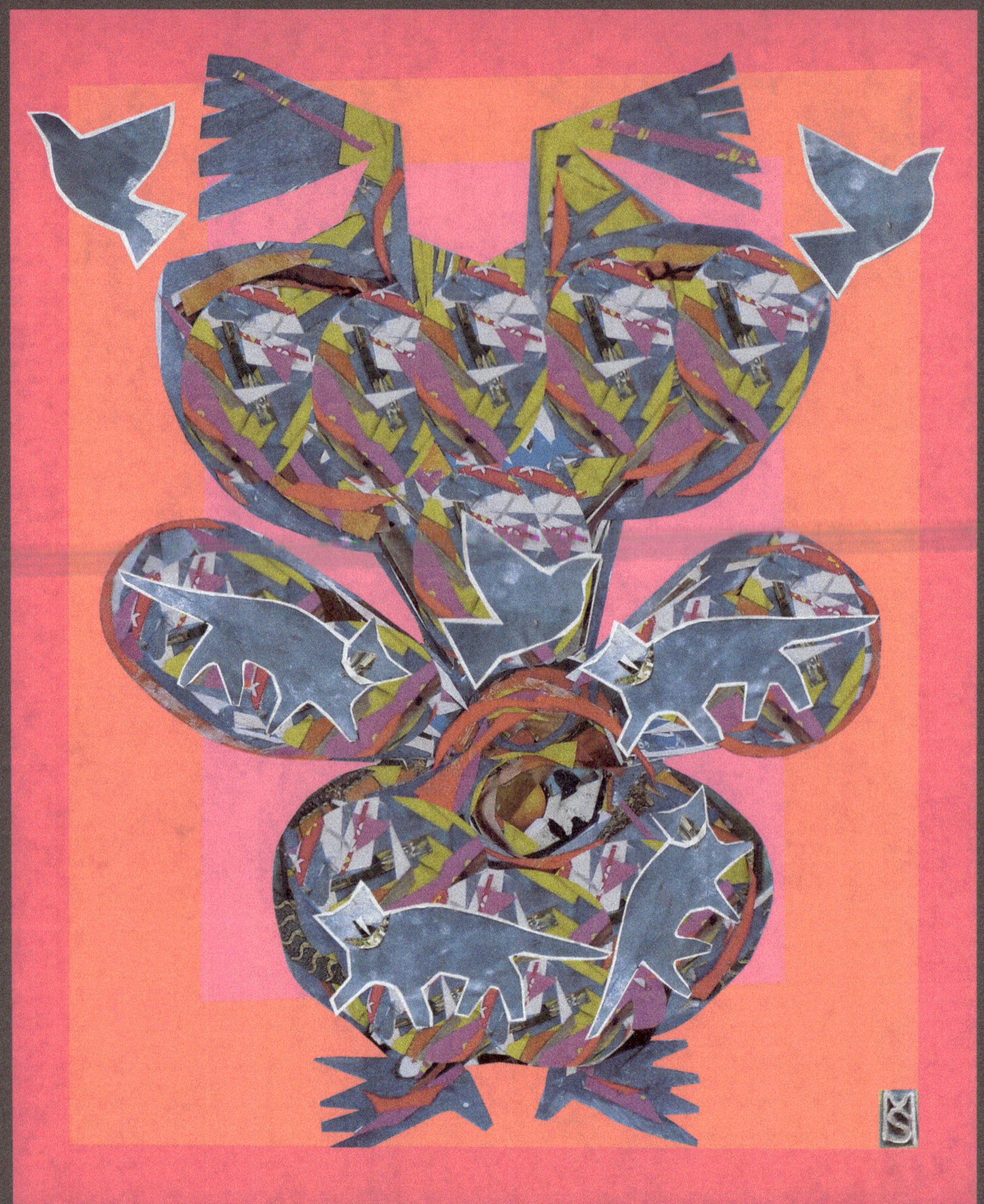

Cropping the Shine
(40cm x 29cm)

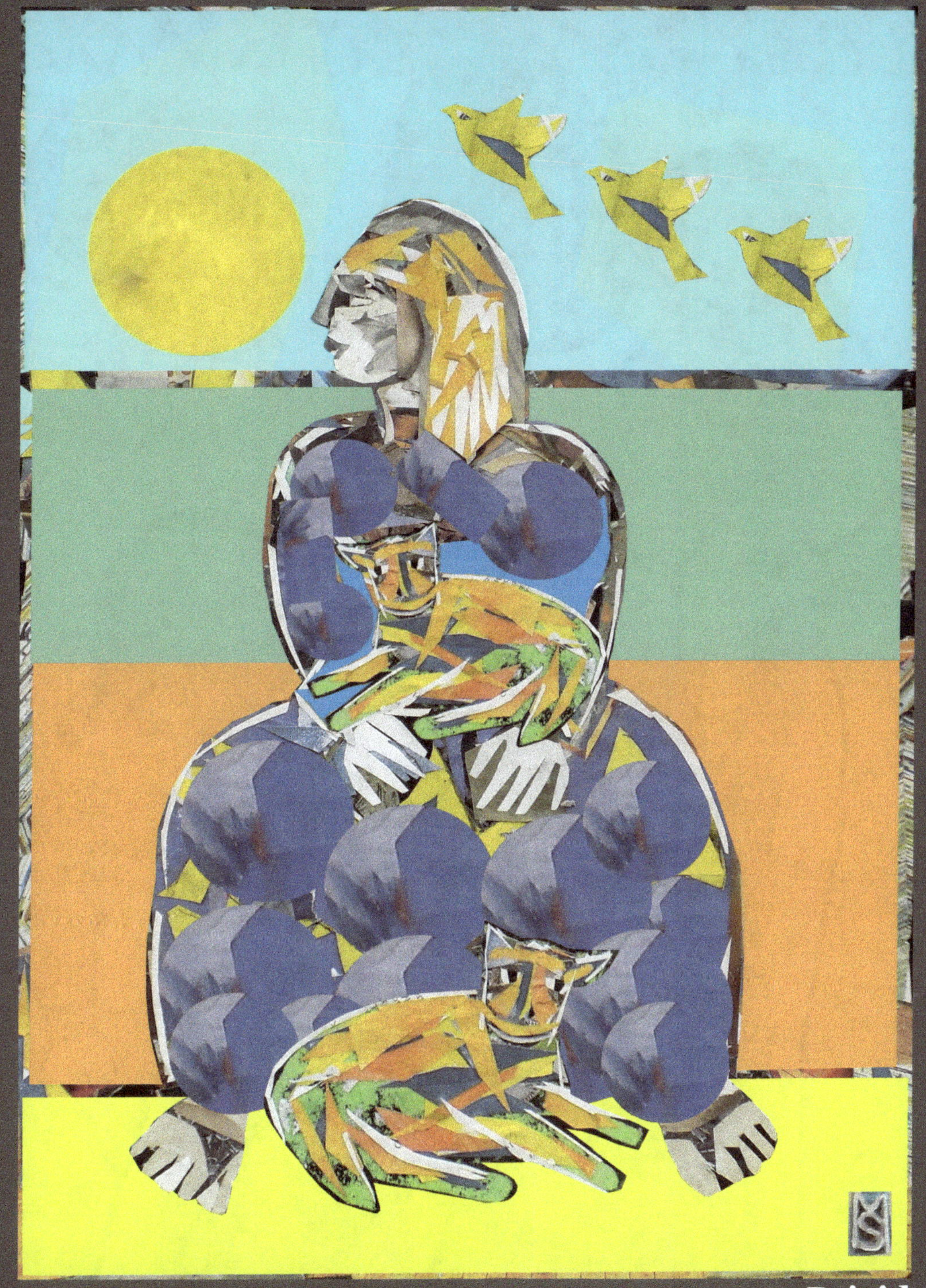

Brigid
(45cm x 34cm)

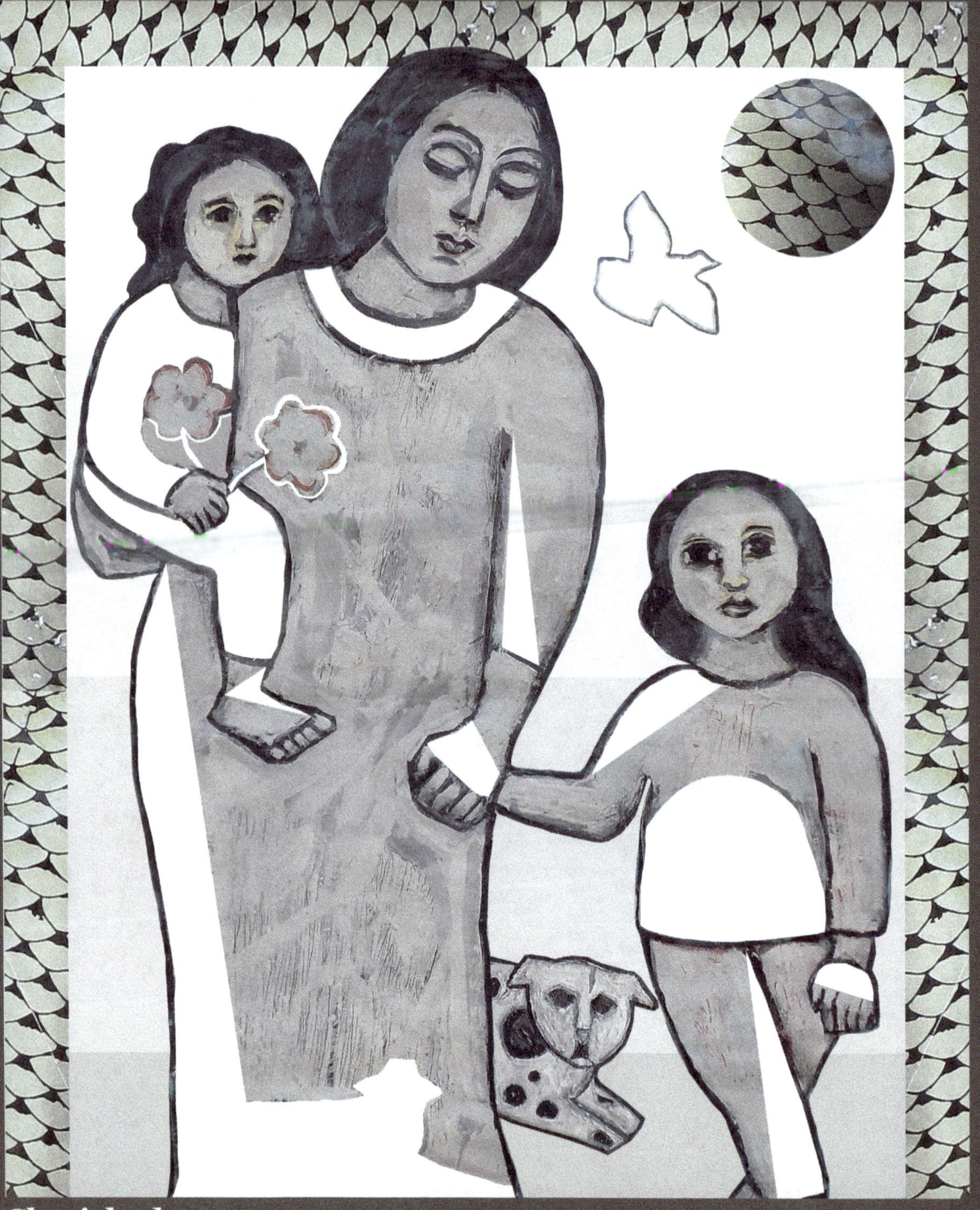

Cherished
(77cm x 55cm)

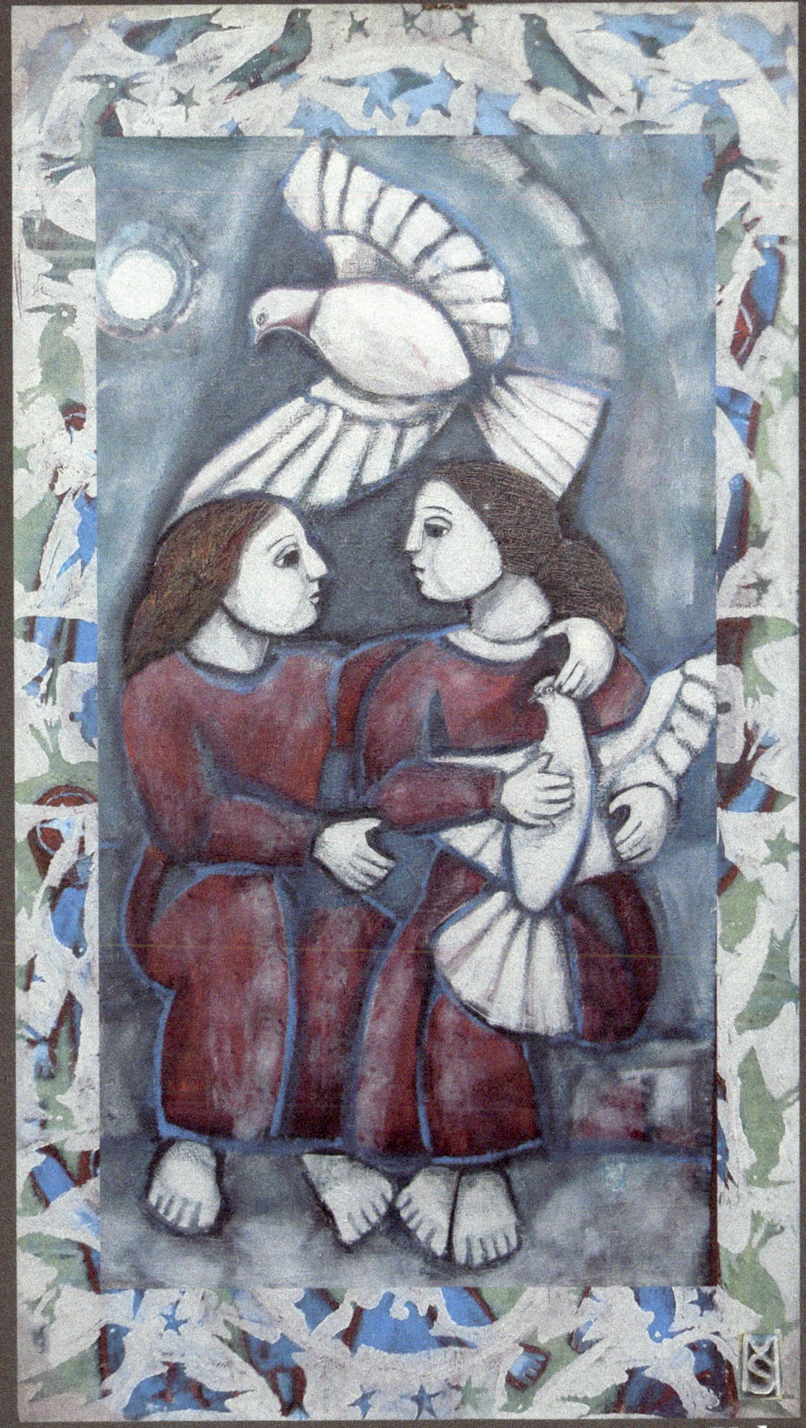

Yebo
(125cm x 70cm)

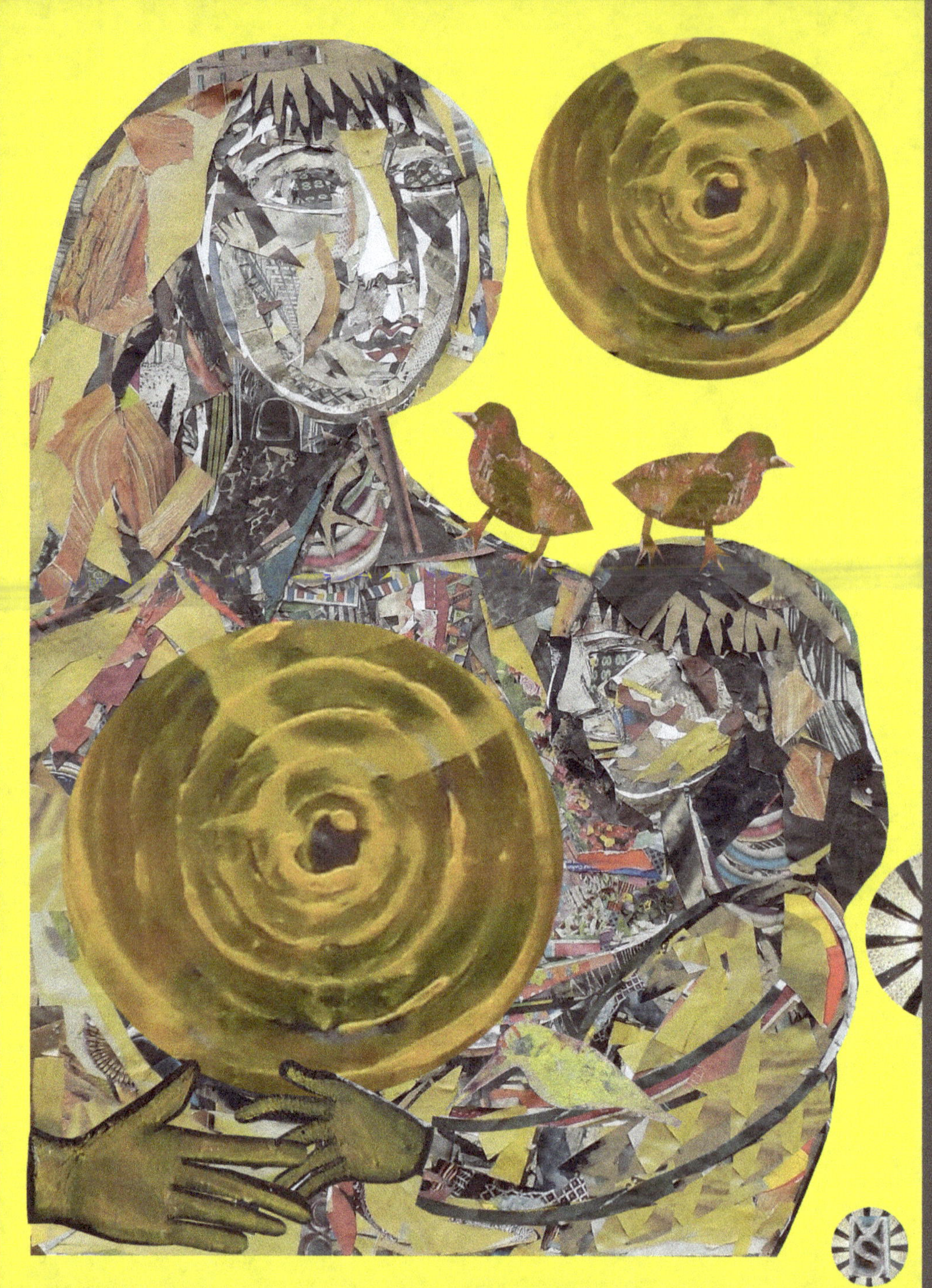

Saved Fragments
(77cm x 56cm)

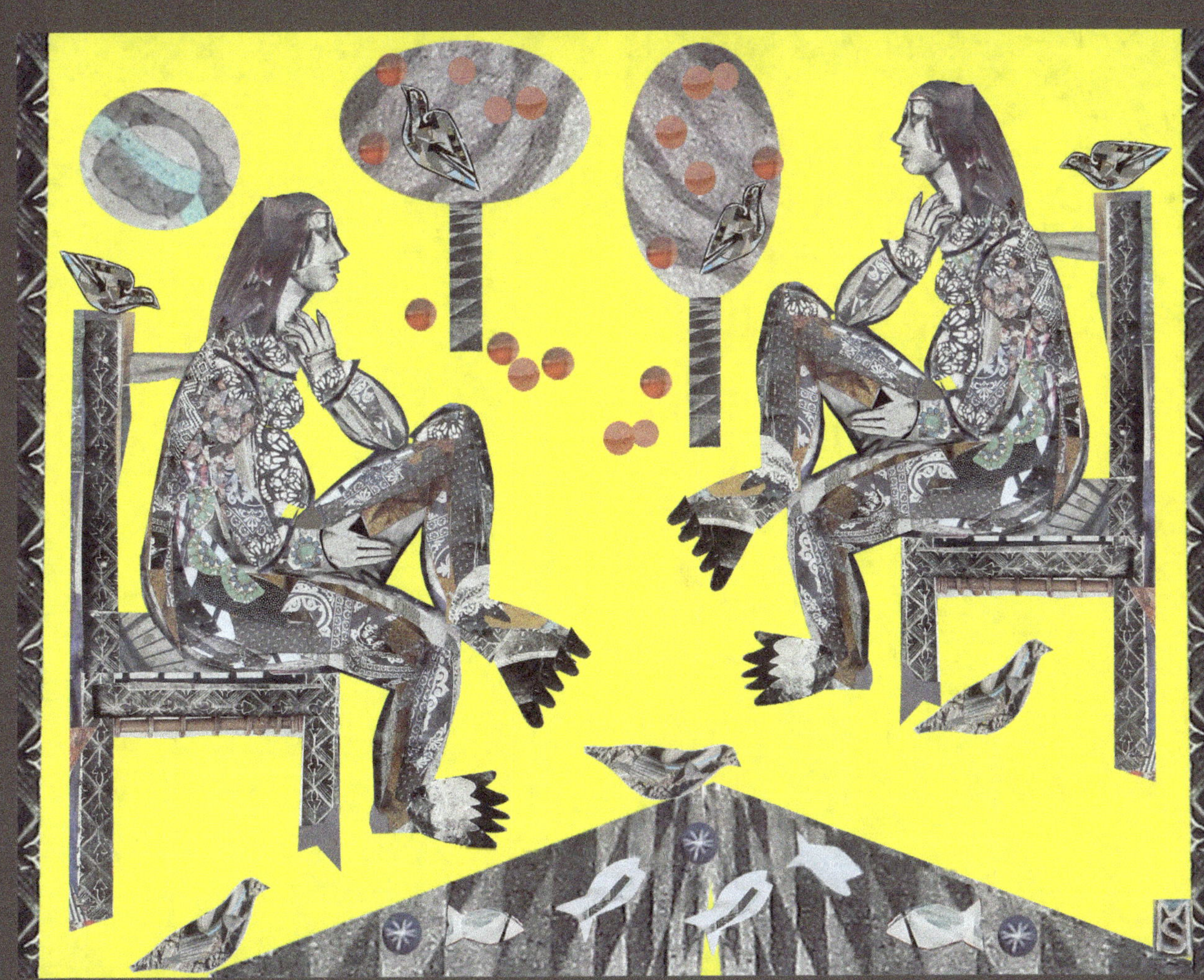

Metis
(36cm x 47cm)

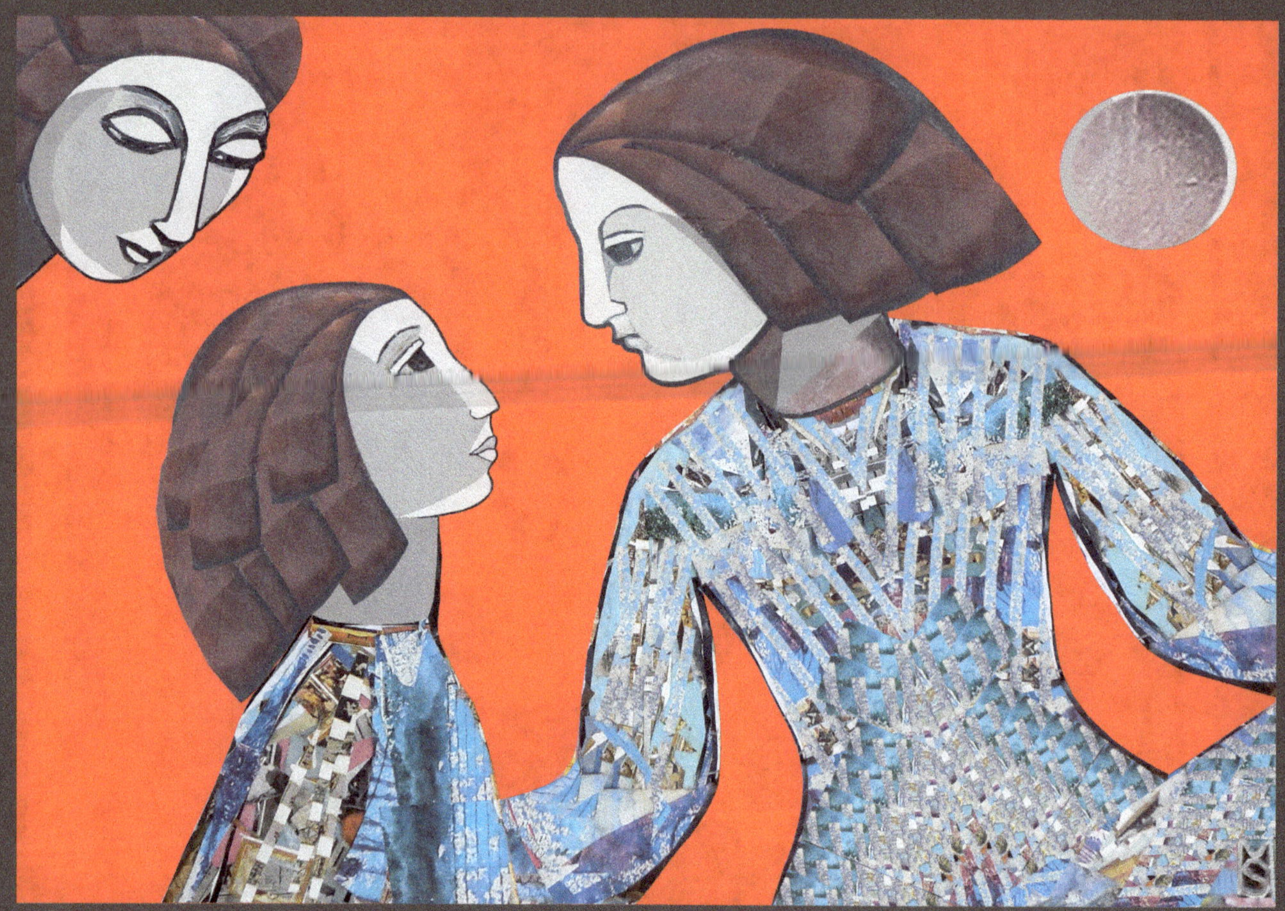

Ginny and Stella
(51cm x 75cm)

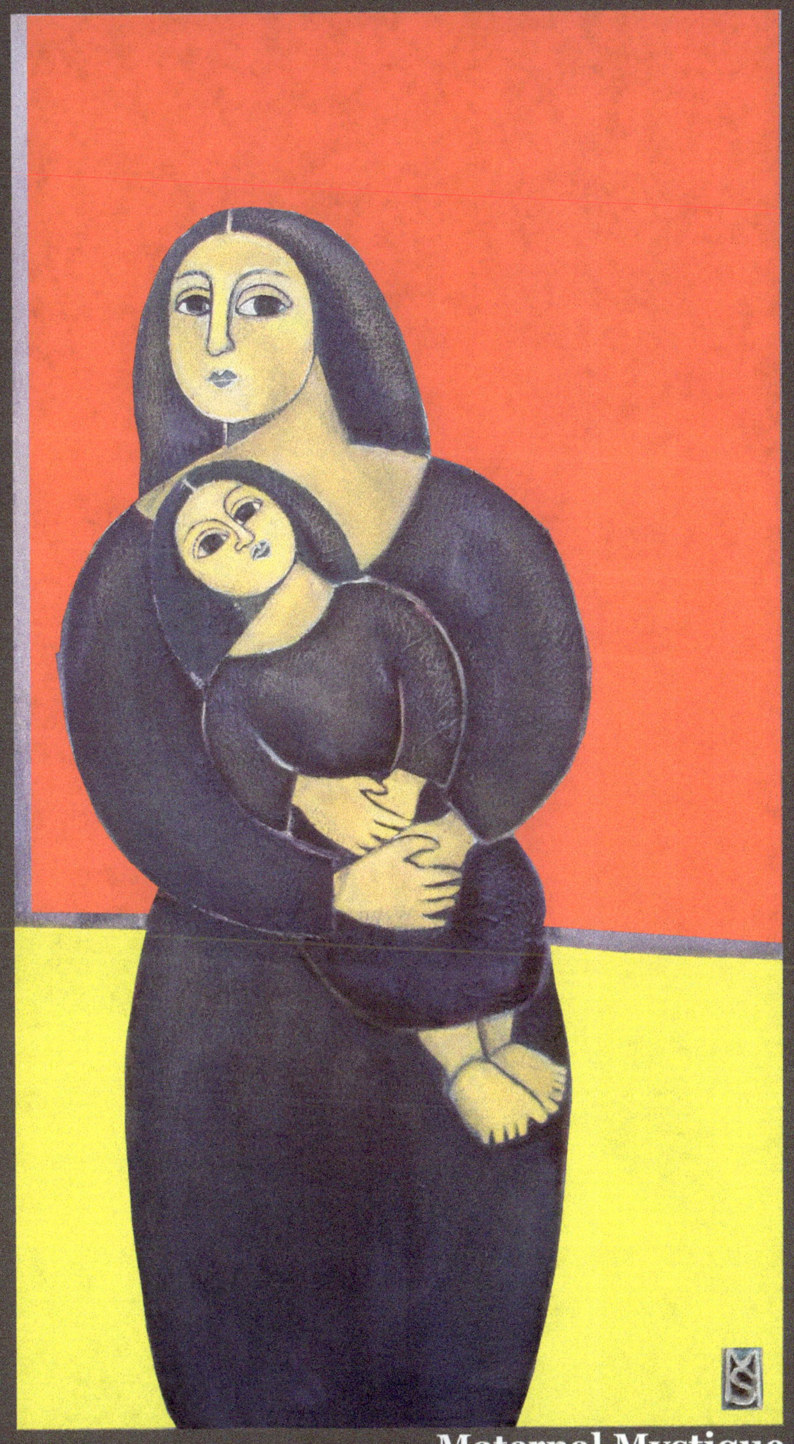

Maternal Mystique
(130cm x 70cm)

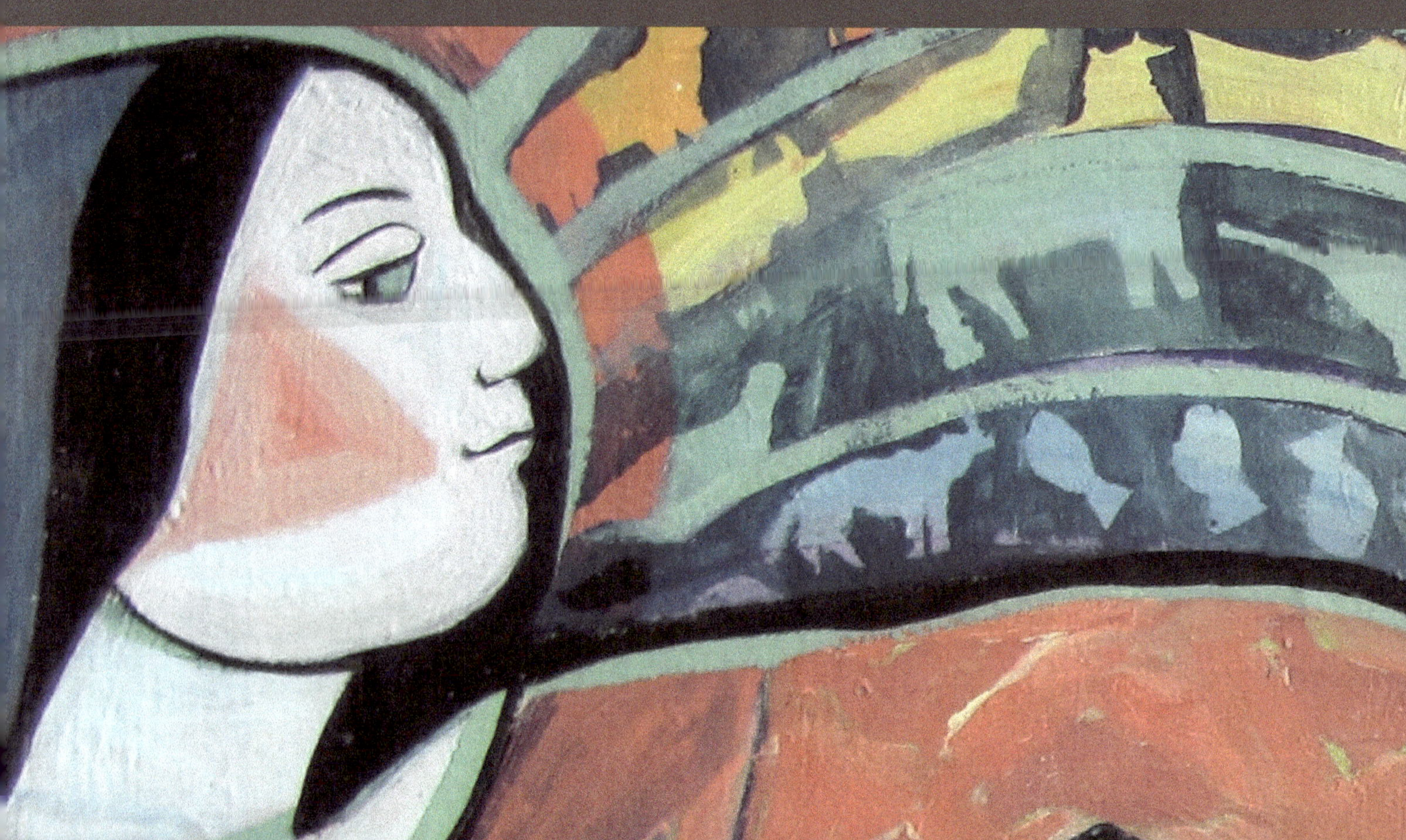

Girlscape
(80cm x 130cm)
Full image on pg.252.

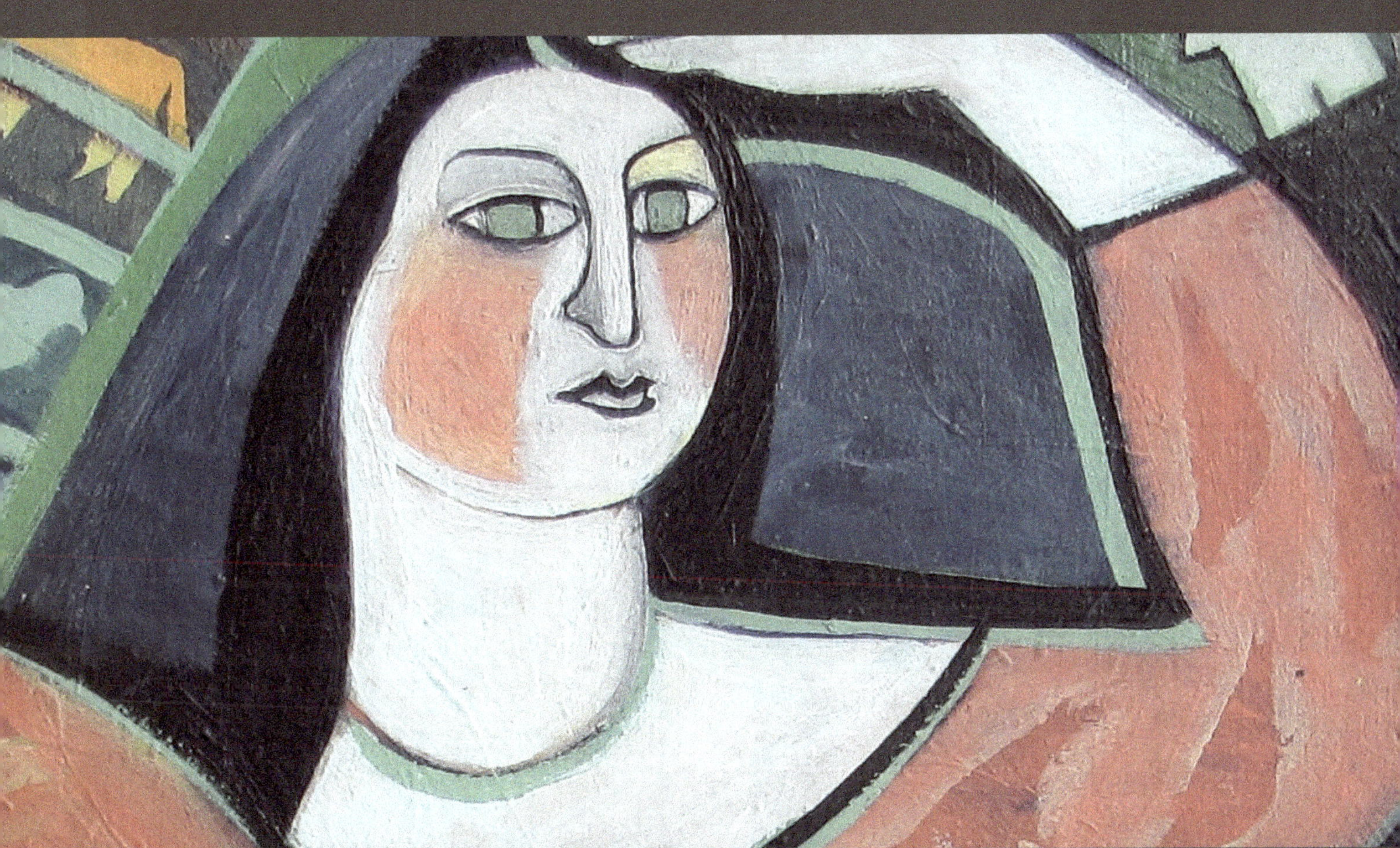

Art Used On Book Covers

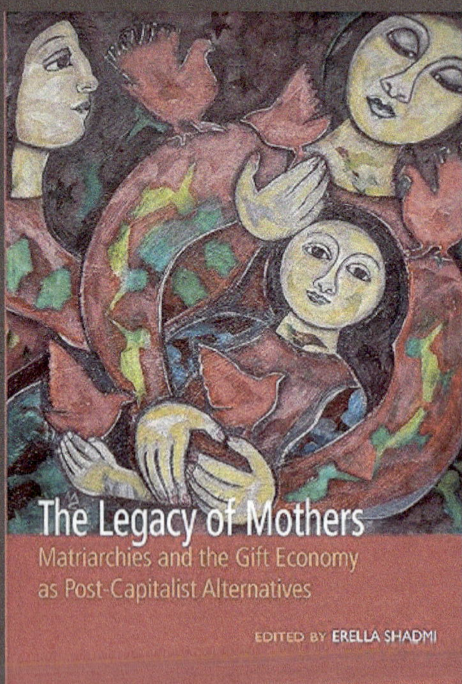
The Legacy of Mothers
Matriarchies and the Gift Economy
as Post-Capitalist Alternatives
EDITED BY ERELLA SHADMI

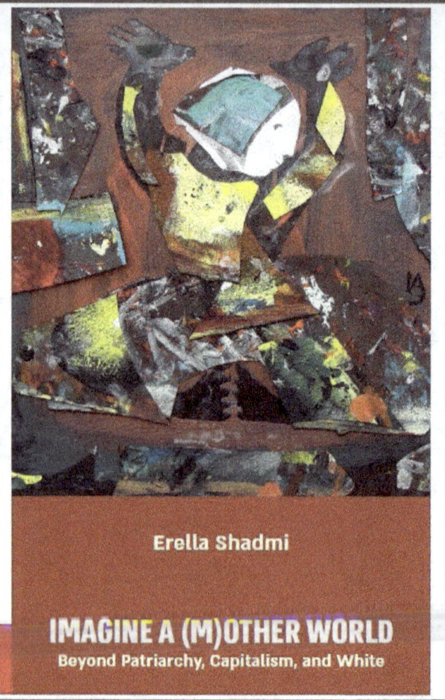
Erella Shadmi
IMAGINE A (M)OTHER WORLD
Beyond Patriarchy, Capitalism, and White

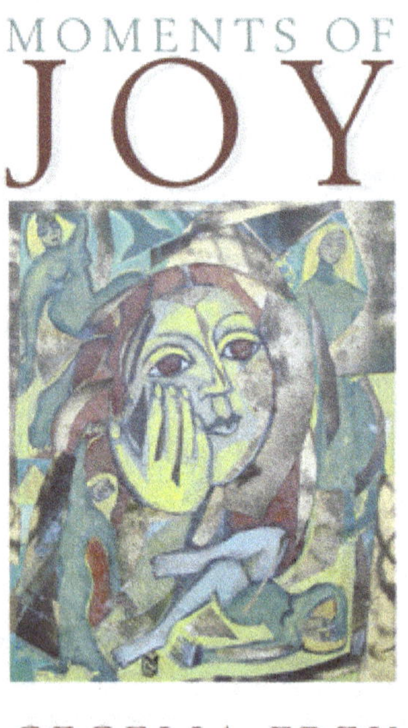
MOMENTS OF
JOY
CECELIA FREY

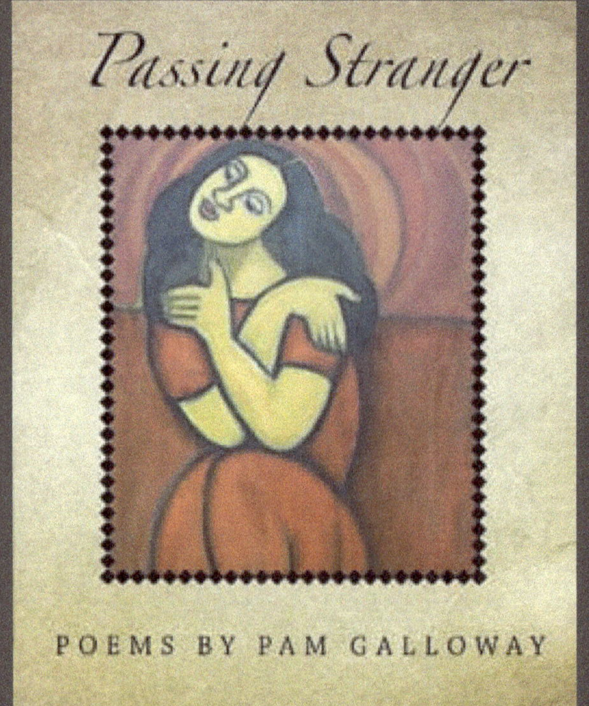
Passing Stranger
POEMS BY PAM GALLOWAY

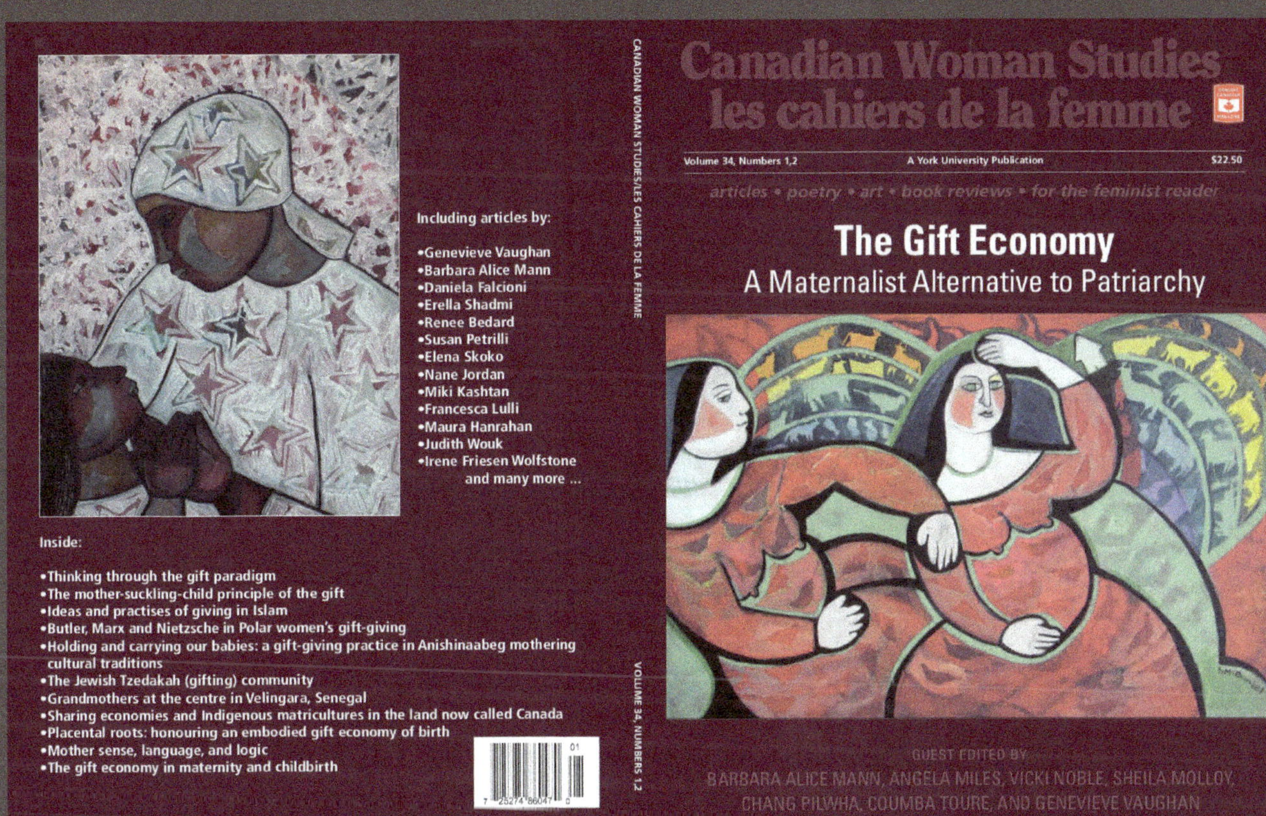

The Legacy of Mothers edited by Erella Shadmi published by Inanna Publications

Imagine a (M)other World by Erella Shadmi published by Pardes Publishing

Moments of Joy by Cecelia Frey published by Inanna Publications

Passing Stranger by Pam Galloway published by Inanna Publications

The Gift Economy: A Maternalist Alternative to Patriarchy edited by Barbara Mann, Angela Miles, Vicki Noble, Sheila Molloy, Chang Pilwha, Coumba Toure and Genevieve Vaughan published by Canadian Woman Studies

Shirley McDaniel

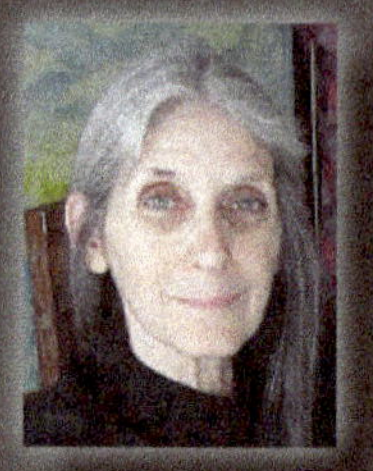

I was born in Port Shepstone, South Africa in 1951, the youngest of five children and developed an interest in art from an early age.

When I was seven years old, my family relocated to Pietermaritzburg, where I attended Athlone Primary School, before moving on to Wykeham (now The Wykeham Collegiate) for my high schooling.

On moving to Johannesburg, I matriculated at the Johannesburg School of Art, Ballet, Drama and Music. I then attended The Johannesburg College of Art, after which I worked at the University of the Witwatersrand as a layout artist on "Wits Student" and other student publications.

I married Barry Mc Daniel in 1973 and our two children, Catherine and Matthew were born in 1976 and 1978 respectively. During this period, I devoted my time to my family, whilst still managing to use my artistic talents, by creating my own unconventional bed-spreads, using recycled fabric. I also created ornate mirror frames (again using recycled materials), along with other artistic endeavours.

In the late 1980's when I felt that my children no longer needed me on a full-time basis, I decided to engage in further studies and graduated, at the age of 38, with a Diploma in Fine Arts at the Witwatersrand Technikon, in 1989.

In 1990, I teamed up with an artist friend and established Greenway Art Studio in Greenside, Johannesburg, where we taught art to students of all ages and also offered adult figure drawing classes on two evenings a week. The studio was successful and I ran it until our family moved to the KwaZulu-Natal south coast in 1996.

Since moving to Trafalgar and then to Cape Town, I have had the opportunity to devote the majority of my time to painting, which has enabled me to build up a substantial body of work. My paintings are mostly acrylic painted on canvas. Their subject matter frequently incorporates images of women, symbolising for me, a larger sort of "human connectedness." My themes are largely about "beings" interacting with each other and often include aspects and motifs of the natural surroundings in which I live.

https://www.art-explorations.com/

Acknowledgments

My beloved Barry . . . I thank you for the website you created in which to house and showcase my art, without which there would be no book as it is the very foundation of this book! Thank you for your time and skill in putting it all together . . . the evolution in building the entire web site: compiling, collecting, and arranging all the components into a whole, an entirety. The integration and cohesion you created in your photography . . . your positioning . . . the detail involved in your careful notating . . . of dimensions . . . titles and numbering of every web site work . . . and the careful placements within the various sections you created for clarity of content . . . correlating the varied work processes . . . all of which evolved into a cohesive and comprehensive whole. Last but not least was the joy of this sharing in the collaboration of it all.

Thank you very dear Jason . . . with incalculable gratitude appreciation and fondness . . . I thank you for this book being born . . . for your patience . . . warmth and generosity of spirit, your skill . . . steadfast support and significant input . . . providing guidance throughout this process . . .

With immeasurable and infinite love to you my ever-beloved Cath and *Liebe Familie* for everything. With much gratitude and thanks - Ca and Gee for all of your art related input.

With boundless and abundant love gratitude and thanks to you for everything my ever-beloved Mat, the excellent editor of our work . . .

Thank you so very much my dearest *Scrimmy* (aka Jayne Galassi a truly amazing artist) for this Foreword and for our timeless ties.

Huge thank you's to you awesome author Lisa De Nikolits my *Lil Li* . . . for our Luciana links that you so generously brought about, and for so much more that we share!

To Paula. Thank you my *Peebs* for our enriching Greenway Art Studio *Twogetherness* times and for our continuing sharings . . .

Hugging you thank you my ever-dearest *Peter-Pumpkin* for the picture-pathways and our ongoing joyous journeying . . .

To my beloved bridesmaids Carly and Annie . . . both lifelong companions.

Thank you my Rubes for the sunny afternoons in the Michaelis Art Library, Fruits and Roots and for Doc Merry.

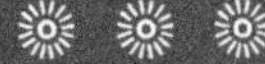

www.ingramcontent.com/pod-product-compliance
Lightning Source LLC
LaVergne TN
LVHW061202120826
845149LV00011B/1881